v

Chapter 4: PROGRAMMING LANGUAGES AND OPERATING SYSTEMS   99

Chapter 5: PROGRAM DESIGN, CODING, AND TESTING   123

Part Three POPULAR MICROCOMPUTER APPLICATIONS   151

Chapter 6: WORD PROCESSING AND DESKTOP PUBLISHING   153

Part Two HARDWARE, SOFTWARE, AND PROGRAMMING   55

Chapter 3: COMPUTER HARDWARE   57

Chapter 7: ELECTRONIC SPREADSHEETS   187

Chapter 8: DATABASE MANAGEMENT   215

Chapter 9: TELECOMMUNICATIONS   243

Chapter 12: COMPUTERS IN ART AND ENTERTAINMENT   321

Chapter 13: COMPUTERS IN INDUSTRY   349

Chapter 14: COMPUTERS IN BUSINESS AND FINANCE   367

Chapter 15: ARTIFICIAL INTELLIGENCE   393

Part Five COMPUTERS AND SOCIETY   417

Chapter 16: COMPUTER CRIME AND SECURITY   419

Chapter 17: COMPUTERS AND EMPLOYMENT 439

Chapter 18: COMPUTERS AND PEOPLE 455

The fifth edition of *The Mind Tool* has been updated to reflect recent developments in the rapidly changing computer industry. Topics that first appear or that receive much greater coverage in this edition include fourth generation languages, programming environments, computer-aided software engineering (CASE), desktop publishing, graphics scanners, Structured Query Language (SQL), integrated services digital networks (ISDN), hypertext, colorization, ATM networks, smart cards, program trading, expert systems, and computer viruses. Several chapters have been completely rewritten to improve coverage and presentation. Important terms are listed in a vocabulary-review section at the end of each chapter. Topics for discussion are now provided at the end of every chapter, and exercises are provided where appropriate.

Part 1, Overview, is just that. Chapter 1 surveys the basic concepts of the computer field. Chapter 2 provides a brief history of computing and introduces additional concepts. Chapter 2 now includes brief introductions to the most popular microcomputers and operating systems.

Part 2, Computer Systems, is devoted to hardware and software. Chapter 3 covers information representation (binary codes), information storage (main memory, tape, and disks), the central processing unit, the overall organization of a computer system, and input/output devices. The technical level of this material has been reduced considerably from that of the previous edition. Chapter 4 covers operating systems and programming languages. Chapter 5, which introduces the student to the art and craft of computer programming, now includes a discussion of computer-aided software engineering.

Part 3, Popular Microcomputer Applications, which is new in this edition, covers the five most popular microcomputer applications: word processing and desktop publishing (Chapter 6), electronic spreadsheets (Chapter 7), database management (Chapter 8), and telecommunications (Chapter 9). Emphasis is on the general capabilities of microcomputers in each application rather than on the specific details of particular hardware and software. The material on desktop publishing has been expanded considerably; Chapter 8 has been rewritten completely to reflect recent developments such as SQL and HyperCard; Chapter 9 now includes a discussion of ISDN.

Part 4, Putting Computers to Work, surveys the use of computers in many areas of human endeavor: health care, education, the arts, industry, business and finance, and artificial intelligence. The chapter on artificial intelligence has been rewritten to reflect the current emphasis on expert systems.

Part 5, Computers and Society, covers the impact of computers on society. Topics covered include computer crime and security (Chapter 16) and effect of computers on employment (Chapter 17). Chapter 16 now includes a full discussion of the various hostile programs (Trojan horses, viruses, worms, and bacteria) that threaten computer systems. Chapter 18 takes up three people-oriented topics: privacy, the impact of computer systems on employees who use them, and the reliability of computer systems whose failure can lead to disaster. Included is a discussion of questions that computer scientists have raised concerning the feasibility of the proposed Strategic Defense Initiative (Star Wars).

The Appendix, Buying a Personal Computer, provides some information about the computer marketplace and some hints for planning the purchase of a personal computer.

A glossary provides definitions for the most important computer terms used in the book. To keep the glossary to manageable size, it does not include terms used in applications areas such as medicine and business.

I wish to thank the following for their helpful comments on the manuscript and on the fourth edition:

Don Brax, Washington High School; Pearl Brazier, Pan American University; Ruby Chittenden, Arkansas State University; Philip East, University of Northern Iowa; June Fordham, Prince George's Community College; Marilyn Foulke, Louisville Collegiate School; Armando Gingras, Metropolitan State College; Earl Hasz, Metropolitan State College; Paul Jones, Towson State University; Kaila Katz, Montclair State College; Jeffrey Morse, Charles Wright Academy; Donald Ploch, University of Tennessee at Knoxville; John Rettenmeyer, Northeast Louisiana University; Charles Riden, Arizona State University; Ralph Szweda, Monroe Community College.

PART ONE

OVERVIEW

COMPUTER CONCEPTS

INTRODUCTION

One of the most important themes in the history of civilization is our ever increasing use of tools to shape and control the world around us. These tools range from the simple hammer and saw of the carpenter to all the complex machines of our modern civilization. We use tools to extend the power of our muscles, the speed and dexterity of our fingers, and the keenness of our sight, hearing, taste, smell, and touch. Tools allow us to engage in activities for which our unaided bodies are totally unsuited, such as traveling through the air, in space, or beneath the surface of water.

Until recently, almost all tools served to extend the powers of our bodies rather than those of our minds. Such mind tools as there were fell into two categories: devices for doing arithmetic, such as the adding machine and the slide rule, and tools for preserving and communicating ideas, such as the technology of writing and printing. In the last ten years, however, a powerful, general purpose mind tool, the electronic computer, has become widely available. In almost any shopping mall we can now buy a machine that will not only do our arithmetic but help us think, write, draw, play music, learn, keep records, and retrieve information.

It is to these mind tools, the electronic computers, that this book is devoted. This chapter is an overview of computer concepts and terminology. All the topics introduced in this chapter are taken up in more detail later in the book.

BACKGROUND

The idea of an automatic computing machine can be traced back to the mid-nineteenth century. But it was only in the 1940s, when electronics

This IBM Personal Computer (IBM PC) illustrates the components of a typical personal computer system. The display sits atop the system unit; the printer rests on a separate stand. The black area on the front of the system unit contains two disk drives. To the left is a diskette drive; you should be able to see the slot into which diskettes are inserted. To the right is a hard disk drive, which contains the permanently installed hard disk.

was applied to the task of automatic computing, that fast, reliable computers became possible. Early computers were used mainly for scientific and technical calculations. In the 1950s, however, businesses, universities, and government bureaus began using computers to store and process such nonmathematical data as orders, invoices, and personnel records. The use of computers for business data processing expanded enormously in the 1960s and has continued to increase at a rapid pace ever since.

The computers of the forties, fifties, and sixties were complex, expensive machines that were practical only for organizations such as businesses and universities. Individuals could use a computer only by virtue of being associated with an organization that owned one, and in most cases the person's use of the computer was strictly controlled. During this period computers provided ever increasing benefits for organizations, but few individuals were able to use a computer as a personal problem-solving tool.

In the 1970s this situation began to change. Responsible for the change were developments in microelectronics, the art of building complex electronic circuits on tiny silicon chips, which could be manufactured in large quantities at low cost. The most important computer chip is the *microprocessor*, which carries out all the calculations and controls the operation of the rest of the computer. Other chips store data and communicate with external devices, such as display screens, keyboards, and printers.

Computer chips have made possible compact, low-cost microcomputers or *personal computers*—computers that can serve as personal mind tools for individuals. Moreover, computer chips can be incorporated in other machines that can benefit from computer control, such as washing machines, microwave ovens, television sets, cameras, and automobiles. Entirely new machines, such as pocket calculators and video games, become possible. The enormous changes in the use of computers made possible by microelectronics are sometimes referred to as the microelectronics

This computer from IBM's new Personal System/2 (PS/2) line has a diskette drive (diskette slot visible on front of system unit) and an internal hard disk drive. The system unit has a smaller "footprint" (takes up less space on the desk) than that of the IBM PC.

revolution. Much of this book is devoted to the microelectronics revolution and what it means to you.

DATA AND PROGRAMS

Computers vary widely in such incidental details as size, shape, cost, and speed of operation. All computers, however, have two characteristics that distinguish them from other machines:

1 A computer is a machine for storing and processing information.

2 The operation of a computer is controlled by a detailed set of step-by-step instructions called a *program.*

Let us look in detail at each of these two major characteristics of computers, information processing and program control.

Information Storage and Processing

As long as information exists only inside our heads, there is no way for it to be processed by a computer. For computer processing, information must be represented by such concrete symbols as words, numbers, drawings, and sounds. These concrete symbols are referred to as *data;** they are represented inside the computer by codes similar in spirit to the familiar Morse code. Computers store and process information by storing and manipulating concrete symbols that represent the desired information. When there is no need to distinguish between abstract concepts and the concrete symbols that represent them, people often use the terms *information* and *data* interchangeably.

The first computers were used for arithmetical calculations. The input data for the computer consisted of the numbers to be used in the calculation; the output data consisted of the final result of the calculation. The results of intermediate steps in the calculation were stored inside the computer until they were needed to produce the final result. Aside from this temporary storage of intermediate results, the first computers were used for calculation rather than data storage.

Computer designers soon realized, however, that much labor could be saved by keeping frequently needed data stored inside the computer. That way, a data item would have to be entered only once, rather than every time it was needed in a calculation. If business files, such as accounts with customers, accounts with suppliers, inventories, time cards, and personnel records, were stored in a computer, the computer could go through the files automatically and print such business documents as orders, invoices, and payroll checks.

One advantage of storing information in a computer is the ease with which the information can be changed. A computer can locate and modify a business record much faster than can a clerk searching through a filing cabinet. Writers, artists, and musicians often use computers for creating

---

*People differ as to whether the word *data* should be singular or plural. We adopt the singular usage in this book, so we will say "This data was manipulated." Those who prefer the plural usage would say, "These data were manipulated."

The display of this Apple Macintosh SE is built into the system unit instead of being separate as with the IBM machines. The system unit also contains a diskette drive (diskette slot visible on front) and a hard disk drive. To the right of the keyboard is a mouse; rolling the mouse over the desktop produces corresponding movements of a pointer on the screen.

and storing their works because of (among other reasons) the ease with which corrections and revisions can be made.

Frequently, input for a computer is typed on a keyboard and the computer's output is displayed on a screen or printed on paper. Although keyboards and display screens are the most familiar means of communicating with a computer, they are by no means the only ones, nor is typed text the only form of data computers can handle. With suitable attachments, such as microphones and cameras, computers can input, output, and store speech, music, drawings, and photographs. Computers can also monitor and control other machines, such as home appliances, laboratory apparatus, and the machines in a factory.

Data can be represented in *digital* or *analog* form. Digital data is represented by discrete codes, such as letters or digits. Analog data is represented by continuously varying quantities, such as the strength of an electrical current or the position of a mechanical part.

Digital clocks (which display the time in numbers) and analog clocks (which use the traditional hands) illustrate the two methods of data representation. The reading of a digital clock is represented by symbols that change abruptly from one minute to the next; for example, all the displayed symbols change to completely different ones as the reading of the clock goes from 7:59 to 8:00. And even the number of symbols displayed changes as the reading goes from 9:59 to 10:00. In contrast, the hands of an analog clock move smoothly, without any abrupt changes; a clock reading 7:59 appears only slightly different from one reading 8:00. If the minute hand is between the marks representing 59 and 60 minutes, we have to estimate how far it is between the marks and hence whether the time is closest to 7:59 or 8:00. No such estimation is necessary or possible with a digital clock.

The adjective *digital* indicates that a device stores or manipulates data in digital form. The computers discussed in this book are called *digital computers* because they store and manipulate digital data. Analog computers, which store and manipulate data in analog form, are discussed briefly in Chapter 2; they are nowhere nearly as important as digital computers.

Some input devices, such as microphones and television cameras, generate data in analog form; before such data can be sent to a computer, it must be converted to digital form, a process called *analog-to-digital conversion*; the converted data is said to have been digitized. Likewise, some output devices, such as loudspeakers, require analog data. Before these devices can be driven with computer output, the digital output data must be converted to analog form, a process called *digital-to-analog conversion*.

Programs and Programming

We say that a computer *runs* or *executes* a program when it carries out the program's instructions. A computer is a truly general purpose information-processing machine in that it can carry out almost any* information-processing task for which we can supply a suitable set of instructions. We can change the computer from performing one task to performing a quite different one just by changing its program. Such a change can be carried out rapidly, sometimes in a fraction of a second.

On the other hand, a computer will do nothing useful for us until we have provided it with an appropriate program. A few programs may come with the computer; beyond these, however, we must write or purchase the programs that we need. Many people purchase all the programs that they need; others write simple programs but purchase more complex ones. It is rare for persons other than professional programmers to write such complex programs as word processors and database managers.

Most stores that carry computer *hardware* (the machines themselves) also carry the programs or *software* needed to control the computer. Computer software can now be purchased in books stores, computer stores (which sell both hardware and software), and in software stores (which sell only software). The cost of the software for a computer may far exceed the cost of the hardware.

It may help to compare computers with other familiar machines that exhibit flexible behavior. A phonograph is a general purpose instrument for reproducing music. Unlike a music box, which can play only a single tune, a phonograph can play any song for which we have a record. If we think of the phonograph as corresponding to a computer, then the record corresponds to a computer program. A motion picture projector provides another example. The hardware (the projector) will show any movie provided only that we supply the necessary software (the movie film). Recognizing these analogies, people nowadays sometimes refer to recordings and films as "software."

We often speak of a program accomplishing a particular result; we say that this program plays chess, that program updates customer accounts, and another program teaches a science lesson. Whenever we say that a

---

*In principle, any computer can—under the direction of the appropriate program—carry out any computing task. In practice, such details as speed of operation, information storage capacity, and provisions for input and output often make one computer better suited than another for a particular task.

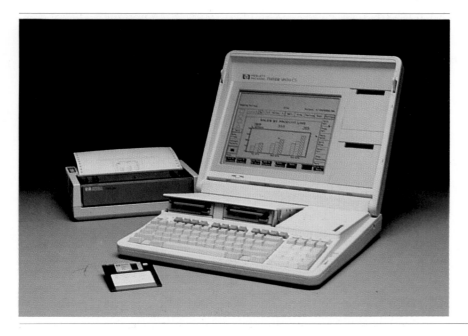

The diskette drives for this laptop computer pop up to the position shown for insertion and removal of diskettes; after the insertion or removal, the drives are pushed down into the body of the computer. A 3½-inch diskette cartridge lies on the table; a printer can be seen in the background.

program does a particular task, we mean that the computer does the task by following the instructions contained in the program.

A person who writes computer programs, either as a profession or a hobby, is a *programmer*. A person who uses computers is a *user*. Most users do not write programs; in fact, they may have little or no knowledge about the internal operation of computers and programs. Such *naive users* (as they are sometimes called) operate the computer by following step-by-step instructions that they have previously memorized or written down. Any untoward event, such as an unexpected error message from the computer, is likely to derail a naive user.

Users who are technically knowledgeable about computer hardware and software are called *power users*. The power users in an organization are often called on to help naive users who are having problems with hardware or software. The trouble with this is that the power users' own jobs may not get done because of the time spent helping other people with their computer problems.

Most users, even those who have no desire to be programmers or power users, can still benefit from greater knowledge of computer hardware and software. One objective of books such as *The Mind Tool* is to remove as many people as possible from the category of naive users.

◣ HARDWARE

The purpose of the sections on computer hardware and software is to introduce briefly many of the concepts and terms that we will be using throughout the rest of the book. Persons who have had some experience with computers may find that they are already familiar with most of this material so that a quick glance through these sections will suffice.

Classification of Computers

Computers can be classified as *special purpose* or *general purpose*. A special purpose computer is dedicated to a single task; the computers built into cameras, television sets, automobiles, and kitchen appliances are of this type. A general purpose computer can be used for a wide variety of different tasks. Computers that are advertised and sold as computers (rather than as parts of other appliances) are general purpose computers.

The crucial difference between special purpose and general purpose computers lies not in their hardware but in their software. A special purpose computer can execute only a single built-in program and so is limited to a single task; a general purpose computer can execute many different programs and so can perform many different tasks. If we compare a general purpose computer to a phonograph, which can play any music we have a record for, then a special purpose computer corresponds to a music box, which can only play the single tune that is built into it, or at best allows the user to select one of a small number of built-in tunes.

When the term *computer* is used without further qualification, it usually refers to general purpose rather than special purpose computers.

Computers are further classified as *embedded computers, microcomputers, minicomputers, mainframes*, and *supercomputers*. The following is a brief description of each category.

- **Embedded computers** Embedded computers are special purpose computers incorporated into other machines, such as automobiles, cameras, and television sets. Most people probably own at least one device that contains an embedded computer. Most embedded computers are microcomputers, although some scientific instruments contain embedded minicomputers. The term *microprocessor controlled* is often used to indicate that a device contains an embedded computer.

- **Microcomputers** A microcomputer is any computer that is built around a microprocessor. Special purpose microcomputers are widely used as embedded computers; general purpose microcomputers, also known as *personal computers*, are widely used in offices, schools, and homes.

- **Minicomputers** Before the invention of the microprocessor, minicomputers were the lowest cost and most widely used computers; now, minicomputers lie between microcomputers and mainframes in cost, speed, and computing power. To reflect this changed situation, minicomputers are now sometimes referred to as *midrange computers*.

- **Mainframes** Mainframes are the large-scale computers found in the computer rooms of most businesses, financial institutions, and universities. Most of the developed world's business and financial records are stored in the auxiliary memories of mainframe computers.

- **Supercomputers** Supercomputers are the most powerful and expensive computers of all. Applications that call for supercomputers include many scientific and engineering calculations, weather prediction, cryptography (trying to break secret codes), and computer animation (computer generation of motion picture and television images). To allow a supercomputer to spend as much of its time as possible calculating, it usually does not communicate directly with the outside world, but uses a minicomputer or a mainframe as an intermediary.

The Central Processing Unit

The heart of the computer, the part that is responsible for carrying out the instructions in the program, is the *central processing unit* or *CPU*. The central processing unit takes its orders from the program; all other parts of the computer take their orders from the central processing unit. In microcomputers the central processing unit is a microprocessor, which is usually constructed on a single silicon chip. The box or cabinet that contains the central processing unit is also sometimes referred to as the CPU, although it usually contains other components as well.

Main Memory

A computer's memory is used for data storage. (In fact, some people prefer to use the term *storage* instead of *memory*.) *Main memory* is used to store the program that the computer is currently executing and the data that it is currently manipulating. Main memory is not usually used for long-term storage of programs and data files. Its storage capacity is too small, and most computers lose the data stored in main memory when the power is switched off.

This computer chip is about the size of a ladybug.

Auxiliary Memory

Auxiliary memory augments main memory by providing long-term storage for programs and data files. Access to data in auxiliary memory is much slower than for data in main memory, but the capacity of auxiliary memory is usually greater than that of main memory, and the contents of auxiliary memory are retained when the computer is turned off.

The most popular medium for auxiliary memory is the magnetic *disk*. For now we will consider only the disks used for personal computers, which come in two forms: *diskettes*, which can be removed from the computer and stored in a file box when not in use, and *hard disks*, which are permanently mounted inside the computer. The hardware components that writes (records on) and reads (plays back from) disks is called a *disk drive*.

Recorded on each disk is a directory showing the names of all the programs and data files stored on the disk. To run a program, the user enters the name of the program to be executed and the names of the data files it is to manipulate; the named program is loaded into main memory, given control of the computer, and given access to the designated data files.

Microcomputer software is usually sold on diskettes.

Input and Output

Input devices and output devices convert between symbols meaningful to people, such as letters and numerals, and the codes that a computer uses internally. The most common input device is a typewriter-like keyboard;

In the 1970s, most computing was done by large mainframe installations such as the one shown here. Although the sizes of some mainframe components have since been reduced, a major mainframe installation still fills a large, specially constructed computer room.

the most common output device is a television-like *video display*. Some home computers allow an ordinary television set to be used as a display. The next most common output device is a printer, which is used to make a permanent record of the computer's output.

Some computers provide a pointing device to allow the user to designate particular items on the screen. For example, the computer may display a menu of operations it can carry out. The user selects the desired operation with the pointing device. The most popular pointing device is a *mouse*, a small, boxlike device that can be rolled around on a desktop. An arrow on the screen follows the movement of the mouse; moving the mouse to the left or right, for example, moves the arrow a proportional distance in the same direction. When the arrow has been properly positioned, the user presses a button on the mouse to select the item at which the arrow is pointing.

A computer terminal is a device for communicating with a remote computer; it consists of a keyboard and either a video display, a printer, or both. Computer terminals are widely used to communicate with minicomputers and mainframes. A microcomputer usually has its own keyboard and display so that it does not need a separate computer terminal. In fact, microcomputers are often used as terminals for communicating with other computers. Programs are available that allow a microcomputer to emulate various brands of computer terminals; the remote minicomputer or mainframe cannot tell the difference between the microcomputer and the terminal it is emulating.

Computer Systems

We refer to a particular combination of hardware components and software programs as a *computer system*. The photographs in this chapter illustrate the hardware components of a number of computer systems. To see in more detail how hardware components can be combined to form a computer system, let's consider a typical personal computer system.

This computer system has a keyboard for input and a video display for output. Other input and output devices may include a mouse for pointing to items on the screen and a printer for producing permanent output. For auxiliary memory there will be one or more diskette or hard disk drives. Even if hard disks are used, there will be at least one diskette drive, since software is usually delivered on diskettes. Somewhere near the computer there will probably be one or more file boxes for holding diskettes. Finally, there may be a modem, a device that allows a computer to communicate with other computers over the telephone lines.

Like all computers, the one we are considering has a central processing unit and main memory, which are contained in an enclosure sometimes referred to as the system unit. The keyboard, video display, and disk drives may be included in the system unit or may be separate. The printer and modem will most likely be separate from the system unit, although a few portable computers do have built-in printers and modems. A mouse must be separate since it has to roll around on the desktop.

◥ SOFTWARE

However diligently we describe the hardware components of a computer system, we can say little about how the system actually works without considering the all important software that controls almost every aspect of the system's behavior.

The Operating System

The operators of early computers used complex control panels to monitor and control the machine's operation. In time, however, computer designers realized that the computer could monitor and control its own operation under the direction of an appropriate program. Thus, aside from a keyboard and possibly a mouse, modern computers seldom have any controls more elaborate than an on-off switch and perhaps a button to reset the system after a malfunction. The user operates the machine by typing in commands for the control program or using a mouse to select commands from a menu displayed by the control program.

The control program is called the computer's *operating system*. It is also sometimes referred to as a *disk operating system (DOS)*, since one of the primary tasks of the operating system is to manage the transfer of data and programs to and from disks. The operating system profoundly influences the way in which users interact with the computer. Two computer systems with the same hardware may seem very different to users if they are running different operating systems.

A copy of the operating system program is kept on a disk. The operating system must be in main memory, however, before the computer can run it. But transferring data and programs between main memory and disk storage is normally the responsibility of the operating system. How then,

A supermini—a computer on the borderline between minicomputers and mainframes.

do we get the operating system from disk into main memory when we first turn on the computer?

A small program for loading the operating system is stored permanently in the computer's main memory. When the computer is turned on, the loading program is run automatically. Under the control of the loading program, the computer copies the operating system from disk into main memory and then transfers control of the computer to the operating system. This process of using a small loading program to start up the computer system reminded people of the phrase "lifting yourself by your own bootstraps," which means starting out with little or nothing and working your way up. As a result, the small loading program is called a bootstrap loader, and the process of starting a computer system is referred to as bootstrapping or just *booting* the system.

From the user's point of view, booting a computer system is usually very simple. If the operating system is stored on a diskette, the proper diskette must first be inserted in the disk drive that the system uses for booting. The user then switches on the computer and waits for the booting process to be completed. Usually a light on the disk drive will turn on while the operating system is being loaded, and you may hear the mechanism of the drive operating. When the operating system has been loaded, it may request the user to enter some preliminary information, such as the current date and time. When this information has been typed in, the operating system will stand by for the user's commands.

On command, the operating system will perform any of a number of useful functions. The following are a few of the most widely used commands that an operating system can carry out:

■ Display a disk directory showing the names of all the programs and data files stored on the disk. Each program and data file has a name that was assigned when the file was created.

■ Run a program, that is, load the program into main memory from disk and give it control of the computer. We must have a program stored on a disk for every task we want the computer to carry out. To have the computer do a particular task, we request the operating system to run the corresponding program. If the program is on a diskette, we must, of course, insert the proper diskette into a diskette drive before requesting that the program be run. When the program finishes running, it returns control to the operating system, which will then stand by for our next command.

■ Copy a program or data file from one disk to another. Since disks can be damaged, thus losing the data stored on them, it is essential to keep more than one copy of important program and data files. Normally one works with one copy of the file while a diskette containing a *backup copy* is kept in a safe place.

■ Display the contents of a file on the screen or print it on the printer. Only files that contain text—those whose codes represent characters such as letters and numerals—can be printed. Files coded in other ways will produce a meaningless display or printout.

There are two basic methods for giving commands to the operating system. In the ''command line'' method, the user types a line giving the operation to be carried out and the files and hardware devices affected. For example, to copy a text file named `chapter3` from the diskette in drive a to the diskette in drive b, we might have to type:

```
copy a:chapter3 b:
```

The `a:chapter3` indicates that the file `chapter3` on the diskette in drive a is to be copied. The `b:` indicates that the copy is to be stored on drive b.

As the example suggests, command lines can get rather cryptic. Also, many people who wish to use computers are not skilled typists and have difficulty typing the command lines correctly. Therefore, some operating

Cray supercomputer (cylindrical object in foreground). The surrounding computers and peripherals feed data to the supercomputer and store the results it produces.

Laptop computers are popular for use on airplanes.

systems allow users to select command and file names from menus. The selection can be made with a mouse or from the keyboard. In the first case, the mouse is used to move a pointer to the desired command or file name; a button on the mouse is then pressed to make the selection. To make the selection from the keyboard, direction keys (keys marked with arrows) are pressed to move a highlighted area up, down, left, or right on the screen. When the desired command or file name is highlighted, a designated key is pressed to make the selection.

Programming Languages

To get a computer to execute our programs, we must state our instructions in a language that the computer can understand. Languages used for this purpose are called *programming languages*. The central processing unit, the hardware component responsible for executing instructions, understands only obscure codes called *machine language*. Since people find machine language very difficult to work with, they have devised a number of easier-to-use *higher-level programming languages*. Some familiar higher-level languages are Ada (named after the computer pioneer Augusta Ada Byron, Countess of Lovelace), Basic (Beginner's All-purpose Symbolic Instruction Code), C (so called because it was inspired by a language called B), Cobol (Common Business Oriented Language), Fortran (Formula Translator), Lisp (List Processor), and Pascal (named after the French mathematician and philosopher Blaise Pascal).*

Although the computer cannot directly understand programs written in higher-level languages, it can do so with the aid of other programs called *language processors*. For example, one type of language processor, called a *compiler*, simply translates a program from a higher-level language into machine language. (That is, the computer performs the translation under the control of the compiler program.) We need a separate language-processor program for each higher-level language in which we wish to write programs.

Applications Programs

The various tasks that we wish a computer to do are called *applications*. Typical applications are printing workers' paychecks, controlling robots, guiding spacecraft, and playing games. The programs that enable the computer to carry out these applications are called *applications programs*. They are to be distinguished from *systems programs*, such as operating systems and language processors, that aid us in using the computer system rather than carrying out applications.

Usually, we need a separate program for each application for which we wish to use the computer. Some programs, however, can be used for several related applications; such multipurpose programs are called *inte-*

---

*Language names that are acronyms (abbreviations) are sometimes spelled with all capital letters: BASIC, COBOL, FORTRAN, LISP; the current trend, however, is toward capitalizing only the first letter of language names. Note that there is no justification for using all capital letters for names that are not acronyms, such as Ada and Pascal.

grated programs. Integrated programs make it easy to switch from one application to another, something that many office workers must do frequently. The commands that the program carries out are similar for the different applications, making them easier to learn and remember than if each application required completely different commands. Finally, integrated programs have provisions for transferring data from one application to another. When separate programs are used, the data for different applications may be stored in incompatible formats, making data transfers between applications difficult or impossible.

◥ USING COMPUTERS

Computers are now being used in so many ways that we have no chance of covering them all in this book, let alone in this chapter. We will, however, look briefly at some of the major areas in which computers are being widely used. Keep in mind that each application mentioned normally calls for a separate program. Often the major obstacle to computerizing a particular application is getting the necessary programs written.

Scientific, Engineering, and Industrial Applications

The first computers were built to carry out the complex calculations of mathematics, science, and engineering. Computers are still used for these "number crunching" tasks with often unexpected influence on our everyday lives. For example, many high quality consumer products, such as cameras, are available at reasonable cost only because computers were used to carry out the complex calculations necessary for their design. And a number of recent techniques in medical diagnosis depend on the ability of computers to convert the mass of data collected by a medical instrument into a picture the physician can interpret.

Many products, including computers themselves, are now designed and manufactured with the aid of computers. In computer-aided design, computers are used to carry out the calculations for the design of a product, produce the drawings that describe it, and simulate its operation before it is actually built. Once designed, the product may be manufactured by robots and other computer-controlled machines, a process called *computer-aided manufacturing.* In this case the computer-aided-design program also produces the instructions for controlling the machines that manufacture the product.

Business and Financial Data Processing

The second major application area to be computerized was record keeping for businesses and financial institutions. By the end of the 1960s, most large organizations were using computers for data storage and processing. In the 1970s and 1980s, the decreasing cost of computers has brought these capabilities to smaller organizations as well.

In addition to duplicating the functions of manual record keeping, computers have provided many additional functions that were not practical with manual systems. Management information systems (MIS) are now

Using a laptop computer on a park bench.

widely used to extract from computerized files the meaningful information that can help managers to make decisions. Electronic mail allows messages and data to be sent from one branch of a company to another at electronic speeds. Automatic teller machines give people access to their bank accounts from convenient locations such as shopping centers. Point-of-sale terminals (electronic cash registers) translate bar codes into prices, print the names of the products purchased on the sales slip, collect statistics on customers' purchasing habits, and verify credit card information.

Computers in the Office

Although businesses have now been using computers for a number of years, the computers have been mainframes operated by the company's data processing department. Data to be entered into the computer was sent to the data processing department, which, in turn, distributed to other departments reports printed by the computer. Only recently have microcomputers come into offices, where they are used for such routine chores as typing, business calculations, and information retrieval. The following are some common applications for office computers.

In word processing, the computer functions as an electronic typewriter. Text is stored in the computer's main memory as it is typed and can be saved on disk for later use. A small segment of the stored text (typically 20–25 lines) appears on the display screen; we can think of the display as an opening through which a small portion of the text is visible. This opening is easily moved through the stored text, allowing any 20–25 line segment to be displayed.

The great advantage of word processing is that the stored text can be corrected and revised without being completely retyped. Additions and deletions can be made at any point, and blocks of text can be moved about or copied from one place to another. When changes are made, the computer

The Apple II was one of the first personal computers to achieve widespread popularity outside the ranks of computer enthusiasts.

automatically adjusts lines and paragraphs to make room for additions and to close up the spaces left by deletions. Thus there is no indication in the final text that any changes were made.

On command, the computer will print out a copy of the stored text, taking care of such routine chores as formatting the text into lines, paragraphs, and pages, numbering pages, and printing a heading at the top of each page. Also, the computer will print multiple copies of a document, inserting information from a disk file at designated points. Given a disk file containing a mailing list, we can use the computer to print multiple copies of a form letter, each addressed to one of the persons on the mailing list. We can even have the computer insert the name of the recipient at appropriate points throughout the body of each letter.

Business data and the results of business calculations are often recorded on a spreadsheet, a sheet of paper divided into rows and columns for convenient presentation of data tables. A spreadsheet program allows the computer's display to serve as an electronic spreadsheet and provides a powerful electronic calculator for computing the results to be displayed.

As with word processing, part of the power of a spreadsheet program lies in the ease with which data entries can be corrected and revised. Even more important, all calculations are carried out automatically according to formulas entered previously. If one data entry is changed, then all values that were calculated from that entry also change. This makes spreadsheet programs popular for business forecasting, for exploring the consequences of assumptions about such variables as income, expenses, and interest rates. To find out what happens if, say, expenses increase by 25%, we just make the appropriate change in the expenses entry on the spreadsheet. The computer then automatically recalculates all quantities that are affected by expenses.

A collection of disk files containing related records forms a *database*. A database management program allows the user to create new files, store new records in files, retrieve and update existing records, print reports based on the contents of files, and delete files that are no longer needed. The files making up the database are stored in the computer's auxiliary memory, usually on disks. A microcomputer, particularly one with a hard disk, may be able to store all the data files required by a small company. Larger companies usually store their databases on mainframes; however, arrangements may be made for office microcomputers to access the database by communicating with the mainframe.

The term *telecommunications* refers generally to electronic communication; in the computer industry it refers to electronic communication between computers. Such communication allows users to share information without having to print it out from one computer and key it back into another. The information can be sent over telephone lines or over local area networks (LANs) specifically designed for linking computers. Electronic mail, which allows letters to sent from computer to computer without ever being printed out, is a natural adjunct to word processing. An office microcomputer can retrieve information from other office microcomputers, from company mainframes, or from commercial information services. A single storage device, such as a hard disk, can serve all the computers on a particular network.

Appropriate charts and graphs often improve business reports and presentations. Business graphics programs make it easy to prepare charts

Because of their quiet operation, computers are ideal for use in libraries, where noisy typewriters may be forbidden.

and graphs from data calculated with spreadsheet programs or extracted from a database.

Sometimes several popular business applications are combined into a single integrated program; such programs typically provide word processing, spreadsheet analysis, database management, telecommunications, and business graphics.

Computers in Education

Computers can aid in teaching traditional subjects such as English, mathematics, and science. They are essential for teaching students about computers in such courses as computer literacy, computer programming, and computer science. Computers can also aid the teacher with many routine chores, such as generating assignments and test questions, grading tests, and record keeping.

Using computers to help teach traditional subjects is called *computer-assisted instruction*. The most common form of computer-assisted instruction is drill and practice, in which the computer asks questions and informs students whether their responses are correct. For incorrect responses the program may provide hints or additional information to help the student get the correct answer without being told. Drill and practice programs are often disguised as computer games in which students earn points with correct answers.

Another popular form of computer-assisted instruction is simulation, in which a computer mimics some real-life system such as a business, an aircraft, or a stock exchange. Simulation allows students to experiment with such activities as running a business, flying an airplane, or investing in the stock market—activities that it would be difficult or impossible for them to experience in real life.

Programmed instruction is a more advanced form of computer-assisted instruction that teaches new material instead of just drilling students in material that they are already supposed to know. Students are quizzed on each topic as soon as it has been presented. If a student does not answer the questions correctly, the topic is reviewed in more detail or from a different point of view.

In the past programmed learning has faced two obstacles: (1) microcomputer memories are often not large enough to hold the amount of text needed for a programmed learning session; and (2) the material is presented only through text and simple diagrams rather than the pictures and sounds available from such media as recordings, movies, and television presentations. A solution to both problems may be provided by optical discs such as the compact discs* now widely used for record albums. A single disc can store computer programs, large amounts of text, still pictures, sounds, and television presentations. Under the control of a computer, an optical disc player can present exactly the text, pictures, and sounds needed at each point in a lesson.

Many schools now offer courses in the use and programming of computers. Computer literacy courses introduce students to the use and operation of computers and to popular applications such as word processing and spreadsheet analysis. *The Mind Tool* is an example of a computer literacy textbook. Computer programming courses teach students to write programs in a particular programming language. Computer science courses teach not only programming but also the theoretical and mathematical foundations of computing.

Home Computers

When the first personal computers appeared, many observers predicted that there would soon be a computer in every home and that such routine domestic chores as keeping recipe files and balancing checkbooks would soon be turned over to computers. These predictions have not been borne out. Although appliances containing embedded computers are in widespread use, only about fifteen percent of all households own personal computers, and those computers are rarely used for routine domestic chores.

Perhaps not surprisingly, recreation is one of the most popular applications of home computers. Personal computers can be used to play not only fast-action video games but also more intellectual games in which careful reasoning is more important that fast reflexes. Commercial information services offer multiperson games that allow computer owners all over the country to play with or against one another. Many computer games are simulations in which, for example, the player may be challenged to fly a simulated airplane, fight a simulated battle, or manage a simulated economy.

Hobbies also provide many applications for home computers. Computer programming is a popular hobby that its adherents find so fascinating and challenging that they are sometimes guilty of ignoring other activities in its favor. A related hobby is telecommunications—communicating with

*The preferred spelling is "disk" for computer products and "disc" for entertainment products. Since optical discs originated in the entertainment industry, the spelling "disc" is often used for them even in computer publications.

This student is using a mouse to point to an item on the screen of a Macintosh. The Macintosh is operated mainly by using the mouse to select commands from on-screen menus.

other computer owners via computer conferencing and electronic mail systems operated by commercial information services and by private individuals. Ham radio operators, weekend pilots, amateur musicians, model railroad enthusiasts, and collectors of all kinds are a few of the other hobbyists that have found good uses for computers.

Many home computers have been bought to help students with their educations. In addition to learning how to use computers (in itself a worthwhile educational objective), students can use computer-assisted instruction to help them master school subjects, word processing to write papers, database management and spreadsheet analysis to organize and analyze information, and telecommunications to obtain research material from information services.

Some people have offices in their homes, either because they are self-employed or just because they bring work home from the office. Computers in home offices are just as useful as in those located in business establishments.

In *telecommuting*, clerical workers do their work at home, using a computer terminal to communicate with the computer system at their place of business. The workers are frequently enthusiastic about telecommuting, but not everybody else is. Managers are often uneasy about workers they cannot keep an eye on. And unions, which have traditionally opposed work in the home, claim that telecommuting workers are paid lower salaries and given fewer benefits that workers in the office. Another reason for union objections is that home workers are difficult to organize into unions.

Some feel that the key to widespread use of home computers is telecommunications. Already, information services allow subscribers to make purchases, carry out banking transactions, buy and sell stocks, make airline reservations, and obtain information on a wide variety of subjects. Currently, however, such services are used by a relatively small number of telecommunications enthusiasts; they are unknown to the public at large.

◣ IMPACT ON SOCIETY

The widespread use of computers is changing many aspects of our everyday lives. People often disagree on which changes should be encouraged as beneficial and which should be discouraged or prohibited as undesirable. The following are some areas of computer use that are of particular concern.

Privacy

Information about each of us appears in many computer files. Such files can be merged to produce a computerized dossier from items of information that were originally collected by different institutions for diverse purposes. Such a dossier could reveal our purchasing preferences, our political sympathies, our credit and medical histories, and our interactions with a variety of government agencies. What restrictions need to be placed on the creation and use of such files to protect our right to privacy and our civil liberties?

Computerized equipment in the workplace allows workers' performance to be monitored much more closely than in the past. For example, workers often enter transactions (such as orders and payments) into a computer via terminals; the computer can easily keep track of how many transactions each worker processes each hour. A computer used for word processing can even record the number of times the typist strikes the keys. Many workers see such electronic monitoring as an invasion of their privacy and claim that it increases the stressfulness of their jobs.

Computer Crime

New technologies present new opportunities for criminals, and computing is no exception. With most financial records stored in computers, criminals

Rather than choose between two rival systems, this executive has both an Apple Macintosh (left) and an IBM PC on her desk.

can steal millions with a few taps on a computer keyboard. Some hackers—computer enthusiasts—have disgraced their hobby by making illegal use of computer systems belonging to other people, sometimes destroying vital data or obtaining confidential information in the process. And software publishers lose millions of dollars each year due to illegal copying of programs by computer users. It has been estimated that as many as half the programs in use are illegal copies.

Employment

Many jobs that once required human labor can now be done better by computers, automated machines, or robots. Although it is sometimes argued that computers have created more jobs than they have eliminated, the newly created jobs usually require far greater skills than the old ones that were eliminated. The result is high unemployment among unskilled and semiskilled workers. What provisions should be made for those whose jobs have been eliminated by computers and automation? And what changes in our economy will be needed to meet the challenge of a future in which the number of available jobs is far fewer than the number of people who need work?

Human Factors in Computer Use

People are by no means always happy with the prospect of using computers in their work. Computers have a reputation for being difficult to learn to operate and unforgiving of minor errors. Workers fear that some slight

A specially designed keyboard and word-processor program allow this Macintosh to be used for writing in the Eskimo language Inuktitut.

mistake will have major consequences for which they will be blamed, that they will "push the wrong button and bring down the entire system." Some office workers have gone so far as to quit their jobs rather than learn to use computers. Computerphobia, the irrational fear of computers, is a recognized psychological condition.

Some fears of computers are indeed irrational, such as the widespread myth that computer displays produce harmful radiation, although repeated studies have failed to discover any radiation danger. On the other hand, it is no myth that glare on a computer display can produce eyestrain and that long, uninterrupted sessions at a computer can produce muscle cramps and backaches. The instructions for operating many computer systems are difficult to understand, and many systems make it all too easy to destroy hours of work with a single careless mistake.

These problems have led to a concern for ergonomics or human factors in computer use. Special lighting and furniture have been designed to reduce eyestrain, muscle cramps, and back problems. Computer programmers are working to make interactions with computer systems easier to learn. One approach is to employ a metaphor in which computer operations are understood in terms of those required for some familiar office task. In the popular *desktop metaphor*, for example, the computer display simulates a desktop containing papers, file folders, in and out trays, and so on. The user can remove a form from the in tray, make additions, deletions, and changes, and then put the form in the out tray, just as one would do with paper forms on an actual desk.

Computer software whose operation is easy to master is said to be *user friendly*. User-friendly programs are often based on a well-chosen metaphor that makes their operation self-evident. One reason for the popularity of spreadsheet programs is that they are based on the simple metaphor of a ledger sheet.

◥ SUMMARY

Computers are mind tools in that they extend the power of our minds rather than the power and dexterity of our muscles or the keenness of our senses. The microelectronics revolution of the 1970s has made these powerful mind tools widely available at a cost almost everyone can afford.

A computer stores and manipulates data under the control of a set of step-by-step instructions called a program. A computer runs or executes a program when it carries out the program's instructions. Under the control of different programs, a single computer can carry out many different information processing tasks. By the same token, a computer cannot carry out a task until we have provided it with an appropriate program. We use the term hardware for the computing machinery itself and the term software for the programs that control it. The combination of hardware and software is known as a computer system.

A person who writes computer programs is a programmer and a person who uses a computer system is a user. A user who can carry out only a few carefully memorized tasks with a computer is a naive user; a user with extensive knowledge of computer hardware and software is a power user.

A computer that can execute programs provided by the user is a general purpose computer; one that only execute a single, built-in program is a special purpose computer. Depending on their cost, memory capacity, and speed of operation, computers can be classified as embedded computers, microcomputers, minicomputers, mainframes, and supercomputers. Embedded computers are usually special purpose microcomputers. General purpose microcomputers are also known as personal computers. Mini-computers are also know as midrange computers.

The most important hardware component of a computer system is the central processing unit or CPU, which is responsible for carrying out the instructions in a program. The program that a computer is executing and the data it is currently manipulating are stored in main memory. Permanent program and data files are stored in auxiliary memory, from which they are moved to main memory for execution or processing. The most popular media for auxiliary memory are disks, which vary widely in size and construction. The most common input device is a keyboard, and the most popular output devices are video displays and printers. A computer terminal is a device for communicating with a remote computer, usually a minicomputer or mainframe. It consists of a keyboard combined with a video display, a printer, or both.

Software is divided into systems programs (systems software), which helps people use the computer system, and applications programs (applications software), which carries out the useful tasks, or applications, for which the system is to be used. The most important systems programs are the operating system and language processors. The operating system manages the flow of programs and data through the computer system. Because one of the main tasks of the operating system is transferring programs and data to and from disk storage, it is often referred to as a disk operating system or DOS.

Computer programs are written in programming languages. Language processors allow people to write programs in convenient higher-level languages rather than in the obscure, coded machine language that the central processing unit can understand. Some widely used higher-level languages are Basic, Cobol, Fortran, and Pascal.

The first computers were used for mathematical, scientific, and engineering calculations. Today computers play an essential role in the design and manufacture of many products, including computers themselves. The second major application for computers was storing and processing business and financial records; today most such records exist only as entries in computer files. The microelectronics revolution brought computers into offices where they are used for word processing, spreadsheet analysis, database management, telecommunications, and business graphics. In education, computers are seeing ever increasing use for teaching traditional subjects as well as computer-related subjects, such as computer literacy, computer programming, and computer science. And computers are being used in many homes for recreation, education, hobbies, and office work done at home.

Widespread computer use is producing many social changes, some of which are undesirable or controversial. Major areas of concern are privacy and civil liberties, computer crime, loss of jobs to automation, and widespread fear and distrust of computers.

A student uses a laptop computer between classes.

◣ Vocabulary Review

analog	disk operating system	naive user
application	(DOS)	operating system
applications program	diskette	personal computer
auxiliary memory	embedded computer	power user
backup copy	general purpose	program
booting	computer	programmer
(bootstrapping)	hard disk	programming
central processing	hardware	language
unit (CPU)	higher-level language	software
computer system	integrated program	special purpose
computer terminal	main memory	computer
data	mainframe	supercomputer
database	metaphor	systems program
desktop metaphor	microcomputer	telecommunications
digital	microprocessor	telecommuting
digital computer	midrange computer	user
disk	minicomputer	user friendly
disk drive	mouse	video display

◣ For Further Reading

Athey, Thomas H., John C. Day, and Robert W. Zmud. *Computers and End-User Software*. Glenview, IL: Scott, Foresman, 1987.

Capron, H. L. *Computers: Tools for an Information Age*. Menlo Park, CA: Benjamin/Cummings, 1987.

Communications of the ACM (special issue on computing in the frontiers of science and engineering). November 1985.

Scientific American (special issue on advances in computing). October 1987.

Sullivan, David R., T. G. Lewis, and Curtis R. Cook. *Using Computers Today*. Boston: Houghton Mifflin, 1986.

◣ Review Questions

1 Why are we justified in referring to computers as mind tools?

2 Describe the microelectronics revolution. What is a computer chip? A microprocessor?

3 What are the two defining characteristics of computers?

4 What are programs?

5 Distinguish between hardware and software.

6 What is a computer system?

7 What is the function of the central processing unit? Of main memory? Of auxiliary memory?

8 What is the most widely used medium for auxiliary memory?

9 What is the most common input device for computers? What are the two most common output devices?

10 What is a computer terminal?

11 Distinguish embedded computers, microcomputers, minicomputers, mainframes, and supercomputers.

12 What is a personal computer?

13 Distinguish between systems software and applications software.

14 What is the function of the operating system? Why is it often referred to as a disk operating system or DOS?

15 What does it mean to boot a computer system?

16 What is a programming language? Contrast machine language and higher-level languages.

17 What is a language processor? A compiler?

18 Name four popular higher-level languages.

19 Describe five application areas for computers.

20 Describe four areas in which concerns have arisen over the adverse effects of computer use.

Topics for Discussion

1 Examine your own attitudes towards computers. Are they based on personal experience or on hearsay? Do you fear or distrust computers and if so, why? Would you be interested in a nontechnical job, such as office worker, that nevertheless required you to interact extensively with computers? Why or why not? How do you think people's attitudes toward computers might change as computers become more and more common at home, at school, and on the job?

2 Consider some familiar technological developments such as the automobile, the airplane, and the telephone. List the effects of each development on society. Which effects are harmful, which are beneficial, and which are controversial—considered beneficial by some and harmful by others?

3 The teaching of computer literacy is controversial. Proponents feel that all students need to be acquainted with the capabilities and limitations of computers to be able to function in the highly computerized society of tomorrow. Opponents argue that most students will use computers only in elementary ways, such as punching the keys on a computerized cash register, and that time and money spent on computer literacy courses could be better applied to teaching reading, writing, and arithmetic. Discuss the pros and cons of teaching computer literacy.

4 Computers are sometimes criticized as "cold" or "unfeeling," yet we do not hear the same criticism about other products of modern technology, such as phonographs, television sets, and video recorders. Why should our attitudes towards computers be different?

DEVELOPMENT OF COMPUTERS

INTRODUCTION

Sometimes the easiest way to understand a branch of science or technology is to consider the steps by which it reached its present stage of development. The form in which a concept is first introduced is often easier to understand than the more complex and sophisticated forms that it takes later. Many aspects of a technology seem far less arbitrary when we are aware of the historical circumstances that motivated their development. It's no wonder, then, that science and technical writers often take a historical approach to their subjects. We follow their lead in this chapter by taking a brief look at the historical development of computers.

IN THE BEGINNING

Before the advent of modern high technology, technical aids were available for only the simplest forms of information processing. The technologies of writing and printing preserved and distributed information. Clockwork mechanisms kept track of times, dates, and the motions of astronomical bodies. Simple mechanical devices helped diplomats and spies to encipher and decipher secret messages. Clockwork-driven robots that wrote letters and played musical instruments entertained the courts of Europe. Automated looms wove complex patterns. Elements of all of these innovations can be found in modern computer systems. The technology that led most directly to the computer, however, was that for carrying out arithmetical calculations.

The Abacus

''Paper and pencil'' calculation was incredibly difficult in ancient times. For one thing, the ancient equivalents of paper and pencil were scarce and expensive. For another, the notations for writing numbers were not well suited to calculation, as anyone who has ever tried to do multiplication or division in Roman numerals can testify. These circumstances almost forced the ancients to develop mechanical aids to computation.

The *abacus*, or counting frame, originated with the Babylonians about five thousand years ago. In its earliest form it consisted of a board with grooves in which pebbles could slide. (In fact, our words *calculate* and *calculator* come from the Latin word *calculus*, which means *pebble*.) Eventually, the pebbles were replaced by beads that slide on wires mounted in a frame.

One reason the abacus was so successful was that its construction embodied the concept of zero as a place holder, which was not present in Roman numerals and most other ancient notations. In the western countries, the widespread use of the abacus persisted until the modern Hindu-Arabic notation for numbers (which includes the concept of zero) and inexpensive writing materials made paper-and-pencil calculation practical. In the Orient, the use of the abacus persisted into modern times; only recently has it largely given way to the pocket electronic calculator.

Chinese abacus. The Japanese abacus has one less bead both above and below the divider.

Mechanical Calculators

The abacus was an adding and subtracting machine. Although its use greatly simplified multiplication and division, it did not relieve the operator of the need to learn the multiplication tables. Also the abacus had no provisions for carrying and borrowing, which had to be done manually by the operator. Calculators with provisions for carrying, borrowing, and automatic multiplication first appeared in the seventeenth century.

The first mechanical calculator was invented by the German astronomer Wilhelm Schickard. Little is known about Shickard's machine, no models of which have survived, but it was said to be able to do addition, subtraction, multiplication, and division.

The next mechanical calculators were invented by two of the most illustrious figures of seventeenth century science: the French mathematician and philosopher Blaise Pascal (pronounced pas CAL), after whom a popular programming language is now named, and the German mathematician, philosopher, and diplomat Wilhelm von Leibniz (pronounced LIPE nits). Pascal's machine could be used only for addition and subtraction; Leibniz's machine was capable of multiplication as well. Neither machine was reliable because the mechanical technology of the time could not produce parts with the necessary precision.

Another area of Leibniz's mathematical work would eventually be of enormous importance for computing. Leibniz was the first western mathematician to study *binary notation*, a method of representing numbers using only two digits, 0 and 1, instead of the usual ten digits, 0 through 9. (The 0s and 1s used in binary notation are called *binary digits* or *bits*.) Binary notation would turn out to be the most effective way to represent numbers in computers. That application lay far in the future, however. Leibniz's calculator, like all calculating devices prior to modern times, was based on the conventional ten-digit decimal notation.

Mechanical calculators were improved by later inventors, although for a long time they continued to be plagued with unreliable operation. Re-

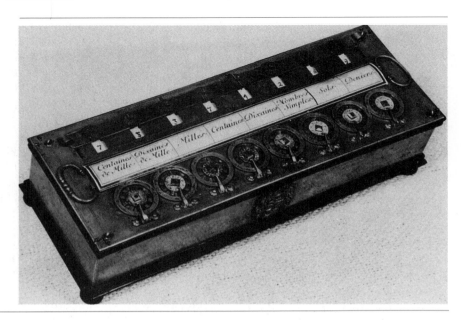

Pascal's calculator. The calculator was operated by turning the dials at the bottom in a manner similar to dialing a telephone.

liable calculators were developed in the late nineteenth century and become commonplace in the early 1900s. They remained in widespread use until replaced by electronic calculators in the early 1970s.

The Slide Rule and Analog Computers

The seventeenth century also saw the invention of the slide rule, which allowed multiplications and divisions to be performed by manipulating strips of wood ruled with special scales. Because of its simplicity, the slide rule did not suffer from the reliability problems that plagued mechanical calculators. Its main drawback was the limited accuracy with which its scales could be read. Slide rules became very popular with scientists and engineers, and remained so until replaced by electronic calculators in the 1970s.

We recall that there are two approaches to representing data in a computing device. Analog data is represented by continuously changing quantities, such as the positions of the hands on a traditional clock; digital data is represented by discrete symbols, such as those that appear on the face of a digital clock. The abacus and the early mechanical calculators were all digital devices. In the abacus, the digits 0 through 9 were represented by different arrangements of pebbles or beads; in the mechanical calculators, each digit was represented by a gear or other part that could be in one of ten possible positions. The slide rule, however, is an analog device, because answers are obtained by measuring the position of an indicator line on a ruled scale—a position that changes continuously as the slide rule is operated.

In the twentieth century, these two approaches to representing data led to two kinds of computers: *analog computers* based on measurement of continuously varying quantities and *digital computers* based on coded

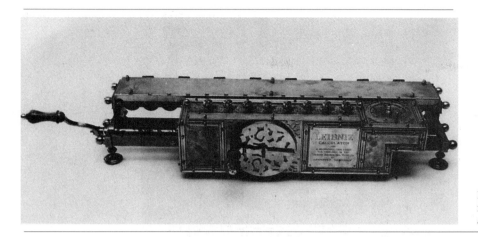

Leibniz's calculator could do multiplication and division as well as addition and subtraction.

representations of data. As with the slide rule and the mechanical calculator, early analog computers often proved simpler, less expensive, and more reliable than early digital computers. As the technology of computing advanced, however, the digital approach proved to be far more accurate, flexible, and powerful than the analog approach. Today analog computers are used only for very specialized purposes. When the word *computer* is used without qualification, it always refers to a digital computer.

The Jacquard Loom

Around the turn of the nineteenth century, the French inventor Joseph-Marie Jacquard devised an automated loom for weaving cloth containing decorative patterns. The loom was controlled by a set of punched cards that were fastened together to form a continuous tape. The patterns of holes in the cards determined which threads were raised and lowered at each step in the weaving process. Changing the cards changed the pattern woven into the cloth. Jacquard looms came into widespread use in the early nineteenth century, and their descendants are still used today.

The Jacquard loom was the first machine whose behavior could be changed by changing its program rather than by redesigning the machine. As such, it was the direct ancestor not only of modern automated machine tools but of the player piano as well. It also has the dubious distinction of being the first automated machine to arouse public opposition. Jacquard looms were smashed and sabotaged by workers whose jobs had been eliminated.

◣ THE ANALYTICAL ENGINE

In the 1830s, the concepts of mechanical calculators and programmable machines came together, and the idea of the automatic computer was born. Like most early calculating devices, however, the computer remained

Jacquard loom. Note the punch cards at top, which are joined to form a belt.

largely an idea only, since the mechanical technology of the time was not up to constructing the machine itself.

Charles Babbage

The inventor of that nineteenth-century computer was a figure far more common in fiction than in real life—an eccentric mathematician. Most mathematicians live personal lives not too much different from everyone else's. They just happen to do mathematics instead of driving trucks or running stores or filling teeth. But Charles Babbage was an exception.

For example, all his life Babbage waged a vigorous campaign against London organ-grinders. He blamed the noise they made for the loss of a quarter of his working power. Babbage was not merely content to write anti-organ-grinder letters to the newspapers and to members of parliament. He personally hauled individual offenders before magistrates, and became furious when the magistrates declined to throw the offenders in jail.

Or consider this. Babbage took issue with this couplet in Tennyson's poem ''Vision of Sin'':

> Every minute dies a man
> Every minute one is born

Babbage pointed out (correctly) that if this were true, the population of the earth would remain constant. In a letter to the poet, Babbage suggested a revision:

> Every moment dies a man
> And one and a sixteenth is born

He emphasized that one and a sixteenth was not exact, but he thought it would be good enough for poetry.

Yet, despite his eccentricities, Babbage was a genius. He was a prolific inventor whose inventions included the ophthalmoscope (for examining the retina of the eye), the skeleton key, the locomotive "cow catcher," and the speedometer. He also pioneered operations research, the science of carrying out business and industrial operations as efficiently as possible. Babbage was a fellow of the Royal Society, and at Cambridge University he held the same chair that was once held by Isaac Newton, the most famous of British scientists.

The Difference Engine

The mathematical tables of the nineteenth century were full of mistakes. Even when the tables were calculated correctly, the printed versions often contained typographical errors. Because people who published new tables often copied from old ones, the same errors cropped up in table after table.

According to one story, Babbage was lamenting about the errors in some tables to his friend Herschel, a noted astronomer. "I wish to god these calculations had been executed by steam," Babbage said. "It is quite possible," Herschel responded.

Intrigued by Herschel's response, Babbage set out to build a machine that would not only calculate, but would automatically print, the entries in the tables. He called the machine the *Difference Engine* because it worked by solving what mathematicians call difference equations. The name is somewhat misleading in that the machine constructs tables using repeated additions, not subtractions.

The word *engine*, by the way, comes from the same root as *ingenious*. Originally, *engine* referred to any clever invention. Only later was its meaning restricted to those particularly clever inventions that change the heat of burning fuel into mechanical energy.

In 1823 Babbage obtained a government grant to build a Difference Engine. He ran into difficulties, however, and eventually abandoned the project. In 1854 a Swedish printer built a working Difference Engine based on Babbage's design.

The Analytical Engine

One reason Babbage abandoned the Difference Engine was that he had been struck by a much better idea. Inspired by Jacquard's punched-card-controlled loom, Babbage wanted to build a punched-card-controlled calculator. He call his proposed automatic calculator the *Analytical Engine*.

The Difference Engine could only compute tables (and only those that could be computed by successive additions). But the Analytical Engine could carry out any calculation, just as Jacquard's loom could weave any pattern. All one had to do was punch the cards with instructions for the desired calculations.

The Analytical Engine had many of the major components found in modern computers. Babbage referred to the machine's main memory as the store; the terms *store* and *storage* are still sometimes used to refer to

Charles Babbage.

Part of Babbage's Analytical Engine, a nineteenth-century computer. Like the Difference Engine, the Analytical Engine was never completed.

main memory. The Analytical Engine's central processing unit consisted of the mill, which carried out arithmetical calculations, and the barrel, which triggered the parts of the machine needed to carry out each instruction. Today we would call the mill the arithmetic/logic unit and the barrel the control unit. Input data for the Analytical Engine was to be on punched cards, and its output was to be printed.

Had the Analytical Engine been completed, it would have been a nineteenth-century computer. But, alas, that was not to be. The British government had already sunk thousands of pounds into the Difference Engine and had received nothing in return. It had no intention of making the same mistake with the Analytical Engine. No working Analytical Engine was ever built, and Babbage's work was forgotten until after the same discoveries had been made independently by the computer pioneers of the twentieth century.

Looking back, the government may have even been right. If it had financed the new invention, it might have received nothing in return. For, as usual, Babbage's ideas were far ahead of existing mechanical technology. This was particularly true because the design for the Analytical Engine was grandiose. For example, Babbage wanted his machine to do calculations with fifty-digit accuracy, which is far greater than the accuracy of most modern computers and far more than needed for most calculations.

What's more, Babbage often changed his plans in the middle of a project with the result that everything that had been done previously had to be abandoned and the work started anew. How ironic that the founder of operations research, the science of industrial management, could not manage the development of his own inventions.

Babbage's contemporaries would have considered him more successful if he had stayed with his original plan and constructed the Difference Engine. If he had done so, however, he would have earned only a footnote in history. It is for the Analytical Engine that he never completed that we honor Babbage as the "father of the computer."

Lady Lovelace

Even though the Analytical Engine was never completed, a demonstration program was written for it. The author of that program has the honor of being the world's first computer programmer. Her name was Augusta Ada Byron, later Countess of Lovelace, the only legitimate daughter of the poet Lord Byron.

Lady Lovelace was a liberated woman in a time when such liberation was hardly fashionable. Not only did she have the usual accomplishments in language and music, but she was an excellent mathematician. The latter was most unusual for a young woman in the nineteenth century. (She was also fond of horse racing, which was even more unusual.) Her mathematical abilities became apparent when she was only fifteen, and she studied with one of the most well-known mathematicians of her time, Augustus de Morgan. She became interested in Babbage's Analytical Engine at about the same time she was studying with de Morgan.

In 1842 Lady Lovelace discovered a paper in French on the Analytical Engine. At Babbage's suggestion she translated the paper and added her

Lady Lovelace, the first computer programmer.

own notes, which were twice as long as the original paper. Much of what we know today about the Analytical Engine comes from Lady Lovelace's notes.

To demonstrate how the Analytical Engine would work, Lady Lovelace included in her notes a program for calculating a certain series of numbers of interest to mathematicians. This was the first computer program, and Lady Lovelace thus became the first programmer. A programming language recently developed for the Department of Defense is named *Ada* in Lady Lovelace's honor.

"We may say most aptly," Lady Lovelace wrote, "that the Analytical Engine *weaves algebraical patterns* just as the Jacquard loom weaves flowers and leaves." Most aptly said, indeed.

◣ BOOLEAN ALGEBRA

Another cornerstone of modern computing was laid in the mid-nineteenth century by the English mathematican George Boole. Boole invented an algebra of logical reasoning in which the truth or falsity of a statement is represented by a *truth value* of 1 for true and 0 for false. The operations of *Boolean algebra*, as the algebra of logic is now called, correspond to logical connectives such as *and*, *or*, and *not*. For example, if A and B represent sentences that can be either true or false, the compound sentence "A and B" is true only if both sentence A is true and sentence B is true. Boole expressed this is his algebra by defining the operator AND as follows:

0 AND 0 = 0

0 AND 1 = 0

1 AND 0 = 0

1 AND 1 = 1

Thus, the compound sentence "A and B" has a truth value of 1 only if both sentence A and sentence B have a truth value of 1.

Boolean algebra is now used not only for reasoning about the truth and falsity of statements but for designing the electronic circuits that make up a computer. Modern programming languages often classify data into *types* depending on the kind of information represented by the data and the operations that can be carried out on it. In many programming languages, the type used to represent truth values is known as type *Boolean*.

◣ AUTOMATIC DATA PROCESSING

In the 1880s, the American engineer Herman Hollerith pioneered what would eventually become the most widespread application of computers. Out of his work grew the company that is now most closely associated with computing in the public mind.

What Hollerith invented were machines to aid in compiling, sorting, and tabulating data collected in the 1890 United States census. Each per-

George Boole, who invented an algebra of logic now known in his honor as Boolean algebra. In programming languages, logical data and operations are often designated by the adjective *Boolean*.

son's responses to the census questions were represented by a pattern of holes punched into a card. Hollerith's machines sensed these patterns of punched holes and carried out the proper action for each card. One machine, after reading a set of cards, displayed on a set of dials the number of people in each category for which statistics were being collected. Another sorted cards by opening a door over the bin in which each card was to be placed.

Hollerith pioneered *automatic data processing*,* the use of machines to process statistical and business data. Hollerith was the first to apply electricity to computing; previous computing devices had been purely mechanical. Hollerith's punched cards remained in widespread use for recording data even after the actual data processing was being done by computers. Only in the 1960s did punched cards begin to be replaced by computer terminals, which allow data to be entered directly into a computer without first being punched onto cards.

Hollerith formed a firm, the Tabulating Machine Company, to sell his machines first to census bureaus throughout the world and then later to private businesses as well. Eventually, after merging with three other companies, Hollerith's firm became the IBM (International Business Machines) corporation, which became the major supplier of punched-card data processing equipment. Because of its preeminence in punched-card data processing, IBM was well positioned to play a major role in the business applications of computers. Although IBM was not the first company to market a computer, and was initially reluctant to enter the computer field, when it finally took the plunge, it quickly became and still remains the major supplier of computing equipment used for automatic data processing.

BABBAGE'S DREAM COME TRUE

Babbage's work was totally forgotten, to be unearthed only after it had been rediscovered by others. Even the use of punched cards for data had to be rediscovered by Hollerith. Automatic computers of the kind envisioned by Babbage first began to be built in the late 1930s, almost exactly a hundred years after Babbage had begun work on the Analytical Engine.

Electromechanical Computers

The Analytical Engine was to have been a purely mechanical device. Data manipulation and moving the data from one part of the machine to another were accomplished by a complex array of moving parts that even a modern mechanical engineer might have trouble getting to work reliably. The first computers actually to be built, however, were *electromechanical computers*. Electricity was used to move data and instructions from one part of the machine to another, replacing the complex mechanical arrangements Babbage had envisioned for this purpose. The actual calculations, however,

---

*Today this application is often referred to as just *data processing*, or *DP*, the "automatic" being taken for granted. The term *electronic data processing*, or *EDP*, is also sometimes used.

were still carried out by moving parts, whose operations were relatively slow compared to those of electric circuits.

In 1936 the German engineer Konrad Zuse began building a series of computers. When his first attempt at a purely mechanical computer did not work very well, he switched to electromechanical designs. Zuse also considered the possibility of completely electronic computers but was not able to acquire the necessary components. Zuse's machines were prophetic in another way: the binary digits 0 and 1 were used for representing data, and data manipulation was governed by the rules of Boolean algebra, which Zuse rediscovered. Numbers were represented in the two-digit binary notation first explored by Leibniz. Alas, as has happened so many times in the development of computing, Zuse's work did not become widely known and the innovations he developed had to be rediscovered later by others.

The most well known and influential electromechanical calculator was the Harvard Mark I, completed in 1944 under the direction of Howard Aiken. The actual construction of the Mark I was done by IBM; this was IBM's first venture into computing.

The Mark I was scarcely finished before it was obsolete. The electromechanical machines were just not fast enough. Their speed was seriously limited by the time required for mechanical parts to move from one position to another. For example, the Mark I took six seconds for a multiplication and twelve for a division; this was only five or six times faster than what a human being could do with a mechanical desk calculator.

Electronic Computers: The Quest for Speed

Much of the later development of computers has been dominated by a quest for ever increasing speed of operation. Why is speed so important? A computer program breaks a complex information processing task down into thousands of very simple operations, such as adding, subtracting, multiplying, dividing, and comparing numbers. If the original complex task is to be completed in a reasonable time, the simple operations into which it has been decomposed must be carried out at high speed.

What was needed was a machine whose computing, control, and memory elements were completely electrical. The speed of such a machine would be limited not by the speed of mechanical moving parts but by the much greater speed of moving electrons.

The elements of such an *electronic computer* were demonstrated in the late 1930s by John V. Atanasoff of what was then Iowa State College. Although Atanasoff's work did not become widely known until much later, it did influence the thinking of John W. Mauchly, one of the designers of the first general purpose electronic computer, ENIAC (Electronic Numerical Integrator and Computer). A patent on ENIAC taken out by Mauchly and coinventor J. Presper Eckert would eventually be invalidated because of, among other reasons, the earlier work of Atanasoff. In the words of the judge's decision, Eckert and Mauchly "did not themselves first invent the automatic electronic digital computer, but instead derived that subject matter from one Dr. John Vincent Atanasoff." Historically, however, ENIAC is considered to be much more important than Atanasoff's work, which did not become widely known until the time of the patent dispute in the early 1970s.

Herman Hollerith, who pioneered automatic data processing.

ENIAC, which was completed in 1945, used vacuum tubes for computing and memory and used an electrical plugboard (like an old-fashioned telephone switch board) for control. The connections on the plugboard specified the sequence of operations that ENIAC would carry out. ENIAC was 500 times faster than the best electromechanical computer. A problem that took one minute to solve on ENIAC would require eight to ten hours on an electromechanical machine.

ENIAC was also the first of many computers to have acronyms for names. The same tradition gave us EDVAC, EDSAC UNIVAC, JOHNIAC, ILLIAC, and even MANIAC.

The Stored-Program Computer

EDVAC (Electronic Discrete Variable Computer) was designed by Eckert and Mauchly in the mid-1940s; delayed by a bitter patent-rights dispute that caused Eckert and Mauchly to leave the project, it was not completed until 1952. EDSAC (Electronic Delay Storage Automatic Computer), a British machine based on the EDVAC design, was actually completed first, in 1949. These machines introduced the important concept of a *stored-program computer*. In all earlier machines, from the Analytical Engine through ENIAC, the program had been stored outside the computer, on punched tape, punched cards, or plugboards. Programs for EDVAC and EDSAC, however, were stored in memory in the same form as data. Like data, the stored program was subject to manipulation by the computer.

The original motivation for the stored-program computer was to allow a program to modify itself. That is, one part of the program could direct the computer to change another part of the program, a technique that could be used to overcome some of the limitations of early computers. Today, self-modifying programs are considered a poor programming technique. Because some of the program's instructions will be modified before they are executed, it is almost impossible for a person reading a self-modifying program to understand what the program will do and hence assure that it will work correctly. On the other hand, the concept of one program manipulating *another* program as data lies at the foundation of all modern systems software, such as operating systems and language processors.

The brilliant Hungarian-American mathematican John von Neumann (pronounced fun NOY mahn) worked with Eckert and Mauchly on the design of EDVAC. In 1945 von Neumann published a preliminary report on EDVAC that for the first time described the stored-program concept in print. As a result of this report, von Neumann was given credit for the stored-program computer, which has come to be called a *von Neumann machine*. It now appears, however, that the stored-program concept was due to Eckert and Mauchly rather than von Neumann.

EDVAC and EDSAC were the first electronic computers to use binary notation, and for all practical purposes they introduced this concept, since Zuse's earlier use of binary notation for electromechanical computers was not widely known. Informed of the choice of binary notation, people often expressed concern over the difficulty of converting between the binary notation used by the computer and the decimal notation that people can

Hollerith's tabulating machine.

understand. Computer pioneers found it difficult to convince others that this conversion presents no problem because the computer itself can be easily programmed to convert between decimal and binary notation.

Although ENIAC was not designed as a stored-program computer, a plugboard program was devised for it that allowed it to carry out instructions stored in its memory. That is, under the direction of the plugboard program, ENIAC would execute another program stored in memory. The plugboard program, what we would call an interpreter program today, was the first example of a systems program and of a language processor. It pioneered a fundamental principle of systems programming, that of providing through software capabilities that could have been, but were not, included in the machine's hardware.

Commercial Manufacture of Computers

The early computers were designed and constructed individually rather than manufactured as commercial products. This era ended in 1951 when the first Ferranti Mark I computer was installed in the University of Manchester in England. In the same year, the first UNIVAC (Universal Automatic Computer) was delivered to the United States Census Bureau by Remington Rand. UNIVAC had been designed by Eckert and Mauchly for manufacture by their own Eckert-Mauchly Computer Corporation; however, they were unable to raise the funds needed to manufacture UNIVACs and so had to sell out to Remington Rand.

UNIVAC was the first computer to gain widespread notice by the general public. The machine received considerable publicity when CBS used a UNIVAC to provide early election-night predictions of the outcome of the 1952 presidential election. When the computer predicted an Eisenhower landslide in what was supposed to be a close race, the skeptical programmers reprogrammed the UNIVAC to produce a more conservative estimate. The computer's first prediction, however, turned out to be nearly correct, only a few electoral votes off from the final election results (Eisenhower did slightly better than even the computer predicted).

In 1953 IBM began delivery of the IBM 701 computer. IBM's preeminent position in punched-card data processing and its large, well-trained sales force gave it a commercial advantage that other early computer companies found impossible to overcome. IBM quickly became the predominant supplier of computers for automatic data processing. In other areas, however, such as scientific computing, IBM encountered much stronger competition.

THE COMPUTER GENERATIONS

From the 1940s to the present, computer technology has gone through a number of major changes, and still further changes are anticipated in the future. People sometimes classify computers according to *computer generations*, each based on a different technology. Although the idea of computer generations is useful for outlining the development of computer technology, its limitations should be noted. The use of different technologies overlapped, so there is no sharp dividing line from one generation to the next. As a result, people sometimes differ as to the time span of each generation and the technologies that should be associated with it. And the announcement of a new generation has sometimes been used purely for publicity purposes by computer manufacturers and researchers.

The Harvard Mark I: Babbage's dream come true.

(Left) J. Presper Eckert standing before ENIAC, the first general purpose electronic computer. (Right) John W. Mauchly (left) and J. Presper Eckert, the inventors of ENIAC, stand before another early electronic computer, BINAC.

The First Generation

First-generation computers prevailed in the 1940s and for much of the 1950s. They used vacuum tubes for calculation, control, and sometimes for memory. A variety of other ingenious devices were also used for memory. One, for instance, stored data as sound waves circulating in a column of mercury. This was the "delay storage" that forms part of the name of EDSAC. Another device stored data as patterns of electric charge on the face of a cathode ray tube, which is similar in construction to a television picture tube. This memory device became obsolete, but the cathode ray tube would return in the third generation as the video display, the primary device for displaying computer output.

The use of magnetism for data storage was pioneered in the first generation. Data was recorded on *magnetic tape* using much the same principles that govern modern audio and video cassette recorders. *Magnetic drums* worked in a similar manner except that the data was recorded on the surface of a spinning drum rather than on tape. Magnetic tape and magnetic drums were important in both the first and second generations; both largely gave way to disks in the third generation.

Vacuum tubes (the "radio tubes" that were once familiar components of radio and television sets) are bulky (about the size of a salt shaker), unreliable (they burn out frequently), energy consuming, and generate large amounts of heat. As long as computers were tied down to vacuum tube technology, they could only be bulky, cumbersome, and expensive.

The Second Generation

In the late 1950s, the transistor began to replace the vacuum tube. Transistors, which are only slightly larger than kernels of corn, generate little heat and enjoy long lives.

UNIVAC, the first computer to be commercially marketed in the United States.

At about this time, *magnetic-core memory* was introduced. This consisted of a latticework of wires on which were strung tiny, doughnut-shaped beads called cores. Electric currents flowing in the wires stored data by magnetizing cores. Data could be stored in or retrieved from core memory in about a millionth of a second.

With the introduction of core memory, a clear distinction formed between main memory for short-term storage with fast access and auxiliary memory for longer-term storage with slower access. Main memory was core memory for the second and much of the third generations; even today oldtimers in the computing field often refer to main memory as "core." Magnetic tape, introduced in the first generation, was the mainstay of auxiliary memory in the second generation.

Higher-level languages appeared during the second generation. In 1951 mathematician and naval officer Grace Murray Hopper conceived the first compiler program for translating from a higher-level language to the computer's machine language. In 1957 John Backus at IBM completed a compiler for Fortran, the first higher-level language to see widespread use. In 1960 an industry-wide committee (on which Grace Hopper played a leading role) published a preliminary draft report describing Cobol. After further revision and extension in the early 1960s, Cobol became the standard programming language for business data processing applications on mainframe computers.

The rudiments of operating systems were also emerging. Loading programs loaded other programs into main memory from external media such as punched cards, paper tape, or magnetic tape. Monitor programs aided the programmer or computer operator to load other programs, monitor their execution, and examine the contents of memory locations. An input-output control system consisted of a set of subroutines for manipulating input, output, and storage devices. A *subroutine* is a program that is called by another program. Control of the computer is passed to the subroutine by the calling program; when the subroutine completes its task, it returns control of the computer to the calling program, which continues executing from the point at which it called the subroutine. By calling the subroutines in the input-output control system, a program could communicate with external devices without becoming involved in the intricacies of their internal operation.

The Third Generation

The early 1960s saw the introduction of *integrated circuits*, which incorporated hundreds of transistors on a single silicon chip. The chip itself was small enough to fit on the end of a finger; after being mounted in a protective package, it would still fit in the palm of a hand. With integrated circuits, computers could be made smaller, less expensive, and more reliable.

Integrated circuits made possible minicomputers, computers small and inexpensive enough to find a place in the classroom and scientific laboratory. In the late 1960s, integrated circuits began to be used for main memory. Except for some older machines still in use, integrated-circuit memory chips have now completely replaced magnetic-core memory.

Beginning in the 1960s, magnetic disks began to replace magnetic tape for auxiliary memory. Today, disks are the dominant technology for auxiliary memory. Magnetic tape is now used mainly for transporting programs and data between computers (software for mainframes and minicomputers is usually delivered on magnetic tape) and for archiving—storing programs and data that must be kept on file but are rarely, if ever, used.

The third generation saw the advent of computer terminals for communicating with a computer from remote locations. The first terminals were typewriter-like devices that produced printed output. During the course of the third generation, the typewriter terminal largely gave way to the *video-display terminal (VDT)* in which the computer's output was displayed on a screen rather than printed. Video-display terminals largely replaced punched cards as the primary means for entering data and programs into a computer.

The use of higher-level languages became widespread during the third generation. Compilers were written for well over 150 higher-level languages, although only about 10 to 20 languages received widespread use.

Operating systems came into their own in the third generation. The operating system was given complete control of the computer system; the computer operator, programmers, and users all obtained services by placing requests with the operating system via computer terminals. The computer's control console was used only for starting up the system and diagnosing malfunctions; eventually, elaborate control consoles disappeared.

Turning over control of the computer to the operating system made possible modes of operation that would have been impossible with manual control. In *multitasking*, for example, the computer is switched rapidly from program to program in round-robin fashion, giving the appearance that all the programs are being executed simultaneously. When one program must wait on a slow external device, such as a keyboard, it loses its turns at the central processing unit until the external operation is complete.

A vacuum tube circuit (left) from a first-generation computer and a transistor circuit (right) from a second-generation computer. A modern computer chip may be the equivalent of ten to a hundred thousand circuits such as these.

Grace Hopper, a pioneer in programming languages and compilers.

(Left) Two computer chips fit on the face of a watch. (Right) Chips in their protective packages, ready for installation in computers.

Thus while one program is waiting, the central processing unit is kept busy working on other programs.

An important form of multitasking is *time sharing*, in which many users communicate with a single computer from remote terminals. Although each user seems to have sole use of the computer, in fact the central processing unit is being switched rapidly from one user's program to another's. While one user is pausing to think, the computer is busy working on other users' programs.

The term *virtual* is used for any computing resource that appears to correspond to a hardware component but is actually simulated by means of software. In the late 1960s and early 1970s, operating systems began to offer *virtual memory*, in which the operating system automatically transfers programs and data between main and auxiliary memory, thus making the system seem to have a much larger main memory than is actually present in the hardware.

The Fourth Generation

The 1970s saw the advent of *large-scale integration (LSI)* and *very large-scale integration (VLSI)*. The first LSI chips contained thousands of transistors; modern VLSI chips contain hundreds of thousands or millions of transistors. VLSI technology led to two innovations: embedded computers inexpensive enough to be used as parts of other appliances and personal computers inexpensive enough to be used as personal tools rather than as resources to be shared by an entire organization.

The most important computer chip is the microprocessor, which corresponds to Babbage's mill and barrel. The first microprocessor, designated the 4004, was introduced in 1971 by the Intel corporation. The 4004 was intended for embedded use in calculators, cash registers, and the like. It was not powerful enough to serve as the central processing unit of a microcomputer. In 1972 Intel introduced the 8008 microprocessor, which was just barely powerful enough for use in microcomputers. An improved version, the 8080, which was introduced in 1974, was much better suited to serving as the central processing unit of a general purpose computer.

In July 1974 *Radio-Electronics* magazine published an article on a home-built computer based on the 8008 microprocessor. Over ten thousand readers purchased detailed construction plans from the magazine. Because of the complexity of the project and the difficulty of obtaining the necessary parts, however, it is doubtful that many who ordered the plans actually built the computer.

The January, 1975 issue of *Popular Electronics* featured the Altair 8800, a microcomputer based on the 8080 microprocessor. A complete kit of parts for building the Altair was offered by an Albuquerque, New Mexico company called MITS (Micro Instrumentation Technology Systems). Reader response was overwhelming; MITS was deluged with phone calls and within a month had received orders for 500 kits. (In a business plan submitted earlier to its bank, MITS had predicted 500 orders within a year.)

The success of MITS inspired many other companies to produce personal computers. The personal computer marketplace became and remains very turbulent with new companies frequently appearing and existing ones frequently failing. Although space does not permit considering these developments in any detail, we will look briefly at a few of the most important personal computers that have appeared to date.

In 1977 Apple Computer Company introduced the Apple II, a compact desktop computer that was self-contained except for a video display and disk drives. The Apple II was one of the first microcomputers to be accepted by business users. This acceptance was largely due to a single program for the Apple II, a spreadsheet program called *VisiCalc*.

In 1981 IBM introduced the IBM Personal Computer, usually referred to as the IBM PC. To the surprise of many, probably including IBM, the IBM PC was enormously successful and quickly became the leading personal computer in terms of sales. The entry of IBM into the personal computer marketplace initiated the widespread use of personal computers by corporations, which were apparently ready to use personal computers but reluctant to purchase them from less well-known companies. The original IBM PC was followed by the IBM PC/XT (eXtended Technology) with a built-in hard disk and the IBM PC/AT (Advanced Technology) with both a built-in hard disk and a faster microprocessor. These machines are largely *compatible*: most software for the IBM PC family will run on the PC, PC/XT, and PC/AT.

To capitalize on the success of the IBM PC, PC/XT, and PC/AT, many other manufacturers now produce *clones*, also known as *IBM PC compatibles*, which imitate many aspects of the IBM PC machines and can run many of the same programs. The tendency to imitate the IBM PC family has provided the industry with needed standardization on the one hand but may have tended to stifle innovation on the other.

In 1981 Osborne Computer Corporation introduced the first *portable computer*, a personal computer (with keyboard, display, and disk drives) built into a carrying case. Portable computers became popular with those who needed to use their computer at more than one location. Other manufacturers quickly introduced portables; these newer portables were more technologically advanced than the Osborne machine and (probably most important of all) were IBM PC compatible. Unable to keep up with the competition, Osborne Computer Corporation went bankrupt in 1983.

Also in 1983, Radio Shack introduced the first *laptop computer*, a battery operated computer that could be used on airplanes and in meetings, news conferences, and hotel rooms. Although early laptops suffered from such problems as small, hard-to-read displays, lack of disk drives, and lack of IBM PC compatibility, they quickly became popular with writers and journalists and with business people who needed to use a computer while traveling. The limitations of the early laptops have now largely been removed; the most recent laptops are IBM PC compatible, have full-size, easy-to-read displays, and have both diskette and hard-disk drives. Some people have gone so far as to suggest that laptops may eventually replace desktop computers; at least, they seem likely to replace the bulkier, heavier Osborne-style portables.

In 1984 Apple introduced the Macintosh computer, which is distinguished by its *user interface*, the way in which information is presented and manipulated on the computer screen. The user interface determines what is sometimes called the *look and feel* of the system—the appearance and behavior of the system as seen through the eyes of the user. The Macintosh user interface, which grew out of research done at the Xerox Palo Alto Research Center, emphasizes *graphics* (pictures, drawings, and a variety of typefaces), *icons* (small drawings representing system components such as files, disks, and printers), and the use of a mouse to select commands from menus. The Macintosh user interface became popular with users (particularly those who were new to computing), even though the original Macintosh suffered from lack of speed, main memory capacity, and disk storage capacity. Later models, notably the Macintosh II introduced in 1987, removed the limitations of the original Macintosh while retaining the distinctive look and feel of the Macintosh user interface.

Also in 1987, IBM introduced its Personal System/2 (PS/2) computers. The PS/2 family features some technological advances over the IBM PC family, which PS/2 is intended to replace. IBM PC users have been slow to switch to the PS/2 line, and manufacturers of IBM PC compatibles have introduced machines that rival or exceed the capabilities of the most advanced of the PS/2 machines. It thus seems that the PS/2 family will not quickly replace the IBM PC compatibles, but that both will continue to claim significant shares of the personal computer market.

To reduce the impact of PS/2 clones, IBM has made extensive use of *proprietary technology** in the PS/2 line. In order to make PS/2 clones legally, other manufacturers must license this technology from IBM. For such licenses, IBM is charging a hefty 5 percent royalty, which (IBM hopes) will reduce the prevalence of PS/2 clones and increase their cost. In any event, IBM will get a percentage of the sales income from PS/2 clones, which it does not get for IBM PC clones.

Every general purpose microcomputer needs an operating system. In some cases the operating system is proprietary to a particular computer

---

*A technology is proprietary if rights to its use (such as copyrights and patents) are owned or controlled by a particular company.

Punch cards were widely used for input and output by second- and third-generation computers.

manufacturer; the operating system is available only from that manufacturer and used only with that manufacturer's computers. For example, Apple computers normally run proprietary operating systems; the distinctive features of the Macintosh user interface derive mainly from the Macintosh's proprietary operating system, which is called simply "the Finder" (it is part of the Macintosh concept to avoid technical terms like *operating system*).

Other operating systems can be used with machines from many different manufacturers; all computers running a given operating system must use the same or closely related microprocessors. Typically, the developer of the operating system licenses it to the various computer manufacturers, each of whom adapts the operating system to its own computer and sells copies to purchasers of that computer. Four important examples of such operating systems are CP/M (Control Program for Microcomputers), MS-DOS (Microsoft Disk Operating System), the Microsoft version of OS/2 (Operating System 2), and UNIX.

CP/M, from Digital Research, was written for the 8080 microprocessor and became extremely popular with owners of 8080-based computers. When the IBM PC (which used a different microprocessor, the 8088) was being developed, IBM approached Digital Research for an operating system. No agreement was reached, however, and IBM turned to Microsoft, a company known till then only for language processors. (The founders of Microsoft wrote the first Basic interpreter for the Altair 8800.) The result was PC-DOS, which is proprietary to IBM, and the very similar MS-DOS, which Microsoft licenses to manufacturers of IBM PC compatibles. Computers are sometimes designated by the operating system they run; thus IBM PCs and compatibles are known as MS-DOS machines, and the older 8080-based computers were known as CP/M machines. MS-DOS machines quickly replaced CP/M machines in the computer marketplace, and leadership in the operating system market passed just as quickly from Digital Research to Microsoft.

With its PS/2 line, IBM introduced a new operating system, OS/2, which runs on most PS/2 machines as well as on the IBM PC/AT and compatibles. Developed jointly by IBM and Microsoft, OS/2 is being marketed in the same way as MS-DOS: IBM will release its own proprietary version and a similar version will be licensed to other computer manufacturers by Microsoft. (One version of OS/2, called the Extended Edition, will be available only from IBM; it is expected that software publishers will produce their own competitive versions of the Extended Edition for use by other computer manufacturers.) Distinctive features of OS/2 are a Macintosh-like user interface, the ability to manage a much larger main memory than MS-DOS, and the ability to do multitasking. Multitasking allows certain routine tasks such as producing printout and communicating with other computers to be done while the user is working on something else. Also, multitasking allows the user to keep several programs loaded into main memory and to switch instantly from one to another as circumstances require.

UNIX, from AT&T, is a multitasking, multiuser operating system. That is, not only does UNIX allow more than one program to run at the same time, it also provides time sharing, allowing many users to work with one computer at the same time via remote terminals. UNIX was developed for minicomputers in the early 1970s and is extremely popular as a minicomputer operating system. UNIX is now also available for microcomputers and is a popular operating system for technical workstations—high-performance microcomputers used by scientists and engineers. UNIX is not widely used for business and home microcomputers, mainly because most software for business and home use is written for other operating systems.

All microcomputers use VLSI memory chips for main memory. The capacity of a memory chip is given as the number of 0s or 1s, or bits, that it can store. In stating memory capacities the symbol K represents 1024. Thus a 1K memory chip can store 1024 bits; a 2K memory chip can store 2×1024 or 2048 bits, and so on. The 1970s saw the introduction of 1K memory chips, which were followed by 4K and 16K chips. During the 1980s, first 64K, then 256K, and, most recently, 1024K chips have come into widespread use; 4096K chips are expected to see widespread use in the late 1980s or early 1990s.

Despite occasional industry flirtations with other technologies, disks remain the preferred medium for auxiliary memory. Microcomputers use two kinds of disks, diskettes and hard disks. Diskettes can be removed from the computer and filed much as one does with paper documents. Hard disks have higher storage capacity than diskettes and offer faster access to stored data; they cannot be removed and filed, however, as they are permanently built into the computer.

The Fifth Generation

In 1982 Japan's Ministry of International Trade and Administration, together with eight leading Japanese computer companies, launched a project to develop the *fifth-generation computers* that they anticipate will be used in the 1990s. Researchers in other countries are pursuing similar goals. The following are some of the expected properties of fifth-generation computers; only time will tell, of course, whether these expectations are correct.

■ Most computers of the fourth and earlier generations can carry out only one arithmetical or Boolean operation at a time. A key to fifth-generation computers is expected to be *parallel processing*, in which hundreds or thousands of operations are carried out simultaneously.

■ Current computers are based on the operations of arithmetic and Boolean algebra. Yet logical reasoning, or inference, is based not so much on Boolean calculations as on discovering patterns of facts that support particular lines of argument. (Think of the detective who discovers in the clues a pattern of facts that implicates the culprit.) The Japanese, in particular, believe that fifth-generation computers will be based on logical inference rather than on arithmetical and Boolean calculations. The Japanese fifth-generation project has adopted a variant of the programming language Prolog (Programming in Logic), which is based on logical inference.

■ Fifth-generation computer systems are expected to make extensive use of the techniques of *artificial intelligence*, which simulate some aspects of human thought. Such systems might communicate with users and programmers in natural languages, such as Japanese or English, rather than in specialized computer languages. They might solve problems without having to be told step-by-step how to arrive at the solution. Instead, they would draw on knowledge and problem-solving techniques previously collected from human experts in the field in which the problem arises. Such *expert systems* are already starting to come into use on fourth-generation computers.

◥ Summary

Before the advent of modern high technology, only a relatively few inventions were devoted to information processing, transmission, and storage. Of these, it was devices for doing arithmetical calculations that led most directly to the development of the modern computer.

In the nineteenth century, the Jacquard loom introduced the concept of a machine controlled by a changeable program. Charles Babbage applied this concept to the design of a programmable calculator, the Analytical Engine, which, alas, was never completed. Babbage's work was forgotten and had to be rediscovered a century later by the pioneers of modern computing. The nineteenth century also saw the invention of Boolean algebra, which plays an important role in the design and operation of modern computers.

Near the end of the nineteenth century, the American engineer Herman Hollerith pioneered the automatic processing of statistical and business data. Today automatic data processing is one of the major application areas for computers.

Babbage's dream began to come true in the 1930s with the construction of the first working computers. The earliest electromechanical computers soon gave way to the much faster electronic computers. Important ideas introduced in early computers were the binary representation of data and the stored-program concept.

The computers that followed the early experimental machines are often classified into generations according to the prevalent hardware technology. First-generation computers used vacuum tubes, second-generation computers used transistors, and third-generation computers used integrated circuits. By the third generation, most of the hardware and software concepts of modern computer systems were in use.

Not everyone agrees as to what technology constitutes the fourth generation, but VLSI, which led to the proliferation of embedded computers and personal computers, seems like the most obvious choice. Work is under way to develop fifth-generation computer systems, which are expected to embody such concepts as parallel processing, computers based on logical inference, and artificial intelligence.

Vocabulary Review

abacus
analog computer
artificial intelligence
automatic data
  processing
binary digit
binary notation
bit
Boolean algebra
clone
compatible computers
computer generations
data processing (DP)
electromechanical
  computer
electronic computer
electronic data
  processing (EDP)

fifth-generation
  computer
graphics
IBM PC compatible
icon
integrated circuit
large-scale integration
  (LSI)
laptop computer
look and feel
magnetic drum
magnetic tape
magnetic-core
  memory
multitasking
parallel processing

portable computer
proprietary
  technology
stored-program
  computer
subroutine
time sharing
user interface
very large-scale
  integration (VLSI)
video-display
  terminal (VDT)
virtual
virtual memory
von Neumann
  machine

For Further Reading

Augarten, Stan. *Bit by Bit: An Illustrated History of Computers.* New York: Ticknor & Fields, 1984.

Feigenbaum, Edward A. and Pamela McCorduck. *The Fifth Generation.* Reading, MA: Addison-Wesley Publishing Company, 1983.

Freiberger, Paul and Michael Swaine. *Fire in the Valley.* Berkeley, CA: Osborne/McGraw-Hill, 1984.

Goldstine, Herman H. *The Computer from Pascal to von Neumann.* Princeton, NJ: Princeton University Press, 1972.

Hodges, Andrew. *Alan Turing: the Enigma.* New York: Simon and Schuster, 1983.

Sculley, John (with John A. Byrne). *Odyssey: Pepsi to Apple.* New York: Harper & Row, 1987.

"Special Section on the Fifth Generation Computer Project." *Communications of the ACM,* September 1983, pp. 629-645.

Tomczyk, Michael S. *The Home Computer Wars.* Greensboro, NC: COMPUTE! Publications, 1984.

Weiss, Eric A. "Self-Assessment Procedure XI: A Self-Assessment Procedure Dealing with One Part of Early Computing History." *Communications of the ACM,* July 1983, pp. 479–482.

◣ Review Questions

1 What was the most widely used method of calculation in ancient times?

2 Name three people who built early mechanical calculators. Which two are also well known for other achievements?

3 Why were most early mechanical calculators unreliable?

4 What, from our point of view, is the most important characteristic of the Jacquard loom?

5 In what century was the automatic computer invented?

6 What facets of Charles Babbage's character might have made it more difficult for him to get his inventions taken seriously?

7 What inspired Charles Babbage to start to work on the Difference Engine?

8 Where did Babbage get the idea of using punched cards to control the Analytical Engine?

9 What functions in the Analytical Engine were performed by the mill, the barrel, and the store?

10 Who wrote a program for the Analytical Engine and, in doing so, became the world's first computer programmer?

11 Who built the first computer to use binary notation?

12 What was the main shortcoming of the Mark I and other electromechanical computers?

13 Trace the early development of the electronic computer.

14 What is a stored-program computer?

15 Describe the technological features characteristic of each of the five computer generations.

16 What memory technology was once so widely used that its name became synonymous with "main memory."

17 In what generation did it become possible for many people to use a single computer at the same time?

18 Outline the development of systems software.

19 What technological developments made personal computers and embedded computers possible?

20 Describe some major events in the development of personal computers.

Topics for Discussion

1 If Charles Babbage had succeeded in building a mechanical computer around the middle of the nineteenth century, how might our present use of computers and our attitudes about them be different?

2 When Babbage conceived the idea of the Analytical Engine, he abandoned the Difference Engine, in which the government had invested a substantial amount of money. Discuss the ethics of this decision.

HARDWARE, SOFTWARE, AND PROGRAMMING

CHAPTER 3

COMPUTER HARDWARE

INTRODUCTION

This chapter focuses on computer hardware, the machinery responsible for carrying out the instructions contained in the software. We begin by looking at the binary codes used to represent information inside the computer, and we see how these codes are stored in main and auxiliary memory. Next we look at the overall logical organization, or *architecture*, of a computer system; we give particular attention to the central processing unit, which not only carries out all the calculations but coordinates and controls the rest of the system. Finally, we look at the most frequently used input and output devices, which enable the computer to communicate with the outside world.

BINARY CODES

A *binary code* represents information by using combinations of the two symbols 0 and 1. When used in a binary code, the symbols 0 and 1 are called *binary digits* or *bits*.

Binary codes are well suited for electronic computers because 0s and 1s are easy to represent electrically. For example, we can represent a 1 by an electrical circuit with a current flowing in it and a 0 by a circuit in which no current is flowing. Other methods of representing bits electrically are by the presence or absence of an electric charge (used for memory chips), by the direction of a magnetic field (used for magnetic tapes and disks), and by the presence or absence of pits in a reflecting surface (used for optical discs).

Representing Alternatives

Representing information boils down to representing alternatives. For example, suppose we want to represent the state in which a person lives. Because there are 50 states, we must be able to represent at least 50 alternatives. The post office uses two-letter codes for the states—FL for Florida, GA for Georgia, WV for West Virginia, and so on. Because there are 26 letters in the alphabet, there are 26×26 or 676 possible two-letter codes. Thus there are far more two-letter codes than are needed to represent the 50 states. We can rest assured that if any reasonable number of new states join the Union in the future, the post office will be able to find two-letter codes for them.

Similar considerations apply to binary codes. With a single bit we can represent two alternatives, one alternative by 0 and the other by 1. For example, we could use a single bit to record the answer to a true-false question by letting 1 stand for true and 0 for false. Two bits give us 2×2 or four alternatives:

00 01 10 11

We could use two bits to record answers to multiple choice questions, each of which has four possible answers. Three bits give us $2 \times 2 \times 2$ or eight alternatives:

000 001 010 011 100 101 110 111

With three bits we could represent the seven wonders of the world or the seven continents, with one three-bit value going unused in each case. (Unused combinations of bits are common; it is rare for the number of alternatives offered by a coding scheme to exactly match the number of alternatives that we need to represent.)

Adding another bit to a binary code doubles the number of alternatives that can be represented. (Why?) Thus it's easy to predict that with four bits we can represent 16 alternatives (16 = 8 × 2), with five bits we can represent 32 alternatives (32 = 16 × 2), and so on.

The ASCII Code

When a key is struck on a computer keyboard, a binary code representing that key is sent to the computer. Conversely, when the computer needs to display a character, it sends the corresponding binary code to the circuits that control the display. Thus, a code is needed for each of the characters found on a computer keyboard

Ideally, all computer systems would use the same coding scheme so that any computer terminal could be used with any system. In reality, unfortunately, there are several coding schemes in use. The most widely used of these is the *American Standard Code for Information Interchange*, usually abbreviated *ASCII* (pronounced AS key). The ASCII code uses seven bits, which give 128 alternatives.

With 128 codes at our disposal, we can represent the uppercase and lowercase letters, the digits, the most commonly used punctuation marks, a handful of mathematical signs, and a number of *control characters*. The control characters are used to issue commands to software and to control hardware devices such as printers and displays.

Figure 3-1 shows the ASCII code. The groups of three bits along the top of the figure give the leftmost three bits of each code value, and the groups of four bits along the left side give the rightmost four bits of each code value. Thus *A* is represented by 1000001, *B* is represented by 1000010, and so on. Notice that the blank space is represented by 0100000. People sometimes erroneously believe that computers ignore spaces; in fact, they treat spaces just like any other character. Figure 3-2 shows a message coded in ASCII.

The two- and three-letter abbreviations in Figure 3-1 represent control characters. For example, CR, LF, and BEL are commands for printers and displays. CR (carriage return) returns the printing mechanism to the left margin, LF (line feed) advances the paper by one line, and BEL (bell) rings a bell or sounds a beep.

Another popular code is the *Extended Binary Coded Decimal Interchange Code (EBCDIC*, pronounced EBB see dick), which is used mainly for IBM mainframes and related equipment. (Note, however, that IBM's popular personal computers use ASCII, which is standard for microcomputers and minicomputers.) EBCDIC represents each character by eight bits giving 256 alternatives, many of which are unused.

ASCII is also sometimes extended to eight bits, providing for 128 more characters. (The IBM Personal Computers use an eight-bit ASCII code.)

Rightmost Four Bits	Leftmost Three Bits							
	000	001	010	011	100	101	110	111
0000	NUL	DLE	*space*	0	@	P	`	p
0001	SOH	DC1	!	1	A	Q	a	q
0010	STX	DC2	"	2	B	R	b	r
0011	ETX	DC3	#	3	C	S	c	s
0100	EOT	DC4	$	4	D	T	d	t
0101	ENQ	NAK	%	5	E	U	e	u
0110	ACK	SYN	&	6	F	V	f	v
0111	BEL	ETB	'	7	G	W	g	w
1000	BS	CAN	(	8	H	X	h	x
1001	HT	EM	)	9	I	Y	i	y
1010	LF	SUB	*	:	J	Z	j	z
1011	VT	ESC	+	;	K	[	k	{
1100	FF	FS	,	<	L	\	l	¦
1101	CR	GS	–	=	M	]	m	}
1110	SO	RS	.	>	N	^	n	~
1111	SI	US	/	?	O	_	o	DEL

FIGURE 3-1
The ASCII code. To find the code for a character, note the column and row in which the character lies. Then write down the three bits at the head of the column followed by the four bits to the left of the row. For example, G lies in the column labeled 100 and the row labeled 0111; thus the ASCII code for G is 1000111.

The additional characters are often used for foreign language characters such as ç, ë, ñ, ô, ú, and ¿; mathematical signs such as ÷ and ≤; Greek letters such as α, β, and τ; foreign currency signs such as £ (pounds) and ¥ (yen); and graphics symbols (such as horizontal and vertical lines, intersecting lines, corners, and solid blocks) that allow simple drawings to be included in text.

Binary Notation

In everyday life we write numbers in decimal notation, which uses the familiar ten digits 0 through 9. For computers, the most efficient representation of numbers—the one that requires the fewest bits and allows the fastest arithmetic—is binary notation, which uses only the two digits 0 and 1 in place of the ten digits of decimal notation.

The easiest way to understand binary notation is to think of how a counting device, such as the mileage indicator on a car, would work in binary notation. If the counter has four dials, one for each digit, then after the counter has been reset to zero the reading will be

0000

If the count is increased by one, the rightmost dial advances from 0 to 1, so that the new reading becomes

0001

What happens when the count increases by one again? Our binary counter has only the two digits 0 and 1 on each dial, so the reading of the rightmost dial cannot get any larger than 1. Our situation is the same as if we had a decimal counter reading 0009; increasing the count by 1 would take the rightmost dial back to 0 and advance the next dial to the left by 1, giving a reading of 0010. The same thing happens for a binary counter, so our next counter reading is

0010

In binary notation, however, this reading represents two, not ten as it would represent in decimal notation.

Increasing the count by one again gives us

0011

which represents three in binary notation. This reading is analogous to a reading of 0099 on a decimal counter, so increasing the count by one again gives us

0100

which represents four in binary notation. Another increase by one gives us

00101

which is five in binary notation.

As in decimal notation, we can drop leading zeros (zeros to the left of the first nonzero digit), so numbers zero through five are written in

c	o	m	p	u
1000011	1101111	1101101	1110000	1110101
t	e	r	s	
1110100	1100101	1110010	1110011	0100000
a	r	e		f
1100001	1110010	1100101	0100000	1100110
u	n	.		
1110101	1101110	0101110		

FIGURE 3-2
The message "Computers are fun." coded in ASCII. Note that the blank spaces between the words are represented by the code 0100000.

binary notation as 0, 1, 10, 11, 100, 101. The following table shows how the numbers 0 through 15 are written in binary notation:

Decimal Number	Binary Number	Decimal Number	Binary Number
0	0	8	1000
1	1	9	1001
2	10	10	1010
3	11	11	1011
4	100	12	1100
5	101	13	1101
6	110	14	1110
7	111	15	1111

How would 16 be written in binary notation?

MEMORY

Computer memory, also called storage, is used to store programs and data until they are needed. Main memory is used for short-term storage of programs and data that are currently in use; auxiliary memory is used for long-term storage of programs and data that must be retained even when the computer is not in operation.

Units of Storage Capacity

The basic unit of information storage is the bit, which represents the capacity for storing a single 0 or 1. We can give the capacity of a storage device by stating the number of bits it can store. For example, the earliest memory chips, which could store 256 zeros and ones, had a capacity of 256 bits.

Many computers store and manipulate bits in eight-bit groups called *bytes*. The byte is a convenient unit of information storage since it is just large enough to hold one character coded in EBCDIC or extended ASCII.* Storage capacity is frequently stated in bytes; when stating storage capacity to persons unfamiliar with the term *byte*, the term *character* is sometimes used instead.

---

*One byte per character is sufficient for American and European languages; Oriental languages, which have many more distinct characters, require two or more bytes for each character. There is a move underway to modify international computer standards to allow for the possibility of multibyte characters, thus assuring that Oriental languages can be accommodated.

When speaking of large multiples of a unit, it is customary to use the prefix *kilo* to represent a multiple of 1000, the prefix *mega* to represent a multiple of 1,000,000, and the prefix *giga* (pronounced JIG uh) to represent a multiple of 1,000,000,000. Familiar examples are the kilometer, which is one thousand meters, and the kilogram, which is one thousand grams.

The numbers 1000, 1,000,000, and 1,000,000,000 are round numbers in decimal notation, but not in binary notation. (For example, 1000 is 1111101000 in binary notation.) In computing, it is more convenient to use values that are round numbers in binary notation. In place of 1000, then, we use 1024, whose binary representation is 10000000000. In place of 1,000,000 (which is 1000 × 1000) we use 1,048,576 (which is 1024 × 1024). In place of 1,000,000,000 (which is 1000 × 1000 × 1000) we use 1,073,741,824 (which is 1024 × 1024 × 1024). Thus *kilo, mega*, and *giga* are defined in the computer field as follows:

Prefix	Exact Multiple	Approximate Multiple
kilo	1024	1000
mega	1,048,576	1,000,000
giga	1,073,741,824	1,000,000,000

For most purposes, we can forget the exact values and think of *kilo, mega*, and *giga* as representing multiples of, roughly, one thousand, one million, and one billion.

In stating memory capacities, *kilo, mega*, and *giga* are usually abbreviated as *K, M*, and *G*, respectively. Thus 4K bits is equivalent to 4 kilobits or 4 × 1024 = 4096 bits. Likewise, 8K bytes is equivalent to 8 × 1024 = 8192 bytes. Note that 1M = 1024K and 1G = 1024M. (Why?).

The terms *kilobyte, megabyte*, and *gigabyte* are sometimes abbreviated as KB, MB, and GB, respectively. Thus a memory with a capacity of 4KB can store 4096 bytes, and one with a capacity of 8KB can store 8192 bytes.

Main Memory

We can think of main memory as the computer's chalkboard in that it is used for temporary storage during the course of a computation. The following are some characteristics of main memory:

- **Fast Access** The central processing unit can transfer a data item to or from main memory in a fraction of a millionth of a second.

- **Random Access** The access time for each item in main memory is the same, regardless of the order in which the items were stored or the location of each item in memory. Since data items can be accessed in any order (even at random) without any speed penalty, we say that main memory has the property of *random access*.

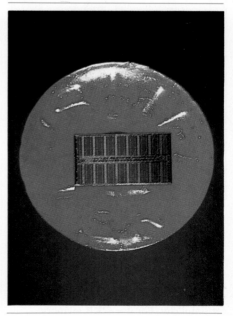

This 256 kilobit memory chip is not much bigger than the hole in a Lifesaver.

■ **Moderate Capacity** Main memory capacity has increased dramatically during the 1980s. (Once a 64KB main memory was large for a personal computer; now 640KB of main memory are the rule, and several megabytes are not unusual.) Nevertheless, the capacity of main memory is still moderate compared to that of auxiliary memory. For example, a typical hard disk for a personal computer stores 20–30MB, and drives with capacities over 100MB are becoming more and more common.

■ **Volatility** The most commonly used type of main memory* is *volatile*—its contents are lost when the electrical power is removed. Normally, this means that everything stored in main memory is lost when the computer is turned off. To retain stored data when the computer is turned off, battery power must be used; some laptops use this approach. The batteries must be kept charged, however, or they will eventually run down and, again, the stored data will be lost.

Main Memory Organization   We can visualize main memory as a set of post-office boxes. Each box, or *memory location*, holds a single data item (a given number of bits). Like post-office boxes, memory locations are often available in several different sizes. Each location has an *address*, which is used to designate that location for the purpose of storing data in it or retrieving data from it.

Figure 3-3 illustrates a *byte-oriented memory* in which the smallest size memory location holds eight bits or one byte. Although not universal, byte-oriented memories are very widely used. The figure shows a 64KB memory, which contains 64×1024 or 65,536 bytes; thus the memory addresses range from 0 through 65,535. Inside a computer, the addresses (like the data) are coded in binary notation; in Figures 3-3 and 3-5, however, the addresses are written in decimal notation for ease of understanding.

Many data items require more than one byte; Figure 3-4 shows the number of bytes needed to store typical data values. When more than one byte is needed to store a data item, adjacent bytes are combined to form larger locations. Figure 3-5 shows how adjacent bytes can be combined to form two-byte, four-byte, and eight-byte locations. Note that the address of a multibyte location is the same as the address of its first byte.

RAM and ROM   Main memory that allows data to be both read from and written to each memory location is called *RAM (random access memory)*. This is a poor term, since all main memory has the property of random access. A better term would be *read-write memory*; the most likely reason why this term is not used is that the corresponding acronym, RWM, is unpronounceable. As we have seen, RAM is volatile—unless battery power is supplied, the contents of memory will be lost when the computer is turned off.

Addresses (decimal)	Memory Locations
0	10111000
1	10101111
2	10000001
3	00000000
4	00110111
65,532	00001111
65,533	10101111
65,534	11111111
65,535	10010111

FIGURE 3-3
In a byte-oriented memory, the smallest sized memory location holds one byte (eight bits). Each byte-sized location has a unique address; although the computer represents addresses in binary notation, the figure shows them in decimal notation for simplicity. For the 64KB memory illustrated here, the addresses run from 0 through 65,535.

---

*See the discussion of RAM and ROM later in the chapter. RAM is volatile; ROM is not.

Data Type	Number of Bytes
Character	1
Small Integer ($-32{,}768$ through $32{,}767$)	2
Large Integer ($-2{,}147{,}483{,}648$ through $2{,}147{,}483{,}647$)	4
Single-Precision Floating-Point Number (Accurate to six significant digits)	4
Double-Precision Floating-Point Number (Accurate to 16 significant digits)	8

FIGURE 3-4
Number of bytes needed to store a character, a small integer, a large integer, a single-precision floating-point number, and a double-precision floating-point number. A floating-point number contains a decimal point; an integer, which represents a whole number, does not. The accuracy of a floating-point number is given as the number of significant digits—digits other than leading or trailing zeros that serve as placeholders. Thus 251,000 and 0.000762 are both accurate to three significant digits.

Main memory that can be read from but not written to is called *ROM (Read-Only Memory)*. The contents of ROM are fixed and cannot be changed. The computer can read from a location in ROM, but it cannot write new data into the location. (Some forms of ROM can be erased and written to with special equipment or in special circumstances; during normal operation in the computer, however, the contents of ROM do not change.) ROM is nonvolatile; its contents remain unchanged regardless of how many times the computer is turned on or off. Some computers come with substantial amounts of software permanently installed in ROM; such permanently stored software is sometimes called *firmware*.

Auxiliary Memory

If main memory is the computer's chalkboard, then auxiliary memory is its filing cabinet. Auxiliary memory is nonvolatile, allowing for long-term storage of programs and data. Auxiliary memory media, such as tapes and disks, can be removed from the computer system and stored separately in files or on shelves. Auxiliary memory provides greater storage capacity at lower cost per bit than main memory. Unfortunately, access to items stored in auxiliary memory may be over a thousand times slower than for items stored in main memory. For this reason, programs and data must be transferred to main memory for processing, then returned to auxiliary memory for permanent storage.

Magnetic Tape   Magnetic tape stores data using the same principles that govern audio and video recording—bits are stored as magnetized areas on the tape. Magnetic tape can store large amounts of data at very low cost: a 2400 foot reel of ½ inch tape can store about 20 megabytes of data and costs about $25. For large computers, magnetic tape is used mainly for transporting programs and data from one computer to another and for archival (very long term) storage. For personal computers, tape is used

(a) Eight 8-bit Bytes

Address

```
0
1
2
3
4
5
6
7
```

(b) Four 2-byte Locations

Address

```
0
2
4
6
```

(c) Two 4-byte Locations

Address

```
0
4
```

(d) One 8-byte Location

Address

```
0
```

FIGURE 3-5

These diagrams show how adjacent bytes can be combined to form two-, four-, and eight-byte locations. Note that the address of a multibyte location is the same as the address of its first byte.

mainly for backing up hard disk units—for providing a backup copy of the data stored on a hard disk so that the contents of the disk can be restored if they are destroyed by a hardware or software malfunction.

Magnetic tape has the property of *sequential access*—data items can be read from the tape only in the order in which they were recorded. Trying to retrieve the items in any other order would require too much winding and rewinding of the tape to be practical (as anyone can testify who has tried to locate a particular selection on an audio or video tape). The restriction to sequential access is the main drawback of magnetic tape; it is this drawback that limits the use of magnetic tape to transporting files and to archival and backup storage.

Magnetic Disks   Magnetic disks (usually just referred to as *disks*) are by far the most widely used medium for auxiliary memory. Disks vary widely in cost, size, construction, and storage capacity, ranging from the pocket-sized disk cartridges used with some microcomputers to the 12-disk packs often used with mainframes. Access times also vary widely with different types of disks but are on the order of thousandths of a second, as opposed to access times of less than a millionth of a second for main memory.

Disks allow random access. Access is not quite so "random" as with main memory, however, in that the access time can vary with the location of the desired data on the disk and with the current position of the access mechanism. For auxiliary memory devices, the term *direct access* is often used instead of *random access*. A disk is sometimes classified as a *direct access storage device* or *DASD* (pronounced DAZZ dy).

Disks are made from aluminum, rigid plastic, or flexible plastic film. The surface of a disk is coated with a magnetic material similar to that used for magnetic tape. Some types of disks allow information to be recorded on both sides, whereas for others, only one side is used. The disk itself, as opposed to the container or mechanism in which it is mounted, is sometimes referred to as a *platter*.

In use, a disk is mounted in a disk drive, which spins the disk like a phonograph record, but much faster. Data is read from and written on the disk with read/write heads. If both surfaces of a platter are used, then there are two read/write heads, one for the top surface and one for the bottom. For some types of disks the read/write head actually touches the disk surface; for others, the head "flies" a few millionths of an inch above the surface. Each read/write head is mounted on an access arm, which can move inward to position the head closer to the center of the disk or outward to position the head closer to the edge of the disk. Figure 3-6 diagrams the read/write heads and access mechanism used for a multiplatter disk pack.

As the disk spins, the part of the disk passing beneath the read/write head forms a circular path called a *track*. As shown in Figure 3-7, the surface of the disk is divided into anywhere from 35 to 200 such tracks. In contrast to the grooves of a phonograph record, the tracks cannot actually be seen by looking at the disk but are merely the invisible paths along which data is recorded. A particular track is selected by the access arm, which moves the read/write head inward to place it over a track near the center of the disk or outward to place it over a track near the edge of the disk.

As shown in Figure 3-7, each track may be divided into *sectors*. Data is normally transferred between main memory and disk in sector-sized blocks. Typical sector sizes are 128, 256, and 512 bytes. Each sector is

A tape library for archival storage.

Floppy disk.

Inserting floppy disk into disk drive.

A 3½-inch diskette cartridge can fit in a shirt pocket.

Interior of a hard disk. The circular brown objects are the platters—the actual disks. An access arm can be seen extended toward the center of the top platter.

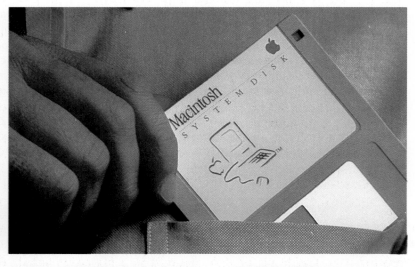

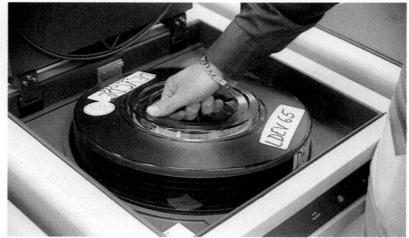

Inserting a disk pack into a disk drive. Disk packs such as this one are widely used with mainframes and minicomputers.

uniquely identified by a sector address, which is recorded at the beginning of the sector. The sector address consists of three components:

- **Head Number,** which designates a particular surface of a particular platter
- **Track Number,** which designates a particular track on the selected surface
- **Sector Number,** which designates a particular sector on the selected track

Before a new disk can be used it must be *formatted* by recording the sector address at the start of each sector.

To read or write a particular sector, the system must first select the proper head, which is done electrically and takes no appreciable time. Next the access arm must be moved until the selected head is over the proper track; this is the slowest part of the access. Finally, the system must wait until the rotation of the disk carries the desired sector past the read/write head. The access time is the time required to position the read/write head over the proper track plus the time until the desired sector has passed beneath the read/write head.

Mainframe computers typically use multiplatter *disk packs.* A 12-platter disk pack has 20 recording surfaces (the topmost and bottommost surfaces are not used) and can store hundreds of megabytes of data.

Microcomputers use hard disks (sometimes called *fixed disks*) and diskettes. A hard or fixed disk is ''hard'' because the platters are made of aluminum and ''fixed'' because the platters are permanently mounted in the disk drive; they cannot be removed and stored separately, as with disk packs or diskettes. (Drives that accept removable hard-disk cartridges are available; so far they have not proved nearly as popular as fixed-disk drives.) Hard-disk drives provide faster access and greater storage capacity than diskettes. Many currently installed hard-disk drives hold tens of megabytes, and the most recent drives to appear on the market hold hundreds of megabytes.

Diskettes come in three sizes: 8 inch, 5¼ inch, and 3½ inch, of which the 5¼-inch size is currently the most popular. An 8-inch or 5¼-inch diskette consists of a flexible plastic disk mounted in a protective jacket. These diskettes are often referred to as *flexible disks* or *floppy disks*. A 3½-inch diskette consists of a rigid plastic disk mounted in a hard plastic cartridge. Typical diskette storage capacities range from ¼ to 2 megabytes. Currently, the 5¼-inch size is most widely used; however, since both IBM and Apple have switched to 3½-inch diskettes, it is expected that this size will be predominant in the future. The small size of 3½-inch diskettes makes them easier to carry about (they fit in a shirt pocket), the rigid platter allows more data to be stored, and the rigid cartridge provides better protection for the stored data.

Optical Discs   Optical discs were developed by the entertainment industry in two forms: videodiscs, which store video data (usually movies) in analog form; and compact discs (CDs), which store audio data (usually record albums) in digital form. Because compact discs already use digital technology, they are more readily adapted to computer applications. A 5¼-

inch compact disc can hold 500–600 megabytes of digtal data—enough to store a 24-volume encyclopedia.

Let's begin by looking at audio compact discs, the ones used for record albums. Before being recorded, the audio analog signal first must be converted to digital data—a stream of 0s and 1s. This stream of digital data is then recorded by using a laser beam to burn pits into the disc's reflective coating; 0s are represented by pits and 1s by unpitted areas. In a CD player, the data is read by another laser beam (this one too weak to burn the coating), which is reflected differently by the pits and the unpitted areas.

An important property of compact discs is that they can be mass produced. The master disc that was recorded with a laser is used to make dies, which are then used to stamp out copies at high speed and low cost. Defects in the stamped copies can cause errors when the data is read back. This problem is alleviated by using error correcting codes: each block of data bits is accompanied by additional check bits that can be used to detect and correct errors.

FIGURE 3-6

Side view of a multiplatter disk pack mounted in a disk drive. The access mechanism can move the read/write heads either in toward the spindle or out toward the outer edges of the platters.

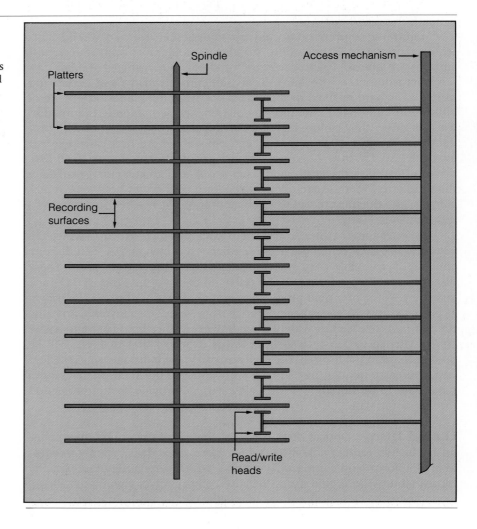

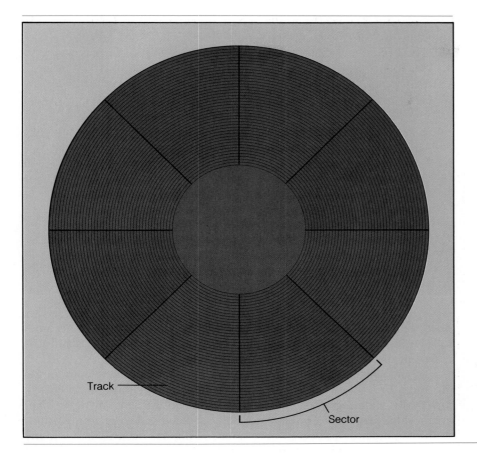

FIGURE 3-7
Tracks and sectors on the surface of a disk. The tracks and sectors are not visible on the actual disk. The tracks are the invisible paths along which data is recorded, and sectors are defined by special codes recorded on the tracks.

Compact discs for computer use are called *CD-ROMs*—compact disc read-only memories. The ROM designation means that the computer can only read data from the disc; it cannot record new data. Thus CD-ROMs are useful for publishing large volumes of information (such as encyclopedias, directories, and other reference works) in computer readable form. CD-ROMs are designed to be completely compatible with audio compact discs so as to take advantage of the CD technology created by the entertainment industry; CD-ROMs can be manufactured by the same factories that make audio compact discs, and many components designed for CD players can also be used in CD-ROM drives. To provide more stringent protection against errors, CD-ROMs incorporate additional error correcting codes, which are used along with those provided for by audio CD technology.

WORM (write once/read many) drives can both write to and read from optical discs. The laser in a WORM drive can be operated at either high or low power. At high power, the laser records data by burning pits into the coated surface of the disc; at low power, the laser reads previously recorded data without damaging the disc. Once data has been written, it cannot be erased or changed (there is no way to remove the pits); it can, however, be read as many times as desired, hence the designation *write*

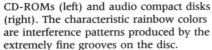

CD-ROMs (left) and audio compact disks (right). The characteristic rainbow colors are interference patterns produced by the extremely fine grooves on the disc.

once/read many. Thus a WORM disc cannot be reused when it becomes full; it either must be filed away (if the recorded information is still valuable) or discarded (if the information is obsolete).

When a file on a WORM disc is updated, an entire new copy of the file must be written to the disc. Since the old copy cannot be erased, repeatedly updating a file will eventually fill up the disc. WORM drives are most useful if a file is only occasionally updated and if previous versions of the file must be preserved even after the file has been updated. Many files of business records satisfy these conditions.

Some have suggested that WORM discs may become sufficiently inexpensive that they can be used like paper notebooks, to be written on as needed and thrown away without a second thought when they become full and the information on them is no longer needed.

Compact discs that can be erased and rewritten are expected to be introduced in the late 1980s.

SYSTEM ORGANIZATION

The logical organization of a computer system refers to the functions performed by the various components and the ways in which they interact with one another. The physical organization refers to the way components are installed and connected inside the computer. Although our main interest is in logical organization, we will also briefly consider physical organization.

Logical Organization

Figure 3-8 illustrates the logical organization of a computer system. The three major system components are the central processing unit, main memory, and the *peripheral devices*. The peripherals are input devices such as keyboards, output devices such as video displays, and auxiliary memory devices such as disk drives. The central processing unit itself consists of two components: the arithmetic/logic unit, which carries out arithmetical and logical calculations, and the control unit, which is responsible for getting the instructions in the program carried out.

The red lines in Figure 3-8 illustrate the flow of control signals from the control unit to other units. By generating appropriate control signals, the control unit can carry out the following operations:

■ Transfer instructions from main memory to the control unit

■ Transfer data between main memory and the arithmetic/logic unit

■ Carry out arithmetical and other operations on data stored in the arithmetic/logic unit

■ Transfer data and control codes between the arithmetic/logic unit and peripheral devices.

Note that the control unit controls peripheral devices only by transferring data and control codes from the arithmetic/logic unit to the peripheral devices as requested by the program. It is up to the program to see that these devices are sent the proper control codes for desired operations, such as printing a character or reading a disk sector.

The blue lines in Figure 3-8 represent the flow of data from component to component. There is a heavy flow of data between the arithmetic/logic unit and main memory, since data stored in main memory must be moved to the arithmetic/logic unit for processing and returned to main memory when processing is complete. Data (such as characters to be printed) and control signals (such as a request to read a disk sector) are transferred from the arithmetic/logic unit to the peripherals. The peripherals send back to the arithmetic/logic unit data (such as the code for the character most recently typed by the user) and status information (such as whether the printer is ready to accept a new character).

Wiring for a supercomputer. Most computers avoid such complex wiring by using printed circuit boards.

Some peripheral devices have the capability for direct memory access, which allows them to transfer data directly to and from main memory, bypassing the arithmetic/logic unit. While such a transfer is in progress, the operation of the central processing unit is suspended, and the peripheral device is given temporary control of the computer system.

Consider the blue lines connecting main memory and the arithmetic/logic unit to the control unit. From main memory, the control unit receives the program instructions that govern its operation. From the arithmetic/logic unit, the control unit receives information about the results of carrying out previous instructions—for example, whether the result of an arithmetical operation was positive, negative, or zero. This information allows *conditional execution* in which the action of the current instruction may be modified by the results of previous instructions. Conditional execution provides computers with their famed capability for making decisions.

The blue line connecting the peripheral devices to the control unit is used when a peripheral device needs attention, as when it has data to send to the central processing unit. The peripheral device demands attention by sending an *interrupt request* to the control unit. When the control unit receives the interrupt request, it begins executing a part of the program called an *interrupt handler*. When the interrupt handler has completed its work, the control unit resumes execution of the program at the point at which the interrupt took place.

Physical Organization

There are many possibilities for organizing the physical components, such as microprocessors and memory chips, that make up a computer system. The organization described here, although not universal, is widely used, particularly for minicomputers and microcomputers.

As shown in Figure 3-9, the system is organized around a *bus*, which is a group of 50–100 wires over which the various components communicate with one another. The bus carries three kinds of information: data,

FIGURE 3-8
Logical organization of a computer system. Red lines indicate paths for control signals, and blue lines indicate paths for data. The control unit controls the operation of the arithmetic/logic unit and also controls data transfers between the arithmetic/logic unit and main memory and between the arithmetic/logic unit and peripheral devices. Some systems feature direct memory access, whereby peripheral devices can transfer data to and from main memory on their own initiative.

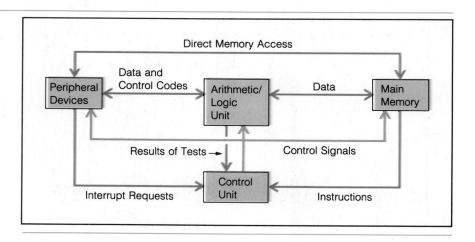

addresses (which designate sources and destinations for data), and timing and control signals (which coordinate the activities of all the components using the bus).

Figure 3-9 shows the simplest bus configuration in which all components are connected to a single bus. More complex configurations are possible; for example, it is not uncommon to use separate buses for main memory and for the peripheral devices.

The chips and other devices making up a computer circuit are mounted on a thin *printed circuit board*. In addition to holding the electronic parts, the printed circuit board contains etched patterns of copper conductors that provide the electrical connections between parts. The basic circuit board for a computer system is the *system board* or *motherboard*, which contains the bus. Along the bus are mounted edge connectors, slots into which other printed circuit boards can be inserted edgewise. Conductors in the edge connector make contact with conductors on the board that is plugged in, thus connecting that board to the bus. It is possible to expand the system by plugging additional circuit boards into edge connectors. For this reason, the edge connectors are sometimes called *expansion slots* and the boards that plug into them are called *expansion boards*.

Systems vary as to which components are on the system board and which are on expansion boards. At one extreme, the system board contains few components; almost everything is on expansion boards. At the other extreme, the entire computer is built on the system board; there are no expansion slots or expansion boards. Many systems follow a course somewhere between these extremes, placing essential components on the system board and leaving the expansion slots free for optional components. For our discussions it will be simplest to consider the first extreme, in which each major component is on a separate circuit board.

The CPU board contains the central processing unit. For a microcomputer, this board contains the microprocessor together with other chips that provide an interface between the microprocessor and the bus.

Most computers contain only one CPU, thus justifying its designation as *the* central processing unit. Some computers, however, have multiple CPUs, which are often referred to as just *processors*, since none is any more central than the others. Multiple processors allow *parallel processing*

Printed circuit boards. The connectors at the bottom of each board plug into slots on the computer's system board.

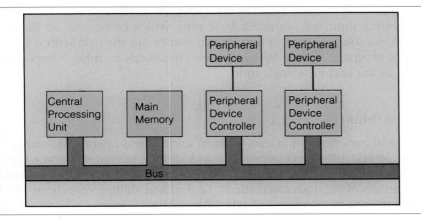

FIGURE 3-9
Physical organization of a typical computer system. The central processing unit, main memory, and the controllers for peripheral devices communicate with one another over a common set of wires called a bus.

whereby the processors simultaneously execute different programs or different parts of the same program. Systems designed for parallel processing must usually use a much more complex bus configuration than shown in Figure 3-9; if all processors were forced to take turns using the same bus and accessing the same main memory, the bus and main memory would become bottlenecks for the entire system. Architectures for systems with multiple processors constitute an active field of computer science research; most of the configurations proposed so far are still experimental, their benefits yet to be established. Consequently, we will confine our attention to the traditional, well-understood systems that have only a single central processing unit.

A main memory board must monitor the address bus for addresses within the range for which the board is responsible. When such an address is detected, a control line informs the memory board whether data is to be read from memory or written to memory. For a memory read, the memory board transfers a data value from the addressed location to the bus. For a memory write, the memory board transfers a data value from the bus to the addressed location.

For each peripheral device, such as a printer or disk drive, there is a *device controller* board that plugs into the bus and is connected by a cable to the peripheral device. The device controller board communicates with the system through on-board memory locations called *registers* (the term *register* is usually used for memory locations other than those in main memory). Registers on device-controller boards have addresses just like locations in main memory, enabling the CPU to transfer data to or from a register on a device-controller board just as it would transfer data to or from a main-memory location.

Many device controllers have a data register, a command register, and a status register. To send or receive data from the device, the CPU writes to or reads from the data register. To send a command to the device, it writes a control code to the command register. To determine the status of the device (such as whether it is busy or ready for the next command), the CPU reads a status code from the status register.

THE CENTRAL PROCESSING UNIT

We now look in more detail at the two major components of the central processing unit: the arithmetic/logic unit, which carries out all the calculations; and the control unit, which carries out the instructions in the user's program, mainly by passing on commands to other components such as the arithmetic/logic unit.

The Arithmetic/Logic Unit

The arithmetic/logic unit can perform arithmetical operations, comparisons, logical (Boolean) operations, and shifting operations. Comparison operations allow a program to make decisions based on its input data and the results of previous calculations. Logical and shifting operations allow a program to manipulate individual bits within a byte.

Interior of IBM PC (left) without and (right) with expansion boards plugged in. The power supply is at the top (rear of machine). At bottom are the diskette drive (center) and the hard disk drive (right). The diskette drive is hidden beneath a circuit board containing the diskette-drive electronics.

Arithmetical Operations The arithmetical operations are the usual addition, subtraction, multiplication, and division. Addition is governed by the following addition table for binary numbers (remember that 10 represents two in binary notation):

$$0 + 0 = 0$$
$$0 + 1 = 1$$
$$1 + 0 = 1$$
$$1 + 1 = 10 \text{ (that is, 0 with 1 to carry)}$$

Notice how simple the binary addition table is compared to the decimal addition table we all had to learn as children. This simplicity makes it easy to incorporate the addition table into the circuits of the arithmetic/logic unit.

Numbers with more than one digit are added as in ordinary arithmetic: the columns are added from right to left, with numbers being carried from one column to the next as required. The following illustrates the addition of two binary numbers, each of which occupies one byte (decimal values are shown in parentheses next to the numbers):

```
  01011111 (95)
+ 00111011 (59)
  10011010 (154)
```

Work through this addition using the binary addition table; note where carries are required.

◥ **Exercise 3-1** Add the bytes 01101011 and 00101001. Don't forget to carry ones when necessary.

Comparisons   A comparison operation determines whether a given binary number is less than, equal to, or greater than another. The result of the comparison is recorded in special bits called *flags*. For example, if the first number is less than the second, the less-than flag is set to 1 and the equal-to and greater-than flags are set to 0. If the two numbers are equal, the equal-to flag is set to 1 and the other two flags are set to 0. If the first number is greater than the second, the greater-than flag is set to 1 and the other two flags are set to 0. The control unit can use the flag settings to determine which instruction will be executed next. Thus the outcomes of comparisons can determine which instructions the computer executes. Instead of being confined to a rigid, preordained sequence of instructions, the program can decide what actions to take based upon the input it receives.

Logical and Shift Operations   Logical and shift operations allow a program to manipulate individual bits within a byte. For example, consider the logical operation AND, which yields 1 only if the two bits being combined are both 1. We can define the logical operation AND with a table similar to the one we used for binary addition.

    0 AND 0 = 0

    1 AND 0 = 0

    0 AND 1 = 0

    1 AND 1 = 1

Now suppose we need to set the middle four bits of a byte to 0, regardless of the values they previously had. We can accomplish this by "ANDing" the byte to be changed with the byte 11000011. For example, if the byte to be changed is 01110110, the AND operation works out as follows:

```
        01110110
AND     11000011
        01000010
```

The first two and last two bits of the byte to be modified remain unchanged in the result. The middle four bits, however, have been set to 0 as desired.

Exercise 3-2   Apply the AND operation to the bytes 11100111 and 10101010.

Exercise 3-3   The OR operation yields 1 if either or both of the bits to which it is applied are 1; it yields 0 only if both bits are 0. Give a table that defines the OR operation.

Exercise 3-4   Apply the OR operation to the bytes 00100100 and 10001101.

Shifting operations shift all the bits in a byte to the left or right by a designated number of places. For example, suppose we are given the byte 00000011 but want to move the two 1s from the right end to the middle of the byte. We can accomplish this result by shifting all the bits three places to the left to get 00011000. (When we shift to the left, 0s are shifted into the right end of the byte, and any bits shifted out of the left end are discarded.)

The Control Unit

Normally, the control unit executes an instruction by signaling other components to carry out the necessary data transfers and manipulations. The control unit itself, however, is responsible for executing jump and call instructions, which affect the order in which the other instructions in the program will be executed. Interrupt requests, which also affect the order in which instructions are executed, are also processed by the control unit.

The Fetch-Execute Cycle   The control unit operates in a fetch-execute cycle. In the fetch part of the cycle, the next instruction to be executed is transferred from main memory to the central processing unit. In the execute part of the cycle, the control unit executes the instruction by sending the necessary control signals to the arithmetic/logic unit, main memory, and device controllers. No matter how complex a job the computer system is accomplishing under the control of its program, the control unit is just going through the same fetch-execute cycle over and over again. We can think of program control as a means by which complex and diverse results can be obtained from a mechanism that operates in a simple, repetitive cycle.

Jump Instructions   Instructions are normally fetched from successive memory locations, just as we might start at the beginning of a list of instructions and work down the list, carrying out each instruction as we come to it. A jump instruction, however, changes the normal order of instruction execution by telling the CPU to jump to another part of the program and continue executing instructions from that point.

Jumps direct the computer to the instructions needed to respond to particular occurrences, such as a particular command from the user. Thus jumps are often conditional; we only want the computer to jump if a certain condition holds. (If the computer doesn't jump, it moves on to the next instruction in memory, the one following the jump instruction.) Computers check conditions by making comparisons. Input data may be compared with values stored in main memory, or calculated results may be compared with one another. The comparisons are done with comparison instructions and the jumps with jump instructions. The jump instructions use the flag bits set by the comparison instructions to determine whether to jump.

For example, an integrated program that can handle several applications might begin by asking the user to select the desired application. Specifically, the user might be asked to enter W to select word processing, S to select spreadsheet analysis, C to select (tele)communications, or D to select database management. The letter entered by the user would be compared, in turn, with the characters W, S, C, and D stored in main memory. If the user entered W, the CPU would jump to the part of the program that handles word processing. If the user entered S, the CPU would jump to the part of the program that handles spreadsheet analysis, and so on.

Jump instructions can also be used to cause the computer to repeat certain sequences of instructions. Consider an embedded computer in a microwave oven; one of the computer's jobs is to turn off the oven at a time specified by the user. Part of the computer's program might be outlined like this:

1 Compare the current reading of the oven's clock with the stop time that was entered by the user (and which is now stored in memory).

2 If the clock reading was less than the stop time, jump to step 1.

3 Turn off the oven.

Steps 1 and 2 will be executed repeatedly, until the clock reading equals the stop time. When that occurs, the computer will not jump back to step 1 but will go on to step 3 and turn off the oven.

Subroutines   A subroutine is a part of a program that is called from elsewhere in a program. When execution of the subroutine has been completed, execution of the program continues with the instruction following the one that called the subroutine. A subroutine is invoked with a call instruction, which causes the CPU to jump to the first instruction of the subroutine. Before jumping, however, the CPU marks its place in the program by saving a return address, which is the address of the instruction immediately following the call instruction. When the subroutine finishes its work, it executes a return instruction. The return instruction causes the CPU to jump to the instruction designated by the previously saved return address. Thus, after the subroutine has finished its work, the CPU picks up where it left off in the execution of the program that called the subroutine.

Subroutines have many uses. Just as a complex machine is assembled from simpler parts, so a complex program can be assembled from much simpler subroutines. A subroutine can be written once but called many times, preventing the instructions in the subroutine from having to be duplicated every time the action performed by the subroutine is needed. A program usually communicates with the computer's operating system by calling subroutines. And, as discussed in the next section, a peripheral device usually requests the CPU's attention by forcing a call to a subroutine.

Interrupts   Each interrupt request specifies a particular interrupt handler subroutine that is to be called to handle the request (usually the interrupt handler is part of the operating system). When the CPU receives an interrupt request, it calls the corresponding interrupt handler subroutine. An interrupt, then, is just a subroutine call that is triggered by a request from a peripheral device rather than by a call instruction in the program.

For example, most computers use interrupts to obtain characters from the keyboard. Each time you strike a key, the device-controller for the keyboard generates an interrupt request. Whatever program is executing is interrupted momentarily while the interrupt handler for the keyboard reads the character that was typed and stores it in a designated area of main memory. When the program needs input from the keyboard, it doesn't read the keyboard directly, but instead obtains its input from the main-memory area in which typed characters were stored by the keyboard interrupt handler.

◥ INPUT AND OUTPUT DEVICES

Input devices convert data from forms convenient for external use into binary codes that a computer can store and manipulate internally. Output devices perform the reverse conversion, translating binary-coded data into such convenient external forms as text and graphs.

In this chapter we will look at the most popular input and output devices. By no means, however, is input and output equipment limited to the devices considered here. Specialized input and output devices designed for particular applications are widely used. Monitoring and control of machinery is one example of an application area in which specialized input and output devices are the rule rather than the exception.

Video Displays

A display presents computer output in a form that can be read by the user. A text display can display only letters, digits, and various special characters such as punctuation marks; a graphics display can also display drawings

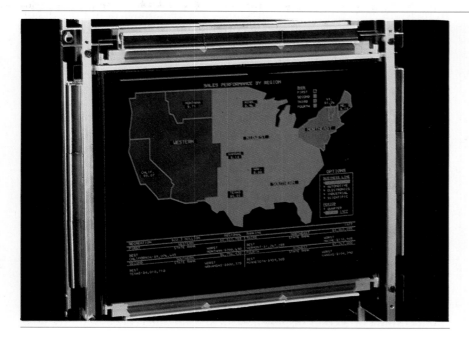

A plasma display, in which light is produced by electrical discharges in a gas (as in a neon sign). Different gases give different colors; neon gas yields the red-orange color seen here.

and pictures. A monochrome display produces output in black and white only, whereas a color display allows other colors as well. For a black and white display, ''white'' is frequently green or amber, which is more restful for the eyes than the white produced by a black and white television set. Also, a monochrome display can show either white text and graphics against a black background or black text and graphics against a white background. A recent innovation is the paper-white display that simulates as closely as possible the appearance of black printing on a white sheet of paper.

The most popular and widely used display device is the *CRT (cathode-ray tube) display*, in which text and graphics are displayed on a video monitor similar in appearance to a television set. In fact, an ordinary television set can be used for a video display, but its performance is poor compared to that of a video monitor specifically designed for computer use. Both monochrome and color monitors are available.

Liquid Crystal Displays (LCDs), similar to those found in calculators and digital watches, are widely used in laptop computers. Early LCD displays were difficult to read under any but the best lighting conditions; this problem has been solved in the most recent displays, however. Currently, LCD computer displays are all monochrome; color LCD displays have been demonstrated and used in miniature color television sets, but color displays large enough for computer use are still prohibitively expensive.

Plasma displays have seen limited use in laptop computers (LCD displays are more popular). Plasma displays work on the same principle as neon lights: light is produced by electrical discharges through a gas such as neon. The gas that is used determines the color of the display; neon gives an orange color.

The *resolution* of a display specifies the degree of fine detail that the display can show; resolution is often specified by stating the number of distinct dots that can be displayed (without running together on the screen) in the horizontal and vertical directions. The remainder of our discussion will focus on CRT displays, which currently are the most widely used and have highest resolution.

Scanning   The screen of a CRT display is coated with a substance that glows when struck by a beam of electrons. The electron beam can strike only one point on the screen at a time. An image on a CRT display must be constantly *refreshed*—each point must be struck by the electron beam sufficiently often to prevent it from fading from the viewer's vision. Thus the electron beam methodically scans the display from left to right and from top to bottom; the beam is intensified when it passes over a bright point in the image, and it is weakened or turned off entirely when it passes over a dark point. The horizontal scanning lines traced out by the electron beam can be seen by closely examining a television picture. Television sets and standard video monitors scan the entire screen thirty times a second; some computer displays scan at different rates.

A video display consists of a video display controller card connected to a video monitor. The display controller card often plugs into the system bus in the same manner as other device controllers. The display controller determines the scanning rate. Many controllers can be set for either a monochrome or a color display and for several different resolutions; such controllers may use different scanning rates for the different display options. Most monitors, however, can scan at only one rate; they will not work (and may burn out) if connected to a display controller that is set to scan at a different rate. To alleviate this problem, manufacturers have brought out *multiscan monitors*, which can scan at any of the rates used by popular video display cards.

Memory-Mapped Displays   The image shown on a video display is stored in display memory, which is part of the video display controller. The controller scans the stored image in step with the electron beam that is scanning the screen of the video monitor. As it scans the stored image, the controller sends to the monitor a video signal that adjusts the intensity of the electron beam so as to give each point the brightness specified in the stored image.

The most popular and versatile form of video display is the *memory-mapped display* in which display memory corresponds to a segment of main memory. Characters and graphics stored in this segment of memory are automatically displayed. At any time the program can check what is being displayed at a given position on the screen by checking the corresponding location in display memory. An image on a memory-mapped display can be changed more rapidly than for other types of displays because the central processing unit has direct access to display memory.

Graphics Displays   How is the image to be displayed stored in display memory? A simple way is to let each bit of display memory correspond to a distinct point in the image. A bit corresponding to a bright point in the image has the value 1 and a bit corresponding to a dark point has the value 0. A display based on this principle is sometimes called a *bit-mapped display*, since there is a one-to-one correspondence, or mapping, between the bits in display memory and the points or dots making up the image.

Each distinct point in the image is called a *picture element*, which is often contracted to *pixel*. The more pixels there are in the image, the greater the resolution or degree of detail that can be shown. Increasing the number of pixels, however, also increases the amount of display memory that is required. A moderate-resolution display of 640 pixels horizontally by 200 pixels vertically requires $640 \times 200 = 128,000$ bits or about 16 kilobytes of display memory.

Color displays require additional bits to represent the color of each pixel. A 16-color display, for example, requires 4 bits for each pixel. Thus a 16-color display needs 4 times as much display memory as does a monochrome display with the same resolution.

The advantage of a bit-mapped display is that it allows the program complete control over the displayed image. By appropriately setting the bits in display memory, a program can display drawings and pictures as well as text. For this reason, a bit-mapped display is often referred to as a graphics display.

Text Displays   A text display stores character codes in display memory rather than the image patterns stored by a bit-mapped display. Normally, each character is represented by its ASCII code, which is stored in a single byte. An additional attribute byte may be used to provide such information as the color of the character or whether it is to be underlined or displayed in reverse video.*

A text display requires much less memory than a graphics display. For example, consider a 25-line display with 80 characters on each line. Suppose that each character is represented by two bytes, one for its character code and one for its attributes. The amount of display memory needed is $80 \times 25 \times 2 = 4000$ bytes or approximately 4KB. Contrast this with the 16KB needed for a 640-by-200 pixel monochrome bit-mapped display and the 64KB required for a 640-by-200 pixel, 16-color bit-mapped display. Text manipulation is much faster for a text display since to change a character, the program need change only one byte (two if the attribute byte is also changed) rather than a bit pattern that is distributed irregularly over a number of bytes.

The display controller maintains the *cursor*, a flashing block or underline that designates a particular character position on the screen. The position of the cursor is set by the program via commands to the display controller. The program, in turn, allows the user to position the cursor with cursor control keys or with a pointing device such as a mouse. It is up to the program to determine the uses to which the cursor will be put. Most programs use the cursor to designate the position at which the next typed character will be displayed or the position that will be affected by a change such as inserting or deleting a character.

Keyboards

Keyboards are the most widely used input device, even though their use is awkward for people who are not trained typists. Some computer keyboards are designed to resemble a typewriter keyboard as closely as possible. Others contain many extra keys that can be used to control various functions of the computer. Those with extra keys are often more convenient to use, but they run the risk of confusing beginners who fear they will never figure out what to do with the extra keys.

A computer keyboard has keys for all the characters that appear on a typewriter keyboard as well as for a few mathematical and foreign-language symbols not usually found on a standard typewriter. The return key, which corresponds to the carriage return key on an electric typewriter, causes the cursor on the display to move to the beginning of a new line. Since many programs require that each command or data entry be terminated by pressing the return key, this key is also known as the enter key. The escape key, which is usually marked *Esc*, is often used to cancel data entries and to terminate the execution of commands and programs.

---

*Reverse video refers to exchanging the background color and the color used for displaying characters. Thus if a display normally shows white characters against a black background, reverse video will consist of black characters against a white background. Reverse video is often used to highlight segments of text, such as an item selected from a menu or a piece of text selected for manipulation by a word processor.

IBM-PC keyboard. To the left are the function keys; to the right are the numeric keypad (white) and the editing keys (grey).

The number keys along the top row of the keyboard are inconvenient for entering large amounts of numeric data. For this reason, many keyboards also provide a numeric keypad in which the number keys are arranged in a square array as on a calculator.

Certain keys do not themselves generate characters but rather modify the characters generated by other keys. Holding down the *shift key* causes the letter keys to type uppercase rather than lowercase letters. Holding down the control key (usually marked *Ctrl*) causes certain other keys, mainly letter keys, to generate control characters. Some keyboards provide still another shift-type key, the Alt key, which, when pressed, establishes

Keyboard for Japanese characters.

an alternate meaning for each key. The Ctrl and Alt keys are often used to indicate that a keystroke represents a command to the program rather than part of the input data.

Many keyboards provide a set of special function keys that serve as push-buttons for requesting various program operations. Unfortunately, different programs use the functions keys in different ways, making it difficult to remember which function key corresponds to which operation for a particular program. One solution is to show the current function key definitions at the bottom of the display. Another is to provide with each program a plastic keyboard overlay on which is printed the operation corresponding to each function key.

Cursor control keys move the cursor on the display up, down, left, and right, allowing the user to position the cursor at the point on the display where data is to be entered or changes are to be made. Commands can be selected from a menu by positioning the cursor on the desired command. The alternative to cursor control keys is to use a pointing device to position the cursor.

Most keyboards will repeat the action of a key that is held down. This is convenient for spacing and underlining and is essential for convenient use of the cursor control keys.

Computer Terminals

A computer terminal is a device for communicating with a computer over a communications channel such as a telephone line. A terminal normally consists of a keyboard for input and either a display or a printer for output. The most popular type of terminal is the video display terminal (VDT), also known as a cathode-ray tube (CRT) terminal. Computer terminals are the standard devices for communicating with mainframes and mini-computers. Separate terminals are seldom needed for single-user micro-computers, since the keyboard and display are integral parts of a micro-computer. Some microcomputers, however, are designed to be used by several people at the same time; as with minicomputers and mainframes, remote users communicate with a multiuser microcomputer by means of terminals.

Terminals designed for particular applications are common. A familiar example of a special-purpose terminal is the automatic teller machine that allows bank customers to obtain information and make transactions by communicating with a remote mainframe or minicomputer.

Pointing Devices

The need frequently arises for a computer user to point out something on the display to the computer—for example, to point to a word to be erased by a word processing program. The computer may display a menu of available commands and allow the user to point to the command to be executed. Most users find this method easier than having to remember which control key or function key corresponds to each command.

Side view of mouse. User's finger points to button that is pressed or released to call the computer's attention to a particular point on the screen.

Bottom view of mouse shows the ball that rolls on the table when the mouse is moved.

Touch-sensitive screen.

Light-pen.

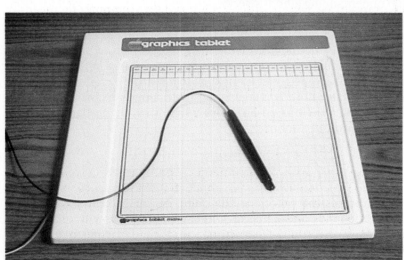

Graphics input tablet (also called graphics pad or digitizer pad) can be used to input drawings to a computer.

One of the earliest pointing devices was the light-pen, which can only be used with CRT displays. As we have seen, the image on a CRT display is produced by an electron beam that repeatedly scans the display screen from left to right and from top to bottom. Because of this scanning action, each point on the display is illuminated at a slightly different time. The light-pen, a penlike device with a light-sensitive cell in its tip, is connected by wire to the computer. The tip of the light-pen is placed over the point the user wishes to designate; when that point is scanned, the light-sensitive cell sends an electrical pulse to the computer. By noting the time at which the pulse arrives, the computer can determine the point over which the light-pen is positioned. Light-pens are frequently used to allow the user to draw on the face of the display (computer software tracks the motion of the light-pen and fills in the line the user is drawing). Light-pens are not so popular for more mundane tasks such as selecting items from command menus.

A display can be made *touch sensitive*, so that the user need only touch the appropriate point on the display to point out an item to the computer. One way to do this is to coat the screen with an electrically conductive film; touching the coating changes its electrical properties and allows the computer to determine the point at which the screen was touched. Another way is to set up a grid of invisible infrared light beams immediately in front of the screen. Touching the screen breaks two light beams, one in the horizontal direction and one in the vertical direction, allowing the computer to locate the point that was touched.

A *touch pad* is a touch-sensitive pad with the same shape as the display but separate from it. Touching a particular point on the pad designates the corresponding point on the screen.

Currently, the most popular pointing device is the *mouse*, a small boxlike object that is connected to the computer by a wire and can be rolled around on a desk. A pointer on the screen follows the movements of the mouse; rolling the mouse left moves the pointer left by an equivalent amount, rolling the mouse right moves the pointer right, and so on. The user presses a button on the mouse when the pointer is at the desired position, such as on the command that is to be selected. Mice work well for such undemanding jobs as selecting commands but not as well for more delicate jobs such as drawing on the screen.

A *trackball* is a metal ball whose top surface protrudes from the panel behind which it is mounted. Moving the exposed surface of the ball in a particular direction produces a corresponding movement in the pointer on the screen. Some people prefer a trackball to a mouse. Certainly, trackballs would seem to have the advantage for portable computers, which are often used in situations such as on airplanes where there is no flat surface on which to roll around a mouse.

Optical Character Recognition

Optical character readers read handwritten, typed, or printed characters directly from source documents, such as filled-out forms. With other forms of data entry, a person must read the source document and strike keys on a keyboard. *Optical character recognition (OCR)* allows us to bypass the error-prone typing process and have the computer read source documents directly. Unfortunately, present optical character readers cannot cope with human handwriting; characters must be carefully hand printed according to certain rules, or they must be typed or printed using typefaces acceptable to the OCR equipment.

OCR typefaces are widely used for printing information on bills; when the bill is returned with the payment, an optical character reader is used to read into the computer the necessary information about the person making the payment. Only the amount that the person paid has to be entered manually.

Magnetic Ink Character Recognition

The banking industry uses magnetic ink character recognition (MICR) to print bank numbers, account numbers, and amounts on checks. The magnetic properties of the ink allow the oddly shaped characters to be read electronically even if they have been written over with ordinary (non-magnetic) ink when the check was made out or during manual processing.

Bar Codes

Bar codes are widely used for printing identifying numbers on items of merchandise; most grocery store, drugstore, and book store items carry such codes. There are two ways to read bar codes. One is with a pencil-like wand, the tip of which the user passes directly over the bar code; such wands, connected to hand-held computers, are often used in taking in-

Machine for reading the magnetic characters printed on checks.

(Left) Using a counter-top bar-code scanner. (Right) The scanner's laser beam traces a complex pattern over the product to find and read the bar code.

ventory. The other, more commonly used method utilizes an automatic scanner built into the counter top; when a product is held or waved over the automatic scanner, a laser beam scans the product in a complex pattern in an attempt to find the bar code. The attempt is not always successful; clerks often have to wave a product over the scanner several times before the scanner indicates (with a beep) that it has found and read the bar code.

Printers

Printers are usually used when a permanent record of computer output is required. High-speed printers can print hundreds, thousands, or even tens of thousands of lines per minute. Printer technology runs the gamut from typewriter-like impact printers to those that use such exotic techniques as laser beams and electrically controlled ink jets to form the characters.

The most popular type of printer for small computers is the *dot-matrix printer*, which forms characters as arrays of dots. The print head, which produces the printed characters, consists of a comblike array of pins (usually 9 or 24), which produce dots by pressing an inked ribbon (similar to a typewriter ribbon) against the paper. A line is printed as the print head sweeps across the page with the pins striking the ribbon wherever dots are needed. Better print quality results if the print head makes two passes over each line; this allows the dots to overlap, so that the individual dots are not as visible. Dot-matrix printers are compact, reliable, and fast. They can print both text and graphics, and some models can print in three or four colors.

The print quality of some dot-matrix printers is poor; the individual dots making up the characters are clearly visible, and some characters appear crude when compared with the corresponding characters on type-writers and typesetting equipment. The number of pins and the number of passes of the print head affect the quality. Thus, a 24-pin printer produces better results than a 9-pin printer, and two passes of the print head produce better results than one.

The quality of dot-matrix printout is often classified as *draft, near letter quality (NLQ)*, or *letter quality (LQ)*. (*Letter quality* refers to the quality produced by an office typewriter and considered satisfactory for business correspondence.) Most dot-matrix printers can be operated in draft mode, in which the print head only makes one pass over each line. Since only one pass per line is needed, the printer runs fastest in draft mode; however, since the dots do not overlap, the output is instantly recognizable as dot-matrix printout. Both NLQ and LQ require two passes of the print head (and hence the printout is produced at about half the speed of draft mode). LQ printout is virtually indistinguishable from the output of an office typewriter; NLQ looks pretty good, but on careful comparison it is not quite as good as LQ. A 9-pin printer can achieve near letter quality; letter quality generally requires 24 pins.

Undeniable letter quality is achieved by solid-face impact printers that, like a typewriter, press a ribbon against the paper by striking it with pieces of type. The most popular of these is the daisy-wheel printer, so named because the type is mounted on bars that extend from the central hub of a wheel in a manner reminiscent of the petals of a daisy. The type font can be changed by changing the daisy wheel. Daisy-wheel printers are usually slower, noisier, and more failure prone than dot-matrix printers. Their output, however, is indistinguishable from typing. Indeed, some recent-model typewriters use daisy wheels instead of the traditional type bars or type balls. Daisy-wheel printers were once standard for business correspondence; their dominance is now threatened by letter-quality dot-matrix printers and by laser printers, which can be used for typesetting as well as business correspondence.

A *laser printer* works like an office copier except that the image to be reproduced is traced out by a computer-controlled laser beam rather than being picked up by a lens focused on a paper original. Laser printers can produce text and graphics having the same high quality found in books and other printed material. Indeed, typesetting—producing the "camera ready" copy that serves as input to the printing process—is one of the major applications of laser printers. Although current laser printers do not have as high a resolution as the phototypesetting machines used for type-

(Left) Dot-matrix printer. (Right) Daisy-wheel printer.

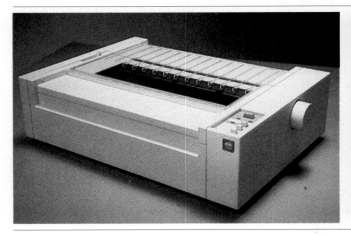
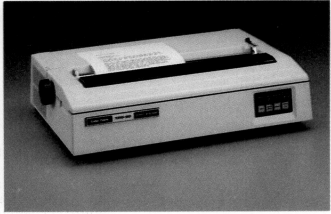

setting books, the difference in quality will often not be noticed except by expert typographers. Even if not appropriate for typesetting fine books, laser printers can meet many of the routine typesetting needs of business and advertising. Laser printers have now dropped in price to the point where they are practical for use with microcomputers (although they are still substantially more expensive than other microcomputer printers). Laser printers driven by microcomputers may have a substantial impact on the typesetting and printing trades.

A laser printer requires an expensive precision optical system to scan the laser beam across the light-sensitive drum on which the image is formed. Other techniques for forming the image, which allow the scanning to be done electronically rather than mechanically, could simplify and reduce the cost of printers using copier technology. For example, in *liquid crystal shutter (LCS)* printers, the part of the image that would be traced out by one horizontal sweep of the laser beam is instead formed with 2400 electronic shutters, each of which can be set electronically to pass or block light.

Ink-jet printers produce characters by bombarding the paper with droplets of ink whose paths are controlled by electric fields. Print quality varies through about the same range as for dot-matrix printers. Clogging of the print head, smearing, and stray droplets can be problems with poorly designed ink-jet printers. A strong advantage of ink-jet printers is that they are quiet; both dot-matrix and daisy-wheel printers are often distractingly loud.

Plotters

Plotters allow computers to make drawings. They are often used to plot graphs, draw maps, and produce engineering drawings. They are also used

Laser printer. Note its resemblance to a tabletop office copier.

to draw the patterns from which microprocessors, memory chips, and other integrated circuits are manufactured. Plotters are used when the highest quality and greatest accuracy are required. For less demanding tasks, other graphics output devices, such as dot-matrix and laser printers, may do just as well.

Speech Synthesizers

Speech synthesizers enable computers to speak. Consumer products that use computer-generated speech include educational toys that pronounce and spell words, electronic phrase books that pronounce phrases in a foreign language, calculators and computers for the blind, and countless electronic games.

With current hardware and software, the speech synthesis is not perfect; the computer seems to speak with an accent. But people who really need a talking computer, such as blind persons, have little trouble learning to follow the machine's accent. And tests have showed that children would rather have their toys speak with a computer accent than have them imitate natural speech more closely.

Most of the computer's accent can be eliminated if the machine has only to utter stock phrases rather than having to be able to read any text. A person chooses the codes to be sent to the synthesizer for each phrase, experimenting with the codes until each phrase sounds as natural as possible. The codes for each phrase are stored in the computer's memory and recalled when needed. Consumer products that use speech synthesis normally follow this method.

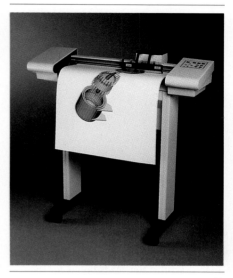

Plotter producing a three-dimensional drawing.

Speech Recognition

Speech recognition enables a computer to understand spoken words, which can be used for both data entry and giving commands to the computer. A word processor, for example, might accept both text and commands for manipulating the text in spoken form. Speech recognition would be welcomed by the many nontypists who find keyboards tedious to use. Business executives, accustomed to leaving the writing and certainly the typing to their secretaries, are usually more at home with spoken than with written communication.

Speech recognition is not yet as highly developed as speech synthesis. Current experimental systems require the user to pronounce each word separately; systems that can process connected speech are not even on the horizon. One experimental speech-operated word processor can recognize about ten thousand words; it is impractical, however, because it requires the full power of a mainframe computer. A similar system that runs on a microcomputer is far too slow, requiring several minutes to recognize each spoken word. The inventor of the latter system hopes that the use of a special-purpose chip will sufficiently speed up the system so that it can be developed as a commercial product.

Speech synthesizer reads books for the blind.

Summary

Information in computers is represented by binary codes, which utilize only the two binary digits (or bits) 0 and 1. Characters—letters, digits, punctuation marks, special signs, and control characters—are represented by binary character codes such as ASCII (7 or 8 bits) and EBCDIC (8 bits). Numbers are most frequently represented in binary notation, a number system that uses only 0 and 1 as digits.

For most modern computers, the basic unit of storage capacity is the byte, which consists of eight bits. Commonly used multiples of one byte are the kilobyte (K or KB; approximately one thousand bytes), the megabyte (M or MB; approximately one million bytes), and the gigabyte (G or GB; approximately one billion bytes).

Main memory consists of a large number of individual memory locations, each of which is designated by a unique address. Typically, the smallest-sized location holds one byte; adjacent bytes can be combined to obtain two-byte, four-byte, eight-byte, and even larger-sized locations. Main memory offers fast access (less than a millionth of a second) and random access (access time for data values does not depend on where they are located in memory or on the order in which they were stored). Most forms of main memory are volatile—unless battery backup power is provided, the contents of main memory are lost when the computer is turned off.

Auxiliary memory provides long-term storage of programs and data that need to be retained even when the computer is turned off. Auxiliary memory is less costly than main memory, but access time may be over a thousand times slower. Consequently, data and programs are moved to main memory for processing; any data that is to be saved is returned to auxiliary memory when processing is complete.

The most common form of auxiliary memory is magnetic disks, which provide direct access (stored values can be accessed in any order, but access time for a value depends on its location on the disk and the current positions of the disk and the access mechanism). Microcomputers use removable diskettes (slow access, low capacity) and built-in hard disks (fast access, high capacity). Large computers use removable disk packs (fast access, high capacity). Large computers also use magnetic tape, mainly for archival (very long term) storage and for transporting programs and data from one computer to another. Magnetic tape is a sequential access medium, since data values must be read back in the same order in which they were recorded. Optical storage, such as CD-ROMs, and WORM drives, are just beginning to be used with microcomputers.

A computer system is built around a central processing unit (CPU), which, in turn, consists of an arithmetic/logic unit (ALU) and a control unit. The arithmetic/logic unit carries out all the calculations; the control unit executes the user's program, passing on to other units whatever commands are necessary to carry out the program's instructions. Input, output, and auxiliary memory devices are called peripherals; each is operated by a device controller, which can receive commands and data from the CPU and can return data and status information. Frequently, the CPU, main memory, and the device controllers are built on printed circuit boards that plug into a bus—a group of 50-100 wires over which the printed circuit boards can communicate with one another.

Input devices and output devices enable computers to communicate with the outside world. The most common input devices are keyboards; the most common output devices are video displays and printers. There are many special purpose input and output devices, such as scanners for reading bar codes and speech synthesizers for producing spoken output.

Speech recognition allows a technician to dictate instrument readings to the computer.

Vocabulary Review

address
American Standard
  Code for
  Information
  Interchange (ASCII)
bar code
binary code
bus
byte
byte-oriented memory
CD-ROM
conditional execution
control character
CRT (cathode-ray
  tube) display
cursor
device controller
direct access
disk pack
dot-matrix printer
draft quality
expansion board

expansion slot
Extended Binary
  Coded Decimal
  Interchange Code
  (EBCDIC)
floppy disk
gigabyte (G or GB)
ink-jet printer
interrupt
kilobyte (K or KB)
laser printer
letter quality (LQ)
light-pen
liquid crystal display
  (LCD)
megabyte (M or MB)
memory location
memory-mapped
  display
motherboard
near letter quality
  (NLQ)

optical character
  recognition (OCR)
optical disc
peripheral devices
plasma display
plotter
printed circuit board
printer
processor
RAM (random access
  memory)
random access
resolution
ROM (read-only
  memory)
sector
sequential access
speech recognition
speech synthesizer
system board
track
trackball

For Further Reading

''In Depth: CPU Architectures'' (special section). Byte, May 1988, pp. 211–268.

Scientific American (special issue on advances in computing). October 1987.

Personal computing magazines such as *Byte*, *Macworld*, and *PC Magazine* frequently feature reviews of microcomputers and peripherals as well as comparisons of all devices in a given category, such as dot-matrix printers. Readers interested in current microcomputer hardware should check recent issues of such magazines in libraries and magazine stores.

Review Questions

1 Explain why information representation can be considered a matter of representing alternatives.

2 Describe the ASCII code. How are the characters X, x, 3, and $ represented in ASCII? How is the blank space represented.

3 What is a control character? What is the function of the control key on a computer keyboard?

4 What decimal values are represented by the binary numbers 101, 111, and 1010?

5 Give the binary representations for six, nine, and fifteen.

6 Approximately how many bytes are there in a kilobyte, a megabyte, and a gigabyte?

7 What do the abbreviations K, M, G, KB, MB, and GB signify?

8 Distinguish between main and auxiliary memory.

9 Distinguish between RAM and ROM.

10 Describe the three steps by which the computer system locates a designated disk sector. Which two of the steps make significant contributions to the access time?

11 Describe the various sizes of diskettes. Which size is most widely used now? Which is likely to be most widely used in the future?

12 Describe CD-ROM and WORM optical storage.

13 What does computer architecture encompass?

14 Name the major hardware components of a computer system.

15 What is the function of the arithmetic/logic unit?

16 What is the function of the control unit?

17 What is the function of the bus?

18 What is the function of a device controller?

19 What is a register? Describe three registers likely to be found in a device controller.

20 What is a condition? A flag?

21 Describe the comparison operation.

22 Describe the fetch-execute cycle.

23 What is a jump instruction? For what purpose is it used.

24 What is a subroutine? What two instructions make subroutines possible?

25 What purpose does an interrupt request serve? What is an interrupt handler subroutine?

26 For what kinds of computers are liquid crystal displays popular?

27 Characterize a memory-mapped display. What is display memory?

28 Contrast a bit-mapped display with a text display.

29 What is a pixel?

30 Describe the keys found on a typical computer keyboard. How do the shift, Ctrl, and Alt keys differ from the other keys?

31 Describe four types of pointing devices. Which is currently the most popular?

32 Give some advantages of dot-matrix printers. What is their main disadvantage? Distinguish draft quality, near letter quality, and letter quality printing.

33 Which type of printer may have a significant impact on the typesetting and printing industries?

34 What output device is used for detailed, accurate drawings such as maps, engineering drawings, and patterns for integrated circuits?

35 What are the advantages of speech recognition and synthesis over other forms of input and output?

Topics for Discussion

1 The most popular computer input device is the typewriter-like keyboard, yet most people cannot type fluently and so find using keyboards to be extremely tedious and error prone. Should schools respond to this situation by teaching typing to all students rather than to just those preparing for secretarial careers?

2 Because of the difficulty of using keyboards, vigorous research is underway to develop speech-recognition as a practical method of input for personal computers. Because of likely limitations of current and near-future technology, connected speech cannot be processed; words will have to be pronounced separately and with carefully controlled enunciation. Some observers find humor in the thought of business executives talking to their computers in robotlike tones. Assuming that the people in question must use computers, do you think they would rather use such unnatural speech than to learn how to type?

3 Discussion questions 1 and 2 raise a larger question: should we insist that computers communicate with us in ways with which we are already familiar (such as everyday speech and handwriting), or should we meet computers halfway such as by learning to type or by using artificial speech patterns that computers can understand?

PROGRAMMING LANGUAGES AND OPERATING SYSTEMS

INTRODUCTION

Systems programs help people to use a computer system. Language processors allow us to program computers in languages that are meaningful to us rather than in the obscure binary codes that the central processing unit requires. The operating system provides both users and programs with a simple means of requesting routine system operations such as transferring data between disk and main memory. The operating system provides the coordination needed for multitasking, in which the system works on more than one program at the same time, and for multiuser systems that serve more than one user at the same time.

PROGRAMMING LANGUAGES

A *computer language* is any notation or set of conventions for conveying instructions or data to a computer. Many applications programs, such as word processors and spreadsheet programs, define sometimes elaborate command languages by which users can make their wishes known to the program. Computer languages used for writing programs are called programming languages, and it is on these that we will concentrate in this section.

Machine Language

The central processing unit can execute binary-coded instructions known as *machine code* or *machine language*. The following is a short sample of machine language:

    10100001 00000000 00000010 00000011 00000110

    00000010 00000010 10100011 00000000 00000010

The codes represent instructions for the computer and the addresses of the main-memory locations that data is stored in or retrieved from as the instructions are carried out.

A machine-language programmer has to know the binary code for each operation the computer can carry out. Since most computers have hundreds of operations, a machine-language programmer must memorize many obscure codes or, more likely, carry around a reference card giving the code for each operation. Machine-language programmers must also be familiar with the internal organization of the computer, such as the central processor registers and the layout of main memory, even though these machine-oriented details have nothing to do with the problem the programmer wants the computer to solve. Because each instruction carries out a very simple operation, such as comparing two numbers, thousands of machine-language instructions are usually required to make a computer do anything useful, and many programs contain hundreds of thousands or millions of instructions.

A machine-language programmer must also keep track of all the addresses of main-memory locations that are referred to in the program. With

A programmer working at a minicomputer.

only the addresses to go by, it is difficult to remember the significance of the data stored in each location. It is easy to make a slip and write an instruction that causes the machine to refer to the wrong memory location.

Still another problem is that if we modify a program, we will probably have to change the addresses of some of the memory locations the program uses. For example, if we insert another instruction in the program, all the instructions and data items following the point of insertion have to be moved forward in memory to make room for the new instruction. The addresses of the instructions and data items that were moved are changed, and the address parts of any instructions referring to those instructions or data items must also be changed. For example, we have to change all jump instructions that jump to parts of the program that have been moved and all call instructions that call subroutines that have been moved. Inserting one new instruction in the program may require us to modify the address parts of many instruction codes.

For these reasons, machine-language programming is extremely tedious. A programmer might write a few machine-language instructions for some special purpose, such as making corrections to an existing machine-language program, but few would write a program of any size in machine language.

Assembly Language

Assembly language allows us to use convenient abbreviations, called *mnemonics*, for operations and memory locations. For example, the following three assembly-language instructions correspond to the machine code at the beginning of the previous section:

```
MOV AX, TOTAL
ADD AX, VALUE
MOV TOTAL, AX
```

The mnemonics MOV and ADD name the machine operations for moving and adding values, and AX names a particular register in the central processing unit. TOTAL and VALUE are names assigned by the programmer to particular locations in main memory. The first line instructs the central processing unit to *move* the contents of the main-memory location named TOTAL to the AX register. The second line instructs the central processor to *add* the contents of the main-memory location named VALUE to the contents of the AX register (the sum is stored back in the AX register). The third line instructs the central processing unit to *move* the contents of the AX register to the main-memory location named TOTAL.

The central processor cannot understand assembly language, of course; it can only execute programs in machine code. Before an assembly-language program can executed, it must be translated into machine language. Fortunately, we can program the computer to do the translation; the program that tells the computer how to do the translation is called an *assembler*. The assembler program is our first example of a *language processor*. Language processors allow computer systems to execute programs written in languages other than machine language.

Assembly language, then, makes it possible for programmers to use convenient mnemonics rather than obscure codes for operations and memory locations. Also, since memory locations are referred to by name rather than by address, the programmer can modify a program without worrying that the modifications will change some addresses and thus require still more modifications. Addresses are assigned by the assembler, which does the job anew each time it translates a modified version of the program.

On the other hand, the assembly language programmer must still write a line of assembly language for each machine instruction,* so assembly language programs that do significant jobs are many thousands of lines long. Assembly-language programmers must also be concerned with the technical details of the computer, such as how the central-processor registers are to be used, how much data will fit into a memory location, and what operations are available for manipulating the data. Thus, although assembly language is vastly superior to machine language and is far more widely used, programming in it is still tedious and requires knowledge of the internal workings of the computer.

Higher-Level Languages

Higher-level languages hide the internal details of computer operation, allowing programmers to phrase a program in the same terms that would be used to describe to a colleague the procedure being carried out. Since

---

*This is not strictly true because most assemblers allow programmers to define *macroinstructions*, or *macros*, each of which can represent a (perhaps lengthy) sequence of assembly-language instructions. A line containing a macro can cause many machine-language instructions to be produced. Convenient as macros can be, however, they are not used frequently enough to affect the magnitude of the task of writing a substantial assembly-language program.

Programmers working at computer terminals.

procedures are stated in different ways in different subject areas and by different groups of programmers, more than one higher-level language is required. Currently there are about 170 higher-level languages in use, although the number in reasonably widespread use is closer to 20. The following table lists seven popular programming languages and gives the principal application areas of each.

Language	Application Area
Ada	military systems
Basic	education, personal computing
C	writing systems programs; often used as an alternative to assembly language
Cobol	business data processing
Fortran	science, engineering, and mathematics
Lisp	artificial intelligence, robot control
Pascal	education, personal computing, computer science research

We recall that adding the contents of memory location VALUE to the contents of memory location TOTAL requires three assembly-language instructions:

```
MOV AX, TOTAL
ADD AX, VALUE
MOV TOTAL, AX
```

The same addition can be expressed as a single line in each of the six higher-level languages:

Debugging a malfunctioning program.

Language	Statement
Ada	TOTAL := TOTAL + VALUE
Basic	LET T = T + V
C	total = total + value
Cobol	ADD VALUE TO TOTAL.
Fortran	TOTAL = TOTAL + VALUE
Lisp	(SETQ TOTAL (PLUS TOTAL VALUE))
Pascal	*total* := *total* + *value*

None of the higher-level language statements refer to any machine components (such as central-processor registers) or machine operations. The business programmer who prefers English-like sentences to algebra-like formulas can have them with Cobol. The scientific programmer who prefers the formulas gets them with Fortran. The personal computer user seeking a simple, easy-to-use language whose language processor will run on a small computer system will be happy with Basic. On the other hand, the systems programmer who does need to work directly with main-memory locations and central-processor registers can do so with C.

Note that, with the exception of the Cobol and Lisp examples, the example statements are all similar. Much of the notation for expressing computations is common to many (although not all) higher-level languages. Once you have learned one higher-level language (unless it's an eccentric one like Cobol or Lisp), you will not find it too difficult to master other, not-too-distantly-related languages. Most programmers find it easy to read programs in many languages, even languages they have not encountered before, although they must usually consult a reference manual for technical details when attempting to write programs in an unfamiliar language.

Higher-level language programs are much shorter than machine-language or assembly-language programs. A single line in a higher-level language program may translate into five, ten, or even hundreds of machine-language instructions.

Fourth-Generation Languages

Higher-level languages provide a convenient notation for telling the computer, step-by-step, how to solve a problem or accomplish a task. So-called *fourth-generation languages (4GLs)* allow the user (who may not be a programmer) to merely describe the problem to be solved or the task to be accomplished; the user does not have to specify step-by-step how the desired results are to be achieved. Since the user does not provide step-by-step instructions, the language processor for a fourth-generation language must incorporate the knowledge and skill necessary to solve the problems presented by the user.

Fourth-generation languages have been most successful in business data processing. Business-data-processing programs are, conceptually, relatively straightforward, although they can be tedious and time-consuming to write in conventional higher-level languages such as Cobol. Often a system of data-processing programs can be described by a diagram showing the flow of data from one stage of processing to the next, along with a description of the various computer screen displays, printed reports, and disk files that are needed.

By allowing users to write their own applications programs, fourth-generation languages are godsends to corporate MIS (management information systems) departments, which are often running years behind in writing the applications programs that have been requested by the various departments in their organizations.

Language Processors

The program that translates other programs from a given computer language into machine language is called a *translator*. A translator program for assembly language is an *assembler*; translators for higher-level languages are often called *compilers*. Translators, assemblers, and compilers are all examples of language processors. The result of the translation process is always a machine-language program that can be executed by the central processing unit just as if it had been coded by hand. As far as the central processing unit is concerned, there is no distinction between hand-coded machine-language programs and those produced by translator programs. The program to be translated is called the *source program*; the program produced by the translator is called the *object program*.

In practice, an additional step called *linking* must often be taken before a translated program can be executed. The object program produced by the translator may call subroutines stored in auxiliary memory. (We recall that a subroutine is just a program that is called by another program rather than directly by the user.) The object program contains references to these subroutines but does not contain the subroutines themselves. Another software program, called a *linker*, must be used to combine the object program with the subroutines it calls. The linker produces an *executable program* that contains not only the object program but all the subroutines that it calls.

The source, object, and executable programs normally reside in files in auxiliary memory; these files are referred to as the *source file*, *object file*, and *executable file*. The user requests execution of a program by typing (or selecting from a menu) the name of the corresponding executable file.

Interpreters are another widely used type of language processor. Instead of translating the statements of the source program into machine language, the interpreter program carries out the operations called for by each statement. Thus the source program is executed when it is processed by the interpreter, instead of being translated into machine language for later execution by the central processor. The central processing unit executes only the interpreter program, which is, of course, written in machine language.* It is the responsibility of the interpreter program to see that the instructions in the higher-level-language source program are carried out.

A programmer working at home.

---

*This doesn't mean that the interpreter program was originally written in machine language; it was most likely written in either assembly language or C, then translated into machine language with an assembler or a compiler.

It can take much longer to execute an interpreted program than a translated one. The reason is that most programs use repetition constructions to specify that some statements will be executed many times. Such repeated statements need to be analyzed only once by a translator, but an interpreter must analyze a repeated statement every time it is executed. And every time the interpreter analyzes a statement, it may have to search a table to find which memory locations are referred to by mnemonics such as TOTAL and VALUE. A translator converts mnemonics into memory addresses that can be used to access the corresponding memory locations directly.

In spite of this drawback, interpreters often provide the most convenient way to develop programs in a higher-level language. The interpreter makes it easy to intermix execution with editing (correcting and modifying a program). (Most interpreters also contain a text editor for entering and changing the source program.) We can execute a few lines of the program, check the results, make some changes, execute the same few lines again, and so on. With a translator, we would have to go through the entire process of translating and linking after each change. When testing an interpreted program, we can use mnemonics such as TOTAL and VALUE to refer to memory locations whose contents we wish to examine. For a translated program, we would probably have to use addresses to specify the locations to be examined. When an error occurs, as when the program requests an impossible operation, the interpreter can tell us which statement in the higher-level language program caused the problem; for a translated program, we may only be given the address of the machine-language instruction that produced the error.

OPERATING SYSTEMS

The operating system is the program that supervises the execution of other programs. It is also known as the *supervisor, monitor, master control program,* or *disk operating system (DOS).* The latter name arises because one of the main functions of an operating system is managing disk storage. By means of *system commands,* the user requests the operating system to execute particular programs and give those programs access to particular data. The operating system takes care of all the details necessary to comply with the user's requests.

Functions of Operating Systems

The following are some of the functions performed by a modern operating system. Not every operating system can perform all the functions listed; for example, the accounting and security functions are usually not provided by microcomputer operating systems.

Program Loading   Programs normally reside in auxiliary memory as executable files. Upon request by the user, the operating system will load a program from auxiliary memory into main memory and arrange for the computer to execute it. The loader program (which is part of the operating system) must allocate an area of main memory to hold the program and its data, copy the program code into that area from auxiliary memory, build a table (for use by the operating system) containing information about the program, and turn control of the computer over to the program. (When the program finishes executing, it will return control to the operating system.) Since the translator and linker do not know where the loader will put a program in main memory, some memory addresses referred to by the program may not be known until the program is actually loaded. It is the responsibility of the loader to compute these addresses (by combining information in the executable file with knowledge of where the program is being loaded) and insert them in the program as it copies the program into main memory.

Operating System Macros   Many operating systems allow the user to define *macrocommands*, each of which represents a sequence of system commands. Giving the macrocommand causes every command in the sequence to be carried out. For example, translation, linking, and execution of a program are often handled by a macrocommand. Macrocommands go by a variety of names, one of the most popular of which is *batch file*.

Control of Peripherals   Peripheral devices often require complex, hard-to-write programs to control the transfer of data between the device and the computer. Writing such a *device-handler* program calls for detailed technical knowledge about the operation of the device. For this reason, device handlers are usually written once and for all and included in the operating system. A user's program transfers information to or from a device by making the appropriate request to the operating system. The form of the request is the same for all devices, even though the coded commands that actually have to be sent to the devices vary widely from

Programmers often write versions of their programs for different computers, such as the IBM PC (left) and the Apple Macintosh on this programmer's desk.

one device to another. Often there are provisions for adding new device-handler programs to the operating system when new types of peripheral devices are installed.

A device handler normally has two parts, both of which are subroutines. One part is called directly by applications programs to send commands to the device, to receive status information from the device, and to transfer data to and from the device. The other part of the device handler is the interrupt handler subroutine that responds to the interrupt requests from the device. The two parts of the device handler allow interactions with the device to be initiated either by an applications program (via a subroutine call) or by the device (via an interrupt request).

Data Management   Not only do computer systems maintain program libraries in auxiliary memory, they store data files there as well. Examples of typical data files include a company's customer accounts or the data collected in a scientific experiment.

When a program needs data from one of these files, it requests it from the operating system. The operating system must first find the desired file in auxiliary memory; then it must find the particular data requested and pass it on to the program. Likewise, the program can pass data to the operating system with the request that it be stored at a particular location in a particular file.

To aid the operating system in managing auxiliary memory, each volume of auxiliary memory (such as a diskette, a disk pack, or a hard disk unit) contains two tables. The *directory* lists all files currently on the volume and gives the area occupied by each. The *allocation table* gives the currently unoccupied areas that are available for storing new files. If the directory is damaged through a hardware or software malfunction, the operating system may be unable to access some or all of the files on the volume. If the allocation table is damaged, the operating system may store new files in areas that are already occupied, destroying the data previously stored there. Utility programs are available that attempt to recover as much data as possible from a disk whose directory or allocation table has been damaged.

Many operating systems handle input and output devices in exactly the same way as disk files. A programmer can write a program to take data from certain files, process it, and store the results in other files. Only when it's time to execute the program does the user have to specify which of these "files" are files in auxiliary memory and which are input or output devices. This specification can be changed each time the program is executed; what was a disk file on one execution of the program can be a printer on the next.

Concurrent Execution   *Concurrent execution* refers to more than one program running on the computer at the same time. Concurrency makes possible multitasking and multiuser systems.

Multitasking allows the computer to work on more that one job, or task, at a time. For example, a microcomputer user might write a report with a word processor and order the word processor to print out the finished report. While the report is being printed, the user might do calculations with a spreadsheet program. To allow the user to do spreadsheet

A single operating system (GEM) is shown running on computers from three different manufacturers: AT&T, Radio Shack, and IBM. Any program that runs under this operating system can run on all three computers.

calculations while the report is being printed, the computer must be able to run both the word processor and the spreadsheet program at the same time.

A *multiuser system* can be accessed from computer terminals by a number of users at the same time. Each user seems to have the entire system to himself or herself. Users can share output devices such as printers and storage devices such as hard disks. Multiuser operation is often referred to as time sharing, since the central processing unit's time is shared among all the users.

Concurrent execution provides challenges for the operating system that go beyond the basic one of sharing the processors' time among a number of programs. For example, if more than one program requests use of the printer, the operating system must give exclusive use of the device to one program until it finishes its printout, then let another program take its turn, and so on. It must not (as an operating system of the author's acquaintance was notorious for doing) print one line of one program's output, then a line of another program's output, then a line of still another program's output, and so on. The users' are guaranteed to be unhappy with their joint printout!

On the other hand, accesses to a disk by different programs often can be interleaved. In this case, the program must schedule the movement of the disk's read-write heads so as to satisfy each program's request as rapidly as possible. In one approach, called the *elevator algorithm*, the read-write heads move inward toward the center of the disk, like an elevator going up. Just as the elevator stops at each floor for which service has been requested, the read-write heads stop at each track for which an access has been requested. When the innermost track for which an access has been requested is reached, the read-write heads reverse direction and begin moving outwards, like an elevator that, having reached the top floor for which service was requested, has switched from "going up" to "going down."

Simultaneous access by programs to a database can present problems. Suppose one program is to make two changes to a record in a database—

say change a person's birthdate and age (presumably to correct previous errors). Suppose that after the first program changes the birthdate, but before it changes the age, a second program accesses the record. The second program will obtain an inconsistent record, since the birthdate and the age will not agree. The operating system must provide a means whereby one program can lock out accesses to a record by other programs until all changes have been completed.

Granting programs exclusive use of system resources, such as devices, can lead to a problem called *deadlock*. Suppose a system has two printers and two programs, each of which needs both printers. Each program requests and is granted one printer. Now each program requests a second printer. The second request from each program will never be granted, however, because the second printer that each program needs is being held by the other program. Neither program will get the second printer that it needs, and so it will never release the printer that it already has and which the other program is waiting for. Neither program can proceed; both are deadlocked. Also, both printers are permanently tied up, although neither is being used. The operating system needs to be able to detect deadlock and take remedial action.

Virtual Memory   Often a program and the data it is manipulating are too large to fit into main memory at one time. Therefore, only the parts of the program and data that are being used at the moment are kept in main memory. The remaining parts reside in auxiliary memory until needed. During execution of the program, parts of the program and data must be swapped back and forth between main and auxiliary memory.

It is tedious for the programmer to have to divide the program in parts and worry about making sure that the needed parts are always in main memory. We would like to free the programmer to concentrate on the

A multitasking operating system allows several programs to run concurrently, with the output from each program appearing in a separate window.

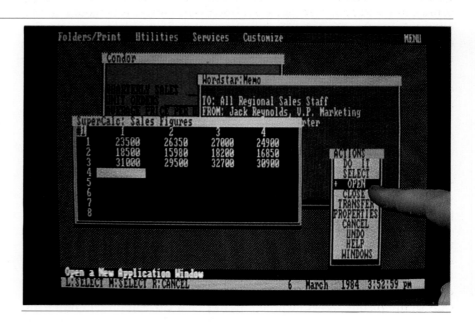

problem being solved without having to worry about computer-oriented technicalities such as main and auxiliary memory.

With a technique known as *virtual memory*, the operating system takes over the task of dividing the program into parts and juggling the parts between main and auxiliary memory. The programmer writes the program as though the computer had a very large main memory. The operating system takes care of the rest. Typically, the program and data are divided into blocks called *pages*. The pages that the program is currently using—that it has referred to recently—are part of the program's *working set* and are kept in main memory. When a page is not referred to for a while, it falls out of the program's working set and becomes a candidate for being "swapped out" to auxiliary memory. If the program refers to a page that is not in main memory, this page becomes part of the working set and is "swapped in" to main memory, preferably replacing a page that has fallen out of the working set and so has become a candidate for being swapped out. If a program refers to many different pages in rapid succession, a phenomenon called *thrashing* takes place, in which the computer spends more time swapping pages than in doing useful work.

We speak of a *virtual* memory, since the computer appears to have a very large main memory that does not actually exist. Any part of a computer system that appears to be present as a result of programming but does not actually exist is said to be virtual. For example, we can think of language processors as implementing *virtual machines*, imaginary computers that accept higher-level languages as their machine languages. Sometimes people use terms such as *Basic machine* or *Pascal machine* to refer to these virtual machines.

Applications Program Interface   A major function of the operating system is providing services to applications programs. As mentioned in connection with peripheral devices, all access by programs to input devices, output devices, and files in auxiliary memory is through commands to the operating system. This is particularly important when concurrent execution is allowed, since only if all devices are accessed through the operating system can the system meet such responsibilities as granting exclusive use of some peripherals, arranging for efficient simultaneous use of others, and detecting deadlock.

Applications programs request operating-system services by calling subroutines that are part of the operating system. In advanced systems, the operating system is protected so that the *only* way an applications program can access the operating system is by calling one of a designated set of subroutines. This protection assures that the applications programs remain subordinate to the operating system; there is no way for one application to bypass the operating system and take actions (such as seizing and refusing to share a peripheral device) that might be disadvantageous to other concurrently executing applications. The subroutine calls—the details of how to call the subroutines to request specific services—are known as the *applications program interface (API)*. We can think of the operating system as a virtual machine whose commands are the subroutine calls in the API.

User-Friendly Interfaces   System commands can be rather cryptic. For example, to edit a file with a word processor, we might issue the system command:

```
wordproc a:report.txt
```

Here wordproc is the name of the word-processor program, that is, the name of the executable file containing the word-processor program. report is the name of the file to be edited, which can be found on the disk in disk drive a; the extension txt, which is given to all files produced by the word processor, distinguishes them from files with the same names produced by other programs. All this is confusing to those who are using a computer for the first time or who do not use the computer regularly. Nor does it help that the very details one is likely to have trouble remembering—where the colon and period must be used, the symbols for designating disk drives, and the name of the word processor program—are likely to vary from one computer system to another.

As a result of the microprocessor revolution, computers have fallen into the hands of many people who want to use them for particular jobs, such as word processing or spreadsheet analysis, without bothering to master the commands and technical details of a particular operating system. They gladly leave the beauties of computer technology to computer science students; they just want to get the mail out, get their reports written, and get next year's budget planned. They demand user-friendly systems whose operation is sufficiently obvious that it can be mastered with brief instruction, a bit of experimentation, and common sense.

One way to make a system user-friendly is to employ a *metaphor*—to make the operation of the system similar to some process with which the user is already familiar. A currently popular metaphor is the desktop metaphor, in which the display simulates the top of a desk. Various papers appear to lie on the desk; these papers are actually *windows*—areas of the display in which programs present their output. The user can adjust the size of each window so that several windows can occupy the desktop simultaneously, or one window can be expanded to fill the entire desk, temporarily covering up the others. If the system supports concurrent execution, programs can be run simultaneously, presenting their output in different windows. Data can be transferred between windows maintained by different programs. For example, a chart produced with a graphics program can be inserted into a report being created with a word processor.

Icons—small pictures on the desktop—represent sources and destinations for data. For example, a picture of a disk represents a particular disk drive; a picture of a printer represents that output device; a trash can represents a destination for data that is to be discarded. Sources or destinations for data can be selected by using a mouse to position a pointer over the desired icon and pressing the button on the mouse.

The mouse is also used to give commands to the operating system and to the various applications programs. A bar across the top of the display lists the types of commands that are currently available. For example, "edit" symbolizes all commands that can be used to edit a program. If the mouse is positioned over the word edit and the button on the mouse is pressed, a menu of all editing commands is "pulled down" (appears in a temporary window below the word "edit"). The user moves the mouse until the pointer is over the desired editing command, then releases the button.

The part of an operating system that interacts with the user is often contained in a program called the *shell*. By changing the shell, one can change completely the *user interface*—the face that the operating system presents to the user. A programmer's shell might allow access to the full power of the operating system but require that requests be in the form of concise, cryptic commands. On the other hand, a user's shell based on the desktop metaphor may be much easier to work with but may not provide for all the operations that are available through the programmer's shell.

Like all applications programs, the shell communicates with the operating system via the API. Thus the API is the primary channel for communicating with the operating system. The shell allows the user to enter commands in a convenient form (such as selecting them from menus), then translates the user's commands into calls to API subroutines.

For consistency, applications should adopt the same user interface as the operating system; the applications and the operating system should have the same "look and feel." The operating system can promote such consistency by providing the API with subroutine calls for maintaining the desired interface. For example, in a system using the desktop metaphor, the operating system can provide commands that enable applications programs to create, delete, and change the size of windows, send output to particular windows, create pull-down menus, determine which menu items or icons have been selected by the user, and so on. These basic display-and-control commands can be used in writing both the operating-system shell and the user interfaces for applications programs.

Accounting   In many organizations it is necessary to keep track of the computing resources (such as computation time and memory space) that each job uses so that each department in the organization can be charged for the resources it consumes. Some companies, by letting other people use their computers, make a business of selling computer resources. Like other utilities, they must prepare monthly bills for their customers. In either case, the job of accounting for who uses how much of what resources falls on the operating system.

Security   You may have gotten the impression that the operating system will try its best to honor any request made by any user. But on large systems with many users, there are usually some requests that should be denied. For example, some files might contain confidential data to which only authorized persons should have access. Others might contain records that someone could benefit from changing, such as bank accounts, student grades, or payroll information. In defense industries, some data and programs might be military secrets. Even in an academic environment, programs and data files must be protected against malicious mischief. It is up to the operating system to require users to identify themselves with passwords, to allow only authorized persons to use the system, and to restrict each user to the files that he or she is authorized to access.

More About Concurrent Execution

The original motivation for concurrent execution came from the enormous disparity between the speed of the central processor and that of most peripheral devices. For example, many computer terminals send and receive characters at the rate of 120 per second. (For sending, this rate is purely theoretical, since nobody can type that fast.) On the other hand, a fast computer can carry out millions of instructions each second. While the computer is waiting for the terminal to send or accept another character, it could have executed at least 10,000 instructions. If the computer is made to wait for the terminal, most of the central processor's time will be wasted.

There are two solutions to this problem. One, made possible by the microprocessor revolution, is to use an inexpensive computer so that the wasted time does not really matter. The other, more interesting solution, is to arrange for the computer to work on other programs while one program is waiting on a peripheral device. Execution of the program that is waiting is not resumed until the request to the peripheral device has been fulfilled.

Multiprogramming　　Multiprogramming refers to the situation in which a single central processor seems to execute a number of programs at the same time. Actually, the central processor is switched rapidly from one program to another. Each program is executed for a short time, called a *time slice* or a *time quantum*. Before the operating system gives a particular program control of the computer, it sets an electronic timer to interrupt the computer when the time slice has expired. When the timer interrupts, control of the computer is returned automatically to the operating system. The operating system then moves on to the next program awaiting execution, sets the timer again, and gives that program temporary control of the computer.

In this way, control of the computer passes from program to program in round-robin fashion. Each program is executed briefly, after which the operating system passes on to the next program. Since it is the central processor that executes the programs, we can think of various programs as taking turns at the central processor.

When a program has to wait on a peripheral device, it loses its turns at the central processor until the request to the peripheral device has been satisfied. But while that program is waiting, other programs are busy taking their turns at the central processor, so the central processor does not remain idle.

Processes and Interrupts　　We have spoken loosely about programs sharing the central processor, but it is more precise to speak in terms of *processes* (also called *tasks*) rather than programs. As shown in Figure 4-1, a process has three components:

1　A program

2　The data the program is manipulating

3　The address of the next program instruction to be executed. Since the address designates, or points out, the next instruction, it is called the *pointer* to the next instruction.

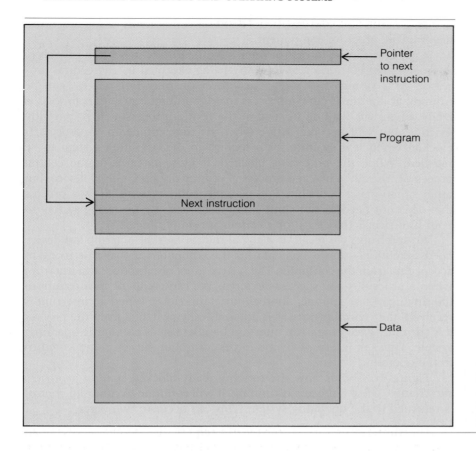

Pointer
to next
instruction

Program

Next instruction

Data

FIGURE 4-1
The three components of a process: the program, the data the program is processing, and a pointer to the next instruction to be executed.

Note that the data component includes not only data stored in main memory but also that stored in the registers of the central processor. Also, the data component contains descriptions of any files in auxiliary memory that the program is processing.

The most important property of a process is that its execution can be stopped at any time and restarted later as if nothing had happened. We say that a process is *active* when it is actually being executed and *inactive* or *suspended* when it is not. The components of an active process reside in the central-processor registers, in main memory, and perhaps partially in auxiliary memory. An inactive process resides in either main or auxiliary memory, or partially in both.

A process leads an independent existence, interacting with users through input and output devices and perhaps exchanging messages with other processes. A process can even create offspring that will carry out their assigned tasks and report back to the parent process. With tongue only slightly in cheek, people have referred to a process as "an organism that lives in a computer system."

Although each process must have its own individual instruction-pointer and data component, a single program can be shared by many processes. Thus a frequently used program, such as a popular word processor, can be placed in memory once and shared by many processes. The only requirement is that the program must never change itself; changes can only be made in the data and instruction-pointer components of the processes, never in the program component.

A process can be in one of three states: *running, ready,* and *blocked.* A process that is running is currently being executed by the central processor. In a system with only one processor, only one process can be running at one time. Only a process that is running is active. A process is ready when it is waiting its turn at the central processor. It is currently inactive, but will become active when its turn comes up. A process is blocked when it is waiting for a request to the operating system to be satisfied. While the process is blocked, it loses its turns at the central processor. Usually a blocked process is waiting on a peripheral device, but other situations are possible. For example, some systems allow a process that does not need to run continually to request the operating system to "put it to sleep" (block it) for a certain period of time.

An interrupt, we recall, is a signal indicating that a peripheral device needs attention—that it has data for the computer or that it is ready to accept data from the computer. The system timer also produces an interrupt when a process's time slice has expired. We can compare an interrupt to the ringing of a telephone, doorbell, or alarm clock. When an interrupt is received, the central processor is automatically switched from the process it is currently executing to an interrupt handler that is part of the operating system. Thus, an interrupt always forces control of the computer to return to the operating system.

Figure 4-2 shows how the running-ready-blocked state of a process can change. Once a process is running, it will continue to run until control is returned to the operating system. This can occur in two ways.

1 The running process can explicitly request the operating system to perform some action, such as an input or output operation. The process is blocked until the requested operation can be carried out.

2 An interrupt can force a transfer of control from the running process to the operating system. The interrupt can be from the timer, indicating that the running process has used up its time slice, or it can be from a peripheral device that needs attention. In either case, the running process is placed in the ready state so that it will be run again when its turn next comes up.*

An interrupt often indicates that a request made by a blocked process has been satisfied—either a peripheral has data for the process or the peripheral can accept data from the process. After carrying out the requested data transfer, the operating system places the process that was waiting in the ready state so that it can resume taking turns at the central processor. Thus an interrupt often results in a blocked process being transferred to the ready state.

When all interrupts have been handled for the moment, the operating system activates the ready process whose turn it is to run. Giving control

---

*In Chapter 3 it was stated that after an interrupt has been processed, execution of the program that was interrupted is resumed. In a multiprogramming system, this is often not true; the interrupt may cause a process switch, so that execution resumes with a different program than the one that was interrupted.

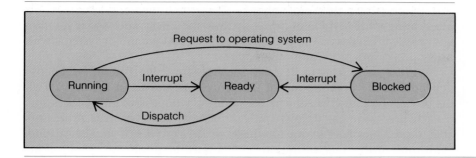

FIGURE 4-2
How processess make transitions among the running, ready, and blocked states. A running process is currently being executed; a ready process is ready to be executed when its turn comes up; and a blocked process is waiting on a peripheral device.

of the central processor to a particular process is called *dispatching*; thus dispatching is the operation that switches a process from the ready state to the running state.

Operating systems are usually organized so that only a small part of the system, called the *kernel*, is responsible for dispatching processes and handling interrupts. The remaining parts of the operating system are processes that are executed in much the same way as user's processes. Thus only the kernel must deal with the rather chaotic situation in which the central processor is rapidly switched from one unrelated process to another, often by interrupts occurring at unpredictable times. Outside of the kernel, we can simply consider all processes as being executed concurrently, without having to worry about how the central processor is switched from one process to another.

Time Sharing   Time sharing is a form of multiprogramming in which users can communicate with their programs while the programs are being executed. (More precisely, users communicate with the processes created when their programs are executed.) Each user seems to have the entire computer to himself or herself and need not be concerned with the fact that the computer is serving many other users at the same time.

What distinguishes time sharing from other forms of multiprogramming is the need for fast response. When a user makes a request of a process, the process should respond promptly—a second or two is the longest tolerable delay. This means that every process must get a turn at the central processor often enough to respond to its user without undue delay. If the number of users and processes is large, the time slice must be short.

Another characteristic of time sharing is that if the number of users is large, all their processes will not fit into main memory at one time. As a result, the operating system continually must swap processes between main and auxiliary memory so that each process will be in main memory when its turn at the central processor next comes up. Note that only ready processes need be swapped; a blocked process can be left in auxiliary memory until it becomes unblocked. At any given time, many of the processes on a time sharing system will be blocked because they are waiting on users who are sitting at their terminals thinking.

Multiprocessing and Distributed Processing   In the past, because of the cost of central processors, each computer system had only one. (If there were others, they probably had specialized functions, such as communicating with peripheral devices.) Now the microprocessor revolution has drastically reduced the cost of processors, and computer systems with many processors are beginning to appear.

We use two terms to describe such systems; which term we choose depends on the organization of the processors and main memory. If all the processors share the same main memory, we speak of *multiprocessing*. If each processor has its own private memory (but with the processors able to send messages to one another), we speak of *distributed processing*. With multiprocessing, all the processors must be in one geographical location—the same location as the shared memory. With distributed processing, the processors with their private memories can be in different cities, states, or countries. Combinations of distributed processing and multiprocessing are also possible, with each processor having access to both private and shared memory.

Writing programs for execution by more than one processor is known as *parallel programming*. In contrast, programming for a single processor is known *sequential programming*, since with a single processor all the steps of the program must be carried out one after the other in a sequence; none can be carried out simultaneously.

Discovering ways of using multiple processors effectively is a subject of continuing research, and the principles of parallel programming are still being hammered out. In everyday life, we know that there are some jobs where several people helping will make the work go faster, and others where the extra people just get in each other's way. In the latter case, we can sometimes rearrange the work in such a way as to allow more people to participate effectively. Likewise, some jobs that computers do have parts that obviously can be carried out simultaneously by separate processors. Other jobs, however, seem at first sight to demand the one-step-after-the-next approach of conventional sequential programming. In some cases, however, researchers have been able to discover other ways of approaching such jobs, ways that allow parallel programming to be used effectively.

Summary

Language processors allow programs to be written in convenient higher-level languages rather than in obscure machine codes. A translator or compiler translates a higher-level-language source program into a machine-language object program that can be executed directly by the central processing unit. An interpreter carries out the instructions in the source program rather than translating it into an object program to be executed directly by the central processing unit. Interpreters are incorporated in many systems and applications programs such as operating systems, word processors, and spreadsheet programs.

The operating system supervises the operation of both hardware and software. Its system commands provide a "control panel" through which both users and programs can operate the computer system. Disk storage mandates a moderately complex operating system, since there is no way for the user to locate disk files manually or to find unused areas in which new files can be stored. The term disk operating system or DOS is often applied to a not-too-complex operating system whose principal function is to manage disk storage.

The operating system can provide virtual devices that appear to be hardware components but are actually simulated by software. An example is virtual memory in which the system seems to have a much larger main memory than is actually present in the hardware.

The operating system provides the coordination needed for multitasking, in which the system works on more than one job at the same time, and for multiuser systems that allow more than one person to use the system at one time. Both multitasking and multiuser systems involve concurrent execution, in which the computer executes more than one process at a time. Concurrent execution can be realized by sharing a single central processing unit among many processes (multiprogramming) or by allowing a number of processors to operate simultaneously (multiprocessing, distributed processing). We speak of multiprocessing when the simultaneously operating processors share the same main memory and distributed processing when they do not.

Programming for one processor is known as sequential programming; programming for multiple processors is known as parallel programming. Computer scientists are still working out the principles of parallel programming and discovering ways to use it effectively.

Vocabulary Review

active process
allocation table
applications program
  interface (API)
assembler
assembly language
batch file
blocked process
compiler
computer language
concurrent execution
deadlock
device handler
directory
distributed processing
executable program

fourth-generation
  language (4GL)
inactive process
interpreter
kernel
language processor
linker
linking
machine language
metaphor
mnemonic
multiprocessing
multiprogramming
multiuser system
object program
parallel programming

process
ready process
running process
sequential
  programming
shell
source program
suspended process
system command
task
thrashing
time sharing
time slice
translator
user interface
window

For Further Reading

Davis, William S. *Operating Systems*. Reading, MA: Addison-Wesley Publishing Company, 1983.

Denning, Peter J. "Third Generation Computer Systems." *Computing Surveys*, December 1971, pp. 175–216

Holt, R. C., et al. *Structured Concurrent Programming with Operating Systems Applications*. Reading, MA: Addison-Wesley Publishing Company, 1978.

Scientific American (special issue on computer software). September 1984.

Tannenbaum, Andrew S. *Structured Computer Organization*. Englewood Cliffs, NJ: Prentice-Hall, 1976.

Tucker, Allen B. *Programming Languages*. New York: McGraw-Hill, 1986.

Review Questions

1 Distinguish between systems software and applications software.

2 What is machine language? What are some of its disadvantages?

3 Contrast assembly language and machine language.

4 What language processor is used for assembly language programs? In what way are the programs processed?

5 Why is assembly language, despite its advantages over machine language, still not convenient for many programmers?

6 Give two advantages of higher-level languages over assembly language.

7 Name seven widely used higher-level languages and give the application areas in which each is most likely to be used.

8 Describe two kinds of language processors used for higher-level languages. Which kind is known by two different names?

9 Distinguish between translators and interpreters.

10 What is an operating system?

11 Why is an operating system sometimes referred to as a DOS?

12 Give ten functions that an operating system performs.

13 What is concurrent execution? Describe multitasking and multiuser systems.

14 Describe multiprogramming and time sharing.

15 What is a time slice?

16 What is a process? Distinguish between active and inactive processes.

17 Describe the circumstances under which the running-ready-blocked state of a process changes.

18 What distinguishes multiprogramming from multiprocessing and distributed processing?

19 What is the difference between multiprocessing and distributed processing?

20 Contrast sequential and parallel programming.

Topics for Discussion

1 Many programmers can program in several programming languages and find little difficulty in learning a new language when the need arises. Others, however, seem to develop an emotional commitment to a single language. They refuse to learn other languages, exaggerate the capabilities of the favored language, and remain faithful to it long after it is generally considered to be obsolete. Anyone who even mildly disparages a programming language in print is apt to be deluged with angry letters from its partisans. Why do people become so committed to a single language? Can you think of other areas in which people develop an emotional commitment to a particular, possibly obsolete, technology? Factors to be considered are the difficulty of learning a new language and the need to maintain (update and correct) existing programs in older languages; however, it is not clear that such practical considerations fully explain the extreme devotion of some programmers to particular languages.

2 Early operating systems for microcomputers were relatively simple and used little memory (tens of kilobytes). They did not offer multitasking, however, and commands had to be given by typing cryptic command lines that often bewildered nonprogrammers. The most recent operating systems emphasize user-friendliness; they support the desktop metaphor, selection of commands from menus with a mouse, multiple windows, and multitasking. On the other hand, these systems require two or more megabytes of memory (more than is currently installed on most microcomputers) just for the operating system; this is over and above the memory required for the applications programs that do the user's work. These advanced operating systems also require faster and more elaborate microprocessors. Is it appropriate to devote so much of a computer's resources to provide a user-friendly interface and conveniences such as multitasking? Bear in mind the decreasing costs of computer memory, the increasing power of microprocessors, and the very significant cost of training employees to use computers, particularly non-user-friendly ones.

CHAPTER 5

PROGRAM DESIGN, CODING, AND TESTING

INTRODUCTION

It would be reasonable to assume that if a program is thoughtfully designed, carefully coded,* and thoroughly tested, it will perform its intended task without error. Unfortunately, this is not the case. Even simple programs are often plagued with *bugs*, errors that make the program behave in some way other than what the programmer intended. For large, complex programs with tens or hundreds of thousands or even millions of lines of code, it becomes almost impossible to find and correct all the bugs. As a result, software projects often run behind schedule and over budget. And when the software is finally released, it still contains bugs with which the user must somehow cope.

The extreme difficulty of producing error-free programs is sometimes referred to as the *software crisis*. Efforts to avert the software crisis have given rise to the discipline of *software engineering*, which attempts to apply to software development the same principles of good engineering practice that govern the design and construction of such artifacts as bridges, highways, and airplanes. Software engineers must apply managerial and economic as well as technical principles to the task of balancing such conflicting factors as performance, reliability, development time, and development cost.

Students of software engineering have not found any magic formula for producing reliable software on schedule and within budget. What they have discovered are systematic techniques of program development that seem to reduce the chance of program errors and make development time and cost more predictable. The hope is that improved versions of these techniques, together with other techniques to be discovered in the future, will eventually make developing a large program as routine as building a bridge or erecting a skyscraper.

CHARACTERISTICS OF GOOD SOFTWARE

Poor-quality software is easy to identify. If a program does not accomplish its intended task, is difficult to use, gives inaccurate results, fails to obey the user's commands correctly, or *crashes*—stops functioning altogether—we may safely assign it a low quality-rating. It is less obvious what characteristics we should insist upon for the highest-quality software. In this section we will look at some proposed criteria for high-quality software.

Reliability

A program is reliable if it is *correct* and *robust*. A correct program meets its specifications: for any valid input (commands or data), the program

---

*The process of actually writing a program, as opposed to other programming activities such as design and testing, is often referred to as *coding*. The printout, or *listing*, of the program is referred to as the program *code*, and the amount of work involved in writing a program is often measured by the number of printed lines or *lines of code* in the program listing.

Software package for Lotus 1-2-3, an integrated program whose spreadsheet-analysis capabilities are very widely used.

produces the specified output. A robust program functions as well as possible in the face of such adverse conditions as invalid input and malfunctioning hardware. When difficulties arise, a robust program informs the user of the problem and suggests what can be done to correct it. Under the same circumstances, a *fragile* program, one that is not robust, is likely to crash, losing some or all of the data with which it has been entrusted.

Testability

For every program we would like to have a set of tests for determining whether the program is correct. Each test would consist of sample input for the program and the corresponding output that the program should produce. A program that passed all the tests in the set could be pronounced correct, if not with certainty at least with a high degree of probability. Unfortunately, for most programs the variety of inputs is so great that an exhaustive set of tests is impossible to construct. One reason for concentrating so much effort on other aspects of the program development process is the extreme difficulty of verifying the correctness of a program by means of testing.

Usability

Regardless of its technical merits, a program must be a practical and convenient tool for accomplishing its designated task. The proper use of the program should be reasonably obvious to someone who understands the task to be accomplished but has little or no experience with computers. It is programs with this characteristic that we call user-friendly.

Designing user-friendly programs can be tricky, since different users may prefer different methods of interacting with the computer. Consider the problem of giving commands to a program. Some users, particularly touch typists, prefer to strike a certain key for each command. Disadvantages of this method are the need to remember which key corresponds to which command and the difficulty for nontypists of finding and striking the proper key. Others prefer to select commands from a menu by moving an on-screen pointer with a mouse. This makes few demands on one's memory or physical dexterity, but moving a pointer down a menu is usually much slower than simply striking the key corresponding to the desired command.

Efficiency

An efficient program executes as rapidly as possible and uses as little memory as possible. Because users of mainframe computers are usually charged according to the central-processor time and the amount of main memory a program uses, an inefficient program may be too expensive to run. A program that is a "memory hog" cannot be run on any computer that does not have the required amount of memory. An interactive program will be very annoying to use if it runs so slowly that there is a long delay between a user's request and the computer's response. A program can be too slow to be useable for its designated task; for example, one experimental program for understanding human speech is impractical because it takes several minutes to recognize each spoken word.

Important as efficiency is, programmers are often prematurely concerned with it. They may write obscure, hard-to-understand programs because the obscure code is marginally more efficient than a more straightforward and understandable version. Experience shows, however, that only a small part of a program's code has a significant effect on the program's running time. Thus, it is best to start out by designing a program for clarity and simplicity. One can then later modify any small sections that testing reveals as bottlenecks for program efficiency.

Portability

A *portable* program is one that can be adapted easily to run on computer systems other than the one for which it was originally written. Clearly, time and money will be saved if a program written for one system can be adapted to others instead of the same program having to be rewritten from scratch for each system.

The most important technique for portability is to program in higher-level languages, which are system independent, rather than in machine or assembly language, which depend on the details of a particular computer system. Another technique is to have the program work through the operating system rather than trying to interact directly with hardware components; often the same operating system is used on systems having a variety of hardware configurations.

Portability sometimes conflicts with user-friendliness. The latter is often served by making maximum use of such hardware devices as a mouse, special function keys, and color and graphics displays. But a program that does this will be difficult to adapt to another system that lacks some of the hardware devices available for the original system and provides others that should be taken advantage of.

Maintainablity

Maintainability refers to the ease with which a program can be modified to correct bugs, adapt it to the changing needs of its users, and implement new features. The programmers who maintain a program are usually not the same as the ones who wrote it originally. For a program to be maintainable, then, its structure must be so simple and clear and its operation so well documented that it can be readily understood by persons other than its authors.

◣ SYSTEMS ANALYSIS AND DESIGN

Before a computer program can be written, someone must decide that a program is needed, determine what role the program will play in the activities (such as business operations) that it is to assist, and draw up the detailed requirements and specifications that the proposed program must satisfy in order to play its designated role successfully. These tasks fall upon the *systems analyst*, who must analyze existing operations, determine what changes may be needed, and specify any computer hardware and software that may be needed to implement the changes.

A *system* is a collection of components (people and machines) organized to accomplish a particular task. We are already familiar with computer systems, collections of hardware and software components organized

Software packages in a Boston computer store.

to meet the users' data processing needs. Some typical business systems are the accounting system, which keeps the company's books, the order fulfillment system, which accepts and ships orders, the billing system, which collects money due the company, and the payroll system, which distributes wages to employees.

A systems analyst is responsible for analyzing and changing existing systems and for designing new systems. The analyst will *analyze* the existing system to see how it works and how it can be improved, then *design* changes that achieve the desired results. A good systems analyst will consider all reasonable approaches to a solution. For example, a change in the manual procedures followed by personnel might bring about the desired improvements without the need for any new equipment. Nevertheless, computers are one of the most powerful tools available for improving the efficiency of information-handling systems, so frequently the systems analyst will specify computer hardware and software to accomplish the desired changes.

During systems analysis and design, the systems analyst determines what programs are required and develops specifications detailing exactly what tasks each program must accomplish. These specifications are turned over to programmers, who design, code, and test the required programs. After the programs have been placed in use, they must be maintained throughout their useful life. We now turn our attention to the *software development life cycle*—the development of a program from the preliminary requirements analysis by the systems analyst through the ongoing maintenance of the installed program.

THE SOFTWARE DEVELOPMENT LIFE CYCLE

Programmers have often been guilty of plunging immediately into coding with only the vaguest idea of the requirements that the program must satisfy, the design best suited to meeting those requirements, and the testing procedures that will assure that the requirements are met. It's little wonder that programs constructed in this haphazard way often fail to satisfy their users. A methodical approach to program development is a hallmark of software engineering.

This methodical approach is summarized in the software development life cycle, which has six phases: *requirements analysis*, *specification*, *design*, *coding*, *testing*, and *maintenance*. Requirements analysis and specification are the responsibilities of the systems analyst. Design, coding, and testing are performed by programmers, with perhaps different groups of programmers specializing in each phase. Maintenance is almost always done by programmers other than those who originally developed the software.

Requirements Analysis

Requirements analysis seeks to understand the problem at hand and produce a *requirements definition* describing an appropriate solution. After studying the system to be improved and deciding what changes are necessary, the systems analyst will develop the requirements definitions for any needed software.

The requirements definition for a program focuses on the program characteristics needed to solve the problem at hand. What operations does the program need to carry out? What kinds of input data does it need to accept and what kinds of output must it produce? On what kind of computer must it be able to run, and what level of performance is required? Details that do not affect the ability of the program to solve the problem, such as the exact forms in which data is entered and displayed, are left to the specification rather than being included in the requirements definition.

Specification

The specification refines the requirements definition by providing additional details of the program's operation, such as the exact formats in which input must be entered and in which output will be displayed. The specification also gives the principles according to which the output is to be computed from the input. Given sample input data, it should be possible to determine from the specification whether that input is valid and, if so, what output the program will produce. The specification confines itself to the external behavior that the program must exhibit. It says nothing about the techniques of programming and data organization that will be used to realize that behavior.

Preparation for testing can begin at the specification stage. Since the specification allows us to determine the output that the program should produce for any input, we can use it to construct test cases for checking the program's operation. Each test case consists of sample input and the output that, according to the specification, the program should produce.

Design

The design may be considered a plan for realizing the behavior called for by the specification. A crucial task of the designer is dividing the program into parts called *modules*, each of which performs a limited, precisely defined function. Dividing a program into modules is similar to determining how to construct a machine from prefabricated parts. The designer may also select the *algorithms*, or step-by-step procedures,* that will be used for major operations. Selection of algorithms for minor or routine operations is usually left to the coding stage.

Coding

In the coding stage, the behavior called for by the specification and the structure set forth in the design are realized by writing instructions in a

---

*Both an algorithm and a program are step-by-step procedures for solving a given problem. A program, however, is in a form suitable for execution by a computer, whereas an algorithm need not be. For example, a program must be coded in a programming language, whereas an algorithm might be stated using English, diagrams, and mathematical formulas.

suitable programming language. The modules are coded individually, with different modules often being coded by different programmers. A programmer need be concerned only with the module that he or she is currently coding. It is the responsibility of the designer, and not the programmer, to see that the various modules interact in such a way as to realize the desired behavior for the overall program.

Testing begins during the coding stage. Each module may have to be tested and corrected many times before a working version is obtained. Errors in the use of the programming language and gross errors that cause the module to function in an obviously incorrect manner are caught during coding. More subtle errors are often missed, however.

Testing

Testing is a systematic approach to finding the errors in a program. In *module testing*, each module is tested individually. Module testing is usually done during coding. *Integration testing* refers to testing groups of interacting modules; when all the modules have been included in integration testing, the entire program will have been tested. Errors often come to light when persons not involved in the development of a program use it in ways not anticipated by the developers. Such errors may be caught by *beta testing*, in which copies of the program are provided to individuals and organizations who agree to use the program and report errors. The organization for which a program was written may conduct *acceptance tests* to determine if the finished program meets their requirements. When several programs are under consideration for a particular application, *benchmark tests* may be used to compare their performance—to see which can perform a certain operation most rapidly, for example.

The quality of a program is the degree to which it adheres to its specifications and is free from bugs. The art of monitoring and improving the quality of software at every stage of the life cycle is an emerging specialty known as *software quality assurance (SQA)*.

Diskette cartridges containing software for the Apple Macintosh.

Maintenance

Hardware requires maintenance because parts wear out and have to be replaced. Software does not wear out but it still requires maintenance for three reasons: (1) errors are found that escaped discovery during testing, (2) the task that the program is to carry out changes, and (3) we wish to add new features to improve the usefulness of the program. The need to adapt to changing conditions occurs frequently in business applications. Changes in the way a business conducts its operations or in the laws that regulate it are likely to require changes in the software it uses.

The programmers who perform maintenance are usually not the same ones who originally developed the program; in fact, maintenance programmers are often the least experienced programmers in an organization, since the more experienced programmers are used to develop new software. A program is easy to maintain, then, if persons unfamiliar with it can with reasonable effort understand it well enough to make corrections or changes. This means that the program's structure must be as clear and logical as possible. The program must be accompanied by documentation that clearly and thoroughly describes its internal operation. And the program should be modular, so that changes in one part will not accidentally affect unrelated parts. With a modular program the maintenance programmers often need only understand the module that needs to be changed or corrected, just as someone changing the tire on a car needs no understanding of the engine or the battery.

STRUCTURED PROGRAMMING

Students of software development have devised a number of systematic techniques for program design, coding, and testing. These techniques often go under the name of *structured programming* to distinguish them from the more haphazard approaches of the past. Structured programming techniques do not provide any sure-fire solution to the software crisis. When thoughtfully applied, however, they do seem to have a positive influence on program reliability and programmer productivity.

Research into programming techniques continues; we may be sure that current techniques will be improved in the future and that new ones will be discovered. The provisional nature of current techniques is important to keep in mind. Some organizations, desperate for relief from the software crisis, adopted the earliest structured programming techniques with near religious zeal. Unfortunately, some of these organizations are now so committed to those early techniques that they resist trying the possibly better approaches emerging from current research.

Modularity

We recall that modularity—breaking a program down into small, nearly independent modules—is a cornerstone of software engineering. There are two approaches to achieving modularity: *subroutines* and *objects*.

Subroutines   A subroutine, we recall, is a program that is called by another program rather than being executed at the request of the user. A call instruction transfers control of the computer to the subroutine; when the subroutine finishes its work, it returns control to the calling program, whose execution continues from the point at which the subroutine was called. Subroutines can call other subroutines, which can call still other subroutines, and so on.

In many higher-level languages, subroutines are known as *procedures* and *functions*. Procedures and functions differ in the manner in which they return the results of their calculations to the calling program, but both are embodiments of the subroutine concept.

Subroutines provide a set of building blocks out of which programs can be constructed. Each subroutine has a precisely defined role in the operation of the entire program, just as the engine, battery, and radiator each plays its role in the operation of an automobile. When writing a subroutine, we can focus our entire attention on its particular role without worrying about the rest of the program. (An engineer who designs batteries spends little if any time worrying about the problems faced by the designers of engines and radiators.) Each subroutine can be tested separately, just as the parts of a car or a computer are tested before being assembled.

Objects   Subroutines provide modularity for the instructions of a program. Objects provide modularity both for the program instructions and for the data the program manipulates. An object is a package containing memory locations for storing data and subroutines for manipulating the stored data. The stored data can be manipulated only by calling the subroutines; it is thus protected from arbitrary tampering by other parts of the program. Programming based on objects is known as *object-oriented programming.* A number of experimental programming languages have been developed to facilitate object-oriented programming; the most well known of these is called Smalltalk.

When a program calls one of the subroutines associated with an object, it is, in effect, sending a message to the object. When the subroutine returns the results of its computations, it can be thought of as replying to the message it received. For example, consider an object that stores a directory of names and telephone numbers. The object can receive four kinds of messages:

- **Insert** a particular name and number into the directory.
- **Find** the number corresponding to a particular name and return that number as a reply.
- **Change** the number associated with a particular name to the one given in the message.
- **Delete** the entry for a particular name.

Each kind of message causes a different subroutine to be called. The subroutine accepts any data in the message (such as a name or phone number), carries out the requested operation, and returns a reply, if any. (The reply to a *find* message is the phone number that was found; the other three kinds of messages do not call for replies.)

Object-oriented programming is based on the concept of *information hiding.* Data (information) and the subroutines that manipulate it are hidden inside an object. Someone working on another part of the program need not know how the data is organized or how the subroutines work, but only what messages the object can receive and what the replies mean. The data inside the object can be manipulated directly only by the object's own subroutines, which reduces the chance of error due to one programmer's misconceptions about the data structures (schemes for organizing data) used by another programmer.

The Top-Down Approach

We can think of a program calling a subroutine as analogous to a superior ordering a subordinate to carry out a certain task. A subroutine returning its results to the calling program is analogous to a subordinate reporting completion of an assigned task to his or her superior. A program whose modules are subroutines consists of a main program, which is invoked directly by the user, and a number of subroutines, each of which is called by the main program or by another subroutine. We can think of the main program as a "chief executive" that calls on a "vice president" subroutine to perform each major task of the program. In turn, each "vice president" subroutine can call on "middle manager" subroutines to aid it with its assigned task, each "middle manager" subroutine can call on "supervisor" subroutines, and so on. At the bottom of this hierarchy are subroutines that can accomplish their assigned tasks without calling on any subordinate subroutines.

We can illustrate the hierarchy of subroutine calls by a *structure chart*, which is very similar to the organizational chart of a business. Figure 5-1 shows the structure chart for a program that plays craps with the user. The main program, *Craps*, manages the overall operation of the game. It calls four subroutines: *GetStartingBankroll*, *GetPlayersBet*, *PlayOneRound*, and *UpdatePlayersBankroll*. *GetStartingBankroll* finds out (by asking the player) how much the player has to bet on the game. *GetPlayersBet* finds out how much the player wishes to wager on the next round. *PlayOneRound* plays one round of the game. *UpdatePlayersBankroll* increases or decreases the player's bankroll by the amount the player won or lost and reports the new amount of the bankroll to the player.

GetStartingBankroll, *GetPlayersBet*, and *UpdatePlayersBankroll* can accomplish their tasks without the aid of any subordinate subroutines. *PlayOneRound*, however, calls two subroutines. *RollDice* simulates the rolling of a pair of dice and informs the player what numbers were rolled. If the outcome of the round is not decided on the first roll of the dice, *PlayRemainingRolls* is called to play the remaining rolls, which are gov-

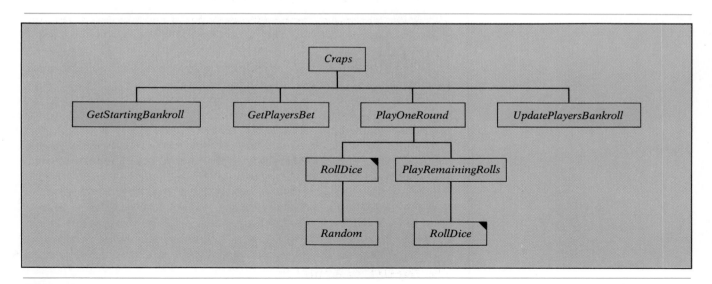

FIGURE 5-1

Structure chart for a program that plays craps. The shaded corner of the box for *RollDice* indicates that this box appears twice in the structure chart. For simplicity, the subroutine *Random* that is called by *RollDice* is shown for only one of the two appearances of *RollDice*.

erned by different rules than the first roll. *PlayRemainingRolls* also calls *RollDice*.

To simulate the unpredictability of dice, the outcome of each roll is determined by a *pseudorandom number*. Pseudorandom numbers appear to have been picked at random even though they are actually generated by a mathematical calculation carried out by a subroutine. Every time *Random* is called, it supplies *RollDice* with a pseudorandom number.

The subroutine *RollDice* occurs twice in the structure chart since it is called by two different subroutines. A corner of the *RollDice* box is shaded to alert the reader to the double occurrence. To save space, the subroutine subordinate to *RollDice* is shown for only one occurrence.

In what order should the subroutines be designed, coded, and tested? The *top-down approach* recommends that we start at the top of the structure chart with the main program. We decide what major tasks the main program must accomplish and have it call a subroutine for each one. While working on the main program, we need be concerned only with what task each subroutine performs and not with the details of how each task is carried out. With the main program completed, we can turn our attention to the subroutines. When working on a subroutine, we need to be concerned only with the task performed by that subroutine; we need not worry about the details of the main program and other subroutines. When writing a subroutine, we can call on still other, yet-to-be-written subroutines to carry out major tasks.

Programs can be coded and tested as well as designed in top-down order. For example, after the main program has been coded, it can be tested before any of the subordinate subroutines have been coded. For testing purposes, each subordinate subroutine is replaced by a special dummy

Screen display produced by project manager software.

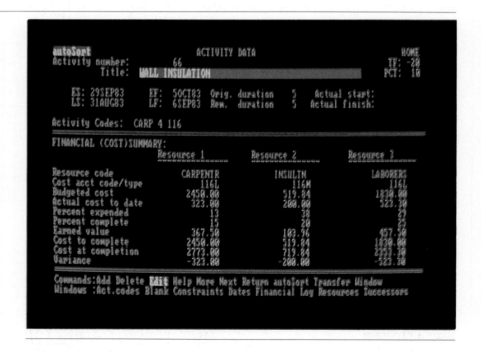

subroutine called a *stub*. A stub prints a message when it is called, prints out the data that was passed to it, and returns a dummy result, but does not actually carry out the assigned task of the actual subroutine. As each subordinate subroutine is completed, it is tested by substituting it for the corresponding stub. (Any subroutines called by the subordinate subroutine, on the other hand, must be replaced by stubs until such time as they are actually written.) As more and more subroutines are completed and substituted for stubs, larger and larger parts of the program can be tested. When the bottom level subroutines, those that do not call any other subroutines, have been installed in place of their stubs, the entire program can be tested.

The top-down approach may be more difficult to apply when modules are objects rather than subroutines. Communications between subroutines always correspond to a superior giving orders to or receiving a report from a subordinate. Communicating objects, however, often function as co-workers, neither of which is subordinate to the other. Sometimes, however, the objects making up a system can be organized into layers. The objects in a given layer can send messages only to each other and to objects on the next lower layer. They can receive messages only from each other and from objects on the next higher layer. When this is the case, we can proceed with a modified top-down approach, designing the objects in the top layer first, then those in the next lower layer, and so on.

Control Structures

Control structures determine the order in which the instructions of a program will be carried out. Some programming languages require programmers to build their own control structures with the aid of so-called "go-to statements" that correspond directly to machine-language jump instructions. However, it is often difficult to comprehend exactly how such do-it-yourself control structures will be executed. For this reason, structured programming advocates three standard, well-understood control structures: *sequencing*, *selection*, and *repetition*. Structured programming is sometimes known as "gotoless programming," although the preference for higher-level control structures over go-to statements is but one aspect of structured programming.

Sequencing   Sequencing refers to carrying out a series of actions in their proper order, one after another. The sequencing control structure causes instructions to be carried out in the order in which they appear in a program or algorithm.

To illustrate sequencing, we will consider an algorithm that might be used to control an automatic washing machine. We will write the algorithm in what is sometimes called a *pseudolanguage*. A pseudolanguage is similar to a higher-level programming language except that instructions are written in informal English rather than in programming-language statements that a computer can process. Since our instructions are not in a form suitable to computer processing, we refer to them as an algorithm rather than a program.

The following is the algorithm for the automatic washing machine:

```
ALGORITHM WashingMachine
    Fill tub with wash water and soap
    Agitate
    Drain wash water
    Fill tub with first rinse water
    Agitate
    Drain first rinse water
    Fill tube with second rinse water
    Agitate
    Drain second rinse water
    Spin dry
END WashingMachine
```

It is convenient to assign names to algorithms and programs; we call this algorithm *WashingMachine*. The heading line

```
ALGORITHM WashingMachine
```

and the closing line

```
END WashingMachine
```

bracket the actual instructions to be carried out.

In accordance with the principle of sequencing, the instructions are carried out in the order in which they appear in the algorithm. Thus the tub is first filled with water and soap, then the clothes are agitated, then the wash water is drained, and so on. Clearly the order in which the instructions are executed is important. Rinsing the clothes before washing them, or drying them before rinsing them, would be as futile as trying to take off your socks before your shoes.

Selection   The behavior of a program will be very inflexible unless the computer can choose between alternate courses of action depending on conditions that prevail at execution time. The control structure that provides for such choices is called *selection*.

A good way to illustrate programming concepts is to write algorithms for various activities that we encounter in everyday life. Consider, for instance, the decision that a driver must make when approaching a traffic light:

```
ALGORITHM StopLight
    IF the light is red THEN
        Stop the car
    ELSE
        Proceed through the intersection
    END IF
END StopLight
```

The words IF and ELSE and the phrase END IF set off a particular grammatical construction in the pseudolanguage, the selection construction. Here is how it works. Immediately following the word IF is a condition, "the light is red." If the condition is true—the light really is red—the instructions between IF and ELSE will be carried out. If the condition is false—the light is yellow or green—the instructions between ELSE and END IF are carried out. Thus, if the light is red, the instruction "Stop the car" is executed. If the light is yellow or green, the instruction "Proceed through the intersection" is executed.

We can improve the algorithm *StopLight* and at the same time look at another form of selection. The previous version of the algorithm treated a yellow light the same as a green light, which is certainly not correct. The following version takes into account that a light can have three possible colors:

```
ALGORITHM StopLight
    IF the light is red THEN
        Stop the car
    ELSE IF the light is yellow THEN
        IF the car has entered the intersection THEN
            Proceed with caution
        ELSE
            Stop the car
        END IF
    ELSE
        Proceed through the intersection
    END IF
END StopLight
```

What we have here is one selection construction nested inside another. The outer construction has the following form:

```
IF the light is red THEN
    (instruction for red light)
ELSE IF the light is yellow
    (instructions for yellow light)
ELSE
    (instruction for green light)
END IF
```

If the light is red, the instruction for a red light (which is "Stop the car") is executed, and the instructions for yellow and green lights are skipped. If the light is yellow, the instructions for a yellow light are followed, and those for red and green lights are skipped. If the light is neither red nor yellow, then the instruction for a green light ("Proceed through the intersection") is followed, and the instructions for red and yellow lights are skipped.

The instructions for the yellow light are themselves given by a selection construction:

```
IF the car has entered the intersection THEN
    Proceed with caution
ELSE
    Stop the car
END IF
```

After we know that the light is yellow, we must determine whether the car has entered the intersection in order to determine which instruction should be followed.

Repetition   Executing instructions repeatedly is a fundamental programming technique. If each step in a program were to be executed only once, it would probably be as easy to do the calculation by hand as to write a program and let the computer execute it.

Let's illustrate repetition with an algorithm for sharpening a pencil. When we write the algorithm, we have no idea how many times the crank of the pencil sharpener will have to be turned to sharpen the pencil. The number of times will surely be different for different pencils. We must find some way of instructing the person or machine executing the algorithm when to stop turning the crank. We can write the pencil-sharpening algorithm like this:

```
ALGORITHM SharpenPencil
    Insert the pencil into the sharpener
    REPEAT
        Turn the crank
    UNTIL the crank turns easily
    Remove the pencil
END SharpenPencil
```

The repetition is controlled by the REPEAT construction. After turning the crank, we know whether it turned easily. If it did, the pencil is sharp and no further repetitions are necessary. If it did not, then we go back and carry out the instruction "Turn the crank" again. The repetitions continue until the condition "the crank turns easily" is found to be true.

Of course, the fact that the crank turns easily does not guarantee that the pencil is properly sharpened. It could be sharp on one side only. An improved algorithm that takes this into account also introduces another repetition construction:

```
ALGORITHM SharpenPencil
    WHILE the pencil is not sharp
        Insert the pencil into the sharpener
        REPEAT
            Turn the crank
        UNTIL the crank turns easily
        Remove the pencil
    END WHILE
END SharpenPencil
```

The WHILE construction differs from the REPEAT construction in two ways. First, the repetition controlled by the WHILE construction continues *while* a given condition remains true rather than *until* a given condition becomes true. Second, the WHILE construction checks the condition before each repetition; the REPEAT construction checks the condition after each repetition.

The improved algorithm, then, starts out by checking whether the pencil is sharp. If it is, then everything between WHILE and END WHILE is skipped, and the algorithm terminates without taking any action. Otherwise, everything between WHILE and END WHILE is repeated as long as the pencil is found not to be sharp when it is taken out of the sharpener.

Structured Walkthroughs

Program errors often occur because of some blind spot in the programmer's perception of the problem or its solution. Errors that the programmer continually overlooks may be immediately obvious to someone else. A useful approach to error detection is to have the programmer explain the program code to a panel of colleagues who raise questions about any parts of the program that they do not understand. In trying to answer the questions, the programmer is often led to errors that would otherwise be missed. A good way to explain a program is to describe how sample data is manipulated by each program instruction. The sample data is "walked through" the program, hence the term *walkthrough*.

The psychological aspects of structured walkthroughs can be tricky. Creative people are reluctant to expose their work to the criticism of their colleagues, particularly when the work is in preliminary form. Someone who feels that his or her competency is being judged may try to avoid, gloss over, or explain away difficulties rather than work to actively seek out and eliminate them.

To avoid a defensive attitude, the other participants in the walkthrough should be the programmer's peers; management personnel should be excluded. The programmer should conduct the walkthrough session. The other participants should not try to rewrite the program, but should confine themselves to pointing out possible problems. Supplying corrections should

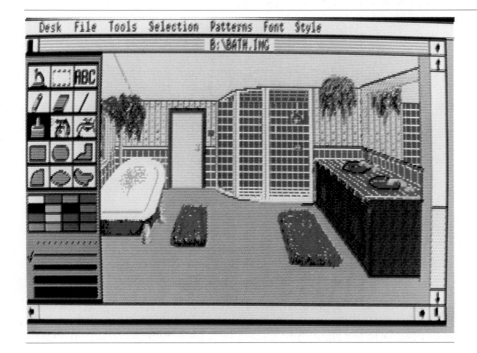

Screen display produced by graphics design software.

be left up to the programmer. Records kept during the walkthrough should be used only for improving the program, not for evaluating the programmer.

SOFTWARE TOOLS AND COMPUTER-AIDED SOFTWARE ENGINEERING

Software developers must sometimes feel like the proverbial shoemaker's children who went barefooted because all the shoes were made for customers, not for the shoemaker's family. Computer-aided design is now a widely used approach to product development, particularly in the electronics, aerospace, and automotive industries. Until recently, however, software developers have used computers only for the most basic tasks of software development, such as compiling higher-level language programs into machine code. And the programs that accomplished these basic tasks often were not very user-friendly and did not work together very smoothly. Fortunately, this situation seems ready to change courtesy of *computer-aided software engineering (CASE)*, which makes extensive use of computers throughout the software life cycle. CASE is an emerging technology; it is not yet very widely used, and current systems do not provide all the capabilities that CASE enthusiasts hope will one day be available. Nevertheless, interest in CASE seems to be growing rapidly, so much so, in fact, that CASE has become a buzzword that is in danger of being applied to any program that can serve in any way to aid software development. In this section we will focus more on the goals toward which CASE seems to be moving rather than on the capabilities and limitations of current CASE systems.

Software Tools

Programs used to aid software development are called *software tools*. The following are some traditional software tools:

- **Text editors,** which enable programmers to enter the text of the source program, save it on disk, and make corrections when errors are discovered.

- **Compilers,** which translate human-readable source programs to machine-coded object programs.

- **Linkers,** which combine object programs that refer to one another into a single executable program.

- **Debuggers,** which enable programmers to analyze the operation of a faulty program, thereby discovering where the errors lie. Debuggers are analogous to the test instruments that a service technician uses to diagnose the problems of a malfunctioning electrical or mechanical device.

In the past, these tools were independent programs that often did not work together very smoothly. Today, these basic software tools are usually combined into an *integrated program development system*, a single program that either contains all the necessary software tools or can invoke them if they are separate programs. The user requests such services as editing and compiling by pressing a command key or making a selection from a menu. The system automatically runs any programs necessary and keeps track of any disk files needed to hold program text or code. The system may supply some steps automatically; for example, if the programmer asks to debug a program that has not yet been compiled, the system will compile and link the program before running it under the control of the debugger.

The software tools that are at the programmer's fingertips, ready to be invoked by command keys or menu selections, are referred to collectively as the *programming environment*. Thus an integrated program development system is often referred to as an *integrated programming environment*.

The Objectives of CASE

The kind of integrated programming environment just described mainly supports the coding phase of the software development life cycle. The goal of CASE is to provide an integrated software development environment that supports all the phases of the life cycle. Additional light is shed on the scope of CASE by two other acronyms that are sometimes applied to the technology: *IDPE (integrated design and programming environment)* and *CADME (computer-aided development and maintenance environment)*.

Integration is a major challenge to CASE technology. A CASE system must govern a diverse variety of software tools, probably procured from separate vendors. Yet all of these tools need to be able to work together smoothly—to exchange data with one another and to respond to commands from the executive program, the program that accepts the user's commands in a user-friendly fashion and passes them on to the individual software tools. Thus work is now underway to develop standards for software tools that will allow tools from a multitude of vendors to fit into a single CASE system.

Microcomputer technology is essential to the success of CASE, since every analyst or programmer using a CASE system needs a powerful computer at his or her disposal. The computer must have good graphics capabilities, since system analyses and program designs are often expressed with diagrams. These requirements are met by *technical workstations*—powerful, graphics-oriented microcomputers so named because they are widely used in science and technology. The workstations on the individual analysts' and programmers' desks exchange data over a computer network,* which may well also include a larger computer, such as a minicomputer or mainframe. One task of the minicomputer or mainframe is

---

*The computers supporting a software development environment are connected by what is called a *local area network*, or *LAN*. Local area networks are discussed in more detail in Chapter 9.

maintaining the data files used by the various software tools and accessed over the network by the various workstations.

Although the ultimate goal of CASE is to support the entire software life cycle, many current CASE systems only support part of the life cycle. The most novel aspect of CASE is its support for systems analysis, which in the past was a purely manual activity. Thus, many current CASE systems focus on systems analysis and design. One occasionally encounters the term *upper CASE* for systems supporting the early phases of the life cycle, and the term *lower CASE* for systems supporting the later phases.

The Database

The software development process creates a large amount of information, which is stored in disk files. For example, the system analyses and designs, requirements definitions, specifications, program designs, and program code would normally be stored. Information that is expressed in formal notations, such as diagrams and computer languages, must be accompanied by documentation in English (or some other natural language) explaining the formal notations to human readers. Often many different versions of a program exist; the different versions could be intended for different (but similar) applications or for use with different configurations of computer hardware. Also, new versions arise whenever errors are corrected in existing versions. In any case, the software development environment must keep track of all the information—specification, design, code, and so on—associated with each version. The CASE system may also maintain information intended to help manage the software development process, such as schedules for coordinating the activities of many analysts and programmers working on the same project.

A set of related data files is known as a *database*;* the information in the database is readily accessible to users and to the various software tools. Users need be concerned only with the logical structure of the information and not how it is stored in disk files. The database maintained by the CASE system is central to the software development process. Normally, each software tool will extract and use certain information from the database and either place new information in the database or update existing information.

Systems Analysis, Requirements, and Specification

CASE environments provide aid for analyzing existing systems, designing new systems, and formulating requirements and specifications for software. Analysis and design are accomplished with the aid of *structured analysis* techniques. In analogy with structured programming, structured analysis provides a methodical approach to systems analysis based on a small number of easily understood concepts.

One such concept, for example, is *dataflow*, the movement of data from one processing station to the next. In noncomputerized systems, the

---

*Databases are discussed in more detail in Chapter 8.

processing stations are workers' desks and the dataflow consists of papers carried from one desk to another; for a computerized system, the data might flow over a computer network connecting microcomputer workstations, minicomputers, and mainframes. The dataflow in a system is expressed by a *dataflow diagram*, which shows the data stores (files, either manual or computerized), the processing stations, and the paths followed by the data in moving to and from the stores and among the processing stations. The diagram—or accompanying documentation—states exactly what kinds of data flow along each path, what processing steps take place at each station, and what data items are filed in each data store. The system analyst would use software tools in the CASE environment to create dataflow and other diagrams and store them in the central database.

When the system analysis and design are complete, the analyst proceeds to create and store in the database the requirements and specifications for the software to be developed. An important goal—and one not fully met by many existing systems—is to store the system design, requirements, and specification in a *formal notation*, one that is mathematically precise. Both diagrams and computer languages can serve as formal notations; natural language descriptions, however, are not sufficiently precise for this purpose. Information stored in formal notations can be, in effect, understood by the various software tools, which can use it for a variety of purposes. Information stored in natural languages (such as documentation) can be stored and retrieved but cannot actually be utilized by the software tools.

Specifically, storing various descriptions of the software in formal notations allow them to be automatically checked for consistency. For example, various tools can check that requirements and specification are

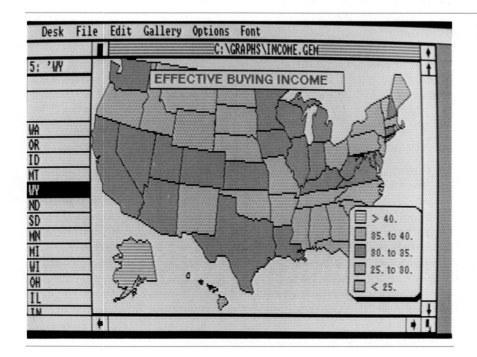

Screen display produced by graphing and charting software.

consistent with the role the software plays in the overall system and that the program design is consistent with the requirements and specification. Software tools can use formal specifications to generate prototypes that demonstrate how the finished program will work and to generate test data that can be used to evaluate the finished software.

Prototyping

People who have something designed for their use often have difficulty in stating their needs completely and in understanding whether a given design will meet all their needs. Architects, for example, frequently must contend with clients who approve the plans but are dissatisfied with the finished building. Likewise, computer users are notorious for saying that a certain program is "not what they really wanted" even though they previously may have approved the requirements and specifications.

This problem can be overcome by demonstrating to prospective users a program that satisfies the requirements and specifications. If the users are not satisfied with the operation of the prototype, the requirements and specifications can be changed appropriately before proceeding with the remaining phases of software development.

A prototyping tool generates a demonstration version, or *prototype*, of a proposed program. Ideally, the prototype should be generated automatically from the specifications. Failing that, the programming of the prototype should be substantially simpler than designing and coding the actual program. In some cases, the prototype may be all that is needed, so it can be delivered as the finished program. More commonly, however, the prototype will be lacking in performance—it may run slowly and be able to handle only a small amount of data. In that case, when the users are satisfied with the prototype, the developers proceed to design and code the actual program based on the specifications arrived at during prototyping.

The use of prototyping may combine requirements definition, specification, and at least preliminary design into a single step, thus somewhat modifying the traditional software life cycle.

Design and Coding

For the design and coding phases of software development, interest centers on two emerging technologies: *program synthesis* and *program verification*.

Program synthesis refers to automatically (that is, with a software tool) designing and coding a program from formal specifications. As discussed in Chapter 4, such program synthesis is also the aim of fourth-generation languages (4GLs). Language processors for 4GLs are designed to obtain program specifications by interacting with naive users in a user-friendly manner. Program synthesis tools in CASE systems would make use of the specifications developed earlier in the life cycle. In either situation, the software tool that performs the synthesis must have extensive knowledge about the problem domain—a synthesizer for accounting programs, for example, must possess considerable knowledge of accounting. Because of this knowledge requirement, most current program-synthesis tools work in relatively straightforward problem domains, such as business data processing.

Program verification refers to proving, by logical reasoning, that a program satisfies its specifications. Unfortunately, as an emerging technology program verification has not emerged very far. Current verification tools are still experimental and unable to verify large programs.

Completely automatic synthesis and verification place severe demands on the software tools, so severe that it may be some time before these technologies become useful outside of highly limited problem domains. An alternative is a tool called a *programmer's assistant* that would aid the programmer in performing synthesis and verification. The human programmer would supply the problem-domain knowledge, intuition, and creativity that are so hard to incorporate into current programs. The programmer's assistant would keep track of the myriad details that, when overlooked, often lead to program bugs.

Testing

Automatic program synthesis or verification could remove the need for much testing, other than to assure that the specified program satisfies the user's needs. That happy state of affairs is not expected to arrive soon, however, so for the foreseeable future we will still need to test programs to detect and correct bugs.

Exhaustive testing of a program is usually impossible; there are simply too many possible sets of input data for the program to be checked for all of them in any reasonable time. With exhaustive testing ruled out, we must try to test as extensively as possible. We must use sets of test data that, as completely as is practical, test that the specifications are satisfied. Such test data can be generated automatically from the specifications stored in the CASE database.

Every time a program error is detected and corrected, a new version of the program is created. Fortunately, version management—keeping track of the different versions and the changes made in going from one version to the next—is an area in which even current CASE systems excel.

Software quality assurance involves such activities as generating test data, statistical analysis of test results, and scheduling of testing activities throughout the life cycle. Software tools for these activities can be integrated into CASE systems, and such tools can make effective use of the CASE database.

Maintenance

The primary prerequisite for maintenance is detailed knowledge of the structure and operation of the program to be modified. The CASE database is an invaluable source of such information; of particular importance are the requirements, specifications, design, and the documentation developed in all phases of the life cycle.

Maintenance programmers may not always have access to the CASE database, since maintenance is sometimes done by a different organization than the one that developed the program. In that case, detailed written documentation of the structure and operation of the program is essential. A goal of CASE systems is to generate such documentation automatically from the information in the CASE database.

A major problem of maintenance is keeping track of the changes that have been made to programs and the new versions that have been created thereby. Again, the version management facilities of CASE systems can come to the rescue.

Summary

Software development projects often run behind schedule and over budget, and the programs they finally produce are often plagued with numerous errors or bugs. Attempts to overcome this software crisis have given rise to the discipline of software engineering, which advocates a systematic approach to the software development process.

High quality software is reliable (correct and robust), testable, useable, efficient, portable, and maintainable.

A systems analyst analyses an existing system, such as a business operation, designs changes to achieve desired goals, and specifies any computer hardware and software needed to implement the desired changes.

A systematic approach to software development often follows the software development life cycle, which has six stages: requirements analysis, specification, design, coding, testing, and maintenance.

Modern programming techniques are often referred to by the term *structured programming*. Modularity involves dividing a complex program into smaller, more manageable building blocks or modules. The top-down approach advocates a particular order in which modules should be designed, coded, and tested. The order in which the instructions of a program are to be executed is specified with three simple, understandable control structures: sequencing, selection, and repetition. In structured walkroughs, a programmer's code is subjected to the scrutiny of his or her fellow programmers.

The emerging technology of computer-aided software engineering (CASE) attempts to apply the power of the computer to the task of creating and debugging software. Important concepts of CASE are (1) a central database that holds all the information relevant to a software project; (2) software tools that work together smoothly, using the central database to provide the input data they need and store the output data they produce; (3) powerful technical workstations that provide each analyst and programmer with access to the software tools and the central database; (4) prototyping—generating demonstration versions of programs early in the life cycle; and (5) consistency checking—checking that the design is consistent with its specifications, for example, and that the program code is consistent with the design.

Vocabulary Review

acceptance testing
algorithm
benchmark testing
beta testing
bug
coding
computer-aided
  software engineering
  (CASE)
dataflow diagram
fragile program
information hiding
integrated program
  development system
integration testing
maintenance
modularity

module
module testing
object-oriented
  programming
portable program
program synthesis
program verification
programming
  environment
prototype
pseudolanguage
repetition
requirements analysis
robust program
selection
sequencing
software crisis

software development
  life cycle
software engineering
software quality
  assurance (SQA)
software tool
structure chart
structured analysis
structured
  programming
structured
  walkthrough
subroutine
systems analyst
technical workstation
top-down approach

For Further Reading

Adrion, W. Richards, et al. "Validation, Verification, and Testing of Computer Software." *Computing Surveys*, June 1982, pp. 159–192.

Hughes, Joan K. and Jay I. Michtom. *A Structured Approach to Programming*. Englewood Cliffs, NJ: Prentice-Hall, 1977.

IEEE Software (special issue on SQA). September 1987.

IEEE Software (special issue on CASE). March 1988.

Lammers, Susan. *Programmers at Work*. Redmond, WA: Microsoft Press, 1986.

Martin, James. *System Design from Provably Correct Constructs*. Englewood Cliffs, NJ: Prentice-Hall, 1985.

"Special Section on Software Testing." *Communications of the ACM*, June 1988, pp. 662–695.

Yohe, J. M. "An Overview of Programming Practices." *Computing Surveys*, December 1974, pp. 221–245.

Yourdon, Edward J. *Techniques of Program Structure and Design*. Englewood Cliffs, NJ: Prentice-Hall, 1975.

Zave, Pamela. "The Operational Versus the Conventional Approach to Software Development." *Communications of the ACM*, February 1984, pp. 104–118.

Zelkowitz, Marvin V. "Perspectives on Software Engineering." *Computing Surveys*, June 1978, pp. 197–216.

Review Questions

1 Describe the software crisis.

2 What are the objectives of software engineering?

3 Discuss some characteristics of good software.

4 Describe the role of the systems analyst in the software development process.

5 Describe the six stages of the software development life cycle.

6 What is structured programming?

7 Give examples of modularity in familiar machines such as automobiles and household appliances.

8 What two programming constructions are often used to achieve modularity?

9 Distinguish between subroutines and objects. What are some other names for objects?

10 Describe the top-down approach. Is this approach more easily applied when modules are subroutines or when they are objects?

11 What is a stub? What function does it serve?

12 What purpose is served by control structures?

13 Give examples of sequencing, selection, and repetition.

14 What is a structured walkthrough? Why is it more likely to be successful than merely having each programmer check his or her own code?

15 Give some of the precautions that must be observed to prevent programmers from taking a defensive attitude in a structured walkthrough.

16 What are software tools? What do we mean by a programming (or software development) environment?

17 What are the objectives of CASE?

18 Why does a database play a central role in CASE systems?

19 How does prototyping help assure that software will meet the needs of the users for whom it was designed?

20 Describe some ways in which CASE can support each of the phases of the software development life cycle.

Topics for Discussion

1 The software crisis arises because it has so far proved impossible to eliminate human error from programming activities. Discuss some other areas of human endeavor in which it has proved impossible to eliminate human error, even though the errors can have the most serious consequences, such as loss of human life. How can computers contribute to complex activities in which the tiniest overlooked detail can have major adverse consequences?

2 The more computers enter into every aspect of our lives, the greater the chance that malfunctioning software can lead to major economic losses or to loss of human life. One suggestion for protecting ourselves against the consequences of disastrous software failures is to license programmers, much as doctors, lawyers, and many other professionals are now licensed. Discuss the pros and cons of this proposal. One difficulty with it is that there is still considerable controversy over the proper approach to software development, so it is not clear on which techniques prospective licensees should be tested. Another difficulty is that programming is now widely practiced by nonprofessionals; since nonprofessional programmers rarely cause any harm and often produce much needed software, there is unlikely to be any support for legislating them out of existence. Thus legislators would have to set guidelines for determining which programs (presumably those whose malfunction could cause serious harm) would have to be written by licensed programmers.

PART THREE

POPULAR MICROCOMPUTER APPLICATIONS

WORD PROCESSING AND DESKTOP PUBLISHING

INTRODUCTION

Microcomputers have been used for a wide variety of applications, and they will be used for many more in the future. Five applications, however, are particularly popular for microcomputers: word processing, desktop publishing, spreadsheet simulation, database management, and telecommunications. In Part 3 we will look at each of these five popular microcomputer applications.

A word processor allows text to be entered, stored, edited (corrected and revised), and formatted (printed in a form specified by the user). Word processors derive their power from the following four capabilities:

1 Corrections and revisions are easy to make.

2 The word processor handles all formatting details, such as printing the proper number of lines on each page and determining how many words to print on each line.

3 Text such as names and addresses can be inserted easily at designated places in standard documents, such as form letters and legal papers.

4 As many copies as needed of a document can be printed. Each copy can have different text inserted, such as a different name and address from a mailing list.

Word processing is available from (1) word processing programs (often just called *word processors*) that run on microcomputers and (2) *dedicated word processors*—special purpose microcomputers that can be used only for word processing. In business, dedicated word processors are being replaced with general purpose microcomputers, which can be used for many other purposes in addition to word processing. In consumer products, however, exactly the opposite trend seems to be in effect, with dedicated word processors supplanting microcomputers on department store shelves.

A word-processor operator enters handwritten corrections that were made on a printout of the first draft of a letter.

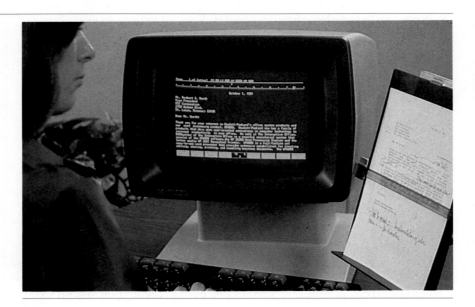

Any changes made to the text being manipulated by a word processor should be reflected instantly on the computer screen. The memory-mapped displays popular on microcomputers allow such rapid screen updates. Although text editing and formatting programs have also been written for minicomputers and mainframes, their performance is much inferior to that of microcomputer word processors owing to the slow speed with which the screen of a remote terminal can be updated.

COMMANDS TO WORD PROCESSORS

In using a word processor, we must provide the computer with two things: (1) text to be inserted into the document being processed and (2) commands requesting various processing operations, such as deletion of a block of text. There are four popular methods of giving commands to a word processor:

1 Use ordinary letter keys for commands. Thus the I key might be used for the command to insert text and the D key might be used for the command to delete text. The problem here is to distinguish commands from text—that is, to determine when the I key represents the insert command and when it represents the letter I. The usual solution is to provide the word processor with a command mode in which all keys are interpreted as representing commands. To insert text, one must switch to an insert or enter mode in which keys are interpreted as representing text to be inserted. This method is popular with touch typists, who are used to typing ordinary letter, digit, and symbol keys without looking at the keyboard.

2 The Ctrl or Alt key is used to switch between commands and text. While the Ctrl or Alt key is depressed, the letter keys represent commands; while it is not depressed, the letter keys represent letters to be inserted. With this method, no special insert mode is required; any keys typed without depressing the Ctrl or Alt key are taken as representing text to be inserted. The disadvantage of this method is that each command requires two key depressions rather than one, and the Ctrl and Alt keys, which usually occur on only one side of the keyboard, can be cumbersome for touch typists to use.

3 Each command is assigned to a special function key. This method, which is popular with dedicated word processors, requires only one key depression per command, and there is no possibility of confusing commands with text. Touch typists, however, must remove their fingers from the typewriter part of the keyboard in order to depress the function keys. Dedicated word processors label each such key with the function it performs; on microcomputers, this usually requires messy stick-on labels or keyboard overlays that invariably get lost. One solution is for the program to display at the bottom of the screen the command associated with each function key.

4 Commands are selected from a menu by moving a pointer or cursor to the desired command. The pointer or cursor can be moved with the

cursor control keys or with a mouse. Selecting one command often causes another menu to be displayed, so that the user may have to make several menu selections to get a command carried out. Menus are popular with newcomers to computing who are intimidated by complex computer keyboards. Moving a pointer to the desired command is slower, however, than typing a command key. For this reason, some programs combine method 4 with method 1 or 2: a command is selected from a menu either by moving the pointer to the command or by typing the first letter of the command. Thus a delete command could be given either by moving the pointer to *Delete* on the menu or by typing the letter D.

For the sake of discussion, we will use method 3 in the rest of this chapter. Thus we will speak of pressing the "Insert key" (the function key for the insert command), the "Delete key" (the function key for the delete command), and so on. Use of any of the other three methods would require only minor changes in the discussions.

TEXT STORAGE

Each document is stored on disk as a *text file*. Some programs load an entire text file into main memory for processing and save the text on disk when requested to do so by the user. An advantage of this method is that all text being processed remains in main memory, so processing is not delayed while the program transfers text between disk and main memory. A disadvantage is that the size of a text file, and hence the size of the largest documment that can be processed, is limited by the size of main memory. Typically, main memory is large enough to hold a term paper or a chapter of a book. For larger documents, such as a book or a long report, each chapter must be stored in a separate text file.

The user must remember to give a Save command frequently to save the current version of the text to disk. Otherwise, if a power failure or computer malfunction occurs, the text in main memory will be lost, taking with it all changes made since the last time the text was saved. When the text is written to disk, the existing text file is not erased but is designated as the backup file (any existing backup file is erased). The backup file can be used if something should happen to the newly written text file or if the user should decide not to keep the changes that have been made.

On the other hand, some word processors leave the bulk of the text on disk, reading into main memory only that portion that is currently being displayed or manipulated. The disk file containing the text is used for reading only; its contents are never changed. Any changes made by the user are stored in main memory; if a computer malfunction occurs, only the changes stored in main memory will be lost, not the text in the disk file. The text displayed for the user consists of text read from the disk file and modified according to any changes currently stored in main memory. When the user gives a Save command, the program reads the entire disk file, modifies the text according to the changes stored in main memory, and writes an entirely new, updated file. Only when the new file has been written successfully does it replace the existing file as the current text file;

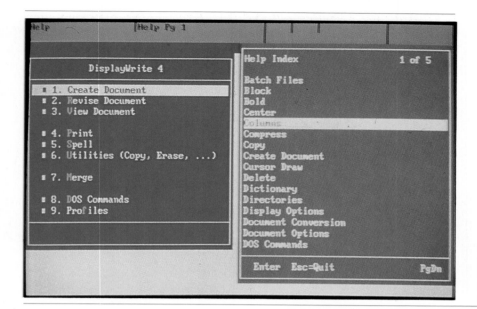

At left is a command menu for the word-processor program DisplayWrite 4; at right is a help menu that allows the user to obtain instructions for using the commands.

the existing file is not erased but is designated as the backup file (any existing backup file is erased).

Word processors that keep the text on disk are somewhat slower than those that keep the entire text in main memory, but they have the advantage of being able to handle files of any size (subject to the limitation of disk capacity). With a hard disk, disk capacity is unlikely to be a limitation and the speed of the hard disk assures that the program will not be slowed down too much by having to read frequently from the disk.

◣ TEXT DISPLAY

The screen serves as a window through which the user can see a small portion of the stored text—typically from 20 to 25 lines. The window can be moved about in the text by *scrolling* or *jumping*. With scrolling, the text moves smoothly up or down the screen. When the text is scrolled downward for instance, the lines move down the screen, with new lines appearing at the top of the screen and old ones disappearing at the bottom. Jumping, on the other hand, causes the entire display to change instantly to show a different part of the text. In general, the user can just think about moving around in the text; the display will always tag along and show the portion of the text on which both the user's and the program's attention is focussed. Some word processors provide for more than one window on the display screen, allowing the user to focus at the same time on several points in the same text file or on points in several different text files.

The displayed text is formatted into lines much as if it were typed on a sheet of paper. Word processors vary as to the degree to which the display is formatted. Some display the text in a format that is convenient for editing

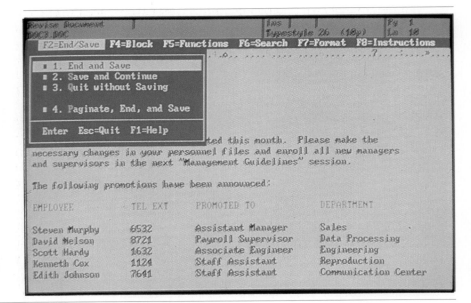

Screen display produced by DisplayWrite 4; note the function-key definitions across the top of the display and the command menu at upper left.

but is not necessarily the same format in which the text will be printed. Other word processors, which display the text exactly as it will be printed, are designated by the phrase *what you see is what you get (WYSIWYG,* pronounced whizzy wig). Some things displayed by this kind of word processor, such as page headings and the spaces between double- or triple-spaced lines, seem to just take up space on the screen without being very informative. Also, the more complex the formatting that has to be done, the more sluggish the program is likely to be in responding to commands. On the other hand, if you need to do complex formatting, such as setting up elaborate tables, a WYSIWYG word processor will help avoid unpleasant surprises when you examine the printed output.

The point in the text on which the word processor's attention is focussed is indicated by the cursor, which is usually a flashing block or underline. Editing commands, such as to insert or delete text, take effect at the point designated by the cursor. The cursor can be moved left, right, up, or down with four *cursor control keys* (one for each direction of movement) or with a mouse. The cursor always remains on the screen. The cursor control keys repeat automatically when held down, so that one just holds down a cursor control key until the cursor has moved as far as desired in the corresponding direction.

Moving the cursor off the right end of a line causes it to go to the beginning of the next line down. Moving the cursor off the left end of a line causes it to go to the end of the previous line. Attempting to move the cursor up from the first line causes the text to scroll down a line, providing a new line for the cursor to rest on. Likewise, attempting to move the cursor down from the bottom line causes the text to scroll up by one line, again providing a new line for the cursor to rest on. The simplest, although not necessarily the fastest, way to reach a given point in the text is to move the cursor to that point. As the cursor moves up or down it will ''drag'' the display window along with it.

For faster movement, many word processors have a Page Up key that moves the display window up by one full screen of text, and a Page Down key that moves the window down by one full screen of text. A Home key moves the window to the beginning of the document, and an End key moves it to the end of the document. Some word processors allow the user to set markers at various points in the text. Later, the user can request the program to jump to the position designated by a particular marker. The cursor is moved to the position designated by the marker, and the display window is moved so that the cursor, and hence the marked position, is on the screen. Allowing multiple windows into a text file is an alternative to markers; by pressing a command key, the user can cause the cursor to jump from window to window, thus instantly shifting the program's attention to different parts of the file.

Some word processors will display the headings and subheadings in a text file as an outline. The user can quickly move the cursor to any part of the outline and then have the word processor jump to the corresponding point in the actual text. Using an outline is one of the quickest and easiest ways to get around in a text file.

◥ TEXT EDITING

Editing commands allow new text to be entered and existing text to be modified by inserting new text, deleting old text, moving or copying text from one part of the document to another, and substituting one block of text for another.

Text Entry

Text entry is the process by which new text is typed into the computer. Some programs allow the user just to move the cursor to where the new text is to be entered and begin typing; nowadays this is by far the most common method. Other programs, usually older ones, require the user to first press a Text Entry key that provides a blank screen on which to type. Clearing the screen eliminates the need to reformat text already on the screen as the user types. This allows for faster typing with programs that are sluggish in reformatting text.

When typing paragraphs, you need not press the Return or Enter key at the end of each line. When the end of a line is reached, the word that is being typed automatically jumps to the beginning of the next line, a process know as *word wrap*. The Return or Enter key is used to mark the ends of *paragraphs* rather than *lines*. More generally, the Return or Enter key is used to terminate any line that you do not wish to extend all the way across the screen. If you were typing a list of names, for example, you would strike the Return or Enter key after typing each name so that the next name would appear on a new line. Figure 6-1 illustrates text entry with word wrap.

Like a typewriter, a word processor allows the user to set tab stops to mark positions on a line. Pressing the Tab key causes the cursor to advance

FIGURE 6-1

Text entry with word wrap. When the typed line reaches the right margin (a), typing another character causes the entire word being typed to jump to the beginning of the next line (b). At the bottom of the screen is a typing scale and an area in which the program can communicate with the user. The T on the typing scale indicates where the user has set a tab stop for indenting paragraphs. The communications area gives the name of the file that is being edited.

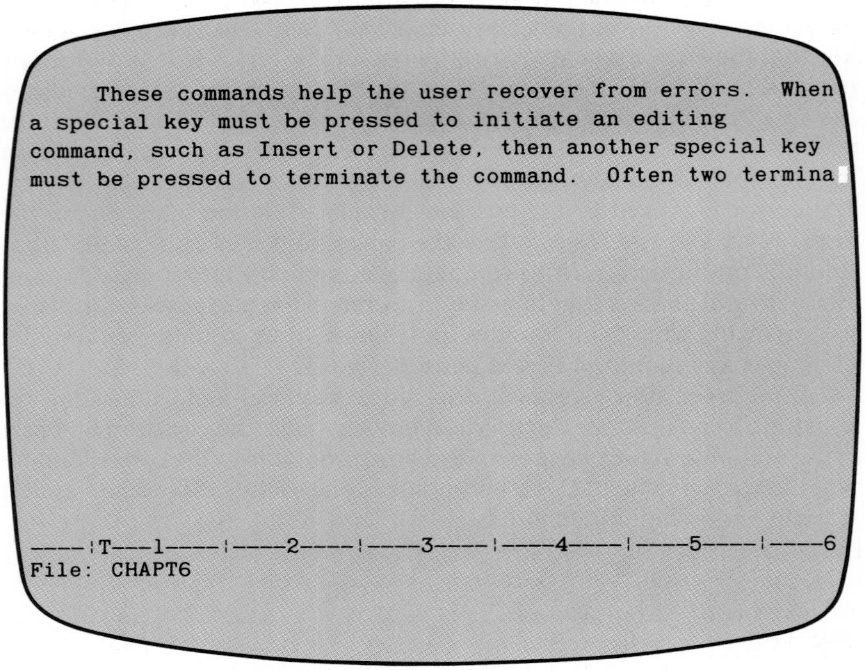

```
        These commands help the user recover from errors.   When
   a special key must be pressed to initiate an editing
   command, such as Insert or Delete, then another special key
   must be pressed to terminate the command.   Often two termina
```

```
   ----|T---1----|----2----|----3----|----4----|----5----|----6
   File: CHAPT6
```

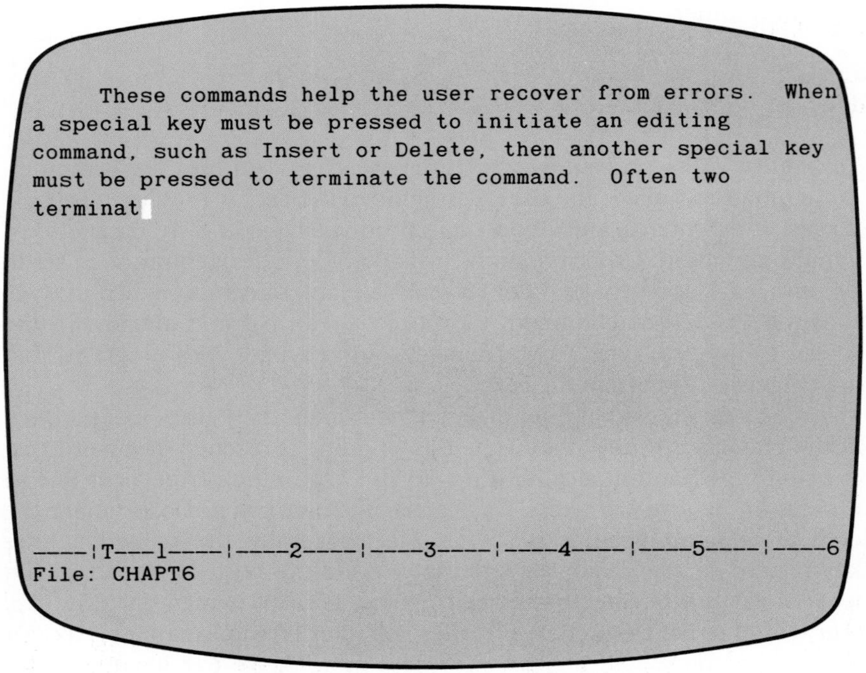

```
        These commands help the user recover from errors.   When
   a special key must be pressed to initiate an editing
   command, such as Insert or Delete, then another special key
   must be pressed to terminate the command.   Often two
   terminat
```

```
   ----|T---1----|----2----|----3----|----4----|----5----|----6
   File: CHAPT6
```

to the next tab stop. The first tab stop is usually used for indenting paragraphs. To start a new paragraph, then, you press the Return or Enter key to terminate the previous paragraph and the Tab key to indent for the new paragraph. Some word processors indent paragraphs automatically, so that the Tab key need not be pressed.

Insertion

Insertion is the process of inserting new text within existing text. As the new text is typed, text following the point of insertion is moved to make room for the new text and reformatted to prevent any lines from becoming too long or too short. Otherwise, insertion is similar to text entry; both word wrap and tab stops are normally provided for both text entry and insertion. Figure 6-2 illustrates insertion with reformatting.

Many word processors make no distinction between text entry and insertion. In either case, one just moves the cursor to the point of insertion and starts typing. Existing text is moved and reformatted as needed. (Again, this is the most common method nowadays.) Other, usually older, word processors require the user to press an Insert key before beginning an insertion. If separate Insert and Text Entry commands are provided, the program will probably respond much more sluggishly during an Insert command than during a Text Entry command. In that case, the Insert command should be used for small amounts of text, such as a single word, and the Text Entry command used for larger blocks of text, such as a paragraph.

Overtyping

Normally, text typed on the keyboard is inserted into the document being edited. Existing text is not changed except to be moved to make room for

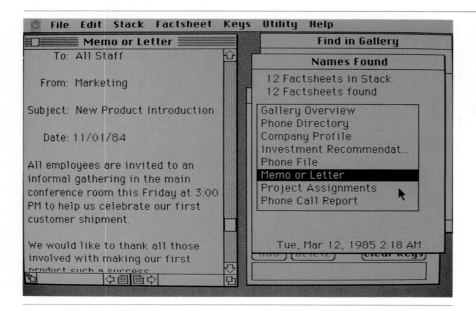

Screen display produced by a word-processor program for the Apple Macintosh. The black arrow, which is positioned by moving the mouse, is used to select items from menus. The selected menu item is shown in reverse video—light characters against a dark background.

FIGURE 6-2

Text insertion. Screen displays before (a) and after (b) inserting the text "very serious" before the word "problem". Note that the text following the point of insertion is reformatted to make room for the inserted text.

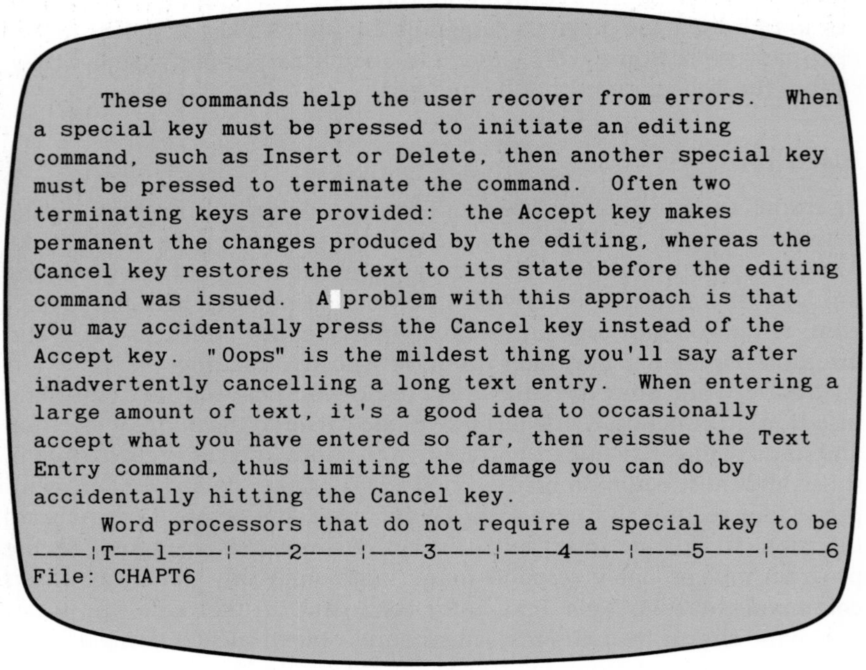

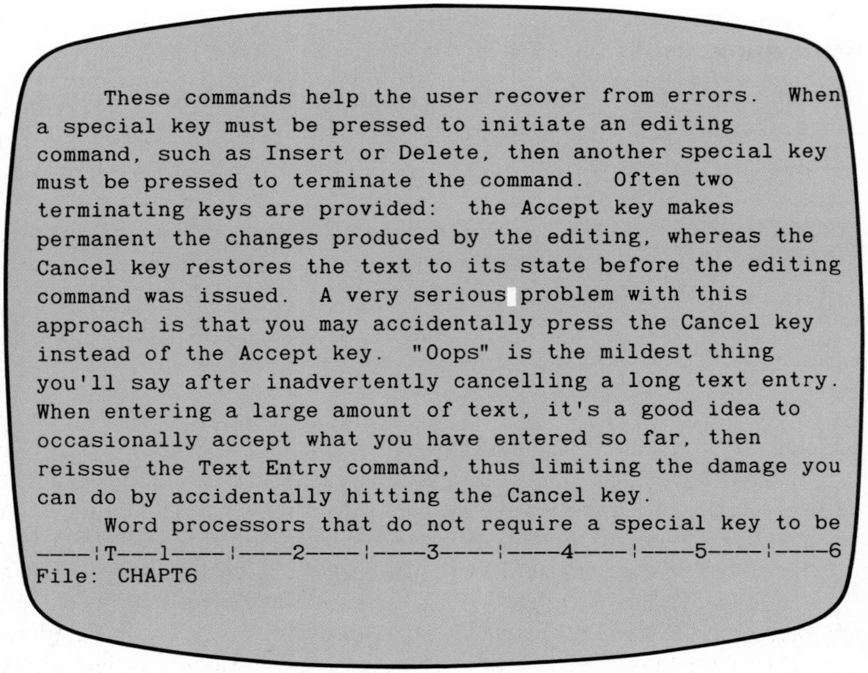

```
      These commands help the user recover from errors.   When
a special key must be pressed to initiate an editing
command, such as Insert or Delete, then another special key
must be pressed to terminate the command.   Often two
terminating keys are provided:   the Accept key makes
permanent the changes produced by the editing, whereas the
Cancel key restores the text to its state before the editing
command was issued.   A problem with this approach is that
you may accidentally press the Cancel key instead of the
Accept key.   "Oops" is the mildest thing you'll say after
inadvertently cancelling a long text entry.   When entering a
large amount of text, it's a good idea to occasionally
accept what you have entered so far, then reissue the Text
Entry command, thus limiting the damage you can do by
accidentally hitting the Cancel key.
      Word processors that do not require a special key to be
----¦T---1----¦----2----¦----3----¦----4----¦----5----¦----6
File: CHAPT6
```

```
      These commands help the user recover from errors.   When
a special key must be pressed to initiate an editing
command, such as Insert or Delete, then another special key
must be pressed to terminate the command.   Often two
terminating keys are provided:   the Accept key makes
permanent the changes produced by the editing, whereas the
Cancel key restores the text to its state before the editing
command was issued.   A very serious problem with this
approach is that you may accidentally press the Cancel key
instead of the Accept key.   "Oops" is the mildest thing
you'll say after inadvertently cancelling a long text entry.
When entering a large amount of text, it's a good idea to
occasionally accept what you have entered so far, then
reissue the Text Entry command, thus limiting the damage you
can do by accidentally hitting the Cancel key.
      Word processors that do not require a special key to be
----¦T---1----¦----2----¦----3----¦----4----¦----5----¦----6
File: CHAPT6
```

```
SPspell
PRMPT 13 words, 0 questionable        NNC:\ADVERT\BROCHURE.TXT               0
· · · · · ·├· · ·┐· · · · ▶ · · ·2· · ·D· · · ·3· ▶ · · · · · · ▶ · · · · · ▶·5· · · ·▶· · · ·6· ▶· · · · ·7·▶· ·┤· · · ·
1-A:\COLUMNS.TXT
▲▲XyWrite III Plus -      ▲▲XyWrite III Plus is        ▲▲Thesaurus - The renowned
                          ideally suited to your       220,000 word Microlytics
The Answer to Your        publishing needs, ┌3-A:\*.*
                          it be the producti│Default drive/directory A:    Directo
Editorial Needs           newspaper with "sn│
                          columns or a busin│AUTOLEAD  PRT         992   6-05-87
                          report that incorp│COLUMNS   TXT        4661   7-13-87
                          ready-to-print fil│CORP      NEW       13164   6-08-87
                          other programs.  A│DEMOBRO   TXT        6162   7-13-87
                          the typesetter is
2-C:\ADVERT\BROCHURE.TXT
     ▲▲▲+
     XyWrite III Plus is a word processor designed for people who write a
        lot.  It responds instantly, reformatting and paginating text
        automatically as it goes.  The commands are simple, logical and
        easy to use and you only need a few of them for everyday writing.
        With the help of the Basic Tutorial booklet and on disk training
        lessons, the average beginner can be working comfortably within
        an hour.  And an extensive, user friendly help system is only a
        keystroke away■+
  +
```

Screen display produced by the word-processor program XyWrite III Plus.

the insertion. However, most word processors also provide an overtype mode in which typed characters replace existing ones. Each typed character replaces the character over which the cursor is positioned. After each replacement, the cursor moves forward in the text by one character, so that successive typed characters replace successive characters in the text.

Overtyping is not nearly as convenient or as widely used as insertion and deletion because the new text must contain the same number of characters as that replaced—we cannot replace a given segment of text with a longer or a shorter segment. Overtyping is sometimes useful for minor corrections, however; it is particularly useful for correcting tables, where insertion or deletion of characters might upset the alignment of the table entries in some columns.

Deletion

Most word processors provide two keys for deletion. The Backspace key deletes the character immediately to the left of the cursor. The Backspace key is frequently used during text entry and insertion to correct mistakes as soon as they are made. The Delete key deletes the character at the cursor position. Holding down the Backspace key repeatedly deletes characters to the left of the cursor position. (The cursor moves left, gobbling up characters as it goes.) Holding down the Delete key repeatedly deletes characters to the right of the cursor position. (The cursor remains stationary; characters to the right of the cursor move to the cursor position where they are gobbled up.)

When characters are deleted, existing text must be moved to close the gap left by the deleted characters and reformatted to prevent any lines from becoming too short or too long. Some word processors allow the

Backspace or Delete key to be pressed at any time; existing text is reformatted as the characters are deleted. Other word processors require a Delete Characters command to be issued before a deletion is started. Reformatting is done only after the Delete Characters command is terminated.

◣ **Exercise 6-1** Use a word processor to type a few pages of text, such as a letter to a friend or a what-I-did-on-my-summer-vacation essay. Try using underlining, italics, and boldface to emphasize important words. Use the backspace key to erase any typing errors that you notice yourself making, but do not try to revise the document at this time. Save the text to disk frequently so that little work will be lost should a power failure or other problem shut down the computer. ◣

Block Selection

The editing operations described so far apply to one character at a time. To apply an operation to more than one character, we must repeatedly strike keys or hold down a key for automatic repetition. Some operations, however, apply to blocks, or segments, of text. Before we can request such an operation, however, we must select the block of text to be affected.

The first step in block selection is to move the cursor to the beginning or end of the desired block and issue a Mark One End command. Next the cursor is moved to the other end of the desired block; all text from the end that was marked through the cursor position constitutes the selected block. This text is highlighted on the screen to make the selected

Screen display produced by one of the most popular word-processor programs, WordPerfect 5.0.

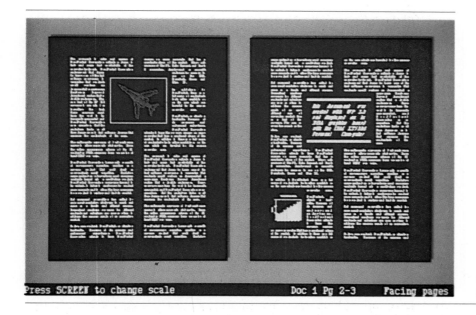

Press SCREEN to change scale   Doc 1 Pg 2-3   Facing pages

WordPerfect 5.0 display showing two facing pages.

block stand out. If the cursor is moved, the selected block, and hence the highlighted portion of text, changes. When the cursor has been positioned so that the desired block is selected, a command for manipulating that block can be issued.

Block Delete, Move, Copy, and Insert

Block Delete, Block Move, and Block Copy each requires a block of text to be selected before the command is issued. Block Delete deletes the selected block. Block Move deletes the selected block but saves a copy of it in a special memory area called the *copy buffer* or, more metaphorically, the *clipboard* or *scrap*. Block Copy saves a copy of the selected block in the copy buffer but *does not* delete the original.

The Block Insert command inserts the contents of the copy buffer into the document at the cursor position. To move a block of text, then, we select the block, issue a Block Move command, move the cursor to the new position for the text, and issue a Block Insert command. Figure 6-3 illustrates moving a block of text. A block of text can be copied in the same way except that we use the Block Copy command, which, unlike the Block Move command, does not delete the original. Note that once a block of text has been placed in the copy buffer, it can be inserted in as many places as desired. Thus a Block Move or Block Copy command can be followed by any number of Block Insert commands to insert as many copies of the selected text as desired.

Some word processors use a single command to move or copy a block directly from one point in the text to another, instead of using one command to store the block in the copy buffer and another to insert it back into the text. The copy-buffer method is the most flexible, however, and seems to be the most widely used.

FIGURE 6-3

Block move. The text to be moved is first selected; the selected text is highlighted on the screen (a). The user deletes the selected text and moves the cursor to the point where the text is to be reinserted (b). Finally, the previously deleted text is inserted at the point designated by the cursor (c). Many word processors break down a move into a deletion followed by an insertion, as illustrated here; others combine the deletion and insertion into a single operation.

```
    These commands help the user recover from errors.  When
a special key must be pressed to initiate an editing
command, such as Insert or Delete, then another special key
must be pressed to terminate the command.  Often two
terminating keys are provided:  the Accept key makes
permanent the changes produced by the editing, whereas the
Cancel key restores the text to its state before the editing
command was issued.  A difficulty with this approach is that
you may accidentally press the Cancel key instead of the
Accept key.  "Oops" is the mildest thing you'll say after
inadvertently cancelling a long text entry.  When entering a
large amount of text, it's a good idea to occasionally
accept what you have entered so far, then reissue the Text
Entry command, thus limiting the damage you can do by
accidentally hitting the Cancel key.
    Word processors that do not require a special key to be
----|T---1----|----2----|----3----|----4----|----5----|----6
File: CHAPT6
```

```
    These commands help the user recover from errors.  When
a special key must be pressed to initiate an editing
command, such as Insert or Delete, then another special key
must be pressed to terminate the command.  Often two
terminating keys are provided:  the Accept key makes
permanent the changes produced by the editing, whereas the
Cancel key restores the text to its state before the editing
command was issued.  A difficulty with this approach is that
you may accidentally press the Cancel key instead of the
Accept key.  When entering a large amount of text, it's a
good idea to occasionally accept what you have entered so
far, then reissue the Text Entry command, thus limiting the
damage you can do by accidentally hitting the Cancel key.
    Word processors that do not require a special key to be
pressed before an insertion or deletion commences often
provide an Undo key to cancel the effects of the most recent
----|T---1----|----2----|----3----|----4----|----5----|----6
File: CHAPT6
```

```
    These commands help the user recover from errors.  When
a special key must be pressed to initiate an editing
command, such as Insert or Delete, then another special key
must be pressed to terminate the command.  Often two
terminating keys are provided:  the Accept key makes
permanent the changes produced by the editing, whereas the
Cancel key restores the text to its state before the editing
command was issued.  A difficulty with this approach is that
you may accidentally press the Cancel key instead of the
Accept key.  When entering a large amount of text, it's a
good idea to occasionally accept what you have entered so
far, then reissue the Text Entry command, thus limiting the
damage you can do by accidentally hitting the Cancel key.
"Oops" is the mildest thing you'll say after inadvertently
cancelling a long text entry. ▮
    Word processors that do not require a special key to be
----¦T---1----¦----2----¦----3---- ¦----4----¦----5----¦----6
File: CHAPT6
```

FIGURE 6-3
(continued)

Search

The Search command scans the document for occurrences of a target word or phrase entered by the user. Searching for a section title is a good way to move quickly to a particular part of the document. (If no outline is available, search may be the only method of finding your way around in a document.) If you fear that you may have used a word or phrase incorrectly or inconsistently, you can locate and check each occurrence of the suspect word or phrase.

When the Search command is given, the program asks the user to enter the target phrase. The search begins at the current cursor position and continues, if need be, all the way to the end of the document. When an occurrence of the target phrase is found, the cursor is positioned on that occurrence and the display window is moved so that the cursor, and hence the occurrence of the target phrase, is near the center of the screen. Since the occurrence that was found may not be the desired one, or because we may need to locate all occurrences of the target phrase, we can have the program continue the search without our having to reenter the target phrase.

In searching for the target phrase, the program ignores the distinction between lowercase and uppercase letters. Thus the target phrase will be found even if it occurs at the beginning of a sentence or if it has been capitalized for emphasis.

FIGURE 6-4

Search and replace. The user enters (in the communications area) the target (text to be found) and the replacement (text to be substituted for each occurrence of the target) (a). Each occurrence of the target is highlighted in turn (b). For each occurrence the user is asked (in the communications area) whether to make the replacement. If the user answers Y (for yes), the replacement is made and the highlight moves to the next occurrence (c). If the user answers N (for no), the replacement is not made and, again, the highlight moves on to the next occurrence.

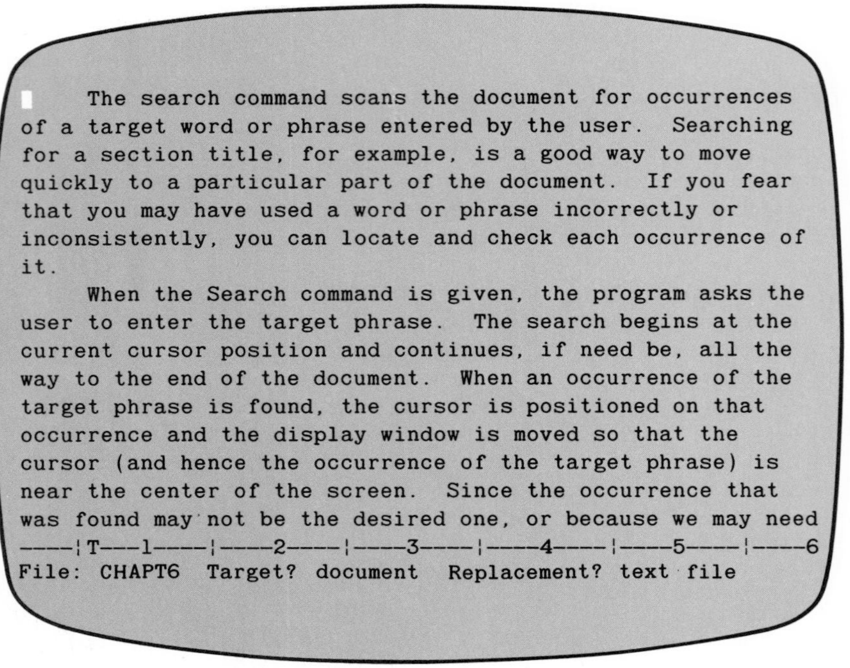

```
    The search command scans the document for occurrences
of a target word or phrase entered by the user.  Searching
for a section title, for example, is a good way to move
quickly to a particular part of the document.  If you fear
that you may have used a word or phrase incorrectly or
inconsistently, you can locate and check each occurrence of
it.
    When the Search command is given, the program asks the
user to enter the target phrase.  The search begins at the
current cursor position and continues, if need be, all the
way to the end of the document.  When an occurrence of the
target phrase is found, the cursor is positioned on that
occurrence and the display window is moved so that the
cursor (and hence the occurrence of the target phrase) is
near the center of the screen.  Since the occurrence that
was found may not be the desired one, or because we may need
----¦T---1-----¦----2-----¦----3-----¦----4-----¦----5-----¦----6
File: CHAPT6  Target? document  Replacement? text file
```

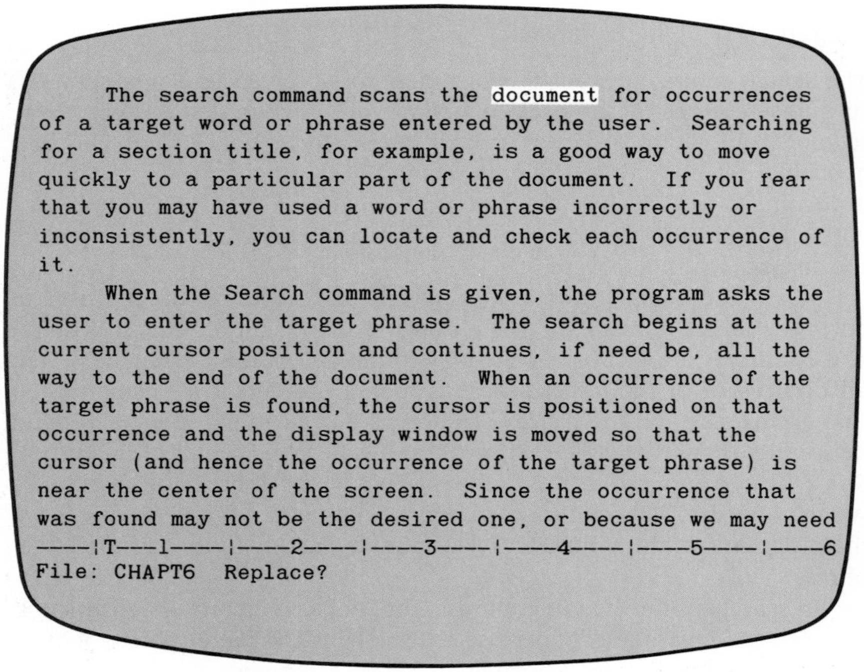

```
    The search command scans the document for occurrences
of a target word or phrase entered by the user.  Searching
for a section title, for example, is a good way to move
quickly to a particular part of the document.  If you fear
that you may have used a word or phrase incorrectly or
inconsistently, you can locate and check each occurrence of
it.
    When the Search command is given, the program asks the
user to enter the target phrase.  The search begins at the
current cursor position and continues, if need be, all the
way to the end of the document.  When an occurrence of the
target phrase is found, the cursor is positioned on that
occurrence and the display window is moved so that the
cursor (and hence the occurrence of the target phrase) is
near the center of the screen.  Since the occurrence that
was found may not be the desired one, or because we may need
----¦T---1-----¦----2-----¦----3-----¦----4-----¦----5-----¦----6
File: CHAPT6  Replace?
```

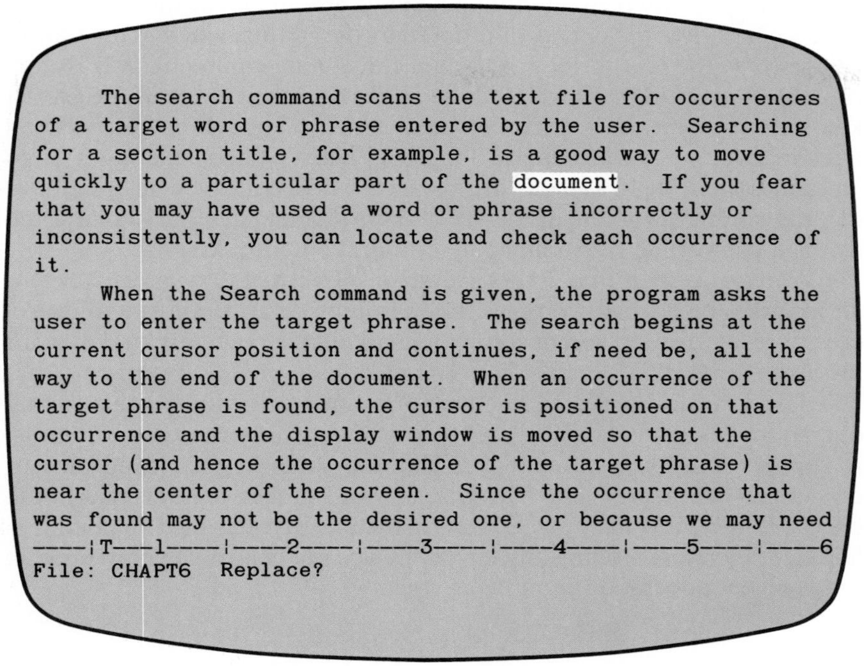

```
      The search command scans the text file for occurrences
of a target word or phrase entered by the user.  Searching
for a section title, for example, is a good way to move
quickly to a particular part of the document.  If you fear
that you may have used a word or phrase incorrectly or
inconsistently, you can locate and check each occurrence of
it.
      When the Search command is given, the program asks the
user to enter the target phrase.  The search begins at the
current cursor position and continues, if need be, all the
way to the end of the document.  When an occurrence of the
target phrase is found, the cursor is positioned on that
occurrence and the display window is moved so that the
cursor (and hence the occurrence of the target phrase) is
near the center of the screen.  Since the occurrence that
was found may not be the desired one, or because we may need
-----¦T---1----¦----2-----¦----3-----¦----4----¦----5----¦---6
File: CHAPT6  Replace?
```

FIGURE 6-4
(continued

Search and Replace

The Search and Replace command finds each occurrence of a target phrase and substitutes for it a replacement phrase provided by the user. If you discover you have consistently misspelled a word or if you need to change the name of a character in your novel, the Search and Replace command will help you set things right. Figure 6-4 illustrates Search and Replace.

Search and Replace can produce surprising results because the word processor knows nothing of the meaning of the text and so will not limit itself to "reasonable" replacements. If you tell the program to change all occurrences of "bad" to "evil," then "badger" will be changed to "evilger" and "Carlsbad Caverns" will be changed to "Carlsevil Caverns." Some word processors avoid this problem by asking the user, for each occurrence of the target phrase, whether the replacement should be made. Others allow the user to specify that only an isolated phrase—one preceded and followed by blank space—will be replaced. Before using Search and Replace, it is a good idea to make a backup copy of your text file in case you should mangle your working copy beyond redemption.

Accept, Cancel, and Undo

The Accept, Cancel, and Undo commands help the user recover from errors. When a special key must be pressed to initiate an editing command, such as Insert or Delete, then another special key must be pressed to terminate the command. Often two terminating keys are provided: the Accept key makes permanent the changes produced by the editing, whereas the Cancel key restores the text to its state before the editing command was issued. A problem with this approach is that you may accidentally press the Cancel key instead of the Accept key. "Oops" is the mildest thing you will say after inadvertently cancelling a long text entry. When entering a large amount of text, it is a good idea to accept occasionally what you have entered so far, then reissue the Text Entry command, thus limiting the damage you can do by accidentally hitting the Cancel key.

Word processors that do not require a special key to be pressed before an insertion or deletion commences often provide an Undo key to cancel the effects of the most recent editing operation. Although this kind of word processor is usually the most convenient to use, one disadvantage is that when an error is discovered, the user may not recall what the last editing operation was. Thus pressing the Undo key may have unexpected results. A popular solution is to allow pressing the Undo key a second time to cancel the first depression. This type of word processor often makes the effects of the previous operation permanent when the next operation is initiated; therefore striking any key, even a cursor control key, can prevent the preceding operation from being undone.

◣ **Exercise 6-2** Use your word processor to load the text file that you created in Exercise 6-1. Now revise the document to improve its accuracy and effectiveness. Read it carefully for spelling and grammar mistakes, and use deletion and insertion to correct any errors found. Try using block moves to rearrange sentences and paragraphs for greater effectiveness. If you find you have consistently misspelled or misused a word, use search and replace to find and change all occurrences of the offending word. Again, frequently save you work to disk so there will be little loss if the computer fails or if you make some drastic mistake in editing. (In the latter case, exit the word processor without saving the text; the file on disk will contain the text as it was the last time it was saved.) ◣

FORMATTING AND PRINTING

Usually, the ultimate aim of word processing is to produce a printed version of the document. The text should be neatly printed with appropriate left, right, top, and bottom margins, and with page headings, page numbers, titles, and so on in their proper positions. Preparing text for printing is known as *formatting*. As mentioned before, WYSIWYG word processors fully format the text displayed on the screen, whereas others save the more complex formatting operations until the text is printed.

It is up to the user to specify such formatting details as the number of lines to be printed on each page and the widths of the left and right margins. There are three popular methods for specifying the desired format:

1 Formatting commands are inserted directly into the document. A command begins with a special character, usually a period, to distinguish it from text to be printed. When the document is printed, the formatting commands are carried out but the command lines are not printed. For example, the command lines

```
.left margin 10
.text length 56
.text width 60
```

specify that the document will be printed with a 10-character-wide left margin and with 56 lines per page. The printed area on the page will be 60 characters wide. Formatting commands constitute a computer language that for advanced typesetting programs can be extremely complex.

2 The user enters values for the various formatting parameters, such as the number of lines per page, in response to queries by the word processing program. A common way to handle this is for the program to display a table showing the *default values* it is currently assuming for the formatting parameters. By moving the cursor about on the screen and typing in new values, the user can change any of the parameter values as needed. No value need be entered for a parameter if the default value is acceptable.

3 Formatting is governed by a special disk file called a *style sheet*. A different style sheet is used for each kind of document—one for a business letter, another for a book manuscript, another for a legal contract, and so on. The word processor has a command that lets the user create a style sheet by responding to queries. Once style sheets have been created and stored on disk, however, all the user needs to do to specify the format of a document is to give the name of the disk file containing the desired style sheet. The style sheet assigns letter

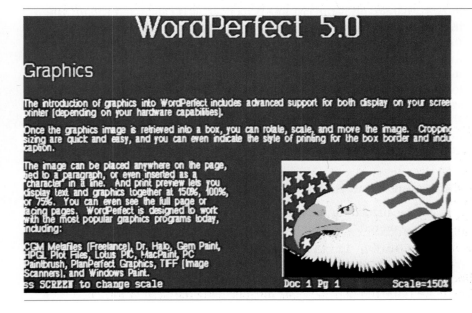

WordPerfect 5.0 display showing text containing graphics.

codes to various character and paragraph styles; for example, *BF* might be the code for boldface type, and *HI* might indicate a paragraph with a hanging indent—every line except the first is indented. During text entry and editing, the user employs these style codes to apply the styles defined in the style sheet to various portions of the text.

Some of the characteristics of printed documents that most word-processing programs allow the user to specify include size and placement of the text area, alignment, centering, hyphenation, and headers and footers. These are discussed below.

Size and Placement of Text Area

The user can specify the size of the printed area and its placement on the page. The size of the printed area is specified by giving its width in characters and its length in lines. Its placement is specified by giving the width of the left margin in characters and the length of the top margin in lines. Some programs also allow lengths and widths to be given in inches, and typesetting programs use a unit called the *pica*, which is traditional in the printing trade and equals ⅙ of an inch.

The user can also specify the amount of space between adjacent lines. Documents being printed in final form usually use single spacing, in which no lines are skipped between consecutive lines of text. Manuscripts, documents that will be edited and then typeset by human compositors, are usually typed double-spaced, with every other line skipped to leave room for editorial changes.

If the program automatically indents paragraphs, then the user can specify the number of characters by which the first line of each paragraph is indented. A negative value for the size of the paragraph indent produces reverse indentation whereby the first line of a paragraph starts to the left of the remaining lines.

Certain problems can arise in breaking text into pages. When the first line of a paragraph is the last line on a page, it is called an *orphan*; when the last line of a paragraph is the first line on a page, it is called a *widow*. Both orphans and widows look awkward and should be avoided in text that is being printed in final form (one need not bother avoiding them in manuscripts). Some word processors will automatically make a page slightly longer or shorter to avoid a widow or orphan; others require the user to specify where this is to be done. Also, certain structures, such as tables, should not be broken between pages. The user should be able to specify that a particular block of text is to be printed entirely on a single page, even at the expense of making the preceding page too short.

Alignment, Centering, and Hyphenation

Text can be aligned on the left, on the right, on both the right and left, or it can be centered. For example, the following text is aligned on the left:

```
Mary had a little lamb
Its fleece was white as snow.
Everywhere that Mary went
The lamb was sure to go.
```

Alignment on the left only is common for typewritten documents. Alignment on the right only is usually used only for special effects:

```
          Mary had a little lamb
  Its fleece was white as snow.
      Everywhere that Mary went
       The lamb was sure to go.
```

Lines that are centered on the page are not aligned on either the left nor the right:

```
        Mary had a little lamb
     Its fleece was white as snow.
      Everywhere that Mary went
       The lamb was sure to go.
```

Centering is usually used for headlines, titles, section headings, and the like.

Text can be aligned on both the left and the right, so that each line has the same length. Such text is said to be *justified*; typeset text is usually (though not invariably) justified.

```
Mary    had   a   little    lamb
Its fleece was white as snow.
Everywhere    that   Mary    went
The   lamb   was   sure   to   go.
```

The appearance of justification will depend on the kind of printer that is available. If only one size space is available, as on most typewriters, then left and right alignment can be achieved only at the expense of irregular spacing within the line. On the other hand, with printers that provide *proportional spacing*, the size of the interword space can be set separately for each line so as to make all lines the same length.

Justified text will look better if all the lines are about the same length to begin with. In aid of this we need to hyphenate long words at the ends of lines and type them partly on one line and partly on another. Although there are rules as to the proper points at which to hyphenate words, the rules have many exceptions, and in many cases a dictionary must be consulted to determine proper hyphenation. Some word processors leave it up to the user to specify points at which a word will be hyphenated. Others, however, handle hyphenation automatically, looking up words in a dictionary on disk when necessary.

Hyphenation and justification should be used only for text that is being printed in final form. Neither should be used for manuscripts, since the extraneous hyphens and spaces will only make the copyeditor's and typesetter's tasks more difficult.

Headers and Footers

A *header* is a line that is printed at the top of every page, and a *footer* is a line that is printed at the bottom of each page. Usually, either headers or footers are used, although occasionally the two are combined on the same page. For example, note the headers on the pages of this book.

Page numbers are printed as part of headers and footers; a special symbol in the header or footer informs the computer where the page number is to be printed. When the header or footer is printed, the computer replaces the special symbol with the current page number.

When pages are to be bound into a book, different headers and footers are usually used for even-numbered (left-hand) and odd-numbered (right-hand) pages. Also, the first page of a chapter usually uses a footer even if headers are used on other pages. Thus a full-featured word processor should accept different headers and footers for use on even-numbered and odd-numbered pages, and it should be prepared to treat specially certain designated pages, such as the first page of a chapter.

◣ **Exercise 6-3** Use the formatting and printing capabilities of your word processor to print out the text that you entered and edited in previous exercises. Try printing the text in more than one format. For example, your essay could be printed double-spaced, as if it were a manuscript being submitted for publication. Or you could print it in several columns, as it might appear in a newspaper. ◣

OTHER FEATURES

Many other features are available in word processors. Competitive pressures often force software publishers to include as many features as possible. Extra features, however, may cause a word processor to take up more memory (leaving less for the text to be processed), may slow its operation, and may make its use more difficult to learn. A word processor with just the features that you need is apt to provide better performance and be simpler to use than one with everything but the proverbial kitchen sink thrown in.

The features discussed in this section are sometimes provided as part of a word processor and sometimes as separate programs intended for use in conjunction with a particular word processor.

Document Chaining

Document chaining allows documents stored in several disk files to be joined and printed as a single document. Document chaining is particularly important for word processors that require the document in each file to fit into main memory, since a long document often must be broken into smaller parts to satisfy this requirement.

Substitution for Parameters

One of the most important applications of word processing is customizing a general-purpose document by inserting such particulars as names and addresses. The points at which text is to be inserted are marked by symbols called *parameters*; for example, the parameter ⟨name⟩ might indicate a point at which a name is to be inserted; the parameter ⟨street address⟩ might indicate a point at which a street address is to be inserted; and so on.

Sometimes we need only a single customized document, as when a legal secretary inserts a client's name in a standard legal form such as a will. In this case, the text to be substituted can be entered at the keyboard. Indeed, the standard search and replace command found in most word processors can be used for this purpose.

Sometimes, however, we need to print many copies of the document with different text inserted in each copy. The most common example is writing form letters to persons whose names and addresses are obtained from a mailing list. As each copy is printed, ⟨name⟩ is replaced by the name of the next person on the mailing list, ⟨street address⟩ is replaced by that person's street address, and so on. Programs for this task are called *mail merge* or *mailing list* programs.

It is helpful if the standard document can be assembled from text stored in several disk files. For example, a legal document may be assembled from the clauses that apply to a particular client, and a form letter can be assembled from paragraphs that address various topics. Such standard blocks of text are called *boilerplate*.

Spelling Checking

A *spelling checker* looks up each word of a document in a dictionary (which is stored on disk) and informs the user of any misspelled words—that is, words that are not found in the dictionary. Each misspelled word is highlighted, and the program may suggest as a correction the most similar

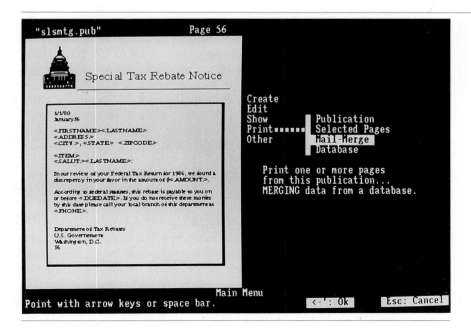

Screen display produced by a mail-merge program. As each copy of the document is printed, information such as the recipient's name and address will be obtained from a database and inserted in the printout at the appropriate places.

word that was found in the dictionary. The user has the option of retaining the original spelling, accepting the suggested correction, or entering still another spelling. If the word is correct as spelled in the document, the user can have the word added to the dictionary. Thus the dictionary will gradually be extended with the specialized vocabulary, such as technical terms, employed by a particular user. Users who are poor spellers must beware of inadvertently putting misspelled words into the dictionary.

Note carefully that a spelling checker can detect an error only if the misspelled word is not in the dictionary. Thus a spelling checker cannot detect the use of the wrong word—of using *too* or *two* instead of *to*, for example, or of using *their* instead of *there*. Since the incorrect words are valid English words, and hence are in the dictionary, they will not marked as misspelled. The same thing applies to typos that change one English word into another; for example, dropping the final *t* of *thought* will not be detected because *though* is also a valid English word.

Some recent programs attempt to check not only spelling but also grammar and style.

Using a Thesaurus

A *thesaurus* lists synonyms for words; writers often use a thesaurus to suggest more interesting or colorful synonyms for commonplace or overused words. Some word processors now provide a thesaurus on disk. To use the thesuarus, you place the cursor on the word you wish to look up and press the designated command key. After a short delay for looking up the word, the word processor displays a list of synonyms. If you wish to use one of the synonyms, you can select it by placing the cursor on it, and the word processor will automatically substitute it for the word that was looked up. In addition, each of the displayed synonyms can itself be looked up, allowing you to explore the thesaurus in search of the word that you want.

A thesaurus must be used with care. The synonyms listed may be only roughly similar in meaning to the word looked up; if the word has more than one meaning, different synonyms may correspond to different meanings. It is up to you to choose the synonym that expresses the exact meaning that you wish to convey; never use a word selected from a thesaurus if you are unsure of its exact meaning and usage. Also, readers quickly tire of elegant or obscure words used where simpler, more familiar ones would do just as well. A thesaurus should be used to remind you of words that are part of your normal vocabulary, not to find words that you would never use in everyday conversation.

Footnotes

Most word processors will keep track of footnotes. The user can enter each footnote at the point in the text where it is referenced. When the text is printed, the user can specify whether each footnote should be printed at the foot of the page on which it is referenced, or whether all footnotes should be collected together at the end of the document.

With regard to footnotes and other mechanisms of academic writing, term papers and theses are often troublesome since they must be formatted to arbitrary standards from which not the slightest deviation is allowed. Students selecting a word processor must make sure that it can format text in accordance with the term paper and thesis requirements to which they must adhere.

Index Preparation

An index-preparation program allows various words and phrases to be marked as index entries. These can be supplemented with additional words and phrases that do not appear in the text but are defined only as index entries. The index-preparation program extracts the index entries from the text, marks each with its page number, sorts the entries into alphabetical order, and combines identical entries. Additional manual editing may be required to combined closely related entries, to introduce cross references, and to add additional entries for completeness and consistency.

This type of index-preparation program is useful only when the text is to be printed in final form. When the material is to be typeset from a printed manuscript, the index must be prepared from the page proofs rather than from the manuscript. For this purpose one needs a program that allows index entries to be made as the proofs are read, then sorts the index and combines identical and related entries.

◣ **Exercise 6-4** Try a spelling checker and thesuarus on the text file created in previous exercises. See if any misspelled words escaped your editing in Exercise 6-2. Use the thesaurus to try to find more effective and colorful substitutes for some commonplace or overused words. Beware, however, of the opposite fault of overusing elegant or obscure words. ◢

◣ DESKTOP PUBLISHING

Desktop publishing, also called *electronic publishing*, is the use of desktop computers for the typesetting and page makeup necessary to publish such material as advertisements, newsletters, newspapers, reports, and books. Although desktop publishing has had little impact on traditional book publishers, it is revolutionizing the publishing done in business and advertising. Publishing activities that once had to be contracted out to specialists can now be performed in-house more rapidly and at lower cost.

Typesetting and Page Makeup

A publisher is responsible for producing one perfect copy of the work to be published. The printer then photographs this *camera-ready copy* and

Two computer systems for desktop publishing. The system at left features a full-page display that can show a complete printed page. The system at right includes a mouse and a laser printer.

uses the resulting films to produce (by photographic techniques) the printing plates required by a particular printing technology.

Traditionally, the manuscript for a work is sent out for *typesetting*, the result of which is long columns of printed text called galleys; drawings and photographs are prepared by other specialists. To prepare the camera-ready copy, artwork, photographs, and blocks of text from the galleys are cut to the proper size and pasted in their proper positions on sheets of cardboard, a process known as *page makeup*.

In desktop publishing, both typesetting and page makeup are done with a desktop computer. The text to be printed is entered into a word processor; artwork is either produced with painting and drawing programs or is scanned from existing printed material. A page-makeup program arranges the text on the pages, inserts artwork in the desired positions, and prints out the camera-ready copy on a laser printer.

Hardware for Desktop Publishing

The Computer   A computer used for desktop publishing must have strong graphics capabilities to display page makeups as well as to display any artwork or photographs that are to be included in the published material. A powerful microprocessor is also essential; graphics processing makes heavy computational demands, so that graphics programs can run very slowly on an underpowered computer. Desktop publishing originated on the Apple Macintosh computer, whose user interface is based on using a mouse for selecting commands from menus and for selecting text and graphics to be manipulated. Desktop publishing software for other computers adopts a similar user interface, so that a mouse is also required.

The Printer   Since the printer is responsible for producing the camera-ready copy, it must clearly be able to print text with typeset quality. It must also be able to handle graphics so that drawings and photographs embedded in the text can be printed. Laser printers satisfy both these requirements and are currently the standard printers for desktop publishing.

The images produced by a graphics printer are made up of large numbers of individual dots. The resolution of the printer, which is a measure of the sharpness of the printed images, is stated as the number of individual dots that can be printed side-by-side for a distance of one inch. Today's laser printers have a resolution of 300 *dots per inch (dpi)*, which is greater than the resolution of other types of graphics printers, such as dot-matrix printers. On the other hand, the phototypesetting machines used in book publishing have typical resolutions of 2000 dpi. Despite the disparity in resolution, laser printers can produce attractive typeset text, particularly if type fonts designed for use with laser printers are employed. The lower resolution is apt to be most evident with graphics, particularly photographs, although the results are satisfactory for many purposes.

Some print shops will accept disk files produced by desktop publishing systems and print them out on phototypesetting machines, thus allowing the higher resolution of phototypesetting equipment to be obtained. When this approach is followed, the in-house laser printer can be used to print preliminary drafts of the typeset material, but the final camera-ready copy is produced by the print shop. The necessary files can be mailed to the print shop on diskettes or transmitted over the telephone. (See the section below on page description languages for why the files produced for laser printers also can be used with phototypesetting equipment.)

Graphics and Text Scanners   A *graphics scanner* (often just called a *scanner*) converts a printed image into digital form and transmits it to a computer; this process is called digitizing the image, and the image transmitted to the computer is said to be *digitized*. Scanners are used to convert photographs and drawings into electronic form so that they can be inserted into text with the page-makeup program. In general, graphics in the pub-

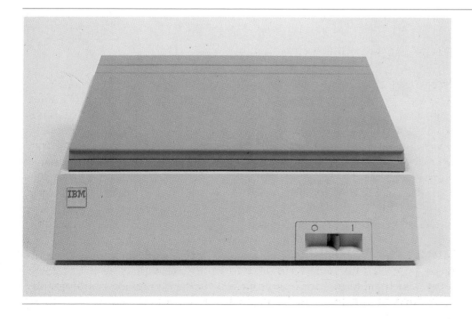

A graphics scanner. The lid lifts to reveal the plate on which the copy to be scanned is placed.

lished material are either created with a painting or drawing program or are scanned from existing photographs, drawings, and printed images.

Likewise, a *text scanner* reads printed text and sends it to a word processor or a page-makeup program. Unlike a graphics scanner, which transmits images unchanged, a text scanner uses optical-character-recognition techniques to identify the text characters and convert them into ASCII (or other) character codes. Thus text obtained with a text scanner is not an exact image of the text that was scanned, but can have any size and style specified by the user.

Software for Desktop Publishing

The Word Processor   Although text can be typed directly into page-makeup programs, such programs are somewhat cumbersome for extensive typing, so that a word processor is usually used for entering, correcting, and revising text. A word processor can produce either unformatted or formatted text files. Unformatted files contain the text that was entered but no information about how the text is to be displayed on the printed page. Formatted files, on the other hand, contain additional information (which was entered by the word processing operator) on type fonts, type sizes, page widths, paragraph indents, and spacings between lines and paragraphs. Unformatted files, which have a standard form for every computer system, generally can be passed from any word processor to any page-makeup program. The same is not true for formatted files, whose structure varies from one word processor to another. A page-makeup

Screen display produced by the Aldus Pagemaker page-makeup program. Note the menu, the mouse pointer, and the way the text "flows" around the graphics.

program usually can read formatted files (if at all) from only a small number of word processors. You should try to choose a page-makeup program and word processor so that the former can read the formatted files produced by the latter. This will allow much of the formatting to be entered when the text is typed and edited rather than later during page makeup.

The Page-Makeup Program   The page-makeup program reads files produced by word processors and graphics programs, and arranges the text and graphics into pages according to the user's instructions; the files read from other programs are said to be *imported* into the page-makeup program. The program allows the user to view the entire page and to zoom in on any part, such as a column of text or an illustration. When viewing the entire page or a large part of it, the individual characters making up the text are usually too small to be displayed on the computer screen. In that case, the text is displayed in *greeked* form where each line of text is represented by a horizontal bar of the proper length and thickness. Thus the user can see how the lines of text are laid out on the page even when the individual characters cannot be made out. If the user zooms in on greeked text, the horizontal bars are replaced by the text they represent.

To use a page-makeup program, you begin by setting up a master page with the margins, column widths, headers, and footers that will be used for every page. For each individual page, text imported from the word processor flows into the predefined columns under the user's direction. Graphics are imported and inserted in their proper places on the page. Some programs will automatically reformat text to make room for the graphics; others require that this be done manually. Other formatting, such as selection of type fonts, must be done now if it was not done in the word processor. Once text and graphics are in place, the user may try changing the position and alignment of text and graphics elements to improve the appearance of the page. When satisfied, the user goes on to the next page in the document. When the entire document is laid out, the page-makeup program is instructed to print it out on the laser printer.

Page Description Languages   The page-makeup program must send to the laser printer (or other output device) complex information about how text and graphics are to be arranged on the printed page. This is accomplished by sending the laser printer a program written in a special programming language called a *page description language (PDL)*. This program contains the text and graphics to be printed along with instructions for such matters as selecting type fonts and positioning graphics on the page. The printer contains a powerful embedded microcomputer and the necessary software for interpreting the program it receives and carrying out the instructions written in the page description language.

The most widely used page description language is Postscript, which is rapidly becoming a *de facto standard*—a standard established by the marketplace even though it is not endorsed by any official standards organization. Postscript has been implemented on both laser printers and phototypesetting machines. Thus, as indicated earlier, Postscript files can be printed out on a phototypesetter when the resolution of laser printers is insufficient.

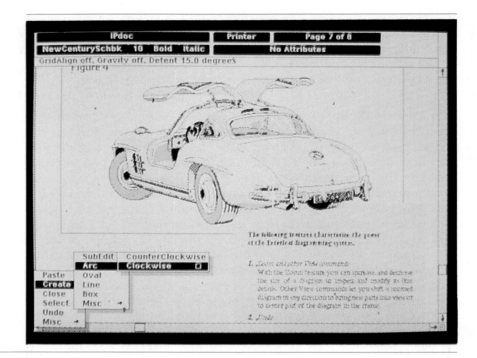

Screen display produced by the Interleaf page-makeup program.

Summary

Word processing allows text to be entered, stored, edited, formatted, and printed. The display screen serves as a window that can be moved about to view different parts of the text. The text on the screen may be formatted exactly as it will be printed or in a simpler form that allows the word processor to operate more rapidly. The phrase *what you see is what you get (WYSIWYG)* is used to describe word processors that display text in the same format in which it will be printed.

Editing operations include inserting and deleting characters, deleting blocks of characters, and moving or copying blocks of characters from one point in the text to another. The word processor will scan the text for occurrences of a given word or phrase, and the occurrences found can be replaced automatically by another word or phrase specified by the user.

The formatting features of a word processor allow the text to be printed in the desired form. Margins, paragraph indents, number of lines per page, headers, and footers can all be specified by the user. Thanks to laser printers, microcomputers are beginning to be used for typesetting, which presents new formatting challenges.

A variety of additional features are available for word processors, either as part of the word processor program or as an additional program designed to work in conjunction with the word processor. Probably the most important of these are mail merge or mailing list programs, which allow form letters to be printed with names from a mailing list inserted into the letters as desired.

Desktop publishing uses desktop computers to produce the camera-ready copy that is used to produce printing plates. Text is entered and edited with word processors, and illustrations are produced with graphics programs. Graphics and text scanners can also be used to input drawings, photographs, and text. A page-makeup program arranges text and illustrations on the printed page. The camera-ready copy is usually produced on a laser printer; however, a phototypesetting machine can be used for higher quality.

◥ Vocabulary Review

block selection	formatting	scrolling
boilerplate	graphics scanner	single spacing
camera-ready copy	greeked text	spelling checker
clipboard	header	style sheet
copy buffer	imported file	substitution for
cursor control keys	insertion	parameters
de facto standard	justified text	text entry
dedicated word	mail merge program	text file
processor	mailing list program	text scanner
default values	manuscript	thesaurus
deletion	orphan	typesetting
desktop publishing	overtyping	what you see is what
digitized image	page description	you get (WYSIWYG)
document chaining	language (PDL)	widow
dots per inch (dpi)	page makeup	word wrap
electronic publishing	pica	
footer	scrap	

◥ For Further Reading

Becker, Joseph D. "Multilingual Word Processing." *Scientific American*, July 1984, pp. 96–107.

_____. "Arabic Word Processing." *Communications of the ACM*, July 1987, pp. 600–610.

Coombs, James H., et al. "Markup Systems and the Future of Scholarly Text Processing." *Communications of the ACM*, November 1987, pp. 933–947

Desktop Publishing (special section). *Byte*, May 1987, pp. 147–202.

Furuta, Richard, et al. "Document Formatting Systems: Survey, Concepts, and Issues." *Computing Surveys*, September 1982, pp. 417–472.

Meyrowitz, Norman and Andries van Dam. "Interactive Editing Systems." *Computing Surveys*, September 1982, pp. 321–415.

Sullivan, David R., et al. *Computing Today: Microcomputer Concepts and Applications*. Boston, MA: Houghton Mifflin Company, 1985.

Wood, Lamont. "Word Processors for Desktop Publishing." *Byte*, May 1988, pp. 102–116.

Review Questions

1 What advantages does word processing have over conventional methods of document preparation?

2 Describe four methods of giving commands to a word processor.

3 Describe two approaches to using main memory and disk storage in word processing. Why does text in main memory need to be saved to disk frequently?

4 Describe how the display screen of a word processor is used.

5 Describe text entry and insertion.

6 Distinguish between insertion and overtyping.

7 Name two keys that can be used for deleting characters and describe the effect of each.

8 Describe how a block of text can be selected for further processing.

9 Contrast block delete, block move, and block copy.

10 Describe the (1) Search and (2) Search and Replace commands.

11 Describe three methods of specifying how text is to be formatted.

12 Describe the major characteristics of the printed text that can be set by the user.

13 What is document chaining?

14 Describe two word-processing applications that hinge on substitution for parameters.

15 How do spelling checkers work?

16 What is the purpose of a thesaurus and what are some ways in which it can be misused?

17 How can word processors help with the preparation of indexes?

18 How is camera-ready copy produced (a) traditionally and (b) with desktop publishing.

19 Describe the use of a page-makeup program.

20 What is the role of page description languages?

Topics for Discussion

1 Some writers claim that word processing reduces the quality of writing. They claim that the greater speed with which text can be entered and corrected causes pieces to be written more hurriedly, with less thought given to content and expression. Discuss.

2 In offices, dedicated word processors are rapidly being replaced by personal computers that can do many other jobs in addition to word processing. On the shelves of department stores, however, personal computers are being replaced by electronic typewriters and dedicated word processors. Why might consumers be more likely to buy dedicated word processors instead of the far more versatile personal computers?

3 Desktop publishing enables even the smallest political or protest groups to turn out professionally polished publications expressing their views. For this reason, well-known science-fiction and computer writer Jerry Pournelle has called desktop publishing a "hardware implementation of the first amendment." Discuss.

4 Some people fear that graphics scanners will result in widespread violation of copyright laws because users of desktop publishing systems will appropriate illustrations from copyrighted publications without permission. Discuss.

CHAPTER 7

ELECTRONIC SPREADSHEETS

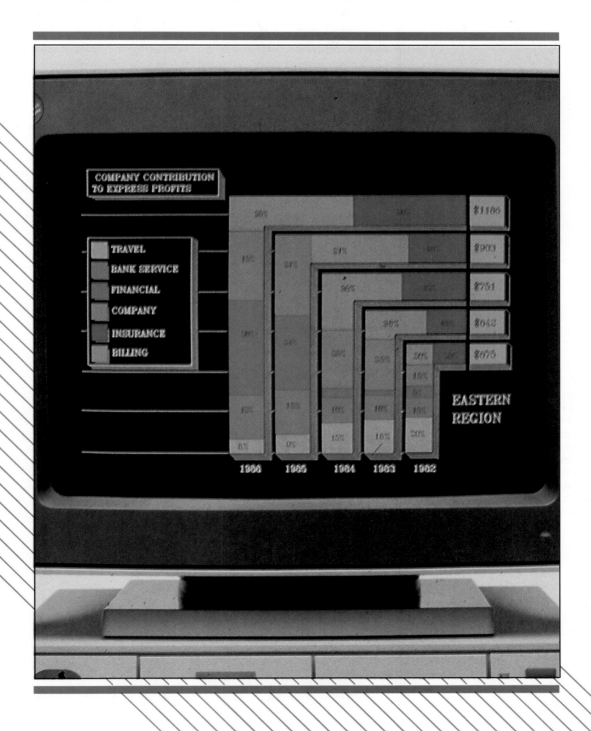

INTRODUCTION

The electronic spreadsheet is the most brilliant software invention of the microcomputer era. Word processing grew out of earlier text editing and formatting programs for minicomputers and mainframes. Database and telecommunications programs address obvious needs. But who would have ever believed that business people would be attracted to microcomputers almost solely for the sake of an automatic calculator combined with an electronic version of an accountant's ledger sheet? No one did believe it, no one except electronic-spreadsheet inventors Dan Bricklin and Robert Frankston, whose Visicalc program was responsible for many of the early sales of Apple and Radio Shack microcomputers.

Today spreadsheet programs are available for almost all microcomputers, and spreadsheet analysis vies with word processing for the distinction of being the most popular microcomputer application. The details of electronic spreadsheets vary somewhat from one spreadsheet program to another. In this chapter we will look at a "generic" electronic spreadsheet that illustrates the major features of all spreadsheet programs but does not necessarily agree with any one of them in every detail.

THE SPREADSHEET

An electronic spreadsheet is a large table typically with 256 *rows* and 64 *columns*. The rows are labeled 1, 2, 3, and so on through 256, or whatever

FIGURE 7-1

Screen display showing the upper left corner of a blank spreadsheet. The highlighted border contains the row and column labels. Each column has a default width of 10 characters. The highlighted rectangle designates the active cell (cell A1). The communications area at the bottom of the screen contains information about the active cell. Since the active cell is blank, only its label is shown.

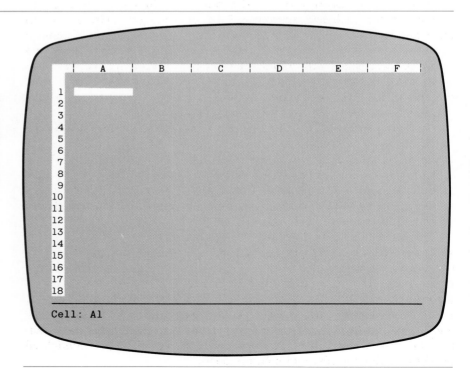

Cell: A1

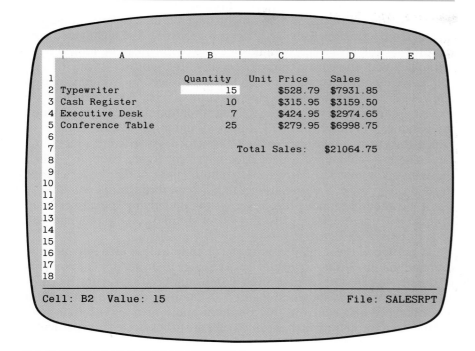

```
        A            B        C          D        E
1                  Quantity  Unit Price  Sales
2 Typewriter           15     $528.79   $7931.85
3 Cash Register        10     $315.95   $3159.50
4 Executive Desk        7     $424.95   $2974.65
5 Conference Table     25     $279.95   $6998.75
6
7                       Total Sales:    $21064.75
8
9
10
11
12
13
14
15
16
17
18

Cell: B2   Value: 15                          File: SALESRPT
```

FIGURE 7-2

A small spreadsheet giving the name, quantity sold, unit price, and sales income for four items of office equipment. The total sales income for all four items is shown at the foot of the Sales column. The active cell is B2; both the label B2 and the contents of the cell are shown in the communications area.

the number of the last row may be. The columns are labeled with letters: the first 26 columns are labeled A through Z, the next 26 are labeled AA through AZ, the 26 after that are labeled BA through BZ, and so on.

Each intersection of a row and a column defines a *cell*, which can hold a number, a label, or a formula. Each cell is designated by its column letter and its row number. Thus, cell A1 lies at the intersection of column A and row 1, cell C7 lies at the intersection of column C and row 7, and so on. A spreadsheet with 256 rows and 64 columns contains $256 \times 64 = 16,384$ cells. A typical application will use only a fraction of these cells, the remainder being left blank. Many computers do not have enough memory to store a spreadsheet in which all the cells are in use.

In word processing, the display screen serves as a window that can be moved up and down to view different parts of the text. In spreadsheet programs, the display serves as a window that can be moved not only up and down but to the right and left, thus allowing all parts of the spreadsheet to be examined. As with word processors, some spreadsheet programs allow the screen to be divided into multiple windows, each of which can show a different part of the spreadsheet.

The screen in Figure 7-1 shows the upper left corner of a blank spreadsheet, and the screen in Figure 7-2 shows the upper left corner of a spreadsheet in which some cells contain labels and numbers. The widths of the columns can be adjusted according to the sizes of the entries that must be accommodated. In Figure 7-1, each column has the 10-character *default width*—the width that the program assumes when the user does not specify another width. In Figure 7-2, columns B and D retain the default width, but columns A and C have been widened. In each figure, a highlighted *border* contains the row and column labels.

The attention of the spreadsheet program is normally focussed on a single cell, the *active cell*, which is highlighted on the display. Commands that apply to a single cell always affect the active cell. The highlighted area that defines the active cell serves as a cursor, which can be moved from cell to cell with the cursor control keys or with a mouse.

As we move the cursor about on the spreadsheet, the window follows along so as to keep the cursor always on the screen. For example, if we move the cursor to the right of the rightmost column shown in the window, the window will move to the right by one column so that the column to which the cursor moved appears on the screen. As in word processing, this column-by-column or row-by-row movement is called *scrolling*. When the window is moved, the row and column labels in the border change to reflect the part of the spreadsheet that is seen through the window.

If we attempt to move the cursor off the underlying spreadsheet—up from row 1, for example, or to the left of column A—the program will beep or otherwise signal an error.

A portion of the display serves as a communications area in which the user and the spreadsheet program can exchange information. The contents of the active cell and its row and column numbers appear in the communications area, as shown in Figure 7-2. Information to be entered into a cell is typed and edited in the communications area, as is certain miscellaneous information, such as which cells are to be affected by a particular command.

ELEMENTARY OPERATIONS

We now turn our attention to the basic operations that are used for entering and manipulating data.

Commands

As with word processors, there are two basic ways of giving commands. We can press a separate key for each command, we can select commands from a menu, or we can use a combination of these two basic methods. If a menu is used, it normally appears in the communications area. Selecting one menu item may cause another menu to appear, so that several menu selections may have to be made before the desired operation is carried out. Before carrying out a command, the program may request additional information, such as which rows and columns are to be affected. Some programs allow the user to respond to such queries by positioning the cursor on the desired row, column, or cell, thus avoiding the need to type in row, column, and cell labels.

Since the exact method of giving commands varies widely from program to program, we will concentrate only on the commands and their effects and not worry about the exact keystrokes by which each command is given.

Using a spreadsheet program on a portable computer at home.

Macros

Spreadsheet users often find that they need to give the same sequence of commands over and over again. Many spreadsheet programs allow such an often-needed sequence of commands to be recorded once and played back whenever needed. Such a recorded sequence of commands is called a *macro*, which is an abbreviation for *macrocommand*. (The prefix *macro* means large, so a macro is a "large" command that the user makes out of the "smaller" commands built into the spreadsheet program.) As with all spreadsheet commands, methods of giving macrocommands vary from one spreadsheet program to another. Some programs allow the user to assign each macro to a particular key. Whenever that key is pressed, the macro is invoked, and the commands in the macro are automatically carried out. We will assume this method in the following discussion.

There are two ways to define a macro. The easiest way is by recording the commands that are to be in the macro. The user gives a command to begin macro recording, then carries out the desired commands exactly as would be done normally, if the commands were not being recorded. When all the commands to be recorded have been carried out, the user gives a command to stop macro recording and specifies the key to which the macro will be assigned. Whenever that key is pressed, the recorded commands will be played back and carried out automatically.

Another way to define a macro is to write it in a *macro definition language*, which is similar to a programming language. This method is more powerful than recording because the user can employ programming techniques such as selection (having different commands carried out under

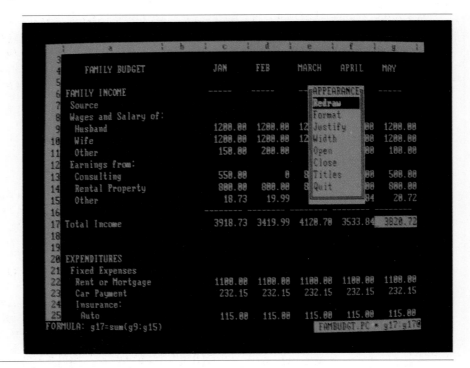

		a		b		c		d		e		f		g	

FAMILY BUDGET   JAN   FEB   MARCH   APRIL   MAY

FAMILY INCOME   -----   -----   ┌APPEARANCE┐   -----
  Source   │Redraw   │
  Wages and Salary of: │Format   │
    Husband   1200.00 1200.00   12   │Justify   │88   1200.00
    Wife   1200.00 1200.00   12   │Width   │88   1200.00
    Other   150.00   200.00   │Open   │88   100.00
  Earnings from: │Close   │
    Consulting   550.00   0   8   │Titles   │88   500.00
    Rental Property   800.00   800.00   8   │Quit   │88   800.00
    Other   18.73   19.99   └──────────┘94   20.72
                       -------- -------- -------- -------- --------
Total Income   3918.73 3419.99 4120.70 3533.84 3920.72

EXPENDITURES
  Fixed Expenses
    Rent or Mortgage   1100.00 1100.00 1100.00 1100.00 1100.00
    Car Payment   232.15   232.15   232.15   232.15   232.15
    Insurance:
      Auto   115.00   115.00   115.00   115.00   115.00

FORMULA: g17=sum(g9:g15)   FAMBUDGT.PC * g17:g17g

Screen display produced by a spreadsheet program. Note the command-menu window that temporarily overlaps the data.

different conditions) and repetition (having a sequence of commands carried out repeatedly). Using programming techniques effectively requires programming skills, however, so this method is usually used only by programmers and power users. Of course, any user can invoke macros that were written by a programmer or power user.

Although macros first became popular with spreadsheet programs, they are also useful with other applications programs, such as word processors and telecommunications programs. Some integrated programs have a macro facility that can be used with any of the applications provided by the integrated program.

Labels and Values

A spreadsheet cell can display either a *label* or a *value*. Labels are entered by the user and serve as titles or to designate particular rows, columns, and cells. A long label may extend over several adjacent cells. User-entered labels should not be confused with the column, row, and cell labels (such as D, 5, and D5) that are generated by the spreadsheet program.

Values are numbers representing the data to be manipulated by the spreadsheet. A value can be entered into a cell directly, or it can be calculated by a *formula* associated with the cell.

Figure 7-2 illustrates both labels and values. The columns and rows are designated by labels such as Quantity, Unit Price, and Sales. The label Total Sales: is used to designate a particular cell. The quantity and unit price figures are values entered by the user. The sales amounts and sales totals are values calculated by formulas.

We enter a value, a label, or a formula by positioning the cursor on the desired cell and typing in the data. Some programs establish some convention for distinguishing among values, labels, and formulas; for example, a label may have to start with a letter, a value with a digit, and a formula with a mathematical sign. For other programs, one must issue a separate command depending on whether a label, a value, or a formula is to be entered. As usual, we will ignore the exact keystrokes required by a particular program and merely assume that the program has some way of classifying each entry for a cell as a label, value, or formula.

As a value, label, or formula is typed, it appears on a line in the communications area. Usually there are some provisions for editing the typed characters to correct mistakes; at a minimum, one can back over and erase incorrect characters with the Backspace key. When satisfied with the value, label, or formula, the user enters it by pressing the Enter or Return key. When a value or label is entered, it appears immediately in the active cell. When a formula is entered, the *value calculated using the formula* (and not the formula itself) appears in the active cell.

Formulas

The crucial idea of electronic spreadsheets is for the values in some cells to be automatically calculated from values in other cells. When a value is changed, all the values that depend on it are automatically recalculated. Formulas specify how these calculations will be carried out. Instead of entering a value or a label for a cell, we can associate a formula with it. The value calculated using the formula is displayed in the cell. We cannot tell just by looking at the spreadsheet which values were entered by the user and which were calculated by formulas. When we position the cursor on a cell, however, any formula associated with the cell is displayed in the communications area.

For example, consider once again Figure 7-2, where the cursor is positioned on cell B2. In the communications area we find

```
Value: 15
```

indicating that 15, the value that occupies cell B2, was entered directly by the user.

Now look at Figure 7-3, which shows the same spreadsheet with the cursor moved to cell D2. In the communications area we find

```
Formula: B2 * C2
```

indicating that the value in cell D2 is calculated as the product of the values in cells B2 and C2. (Multiplication is usually represented by an asterisk in computer languages, since most computer keyboards do not have a times sign.) A quick check shows that the value in cell D2 is indeed the product of those in cells B2 and C2. If the value in cell B2 or C2 is changed, the program will automatically calculate and display a new value for cell D2 as well. Thus any change in the contents of cell B2 or cell C2 automatically changes the contents of cell D2 as well.

In fact, all the values in the Sales column of the example spreadsheet are calculated from the corresponding values in the Quantity and Unit

FIGURE 7-3
The spreadsheet in Figure 7-2 with D2 as the active cell. The communications area shows not the value in the active cell but the formula by which that value is calculated.

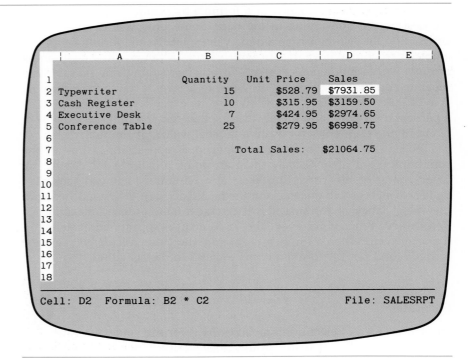

```
                A            B           C            D          E
 1                        Quantity   Unit Price   Sales
 2  Typewriter              15        $528.79    $7931.85
 3  Cash Register           10        $315.95    $3159.50
 4  Executive Desk           7        $424.95    $2974.65
 5  Conference Table        25        $279.95    $6998.75
 6
 7                                   Total Sales:  $21064.75
 8
 9
10
11
12
13
14
15
16
17
18
─────────────────────────────────────────────────────────────
Cell: D2   Formula: B2 * C2                    File: SALESRPT
```

Price columns. Thus if we move the cursor to cell D3, we will find that the communications area shows

    Formula: B3 * C3

indicating that value in cell D3 is calculated as the product of the values in cells B3 and C3. Likewise, if we move the cursor to cell D4, we see

    Formula: B4 * C4

and if we move the cursor to cell D5, we see

    Formula: B5 * C5

Now suppose we move the cursor to cell D7 (the cell labeled Total Sales) as shown in Figure 7-4. In the communications area we find

    Formula: D2 + D3 + D4 + D5

This tells us that the value in cell D7 is calculated as the sum of the values in cells D2, D3, D4, and D5. If any of those values are changed, the value in cell D7 will be changed as well. Note that changing any of the values in the Quantity and Unit Price columns will change the corresponding value in the Sales column, which in turn will change the value of Total Sales.

In general, values in formulas can be represented by constants, such as 2.5, or by cell labels, such as B2. Arithmetical operations are indicated by operators such as the following:

  +   addition
  −   subtraction

* multiplication
/ division

A precedence rule governs the order in which the operations in a formula will be carried out: multiplications and divisions are always done before additions and subtractions. When the precedence rule does not apply, as with successive multiplications and divisions, the operations are carried out in left-to-right order. Parentheses can be used to override the other rules: a part of a formula enclosed in parentheses is evaluated before any parts outside the parentheses.

The following are a some formulas together with descriptions of the calculations that they specify:

Formula	Calculation
1.08 * A5	Multiply the value in cell A5 by 1.08
A1 * A2 + 5	Multiply the values in cells A1 and A2, then add 5 to the product. Note that, in accordance with the precedence rule, the multiplication is done before the addition.
B3 * B5 + C2 * D4	Multiply the values in cells B3 and B5, multiply the values in cells C2 and D4, and add the two products. The precedence rule dictates that the multiplications be done before the addition.
A3 * (B2 + C9)	Add the values in cells B2 and C9, then multiply the result by the value in cell A3. Note that the parentheses cause the addition to be done before the multiplication, in defiance of the precedence rule.

Exercise 7-1 Create a simple spreadsheet, which should have several columns of data (which you fill in) and results (which are calculated by formulas). For example, the data columns might contain the names, prices, and percentage discounts for items of merchandise. The result columns might show the amount of discount and discounted price of each item. There should be a total displayed at the foot of at least one of the result columns. Save your spreadsheet on disk for use in later exercises.

Recalculation

Recalculation is the process by which a value defined by a formula is calculated anew after one or more of the values referred to by the formula have been changed. In Figure 7-3, for example, we see that the value in cell D2 depends on the values in cells B2 and C2. If either of those values is changed, the value in cell D2 will need to be recalculated. This, in turn, requires that the value in cell D7 be recalculated, since the value in cell D7 depends on the value in cell D2.

Normally we specify *automatic recalculation*: any time we change one value, all the values that depend on it are automatically recalculated. From the user's point of view, changing one data entry causes other entries to change as needed to reflect the new data.

When entering large amounts of data, we may wish to disable automatic recalculation. Otherwise, each data entry will trigger a possibly time-consuming recalculation. We will have to wait for the recalculation triggered by one entry to be completed before we can make the next entry. In this situation, it is best to disable automatic recalculation until all the new data has been entered, then either request a recalculation or reenable automatic recalculation. In either case, all the calculations needed to reflect the new data entries will be carried out at one time.

The formulas determine the order in which values must be recalculated. In our example spreadsheet, for instance, the values in cells D2, D3, D4, and D5 must be recalculated before the value in cell D7. If the value in cell D7 were recalculated first, it would be computed from the old values in D2, D3, D4, and D5 rather than from the new values produced by recalculation. Unless directed otherwise, most modern spreadsheet programs follow the *natural recalculation order* dictated by the formulas themselves. Older spreadsheet programs used other recalculation orders, such as recalculating the formulas in row-by-row or column-by-column order.

Screen display produced by Lotus 1-2-3, one of the most popular spreadsheet programs.

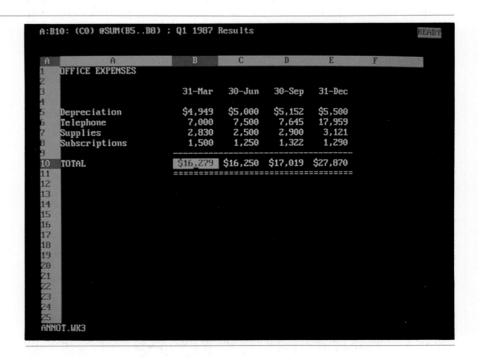

```
            A            B           C           D           E
 1                    Quantity   Unit Price    Sales
 2 Typewriter           15        $528.79    $7931.85
 3 Cash Register        10        $315.95    $3159.50
 4 Executive Desk        7        $424.95    $2974.65
 5 Conference Table     25        $279.95    $6998.75
 6
 7                        Total Sales:    $21064.75
 8
 9
10
11
12
13
14
15
16
17
18
───────────────────────────────────────────────────────────
Cell: D7   Formula: D2 + D3 + D4 + D5        File: SALESRPT
```

FIGURE 7-4
The formula in the communications area shows how the total sales amount in cell D7 is calculated from the sales amounts in cells D2, D3, D4, and D5.

Exercise 7-2 Experiment with the spreadsheet created in Exercise 7-1 by changing some of the data values and noting how the results are recalculated. Note also the time required for recalculation. Now turn off automatic recalculation, enter a completely new set of data values, then turn automatic recalculation back on to have all the results calculated at once.

Circular References

A circular reference is a series of formulas that define the value of a cell in terms of itself. For example, the value in B1 might be calculated from the value in B2, the value in B2 calculated from the value in B3, and the value in B3 calculated from the value in B1. When circular references exist, natural-order recalculation fails and the user is given an error message. Other recalculation orders can be used, but care must be taken if the results are to be meaningful.

To be meaningful, a calculation involving circular references must be repeated or *iterated* until the values stabilize—do not change when the spreadsheet is recalculated. Some spreadsheets will carry out this iteration automatically. There is no guarantee that the values in an iterative calculation will ever stabilize. Circular references and iterative calculations can be extremely powerful, but the spreadsheet designer must be suffi-

FIGURE 7-5
The highlighted blocks illustrate the ranges
B1:D3 (a) and A1:A4 (b).

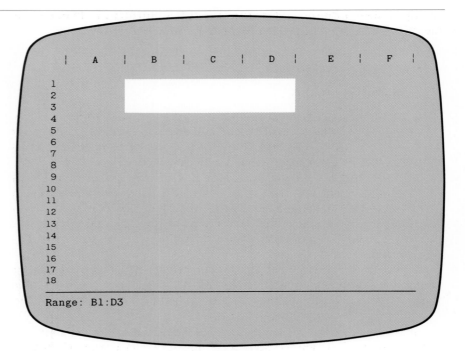

(a) B1:D3

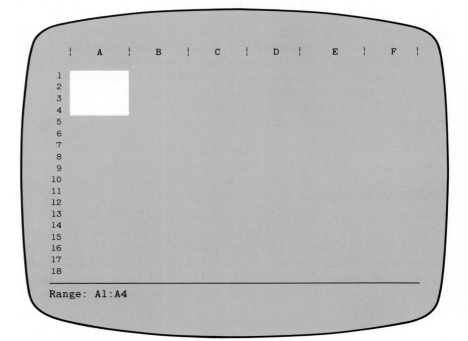

(b) A1:A4

ciently familiar with the mathematical principles involved to know when the calculation can be expected to yield a meaningful result.

Ranges and Functions

A *range* allows us to refer to a block of cells rather than to just a single cell. Ranges can be used in commands and formulas. They are particularly useful in connection with *functions*, which designate predefined calculations that can be carried out on cells and ranges of cells.

A range specifies a rectangular block of cells by giving the labels in the upper left-hand corner and in the lower right-hand corner of the block. The two cell labels are separated by a special symbol such as a colon or a series of periods. If both labels lie in the same row, the entire block will lie in that row. Likewise, if both labels lie in the same column, the entire block will lie in that column.

Figure 7-5 illustrates ranges. The range B1:D3 refers to the block containing the nine cells B1, B2, B3, C1, C2, C3, D1, D2, and D3. The range A1:A4 refers to the block containing the four cells A1, A2, A3, and A4; this block lies entirely in column A.

A function specifies a calculation for the computer to carry out. To distinguish function names from other symbols that can appear in formulas, the name of a function often starts with a special symbol, such as @. Two common functions are @SUM, which adds up the values in a range of cells, and @AVERAGE, which computes the average of the values in a range of cells. Following the function name and enclosed in parentheses are one or more *parameters* that specify cells whose values will be used in the calculation. Parameters often specify ranges of cells.

For instance, in our example spreadsheet the formula for cell D7 is

    D2 + D3 + D4 + D5

We could get the same result by writing

    @SUM(D2:D5)

which instructs the program to compute the sum of the values in cells D2 through D5. As long as only four cells are involved, it does not matter which way we write the formula. But if we needed to add a hundred values instead of just four, the @SUM function would prevent us from having to write an extremely lengthy formula.

In general, functions automatically skip blank cells. Thus, the ranges specified in formulas can include blank cells, allowing us to leave room for additional data that we might need to enter later.

◥ **Exercise 7-3** Use functions to compute the largest, smallest, and average values for one of the columns of your spreadsheet. ◥

Saving, Loading, and Printing

A spreadsheet resides in main memory while it is being manipulated by the spreadsheet program. To retain the spreadsheet for later use, we must save it in a disk file, which we can do by means of a command to the spreadsheet program. Like text being manipulated by a word processor, a spreadsheet should be saved frequently because a power failure or a computer malfunction will cause all changes made since the last save to be lost.

At any time we can request a spreadsheet program to load a new spreadsheet from a disk file. The spreadsheet that was previously in memory will be lost, so we must make sure to save it before loading a new spreadsheet. We usually begin a spreadsheet session by loading the spreadsheet with which we are currently working.

A spreadsheet can be printed in two forms, both of which are illustrated in Figures 7-6 and 7-7. In the form shown in Figure 7-6, the values in a specified range of cells are printed exactly as they appear on the screen. This form of printout allows us to convert a spreadsheet into a printed report that can be passed on to others who might be interested in the data and the results of the calculations.

The form of printout illustrated in Figure 7-7 lists the nonblank cells of the spreadsheet and gives the label, value, or formula that was entered for each one. This form of printout is useful for checking the formulas and for showing someone else how to set up a spreadsheet for a particular problem. It cannot be used to display the results of calculations carried out with the spreadsheet, however, because the formulas themselves are printed rather than the values calculated by the formulas.

All spreadsheet programs will produce the form of printout in Figure 7-6; not all will produce the form in Figure 7-7.

The printout produced by a spreadsheet program can be stored in a disk file, from which it can be imported into (read by) another program, such as a word processor. Thus a table created with a spreadsheet program can be inserted in a report being written with a word processor. Integrated programs that provide both spreadsheet analysis and word processing make it particularly easy to transfer data between a spreadsheet and a document.

FIGURE 7-6
In this printout of the spreadsheet in Figure 7-2, the labels and values in a specified range of cells (here the entire spreadsheet) are printed exactly as they appear on the screen. In this way the spreadsheet is converted into a printed report.

	Quantity	Unit Price	Sales
Typewriter	15	$528.79	$7931.85
Cash Register	10	$315.95	$3159.50
Executive Desk	7	$424.95	$2974.65
Conference Table	25	$279.95	$6998.75
		Total Sales:	$21064.75

```
B1 = "Quanity
C1 = "Unit Price
D1 = "Sales
A2 = "Typewriter
B2 = 15
C2 = 528.79
D2 = +B2 * C2
A3 = "Cash Register
B3 = 10
C3 = 315.95
D3 = +B3 * C3
A4 = "Executive Desk
B4 = 7
C4 = 424.95
D4 = +B4 * C4
A5 = "Conference Table
B5 = 25
C5 = 279.95
D5 = +B5 * C5
C7 = "Total Sales:
D7 = +D2 + D3 + D4 + D5
```

FIGURE 7-7
This form of printout, which shows the label, value, or formula in each nonblank cell, is useful for checking the formulas or for showing someone else how to set up a spreadsheet for a particular problem. Not all spreadsheet programs will produce this form of printout.

◣ **Exercise 7-4** Print out a copy of the spreadsheet created in previous exercises. ◥

◣ EDITING

Editing operations allow a spreadsheet to be modified by changing labels, values, and constants, and by erasing, inserting, deleting, moving, and copying cells and ranges of cells.

Editing and Erasing

When the cursor is positioned on a cell, the label, value, or formula for the cell appears in the communications area. The label, value, or formula can be edited word-processor style by moving a cursor (not the same one that marks the active cell) over the line and inserting, deleting, and overtyping characters as needed. When the line has been edited to our satisfaction, pressing the Enter or Return key will enter a label or value in the active cell or attach a formula to it.

Erasing a cell returns it to the blank state in which it contains no value at all and is ignored by functions such as @SUM and @AVERAGE. We can specify either a single cell or a range of cells to be erased. As with any command that destroys data, we must be careful to avoid inadvertently erasing cells whose contents we wish to retain.

```
A:C5: [W11] +"   "&@STRING(C7,0)&" YEARS" ; String formula which ties into teEDIT
+"   "&@STRING(C7,0)&" YEARS" ; String formula which ties into term of loan.
    Note that this value is bounded by a lower limit of 2 and an upper limit of
100, due to the formulas which prints the hardcopy report._
```

A	A	B	C	D	E	F
1						
2						
3				------- MONTHLY PAYMENT -------		
4	LOAN AMOUNT	INTEREST	TERM:			
5		RATE	20 YEARS	25 YEARS	30 YEARS	35 YEARS
6						
7						
8	$100,000	9.00%	$900	$839	$805	$784
9		9.25%	$916	$856	$823	$803
10		9.50%	$932	$874	$841	$822
11		9.75%	$949	$891	$859	$841
12		10.00%	$965	$909	$878	$860
13		10.25%	$982	$926	$896	$879
14		10.50%	$998	$944	$915	$898
15		10.75%	$1,015	$962	$933	$918
16		11.00%	$1,032	$980	$952	$937
17						
18	$125,000	9.00%	$1,125	$1,049	$1,006	$980
19		9.25%	$1,145	$1,070	$1,028	$1,003
20		9.50%	$1,165	$1,092	$1,051	$1,027
21		9.75%	$1,186	$1,114	$1,074	$1,051
22		10.00%	$1,206	$1,136	$1,097	$1,075
23		10.25%	$1,227	$1,158	$1,120	$1,099

2D_PAYMT.WK3

Lotus 1-2-3 spreadsheet showing how the monthly payment for a loan varies with the amount of the loan, the interest rate, and the term.

Inserting, Deleting, and Moving

Blank rows and columns can be inserted to make room for new data, the need for which was perhaps not anticipated when the spreadsheet was originally set up. When a new column is inserted, all the following columns are moved right to make room. For example, if a new column is inserted after column C, then the new column becomes column D, the former column D becomes column E, the former column E becomes column F, and so on. Likewise, when a new row is inserted, all the following rows are moved down to make room.

We can delete rows and columns to eliminate parts of the spreadsheet that we have decided are no longer needed. When a column is deleted, the following columns are moved to the left to eliminate the gap left by the deletion. When a row is deleted, the following rows are moved up to eliminate the gap.

We must keep in mind that a row will be deleted all the way across the spreadsheet and a column will be deleted all the way down. Frequently, separate tables are placed side by side or one above the other on the same spreadsheet. In deleting a row or column from one table, we must make sure that we are not accidentally deleting a row or column from another table on the same spreadsheet.

When a row or column is inserted, some rows, columns, and cells must be moved to make room, and as a result they receive new labels. Formulas are automatically adjusted to reflect the new labels. For example, suppose a new column is inserted after column C. The cell reference C5 remains unchanged, since column C is not moved. The reference D7, however, is changed to E7 because column D had to be moved to column

E so that the newly inserted column could be labeled D. Likewise, the insertion caused column E to become column F, column F to become column G, and so on. Thus the range A4:F7 is changed to A4:G7 since column F had to be moved but column A did not. Note that the range A4:G7 contains part of the newly inserted column.

Some spreadsheet programs allow the entries in a range of cells to be moved from one part of the spreadsheet to another. The cells whose entries are moved are left blank after the move. The previous contents of the cells in the destination area are replaced by the entries that were moved. Thus any labels, values, or formulas previously stored in the destination area are lost. You must always be careful that a block move does not accidentally overwrite any entries that you wish to retain.

Copying

Copying allows the contents of a cell to be replicated throughout a given range. Although labels and values sometimes can be usefully copied, the most important application of copying is for formulas. Frequently many cells require identical or similar formulas, which would be extremely tedious to enter individually.

Let's return to our example in Figures 7-2 through 7-4. The sales value in cell D2 is calculated as the product of the quantity in cell B2 and the unit price in cell C2. Thus the formula associated with cell D2 is

    B2 * C2

Now consider the sales value in cell D3. This is calculated as the product of the quantity in cell B3 and the unit price in cell C3. Thus the formula associated with cell D3 is

    B3 * C3

Likewise, the formula for cell D4 is

    B4 * C4

and the formula for cell D5 is

    B5 * C5

We see that the formulas for cells D2 through D5 have the same form but are not identical. Each formula refers to columns B and C. But the formula in row 2 refers to cells in row 2, the formula in row 3 refers to cells in row 3, and so on.

Normally, when a formula is copied, we want to adjust the row and column labels to reflect its new position. If a formula is moved down by one row, each row number in the formula should increased by one; if a formula is moved to the right by one column, each column label should be changed to refer to the next column to the right.

Thus we can enter the formula

    B2 * C2

in cell D2 and copy it to all cells in the range D3:D5. The row numbers will be adjusted appropriately in each copy. If there were a hundred entries in the sales column instead of only four, the ability to copy and adjust formulas would be essential rather than merely convenient.

Relative and Absolute References

Let's look in a bit more detail at the principles according to which cell references are adjusted when a formula is copied. In a formula, references such as B2 and C2 are called *relative references* since they are interpreted relative to the cell containing the formula. If the formula is in cell D2, then B2 is taken to represent "the cell in the same row as and two columns to the left of the cell containing the formula." Likewise, C2 is taken to represent "the cell in the same row as and one column to the left of the cell containing the formula." If the formula is copied to a new cell, the relative cell designations remain the same although the actual cell labels change. Thus if the formula

        B2 * C2

were copied to cell F9, the copy would be changed to

        D9 * E9

In the copy, D9 (like B2 in the original) refers to the cell in the same row and two columns to the left of the cell containing the formula, and E9 (like C2 in the original) refers to the cell in the same row and one column to the left.

A cell reference that does not change when a cell is copied is called an *absolute reference*. We designate a row or column reference as absolute by preceding the label with a special sign, typically a dollar sign. Thus B2 always refers to the cell at the intersection of column B and row 2 since both the column and row references are absolute. In $B2, the column reference is absolute, but the row reference is relative and will change if the formula is copied to a cell in a different row. Likewise, in B$2 the row reference is absolute, but the column reference is relative and will change if the formula is copied to a cell in a different column.

◣ **Exercise 7-5** Add a new result column to your spreadsheet (it can duplicate an existing column if there are no more reasonable results to be calculated). Enter the formulas in the new result column as follows: enter a formula in the uppermost cell that is to display a calculated value and then copy the formula to the remaining cells in the column. Use relative references so that the references will be adjusted appropriately when the formula is copied. ◥

FORMATTING

Printed copies of a spreadsheet are often used to communicate data and results in tabular form. The formatting features of spreadsheet programs help us to achieve a neat, clear layout for our tables and to present numerical data in accepted formats.

Most spreadsheet programs can display numerical data in the following formats:

Format	Application	Example
Integer	Whole numbers	123456
General Fixed	Numbers with decimal places	4.0579
Currency	Amounts of money	$345.22
Scientific	Technical applications	3.5E+25

Integer format, which does not provide for decimal places, is used only for whole numbers. *General format* displays a number as accurately as possible within the available width of the cell. *Fixed format* is similar to general format except that the number of decimal places is fixed by the user rather than being chosen by the program. With fixed format, the number of decimal places displayed in a cell is always the same; with general format, the number of decimal places can vary with the value stored in the cell. *Currency format* is essentially fixed format with the

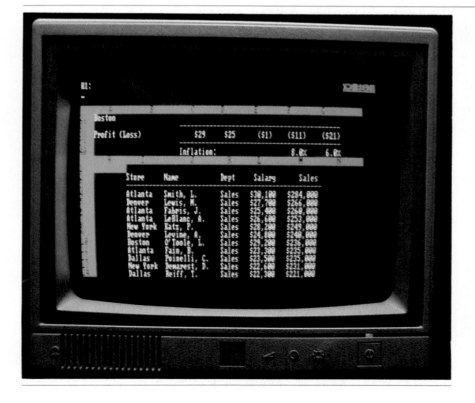

Many spreadsheet programs allow parts of more than one spreadsheet to appear on the screen at the same time.

numbers preceded by a dollar sign. Also, negative numbers in currency format are placed in parentheses rather than being preceded by a minus sign. *Scientific format*, which we will not discuss in detail here, allows very large and very small numbers to be displayed within the confines of a cell.* For some spreadsheet programs, general format will change automatically to scientific format for numbers that are too large or too small to be displayed accurately otherwise.

For labels, the main formatting question is *alignment*. With left alignment, the label is positioned in its cell as far to the left as possible; with right alignment, the label is positioned as far to the right as possible; with centering, the label is centered in its cell. Column headings are often centered, although left alignment sometimes looks best when the column contains alphabetic data (labels), and right alignment sometimes looks best when the column contains numerical data. Labels other than column headings are usually aligned on the left.

Some spreadsheet programs provide a *continuous format* that allows a long string of characters, such as a title, to extend over as many columns as needed. This prevents the user from having to break a long string into pieces that will fit into adjacent columns. If the widths of some columns are later changed, the manner in which the long string is apportioned among the columns will be adjusted automatically.

Spreadsheet programs provide commands for setting the display formats of cells and ranges of cells. When the spreadsheet program begins execution, it establishes a *default format* that applies to all cells for which no other format has been explicitly specified. The default format can be changed by the user. A typical default format would be general format for numbers and left alignment for labels.

Frequently, the same format is specified for all entries in a row or column. If the entries in a column represent amounts of money, for example, currency format might be selected; if they represent whole numbers, integer format might be selected. Sometimes a different format is selected for one or more entries in a column. For example, one might use fixed format (no dollar sign) for most of the entries in a column but currency format (with a dollar sign) for the first entry in the column and for the total at the foot of the column. The number of decimal places could be set to two for the entire column.

The widths of the columns can be adjusted to allow each column to hold data items of the desired size. The spreadsheet program establishes a default width, which can be changed by the user. The default width can be overridden by setting the widths of some columns individually.

Column widths can be changed after data has been entered, but one should be aware of some problems that can arise. With general format, reducing the width of a column may reduce the accuracy with which a value is displayed or require an automatic switch to scientific format. With other formats, reducing the width may make it impossible to display the value in the cell, causing an error. (The spreadsheet program usually fills

---

*In 3.5E+25, the E+25 indicates that the decimal point is to be moved 25 places to the right, adding zeros as necessary. Thus 3.5E+25 stands for 35,000,000,000,000,000,000,000,000.

a cell with repetitions of some error symbol, such as * or #, if the value stored in the cell cannot be displayed.) Reducing column widths can cause some characters of a label not to be displayed. If the user has manually broken a long character string into parts that will fit into adjacent columns (rather than using the continuous format), reducing column widths will lose characters and increasing column widths will introduce extraneous spaces.

The example spreadsheet in Figure 7-2 illustrates several formatting features. The column headings in row 1 are centered; all other labels are aligned on the left. Integer format is used for the numerical entries in column B; currency format is used for the numerical entries in columns C and D. The number of decimal places has been left as two, which was the default setting when the spreadsheet program was started. Columns B and D have the default width of 10 characters. The width of column A, however, was increased to 20 characters to make room for the column entries. The width of column C was increased to 14 characters to make room for the column heading and for the label "Total Sales:".

◣ CONSOLIDATING MULTIPLE SPREADSHEETS

Frequently, a complex problem or report can be broken into smaller parts, each of which can be handled by a separate spreadsheet. The breakdown is often along the lines of company organization: each department solves the part of the problem or produces the part of the report that applies to its activities. The figures arrived at by the various departments must then be consolidated onto a single spreadsheet that provides the desired information for the entire company. To handle this kind of situation, most

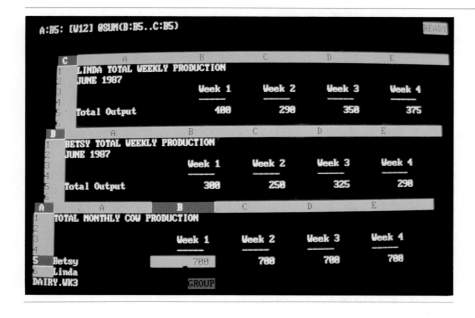

A three-dimensional spreadsheet is displayed as a series of ordinary spreadsheets arranged one behind the other.

spreadsheet programs provide several means for transferring information from one spreadsheet to another.

Values can be copied from one spreadsheet to another. Typically the source spreadsheet is on disk and the target spreadsheet is in main memory. The user specifies the cells of the source spreadsheet whose values will be copied and the cells of the target spreadsheet in which the values will be placed. Incoming values replace the previous values in target cells, so the user must be careful not to overwrite important data when copying from one spreadsheet to another.

Values from one spreadsheet can be arithmetically added to values on another, a process sometimes referred to as *merging*. Merging is similar to copying except that incoming values do not replace the values in the target cells but are added to them. If a target cell is blank, the incoming value is simply stored in it. Suppose that a single target spreadsheet is merged with a number of other spreadsheets. If a target cell was initially blank, then after the mergings it will contain the sum of values obtained from the other spreadsheets.

Certain target cells can be permanently *linked* to source cells on another spreadsheet. Whenever the target spreadsheet is loaded, the values in the source cells will be automatically copied to the target cells. (The source spreadsheets must be available to the system on disk, of course.) Linking is useful when spreadsheets are subject to frequent change. It assures that one is always working with the latest version of any figures that originate on other spreadsheets.

TEMPLATES

Writing the formulas for a spreadsheet often requires technical knowledge in such areas as engineering, economics, finance, and accounting. Spreadsheets users, however, are frequently managers and office workers without specialized technical training. Thus we often need for a specialist to produce a *template*, a spreadsheet with the labels and formulas filled in. Given a template for a particular problem, all the user has to do is fill in the input data for the problem and watch the answers magically appear.

Faced with a template, the user is apt to be confused as to which cells are for input values and which are for calculated results. Accidentally storing an input value in a result cell would be disastrous since the input value would replace a formula, which would prevent future calculations from being carried out properly. To prevent this problem, the template designer can *lock* or protect certain cells, preventing their contents from being routinely modified. All cells containing labels and formulas are usually locked; cells containing values are locked if the values should not be changed by the user. Some programs require the user to supply a password before changing the contents of a locked cell. Others just require that the cell be first unlocked with a special command, thus assuring that the change is not made accidentally.

Most spreadsheet programs provide a command key that will move the cursor to the next unlocked cell. Pressing this key repeatedly will step the user through just those cells into which input data can be entered. Locked cells are passed over automatically.

Some cells may be used only in the spreadsheet's internal calculations. The user neither enters data into them or makes use of results displayed in them. Such cells should be *hidden* so that the user does not have to worry about them. For some spreadsheets, all the cells in a column can be hidden by setting the column width to zero.

The part of a spreadsheet into which data is entered can be arranged as a form that can be filled in conveniently by the user. The cells into which values are to be entered constitute the "blanks" of the form; adjoining labels describe the data that is to go into the blanks. The key that moves the cursor to the next unlocked cell steps from one blank to the next.

As spreadsheets have become more and more widely used, errors in spreadsheet formulas have become an ever increasing problem. It is estimated that a substantial percentage of the spreadsheets now in use contain errors. Designers of spreadsheets and templates are being cautioned to spend more time checking formulas and using test cases to verify that the formulas are producing correct results. Users will find it prudent not to rely blindly on templates but to check their accuracy with test data for which the correct results are known

◣ ADVANCED FUNCTIONS

Most spreadsheet programs simplify writing formulas by providing a variety of advanced functions. Mathematical functions include most of the functions that would be found on a scientific calculator, such as logarithmic and trigonometric functions. Statistical functions compute such statistical parameters as average and standard deviation. Financial functions carry out complex financial calculations such as those for net present value and internal rate of return.

A table-look-up function will look up values in a table. For example, a portion of a spreadsheet can be set up as a tax table, which gives for each tax bracket the base amount and tax rate to be used in calculating income tax. With the aid of a table-look-up function, we can look up a taxable-income value in the table and extract the corresponding base amount and tax rate. These can then be used in a formula for calculating income tax.

Conditions and *logical functions* provide spreadsheet formulas with a decision making capability akin to that provided by selection constructions in programming languages. The formula

```
B1 = B2
```

is an example of a condition. When its value is calculated, the computer checks to see if the values in cells B1 and B2 are equal. If they are, the formula yields the value 1, which represents *true*. If the values in question are not equal, the formula yields the value 0, which represents *false*.

Conditions are used in logical functions such as @IF. When the value of the formula

```
@IF(B1 = B2, A3 + A4, A3 − A4)
```

is calculated, the spreadsheet program first finds the value of the condition B1 = B2. If the condition is *true*, the value produced by the first formula, A3 + A4, is returned as the value of the @IF function. If the condition is *false*, the value produced by the second formula, A3 − A4, is returned as the value of the @IF function. Thus the condition selects which formula will be used to calculate the value of the @IF function.

At least one recent program allows users to define their own functions in terms of existing functions and operations. With the aid of user-defined functions, a full-fledged programming language can be incorporated in a spreadsheet program. Conditions and logical functions provide selection. Repetition is provided by recursion, a technique by which a function is defined partially in terms of itself.

CHARTING

The meaning of data and results is often easier to see when they are presented as *charts* rather than as tables of numbers. Charts are particularly useful when your calculations are to be used as the basis of a printed report or an oral presentation. Consequently, some spreadsheet programs and integrated programs will automatically produce charts from spreadsheet data.

Most charting programs offer line graphs, bar charts, and pie charts, each in several variations. You choose the kind of chart to be created and select the data items on the spreadsheet that are to be charted. You can then enter additional information such as a title, a subtitle, and labels for the horizontal and vertical axes. On request, the program will create a

A Lotus 1-2-3 display showing a spreadsheet and a chart produced from it.

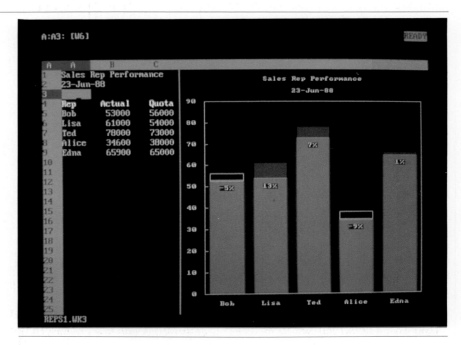

A charting program displays a chart that it has just finished printing.

legend showing the significance of the different colors or patterns of shading used for bars or pie segments. When you have specified all the information to appear in the chart, the program will draw it on the screen for your approval. Several tries at specifying the chart may be needed to get it to look exactly the way you want.

Charts can be drawn with plotters or printed out with dot-matrix or laser printers. Some plotters and dot-matrix printers can print in multiple colors. Laser printers give very high quality charts, but current laser printers print only in black and white.

We often wish to put charts on slides that can be shown during oral presentations. Slides can be made in several ways:

- There are special cameras designed for photographing video displays; you can have the program draw the chart on the screen and use such a camera to photograph it.

- There are peripherals called *film recorders* that record images directly on photographic film. The film is then developed and the slides mounted in the usual way.

- There are companies that will make slides from disk files produced by popular charting programs.

Summary

An electronic spreadsheet combines automatic calculation with a convenient format for presenting data and results. Spreadsheets are particularly useful for ''what if'' type calculations in which one wishes to explore the effect on the results of various changes in the input data.

A spreadsheet is composed of cells, which are arranged in rows and columns. The screen serves as a window through which a portion of the spreadsheet can be viewed. The active cell, the one on which the program's attention is currently focussed, is highlighted. This highlighted block serves as a cursor that can be moved about on the screen with the cursor control keys. Attempting to move the cursor off the screen drags the screen window over the spreadsheet (scrolling).

For each cell the user can enter a numerical value, an alphabetic label, or a formula. A value or label appears in the cell in exactly the form entered by the user. A formula, however, is used to calculate the value that appears in the cell from values appearing in other cells. Recalculation is the process of carrying out all the calculations called for by formulas.

Editing operations allow the contents of cells to be modified or erased. Rows and columns can be inserted and deleted, and the contents of a range of cells can be moved from one part of the spreadsheet to another. The contents of one cell can be copied to all the cells in a particular range. Copying is particularly important for formulas since frequently many cells must have the same or similar formulas.

Most references to cells in formulas are relative references; the actual cells referred to change when the formula is copied. The user must insert special symbols in a reference to produce an absolute reference that remains unchanged when the cell is copied.

Capabilities for formatting allow the user to adjust the widths of columns and specify the exact form in which labels and numbers will be displayed.

Frequently, a spreadsheet contains values obtained from other spreadsheets. Most programs provide facilities for transferring values from one spreadsheet to another. A particularly useful feature is linking, which causes values obtained from other spreadsheets to be updated automatically each time the target spreadsheet is loaded.

Templates provide the spreadsheet layout and formulas needed for a particular problem. Provisions for locking cells containing labels and formulas help prevent the user from inadvertently damaging the template. Provisions for hiding cells allow the template designer to conceal cells about which the user does not need to know. A key that automatically moves the cursor to the next unlocked cell helps the user step quickly through those cells for which data must be entered.

A variety of advanced functions makes it easy to write formulas for complex statistical, financial, and scientific calculations.

Charting programs make it easy to create charts from spreadsheet data; the charts can be included in printed reports or made into slides for showing during oral presentations.

Vocabulary Review

absolute reference	cell	default format
active cell	chart	default width
alignment	column	film recorder
automatic	condition	fixed format
recalculation	continuous format	formula
border	currency format	function

general format
hidden cell
integer format
iterated calculation
label
linked spreadsheets
locked cell
logical function

macro
macro definition
  language
merging
natural recalculation
  order
parameter
range

recalculation
relative reference
row
scientific format
template
value

For Further Reading

Stewart, William. "Analyzing Data from All the Angles." *PC Magazine*, 27 October 1987, pp. 141–152.

Taylor, Jared, et al. "Challenging 1-2-3 on Price and Power." *PC Magazine*, 27 October 1987, pp. 94–138.

Review Questions

1 Sketch the appearance of the display when the cursor is positioned at the upper left corner of an empty spreadsheet. In your sketch, identify cells A4, B1, and D7.

2 What purpose is served by the border of a spreadsheet display?

3 What is the active cell?

4 What highlighted area serves as a cursor?

5 Describe scrolling for a spreadsheet and compare it with the corresponding operation for a word processor.

6 What is the purpose of the communications area?

7 Distinguish values, labels, and formulas.

8 Describe the calculation carried out by each of the following two formulas:

```
B2 * B3
D2 + D3 + D4 + D5
```

9 Describe natural-order recalculation.

10 What is a circular reference? An iterative calculation?

11 What is a range? What cells are referred to by each of the following ranges: A3:A11, B2:F2, and C4:F9?

12 What is a function? What calculation is performed by the formula @SUM(B1:B6)?

13 Describe the editing operations that can be carried out on a spreadsheet.

14 Describe four formats in which numbers can be displayed.

15 Describe three options for aligning labels within cells. What format is appropriate for very long labels such as titles?

16 What precautions must be observed when changing the widths of columns that already contain data?

17 Describe three features that are useful for consolidating multiple spreadsheets. Which one is particularly useful when some of the spreadsheets involved are subject to frequent change?

18 Why are templates useful?

19 For what purposes are cells locked or hidden? Why may a spreadsheet be arranged to simulate a form?

20 Describe some types of calculations that can be carried out with the aid of advanced functions. What advanced functions provide spreadsheets with a capability for selection?

21 Describe how charts can be produced from spreadsheet data.

Topics for Discussion

1 When you create a spreadsheet or spreadsheet template, you are programming the computer to carry out certain calculations. In short, creating spreadsheets is a form of programming. Yet many people who work with spreadsheets, even very complex ones, will have nothing to do with conventional programming languages. Discuss.

2 It is feared that many existing spreadsheets contain errors that cause them to perform their calculations incorrectly. What are some steps that individuals and companies can take to help assure the accuracy of their spreadsheets? How can a user try to check the accuracy of a spreadsheet template prepared by someone else?

DATABASE MANAGEMENT

INTRODUCTION

One of the most important applications of computers is storing and organizing the masses of facts and figures that once bulged the filing cabinets of even the most modest organization. With current technology, we store such data on disks in the form of *files*, which are named collections of data that can be read from and written to via the computer's operating system. A collection of related files, such as those containing the financial records of a company, is called a *database*. Recall that we previously encountered the term *database* in our discussion of computer-aided software engineering, where we considered the database containing all information relevant to a software development project.

Although the operating system can transfer data to and from files, we often need other programs to effectively manage the information stored in files and databases. A *file manager* is a program that enables the user to manipulate the data stored in a single file. A *database management system (DBMS)* is one or more programs for managing the data in a possibly large collection of files. A file manager is usually used interactively, responding immediately to user commands by displaying data on the screen or printing it on the printer. A database management system not only can be used interactively, but also can be used by other programs, such as accounting, billing, and payroll programs. Instead of reading and writing files directly via the operating system, these applications programs call upon the database management system to store and retrieve data.

FIELDS, RECORDS, FILES, AND RELATIONS

A file is a collection of *records*, each of which pertains to a single person, place, or thing. In a file of customer accounts, for example, each record

Mainframes often store databases on disk packs using disk drives such as the ones shown here. Stacked atop the drives are disk packs and disk-pack covers; the latter are removed when the disk packs are inserted into the drives.

contains the account of one customer. Likewise, each record in an employee file provides information about one employee.

A record, in turn, is broken down into *fields*, each of which contains one data value. Each field also has a *field name*, which we can use to refer to the data stored in that field. We can think of a record as a form in which the fields are the blanks to be filled in and the field names are the labels that tell what kind of information is to go into each blank.

For example, an employee record might give the employee's ID number, name, division in which employed, and hourly pay rate. The following is a typical employee record:*

Field Name	Value
ID_Number	139425
Last_Name	Smith
Division	Automotive
Pay_Rate	14.29

The field names identify the fields and indicate the significance of the data stored in each field. The field names are the same for every record in the file and so have to be stored only once for the entire file. The values provide the data pertinent to a particular employee. Since each record refers to a different employee, the values will generally be different for each record.

We can visualize a file as a table whose rows correspond to records and whose columns correspond to fields. In database theory, such a table is called a *relation*. Figure 8-1 shows the relation Employee, which contains eight employee records. The first row of Employee contains the record for Smith, the second row contains the record for Jones, the third row contains the record for Roberts, and so on. The first column corresponds to the

Employee

ID_Number	Last_Name	Division	Pay_Rate
139425	Smith	Automotive	14.29
276931	Jones	Automotive	9.45
342635	Roberts	Aerospace	29.93
398762	Young	Electronics	10.35
409112	Clark	Aerospace	7.69
783215	Sims	Electronics	8.97
864732	Roth	Automotive	35.46
993812	Thompson	Aerospace	21.95

FIGURE 8-1
The relation Employee. The rows correspond to records; the columns correspond to fields. The primary key is ID Number; each value in the ID_Number column uniquely identifies the employee to whom the information in the corresponding row applies.

---

*An actual employee record would, of course, contain much more information, such as first and middle names, address, social security number, and information related to taxes and fringe benefits. The underscores in field names, such as in ID_Number, serve to link two or more English words into a single field name. Computer languages often use underscores where hyphens would be used in English because hyphens are too easily confused with minus signs.

Last_Name	Division
Smith	Automotive
Jones	Automotive
Roberts	Aerospace
Young	Electronics
Clark	Aerospace
Sims	Electronics
Roth	Automotive
Thompson	Aerospace

FIGURE 8-2
The derived relation obtained from Employee by a projection operation selecting the Last_Name and Division columns.

ID_Number field, the second column corresponds to the Last_Name field, and so on.

A database that is organized as a set of relations is called a *relational database*. Relations are now the most popular method of database organization; indeed, *relational* has become a buzzword that is applied to any database management system that even remotely qualifies (and to some that do not). Because of the simplicity and clarity of relational-database concepts, we will find use for them throughout the chapter, even when discussing databases with other organizations.

Simple database management systems usually store each relation in a separate file. More sophisticated systems, however, can create a relation out of data stored in several files. This allows the logical organization of the data—the relations perceived and manipulated by the user—to be considerably different from the physical organization—the organization of the data into disk files. The physical organization can be changed substantially without affecting the logical organization, a property known as *data independence*.

Each relation has a field (or group of fields), called the *primary key*, whose value uniquely identifies the *entity* (person, place, or thing) to which a particular record applies. In our example, the primary key is ID_Number; each ID number identifies one and only one employee. The primary key is used to locate information about a particular entity. For example, if we want to know the pay rate of employee number 409112, we locate the employee record whose ID_Number field contains 409112 and obtain the hourly pay rate, $7.69, from the Pay_Rate field.

The primary key can consist of more than one field. For example, a cash register in a store may assign a different number to each transaction; different cash registers may assign the same numbers, however. Thus to identify a transaction uniquely, we must give both the cash-register number and the transaction number; taken together, these two fields are the primary key of a transaction record.

All the information in a record should be about the entity identified by the primary key; we must not try to cram information about more than one entity into the same record. This means that the values of all nonkey fields should depend on the value of the primary key. If the primary key contains more than one field, the values of the nonkey fields should depend on the entire primary key, not on just some of the fields making it up. Nor should the value of a nonkey field depend on the value another nonkey field. These restrictions are sometimes summarized by saying that the values of nonkey fields should depend on the *key, the whole key, and nothing but the key*. Relations that satisfy these restrictions are said to be in *third normal form*.

The *base relations*—those permanently stored in the database—should always be in third normal form; if they are not, deleting information about

FIGURE 8-3
The derived relation obtained from Employee by a restriction operation selecting the rows for which the value in the Division column is Aerospace.

ID_Number	Last_Name	Division	Pay_Rate
342635	Roberts	Aerospace	29.93
409112	Clark	Aerospace	7.69
993812	Thompson	Aerospace	21.95

ID_Number	Last_Name	Division	Pay_Rate
139425	Smith	Automotive	14.29
864732	Roth	Automotive	35.46

FIGURE 8-4
The derived relation obtained from Employee by a restriction operation selecting the rows for which the value in the Division column is Automotive and the value in the Pay_Rate column is greater than 10.

one entity may cause information about another entity to be deleted accidentally (because we have crammed information about more than one entity into each record). When we need a relation containing information about more than one entity, we use a *derived relation*, which is a relation created from the base relations by database operations.

OPERATIONS ON RELATIONAL DATABASES

It may happen that one of the permanently stored base relations contains exactly the information that we are looking for. More commonly, however, we must use database operations to create a derived relation containing the information we want. The basic operations on relational databases are *projection*, which selects certain columns from a relation; *restriction*, which selects certain rows from a relation; and *join*, which combines columns from different relations.

Projection

Often we are not interested in all the information in a relation. For example, we might want to know what division each employee works in, but we may not be interested in the ID numbers or pay rates. A projection operation allows us to select the particular columns in which we are interested. Figure 8-2 shows the derived relation constructed from the Employee relation by using a projection operation to select the Last_Name and Division columns.

Restriction

A restriction operation picks out those rows of a relation that satisfy a certain condition. For example, suppose we are only interested in employees of the Aerospace division. Figure 8-3 shows the derived relation obtained from Employee by restricting the rows to those containing Aerospace in the Division column.

We can require the rows to satisfy more complicated conditions involving values of more than one field. For example, suppose we are interested only in employees of the Automotive division who make more than ten dollars an hour. Figure 8-4 shows the derived relation obtained from Employee by restricting the value of Division to be Automotive and the value of Pay_Rate to be greater than 10.

Join

The join operation allows us to combine information stored in separate relations. For example, suppose our database also contains the relation

FIGURE 8-5

The relation Boss gives the manager of each division; the primary key of Boss is Division.

Boss

Division	Manager
Aerospace	Bligh
Automotive	Scrooge
Electronics	De Sade

Boss (Figure 8-5), which gives the manager of each division. We wish to find the name of each employee's manager. Neither Employee nor Boss by itself contains the desired information: Employee does not contain managers' names and Boss does not contain employees' names. To get the information we want, we have to pair off Employee and Boss records that refer to the same division.

Our first step is to join the Employee and Boss relations on the Division column. This means that we join the Employee and Boss records having the same entry in the Division field. Figure 8-6 shows the result, which contains columns of both Employee and Boss; for ease of reading, a double line separates the columns that were derived from Employee from those that were derived from Boss. Note that the entries in the two Division columns are the same since we only joined records that refer to the same division.

The relation in Figure 8-6 contains the names of both employees and managers, and so it can be used to determine the manager of each employee. It contains many columns that we do not need, however, so our second and last step is to use a projection operation to select the Last_ Name and Manager columns; Figure 8-7 shows the result, which lists the names of employees and their managers.

Queries

A request for information from a database management system is called a *query*; queries can be posed by interactive users and by applications programs. Queries are expressed in a *query language*; the database management system must translate requests in the query language into the projections, restrictions, and joins that will produce the desired result. The database management system is also responsible for *query optimization*— for choosing the sequence of database operations that gives the greatest

FIGURE 8-6

The result of joining the records of Employee to those of Boss subject to the requirement that two records be joined only if they have the same value in the Division column. The columns to the left of the double line come from Employee; those to the right come from Boss.

ID_Number	Last_Name	Division	Pay_Rate	Division	Manager
139425	Smith	Automotive	14.29	Automotive	Scrooge
276931	Jones	Automotive	9.45	Automotive	Scrooge
342635	Roberts	Aerospace	29.93	Aerospace	Bligh
398762	Young	Electronics	10.35	Electronics	De Sade
409112	Clark	Aerospace	7.69	Aerospace	Bligh
783215	Sims	Electronics	8.97	Electronics	De Sade
864732	Roth	Automotive	35.46	Automotive	Scrooge
993812	Thompson	Aerospace	21.95	Aerospace	Bligh

possible efficiency, so that the requested information can be returned as fast as possible.

◣ SQL

A database management system often provides a computer language in which we can express our instructions to the system. With interactive commands or programs written in this language, we retrieve data from the database, insert new data, update existing data, and delete data that is no longer needed. A database language also allows us to describe the structure of the relations in the database, something we need to do when designing a new database or extending an existing one.

In the past, each database management system provided its own database language; this was particularly true for microcomputer systems. In recent years, however, a standard has begun to emerge. *Structured Query Language (SQL,* pronounced ess-cue-ell or sequel*) is now widely used on mainframes and minicomputers. IBM plans to include SQL in the extended edition of its new OS/2 operating system (which will have built-in database management capabilities); this action will undoubtedly make SQL a de facto standard for microcomputers as well. Seeing the handwriting on the wall, many vendors of microcomputer database management systems are now converting their programs to use SQL.

In this section we will look at the elements of SQL. Our objective is not to master all the technicalities of SQL, but rather to get some feeling for how a database language can be used to define and manipulate the values stored in a database.

Query Expressions

SQL uses *query expressions* to construct derived relations. In interactive implementations of SQL, query expressions can be typed in at the keyboard, and the computer will display the derived relations. In noninteractive implementations, intended to be used by other programs rather than directly by the user, query expressions must be included in other SQL constructions that specify how the derived relations will be used. We will assume an interactive implementation so that we can consider query expressions by themselves, rather than as parts of more complex constructions.

The easiest way to understand query expressions is to see how to use them to carry out the relational operations that were described and illustrated in the preceding section. To illustrate the projection operation, for example, we constructed the relation in Figure 8-2 by selecting the Last_Name and Division columns from the relation Employee (Figure 8-1). We can describe this projection with the following SQL query expression:

---

*The language was formerly known as SEQUEL, for Structured English Query Language. A legal conflict caused the name to be changed to SQL, but many people still pronounce it *sequel.*

FIGURE 8-7
The result of a projection operation that selects the Last_Name and Manager columns from the relation in Figure 8-6.

Last_Name	Manager
Smith	Scrooge
Jones	Scrooge
Roberts	Bligh
Young	De Sade
Clark	Bligh
Sims	De Sade
Roth	Scrooge
Thompson	Bligh

```
SELECT  Last_Name, Division
FROM    Employee
```

We see that the query expression has two distinct parts, which are called clauses. A clause is usually named by the word that begins it, so we have a SELECT clause and a FROM clause. The SELECT clause states which columns will appear in the derived relation; the FROM clause tells which relations will supply the columns mentioned in the SELECT clause. Thus the preceding query expression tells the database management system to construct a derived relation by selecting the Last_Name and Division columns from the relation Employee.

We can easily specify any projection operation with a query expression. Thus

```
SELECT  ID_Number, Division, Pay_Rate
FROM    Employee
```

specifies a derived relation constructed from the ID_Number, Division, and Pay_Rate columns of Employee. Likewise, the query expression

```
SELECT  ID_Number
FROM    Employee
```

constructs a one-column relation that lists the ID numbers of all employees.

If we want all available columns to appear in the derived relation, we can use an asterisk in the SELECT clause instead of naming all the columns. Thus

```
SELECT  *
FROM    Employee
```

specifies a derived relation that contains all the columns of the Employee relation; that is, the derived relation is just a copy of Employee.

Exercise 8-1 Write a query expression to list the ID numbers and pay rates of all employees.

We recall that a restriction operation picks out rows that satisfy a given condition. To represent a restriction by a query expression, we need another clause, the WHERE clause, to give the condition that the selected rows must satisfy. For example, we constructed the derived relation in Figure 8-3 by taking those rows of Employee that had the value Aerospace in the Division column. We express this restriction in SQL as follows:

```
SELECT  *
FROM    Employee
WHERE   Division = 'Aerospace'
```

The SELECT clause says that all the columns of Employee are to be included in the derived relation; the WHERE clause says that the only rows to be included are those for which the value in the Division column is Aerospace.

When the name of a column appears in a condition, it stands for the value in that field. Also, nonnumeric values such as Aerospace are enclosed in single quotation marks (apostrophes) to prevent the data values from

The INGRES database management system is available for microcomputers, minicomputers, and mainframes; here it is shown running on both a laptop and a desktop computer. Note the plasma display on the laptop.

being confused with other words such as column names. Thus the condition

```
Division = 'Aerospace'
```

means that in each row of the derived relation the value in the Division column must be Aerospace.

We derived the relation in Figure 8-4 from Employee by taking only those rows that satisfied two conditions: the value in the Division column must be Automotive and the value in the Pay_Rate column must be greater than 10. In a query expression, the two conditions are joined by the logical connecting word AND (the symbol > means "is greater than"):

```
SELECT  *
FROM    Employee
WHERE   Division = 'Automotive'
AND     Pay_Rate > 10
```

Exercise 8-2 Write a query expression to retrieve the records of all employees of the Electronics division whose pay rate is less than $9.00 an hour. The symbol for "is less than" is <.

Joins are easily expressed using the clauses that we have already discussed. A join is usually followed by a projection to select the desired columns from the joined relations; in SQL, we can accomplish both the join and the projection with one query expression; the SELECT clause specifies the projection and the FROM and WHERE clauses specify the join.

To illustrate the join operation, we first derived the relation in Figure 8-6 by joining Employee and Boss in such a way that records would be joined only if they had the same value in their Division fields. We then derived the relation in Figure 8-7 by selecting the Last_Name and Manager columns from the result of the join. The following query expression accomplishes both the join and the projection:

```
SELECT  Last_Name, Manager
FROM    Employee, Boss
WHERE   Employee.Division = Boss.Division
```

When more than one relation is named in the FROM clause, the rows of all the relations named are joined in every possible way, without regard for the values in each row. Thus each of the eight rows of Employee would be joined, in turn, to each of the three rows of Boss, giving 8×3 or 24 joined rows. From the joined rows formed in this way, the WHERE clause picks out those that are actually of interest, which in this case are those that have the same entry in the two Division columns. Since we have two Division columns, we have to distinguish them in some way; Employee.Division refers to the Division column derived from Employee, and Boss.Division refers to the Division column derived from Boss. The condition

```
Employee.Division = Boss.Division
```

says that the values in the two Division columns have to be the same. The SELECT clause, as usual, specifies which columns are to be included in the final derived relation.

◤ **Exercise 8-3** Write a query expression to list the ID numbers, pay rates, and managers of all employees. ◣

Modifying Stored Data

Although the full name of SQL refers to it as a query language, it is actually far more, since it can be used for modifying stored data and for defining new relations as well as for posing queries. We now look very briefly at the three SQL operations that change the data stored in the database.

An INSERT operation inserts a new row in a relation; that is, it stores a new record in the database. For example, the operation

```
INSERT
INTO    Employee
VALUES ('532905', 'Burns', 'Automotive', 25.35)
```

inserts a new row into the relation Employee. The VALUES clause gives the row to be inserted; note that ID numbers are often treated as non-numeric data (because we do not do arithmetic with them), hence the single quotation marks around the ID number 532905.

Exercise 8-4 Write an SQL command to insert into the relation Boss a record for the Chemicals Division, whose manager is named Legree.

The following DELETE operation deletes the record for the employee with ID number 276931:

```
DELETE
FROM    Employee
WHERE   ID_Number = '276931'
```

Exercise 8-5 Write an SQL command to delete the records of all employees who make more than $25 an hour.

An UPDATE operation modifies some of the values stored in a relation. The following UPDATE operation gives a $5.25 an hour raise to everybody in the Automotive division:

```
UPDATE EMPLOYEE
SET     Pay_Rate = Pay_Rate + 5.25
WHERE   Division = 'Automotive'
```

The SET clause says that the new value in the Pay_Rate column should be the current value plus 5.25.

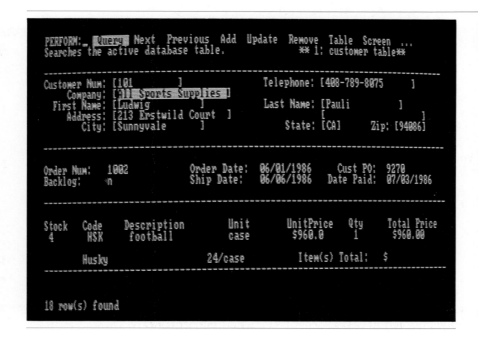

Screen display produced by the Informix-SQL database management system.

◥ **Exercise 8-6** Write an SQL command to give a $5.00 an hour raise to every employee who now makes less than $10.00 an hour. ◥

Data Definitions

A database language has two parts: a *data manipulation language* with which we can tell the system how to manipulate the stored data, and a *data definition language* with which we can describe the structure of the database. So far we have been working with SQL's data manipulation language. Now, we look very briefly at the data definition language by seeing how to define the structure of the Employee relation.

New relations are defined with the CREATE TABLE command. Since the complete command can be somewhat complicated, let's build up the information that it must contain item by item. The first step in defining the Employee relation is listing the names of its columns:

```
ID_Number
Last_Name
Division
Pay_Rate
```

Next, we have to say which columns contain nonnumeric data, such as 'Smith', and which contain numeric data, such as 29.95. Nonnumeric data is referred to as *character data* in SQL. Remembering that ID numbers are treated as character data, we get:

```
ID_Number CHARACTER
Last_Name CHARACTER
Division CHARACTER
Pay_Rate NUMERIC
```

In order for the system to know how much memory will be needed for each field, we must tell it the how many characters can be stored in a character field and how many digits can be stored in a numeric field. For a numeric field, we must also tell it how many of the digits are decimal places, so that arithmetic will be carried out correctly. Let's allow 6 characters for an ID number and 15 characters for a last name or a division name. For a pay rate we allow 4 digits, two of which are decimal places. This information is entered in the definition as follows:

```
ID_Number CHARACTER(6)
Last_Name CHARACTER(15)
Division CHARACTER(15)
Pay_Rate NUMERIC(4, 2)
```

Finally, we must identify which field is the all-important primary key. SQL allows data to be missing from some fields; when data is missing from a field we say that the field has a null value. The value of the primary key must always be present, however; the primary key must be NOT NULL. Also, each primary-key value must be UNIQUE; no two rows can have the same value for the primary key. We specify these two properties of the primary-key field as follows:*

```
ID_Number CHARACTER(6) NOT NULL UNIQUE
Last_Name CHARACTER(15)
Division CHARACTER(15)
Pay_Rate NUMERIC(4, 2)
```

We have now completely defined the structure of the Employee relation. To make our definition into an SQL CREATE TABLE command, we need only to add a few words and some punctuation:

```
CREATE TABLE Employee
  (ID_Number CHARACTER(6) NOT NULL UNIQUE,
   Last_Name CHARACTER(15),
   Division CHARACTER(15),
   Pay_Rate NUMERIC(4, 2))
```

The CREATE TABLE command defines the new relation Employee and orders the database management system to create it. The newly created relation will, of course, be empty until data is inserted into it with INSERT operations.

Exercise 8-7 Write a CREATE TABLE command to define the relation Boss. Allow 15 characters for both the division name and the name of the manager. The primary key of Boss is the name of the division.

Interfacing with Applications Programs

Some database management systems provide full-fledged programming languages; any application that uses the database has to be written in the database programming language. Other systems provide means whereby programs written in other languages (such as Cobol for business applications) can call on the database management system to store, retrieve, and modify data.

SQL systems follow the second course; SQL is not a full programming language, but is limited to database operations. To write an applications program using SQL, we must have some way of invoking SQL commands from other programming languages.

SQL takes advantage of the fact that most programming languages provide means for calling subroutines written in other languages. To provide database services to an applications program, the programmer writes a series of SQL statements (called a *module*) that define a subroutine (called a *procedure* in SQL) for every SQL operation the applications program needs to invoke. The applications program then calls the procedures as needed to query and manipulate the database.

---

*We follow standard SQL in specifying UNIQUE in the CREATE TABLE command, which is where it logically belongs; some popular implementations specify it elsewhere.

The programmer's task can be simplified considerably by using a preprocessor, an auxiliary language processor that translates an extended, nonstandard version of a programming language into the standard version. With the help of a preprocessor, a programmer can include SQL commands in programs written in some other language, say Cobol. The resulting programs are in a nonstandard version of Cobol and cannot be compiled by standard Cobol compilers. A preprocessor, however, can translate the nonstandard Cobol program into (1) a standard Cobol program that calls SQL procedures in the places where the programmer wrote SQL commands, and (2) an SQL module that defines the needed procedures. The Cobol program produced by the preprocessor can then be compiled with a standard Cobol compiler.

FILE MANAGERS AND FLAT-FILE DATABASES

A file manager works with a single file containing a single relation-like table. Such a file is often called a *flat-file database* because the data is stored in a single flat table rather than in the collection of tables required for a relational database. Of course, the file manager program can be used with different database files, but it can only work with one file at a time. There are no commands (such as the relational join) for coordinating data in different files.

A file manager is intended for interactive use only; it cannot be called on by applications programs as most database management systems can. It may be possible for other programs to use data from the file created by the file manager, but they will have to manipulate the data themselves— they cannot turn to the file manager for help.

There is considerable variation among file-manager programs. The features discussed in this section are typical of many file-manager programs; however, the exact features offered by a particular program, as well as the way those features are implemented, may not be exactly as discussed here.

Database management system in use at a baseball game.

Using a File Manager

A file manager normally displays the file as a table such as in Figure 8-1.* Of course, an actual data file will usually be much too large for the table to fit on the screen. Therefore, as with word processors and spreadsheet programs, the display screen serves as a window through which we can see a part of the much larger underlying table. As usual, this window can be moved about to view whatever part of the table we wish. Usually we will be moving it up and down to view different records. If, however,

---

*We will let some of our example relations do double duty as examples of flat-file databases. Note, however, that the underscores in the column names, which are required by SQL, are not usually required by file managers. In our discussion, then, we will refer to the ID_Number column in the figures as ID Number, and refer to the Pay_Rate column in the figures as Pay Rate.

the table is too wide for all the columns to fit on the screen, we may have to move the screen sideways to view the columns that we wish.

Some file managers display files in much the same form as spreadsheets. The column names appear across the top of the screen and are highlighted. Highlighted record numbers (row numbers) appear down the left side of the screen and can be used to refer to a specific record. A rectangular cursor, like that of a spreadsheet, highlights one field—the intersection of one row and one column. The value in the highlighted field can be edited by the user, or if the field is blank, a new value can be entered. The cursor can be moved about in the table at will, and the window will always tag along so as to keep the cursor on the screen. Some programs allow several windows on the screen so that several parts of the file can be viewed at the same time.

Most file managers also allow records to be displayed individually, rather than as a part of a table. Using Figure 8-1 as an example, the first record in the file might be displayed as:

```
Id Number: 139425
Last Name: Smith
 Division: Automotive
 Pay Rate: 14.29
```

The user can display any selected record in this format, and there are commands for moving forward to the next record or back to the previous one while retaining this form of display. The user can edit records in this form by moving a cursor to the desired field and making the necessary changes.

The single-record display form also can be used for data entry. For each record to be entered, the user is presented with a blank form with underlines or highlighted areas showing where values can be entered:

```
Id Number: _____
Last Name: _____
 Division: _____
 Pay Rate: __.__
```

The user moves from field to field filling in the blanks until all the data for the record has been typed in. When the user gives a command to enter the record, the file manager stores the new record in the database and presents the user with a new blank form for typing the next record.

Usually, users have complete freedom to lay out the single-record display form in any way that they wish. Thus, if the user had desired, the example record could be displayed as:

```
Id Number: 139425    Last Name: Smith
 Division: Automotive  Pay Rate: 14.29
```

or in any other format that the user happened to choose. All records will be displayed in the same format, however.

In creating a single-record display form, the user is actually defining the structure of the file. When the user wants to start a new file, the program presents a blank *form-design screen* on which the user can enter and position field names as desired. For each field the user indicates the

All the computer terminals in this office can access a database stored on the minicomputer in the foreground.

size and position of the area in which the corresponding data is to be entered. The user also specifies the type of data (such as numeric or non-numeric) to be entered in each field. The information entered in this way determines the structure of the records in the disk file as well as the way in which individual records and the entire table are displayed.

When the user poses a query to the file manager, it displays all the records satisfying the query. Methods of handling queries vary, but a very simple and elegant one is to treat the query operation as a restriction operation on the displayed table. All records that do not satisfy the query are hidden and do not show on the screen; the hidden records remain in the file, however, and can be redisplayed when the user wishes. The user can move about freely in the restricted table just as in the full table.

To pose a query, we have to state the conditions that the values certain fields must satisfy. Methods for stating queries vary, but a particularly straightforward one uses the single-record display. The program displays a blank form; instead of entering data values, however, the user enters a condition for each field whose values are to be restricted.

For example, suppose we wish to generate the table in Figure 8-4 from the table in Figure 8-1 by requiring that the value of the Division field be Automotive and that of the Pay Rate field be greater than 10. We enter these conditions in the Division and Pay Rate fields as follows:

```
Id Number:
Last Name:
 Division: = 'Automotive'
 Pay Rate: > 10
```

(Remember that > means "is greater than.") When the user indicates that all the conditions have been entered, the program acts on the query and modifies the display screen accordingly.

Some programs also allow selected columns to be hidden, thus allowing the user to apply a projection operation to the displayed table. With both projection and restriction at the user's disposal, it is easy make the screen display only the data in which the user is interested.

Some file managers allow the values of some fields to be specified by formulas, as in spreadsheets. The user cannot (and must not) enter values for those fields; the values of those fields are calculated automatically from the values entered in the other fields.

The file can be sorted on any field or combination of fields. For example, the table in Figure 8-1 is sorted on the ID number field; the records are arranged so that the ID numbers are in ascending order. Figure 8-8 shows the same table sorted on the Division and ID Number fields: the division names are in ascending order, and records with the same entry in the Division column are sorted so that their ID numbers are in ascending order. The overall effect is to group together the records of employees who work in the same division. When we discuss printed reports, we will see an application of this kind of grouping.

At any time you can have the computer print out the file as it appears on the screen. (All the file is printed, however, not just the small portion that can fit on the screen at one time.) If projection and restriction operations can be applied before printing, it is easy for the user to print out just the data that is of interest.

Other forms of printout may be available. Some file managers provide for using the data in the file to print mailing labels or to insert names and addresses in form letters. And most provide means for producing printed reports.

Printing Reports

Although you can print out the file as it appears on the screen, there is often need for more elaborately formatted reports. Most file managers offer a report-generator that gives you considerable freedom in formatting reports.

A report is generated from the records in the file, with each record generating a line on the report. However, you can apply a restriction before

ID_Number	Last_Name	Division	Pay_Rate
342635	Roberts	Aerospace	29.93
409112	Clark	Aerospace	7.69
993812	Thompson	Aerospace	21.95
139425	Smith	Automotive	14.29
276931	Jones	Automotive	9.45
864732	Roth	Automotive	35.46
398762	Young	Electronics	10.35
783215	Sims	Electronics	8.97

FIGURE 8-8
The relation Employee sorted on Division and ID_Number. The values in the Division column are in alphabetical order. Rows that have the same value in the Division column are sorted so that the values in the ID_Number column are in order.

printing a report so that only those records satisfying a given query give rise to lines in the report.

You have complete freedom to define the columns to appear in the report; the columns in the report need not correspond to columns in the file. The values that are to appear in each column are defined by a formula that tells how each value in the column is to be computed from the values in the corresponding record of the file; there is one such formula for each column. In practice, most columns in the report will duplicate columns in the file. However, some columns may contain values that do not appear in the file at all, but are calculated from values that do appear.

You can specify a title to appear on the first page of the report and possibly a running head that appears at the top of each page. The running head can contain the name of the report, the page number, and perhaps the date on which the report was printed.

You can specify a column heading for each column of the report; for reasons already mentioned, the column headings in the report do not necessarily correspond to those in the file.

You can specify summary information, such as counts, totals, and averages, to be printed at the end of the report.

You can also specify *control breaks*, which print summary information at appropriate points throughout the report. These are best illustrated by an example. Consider the file in Figure 8-8; as previously explained, the file has been sorted so that the records for the Aerospace division come first, then those for the Automotive division, and finally those for the Electronics division. When we print a report for this file, we can have summary information printed after the data for each division. The summary line might contain, for example, the number of employees in the division and their average pay rate.

During printing, the report generator monitors the value in the Division column. As long as that value remains the same, the report generator

File managers can display stored data on the screen or use it to generate printed reports.

proceeds normally, printing one report line for each record. But when a new value is encountered in the Division column, the report generator prints the summary information for the old division before processing the first record of the new division.

Note that the file must be sorted properly for control breaks to work properly. What would happen if we specified a control break for each division, but the file was sorted as in Figure 8-1 instead of as in Figure 8-8?

We can specify several levels of control breaks. For example, a large company may have several divisions, stores within each division, and departments within each store. By using three levels of control breaks, we could print a report with summary information for each department, store, and division.

◣ FREE-FORM DATABASES AND HYPERTEXT

The *record-oriented databases* we have considered so far are highly structured into fields, records, and relations; an item of information can be stored only if a field was reserved for it when the database was designed. But we also often need to store unstructured information, such as news stories, encyclopedia articles, scientific papers, researchers' notes, and messages posted on an electronic bulletin board.

A *free-form database* stores unstructured prose in English or some other natural language. A common application of free-form databases are the *on-line databases* maintained in many specialized fields, such as medicine and law. The operators of these databases keep them up to date with the latest information in the corresponding specialties and, for appropriate fees, allow subscribers to access the data with their computers by telephone. Free-form database programs for microcomputers are often used to organize the notes of students, authors, journalists, and researchers. An emerging business activity is marketing CD-ROM compact discs containing information resources such as encyclopedias and handbooks. Such information resources often will have to be organized as free-form databases so that customers will have convenient access to the information they have purchased.

With a structured database, it is usually not difficult to formulate a precise query that will select exactly the records needed for a particular application. Retrieving information from a free-form database is much more problematical; it is not uncommon for the desired information to be obtained only after several failed searches that returned the wrong information or no information at all. Traditional methods of locating information in free-form databases are *menu classification* and *keyword searches*. An emerging technique—which has been around a long time but is just now gaining attention—is *hypertext*, which establishes direct links between pieces of text.

Menu Classification

Let's use the term *items* for the pieces of text stored in a free-form database; depending on the purpose of the database, items can range from short

On-line databases can be accessed from homes and offices via telephone connections.

messages to lengthy articles. A common approach to information retrieval—both manual and computerized—is to classify the items so that users can quickly narrow their search down to the items that may be of possible interest.

Selecting the proper classification is often done through a series of menus. The user is first presented with a menu listing the broad classifications of information that are available. After selecting one of these classifications, the user is presented with another menu listing narrower classifications. This process may continue through several more menus until the user's search has been narrowed down to a collection of items that has not been further subdivided.

The menu technique is used frequently by general-purpose information services that offer information on a wide variety of topics. There is usually a command whereby experienced users can bypass the menus and proceed directly to the desired collection of items. Also, since searches may very well fail, there are usually commands for returning to the previous menu and to the starting menu, making it easy for users to back up and try again.

Keyword Search

When the classification system has been used to its fullest (or if the items are not classified), the user will still be faced with a large number of items to search through. The user can further narrow down the items by a series of searches for *keywords*—words likely to be present in the desired items. To locate information on free-form databases, for example, you might first search for "database" to narrow the search to databases, then for "free-form" to narrow the search to free-form databases.

After each search the database program may indicate the number of items that were found. If the number is large—in the hundreds, say— then you will probably have to think of additional keywords that will further narrow the search. If the number is relatively small—ten or twenty items, say—you may prefer to read them all rather than risk overlooking some items that would be of interest. If the number is zero, you will have to try another keyword, perhaps a synonym of the word that caused the search to fail.

For some databases, a keyword search examines every word of an item; for others, the author of each item is responsible for providing a list of keywords, and only the keywords supplied by the author can be found by keyword searches. Free-form database programs may use one or more indexes (like the index of a book) to locate quickly items containing particular keywords. Indexes permit rapid keyword searches but slow down updating of items, since any changes in a stored item may require many index entries to be changed. Indexes are most suitable for *archival databases*, whose items are not changed once they have been stored.

Hypertext

Conventional books are sequential; the reader is expected to start at the beginning and follow the sequence of topics laid down by the author. Hypertext is nonsequential text. The items are not arranged in any particular order, but related items are joined by direct links that readers may or may not follow as their interests dictate. References to footnotes, cross references between encyclopedia articles, and for-further-reading references in books are noncomputerized examples of hypertext links.

On a computer screen, hypertext looks like ordinary text with certain words highlighted; each highlighted word represents a link to text providing further information about the word in question. For example, in a history text the names of important people might be highlighted, with each linked to a detailed biography of the person in question. To find out more about a person, the reader could click on the name with a mouse (position the mouse pointer on the name, then press and release the mouse button); the screen would change immediately to show the beginning of the biographical article. After finishing with the biographical article, the user could have the computer return to the original history text at the point at which it was left.

Hypertext has long been promoted for educational and information retrieval applications by researcher and visionary Theodor H. Nelson, who advocates a nationwide computer network on which authors can publish their works by storing them in a large hypertext database. Authors can freely refer to other authors' work by means of hypertext links and even incorporate other authors' work into their own. Regardless of such linking or inclusion, the fee paid by a user would be apportioned automatically among the original authors of whatever text the user read.

On a more modest scale, hypertext linking is emerging as an important technique for organizing information stored in databases.

◣ HYPERCARD

Much of the current interest in hypertext is due to *HyperCard*, a much-talked-about data management program provided with Apple Macintosh computers. HyperCard has properties in common with all the file and database managers already discussed. Like file managers, HyperCard is designed for interactive use; although it can print reports, that is not what it does best. Although HyperCard records are structured into fields, they can also store free-form text. Like database management systems, HyperCard can handle records having different structures; it is not restricted to a single, uniform table. Although HyperCard cannot be used by applications programs written in conventional programming languages, it comes with its own programming language (called *HyperTalk*), which allows applications programs to be incorporated into a HyperCard database.

HyperCard uses a variation of hypertext. Whereas hypertext links are traditionally used with free-form text, HyperCard uses them to link structured records. Yet HyperCard records are more flexible than those found in many other databases. A HyperCard record can contain text, graphics, and even sounds. Although a HyperCard record has fields and values like conventional database records, some fields (called scroll fields) act as windows that can be used to scroll, word-processor style, through large blocks of text—thus any amount of free-form text can be stored in a HyperCard scroll field.

A HyperCard database is an example of a *network database* in that related records are joined by a network of explicit links. This is in contrast to a relational database, in which records are related by join operations using fields that occur in more than one relation (thus in our previous examples, the Division field is used to relate records in Employee and Boss).

Like many other Apple Macintosh programs, HyperCard is based on a metaphor—a visual image that helps users grasp what the program does and how it works. The metaphor for HyperCard is stacks of 3-by-5 cards. Each HyperCard file is regarded as a stack of cards; each card holds one record and occupies the full computer screen when displayed. A stack can contain different kinds of cards—it is not limited to a single record structure as is a file maintained by a file-manager. Hypertext links can be established between cards in the same stack and between cards in different stacks. Stacks contain programs as well as data; data and programs provided as HyperCard stacks are referred to collectively as *stackware*.

A card has a background of text, graphics, and fields. The background determines the overall layout of the card. Usually many different cards in a stack will share the same background; however, cards with different backgrounds can appear in the same stack, so the cards in a stack do not all have to have the same structure.

The text and graphics in the background are the same for every card sharing the same background. Fields are slots in which text can be entered; the locations and sizes of the background fields are the same for all cards sharing the background; the actual text in a field, however, varies from card to card. Most fields hold only a fixed amount of text, namely, the amount that can fit into the area reserved for the field on the card. Such fixed-size fields correspond closely to the fields in relational and other kinds of databases. As mentioned, however, a scroll field serves as window past which any amount of text can be scrolled. Thus although a card cannot be larger than the computer screen, an arbitrarily large amount of text can be stored in a scroll field.

The user can search a stack for occurrences of a particular string of characters; thus keyword searches can be conducted. The search can examine all the text in a record or just that stored in a particular field. HyperCard's search facilities are not as powerful as those offered by many conventional record-oriented and free-form database management systems.

Graphics can be any pictures or drawings that can be displayed on the Macintosh screen; HyperCard includes a painting program that can be used to create graphics. Typical graphics might be maps or drawings of buildings, machines, plants, or animals. Also widely used are icons—small pictures representing information the user may wish to access or actions the user may wish the computer to take. HyperCard provides a selection of ready-made icons.

Links between cards, as well as actions to be taken by applications programs, are represented by areas on the card called *buttons*. When the user places the mouse pointer in a button area and clicks the mouse button down and up, HyperCard goes to a related card or carries out some other specified action. Buttons can be opaque (they cover up the background) or transparent (the background shows through). Opaque buttons carry

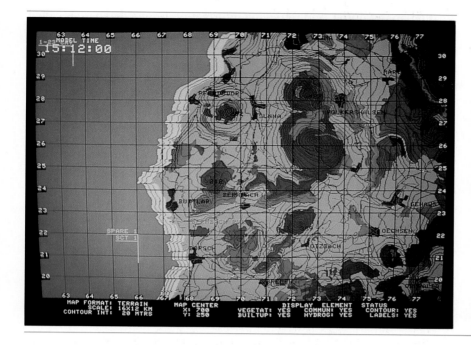

This map was generated from a large database of numerical data.

labels or icons indicating what each button does. Transparent buttons overlay other text and graphics on the card; the buttons themselves are invisible, but clicking on the underlying text or graphics activates the button. For example, a map might have a transparent button over the name of each country; clicking on the name of a country would take the user to a card giving further information about that country.

Attached to each button is a HyperTalk program, called a *script*, which is run when the user clicks on the button. If the button represents a link to another card, the script simply tells the computer to go to that card; such scripts can be created automatically so that users can establish links between cards without having to understand HyperTalk. Because HyperTalk is a full-featured programming language, many other actions, such as searches through stacks and mathematical calculations, can be carried out by HyperTalk scripts. It is in this way that applications programs can be incorporated into HyperCard stacks; the user operates the applications program by clicking on buttons to get various operations carried out.

HyperTalk is an English-like, easy to understand, yet powerful, programming language. Many of the operations it can carry out, such as manipulating cards in stacks, are easily visualized. For this reason, some educators are starting to use HyperTalk to teach programming to beginners, particularly those in fields other than computer science.

◣ Summary

A database is a collection of related files, such as those containing the financial records of a company. A program or system of programs for creating, maintaining, and retrieving information from a database is called a database management system (DBMS).

A record-oriented database is organized into records, each of which applies to a particular entity (person, place, or thing). Each record contains several fields; each field can contain a data item such as a name or address. A collection of records with the same structure can be visualized as a table with one row for each record and one column for each field. Such a tabular arrangement of data is called a relation; a database organized as a collection of relations is called a relational database.

Simple database management systems store each relation in a separate file. More sophisticated systems allow the logical organization of the data (the relations seen by the user) to differ from the physical organization (the files stored on disk). The physical organization can be changed without affecting the logical organization, a property known as data independence.

Each relation has a primary key whose value uniquely identifies the entity to which the record applies. Values of nonkey fields should depend on "the key, the whole key, and nothing but the key." This is a precise way of saying that each record should contain information about one and only one entity. A relation that satisfies this requirement is said to be in third normal form.

The relations stored in a database are called the base relations; temporary relations constructed from the base relations by database operations are called derived relations. A request for data from a database is called a query. The database management system answers a query by constructing a derived relation containing the requested data. The construction is accomplished with combinations of three basic database operations. A projection operation selects certain columns from a relation and discards the rest. A restriction operation selects only those rows of a relation that satisfy one or more relations. A join operation combines records from two relations for the purpose of coordinating information stored in different relations. Two records are combined only if each has the same value in a designated field.

Structured Query Language (SQL) is rapidly becoming a standard language for interacting with relational databases. Query expressions are used to extract information from the database; projection, restriction, and join operations are easily expressed as query expressions. Other SQL operations allow new records to be inserted in relations, existing records to be updated (modified) or deleted, and new relations to be defined.

A file manager maintains a flat-file database—a database consisting of a single relation stored in a single file. A file manager is intended for interactive use rather than use by applications programs. A file manager can insert, update, and delete database records; display the results of queries; and print reports based on the contents of the database.

A free-form database stores unstructured prose rather than structured records. Finding the information that you want is usually more difficult than for structured databases. Three aids to information retrieval are (1) menu classification, which allows the search to be narrowed down to successively smaller categories of items; (2) keyword search, which allows users to find items containing particular words; and (3) hypertext, which allows users to follow links between related items.

One of the currently most-talked-about database systems is HyperCard, which combines features of both structured and free-form databases. Users think of the data as being stored in stacks of cards; one card exactly fills the computer screen. Cards contain background text and graphics along with fields—areas reserved for the card's data. One kind of field, a scroll field, serves as a window through which any amount of free-form text can be viewed. Records in the same stack and in different stacks can be joined by hypertext links.

◥ Vocabulary Review

archival database	file	query expression
base relation	file manager	query language
button	flat-file database	query optimization
character data	form-design screen	record
control break	free-form database	record-oriented
data definition	HyperCard	database
language	HyperTalk	relation
data independence	hypertext	relational database
data manipulation	join	restriction
language	keyword	script
database management	keyword search	stackware
system (DBMS)	network database	Structured Query
derived relation	on-line database	Language (SQL)
entity	primary key	third normal form
field	projection	
field name	query	

◥ For Further Reading

Communications of the ACM (special issue on hypertext), July 1988.

Computing Surveys (special issue on database management systems), March 1976.

Date, C. J. *A Guide to the SQL Standard*. Reading, MA: Addison-Wesley, 1987.

Finkelstein, Richard and Fabian Pascal. "SQL Database Management Systems." *Byte*, January 1988, pp. 111–118.

Harvey, Greg. *Understanding HyperCard*. San Francisco: SYBEX, Inc., 1988.

Kent, Willian. "A Simple Guide to Five Normal Forms in Relational Database Theory." *Communications of the ACM*, February 1983, pp. 120–125. This paper is the source of the "key, whole key, and nothing but the key" characterization of third normal form.

Review Questions

1 Contrast a file and a database.

2 What software program is responsible for transferring data to and from files?

3 What software program is responsible for transferring data to and from a database?

4 What is a record? A field? How do we refer to a particular field in a record?

5 What is a relation? Characterize a relational database.

6 Contrast the logical and physical organizations of data. What is meant by data independence?

7 What is the primary key of a relation? What do we mean when we say that a relation is in third normal form?

8 Describe the projection operation and give an example of its use.

9 Describe the restriction operation and give an example of its use.

10 Describe the join operation and give an example of its use.

11 Give an example of an SQL query expression that performs a projection operation.

12 Give an example of an SQL query expression that performs a restriction operation.

13 Give an example of an SQL query expression that performs a join operation.

14 Describe the functions of the SQL INSERT, DELETE, and UPDATE commands.

15 Describe the function of the SQL CREATE TABLE command.

16 Contrast a file manager with a database management system.

17 Contrast structured and free-form databases.

18 Describe three ways of locating information in a free-form database.

19 Contrast hypertext with conventional documents such as books and magazines.

20 Briefly describe HyperCard.

Topics for Discussion

1 Hypertext researcher Theodor H. Nelson advocates hypertext as a means of liberating readers from the rigid sequence of topics imposed by conventional books. He seems to feel that all readers will enjoy the ability to jump from topic to topic at will. But might this freedom prove intimidating and confusing to some readers, particularly those not used to digging the information they need out of libraries and reference books?

2 The HyperTalk programming language has raised some eyebrows because its statements are designed to read like English sentences. The best known English-like programming language is Cobol, which is widely used in business programming but is not highly regarded by advanced programmers. Beginners are comforted by the familiar appearance of English-like programming langauges, but are apt to become confused when they try variations in phrasing that are permissible in English but not in the programming language. Also, English-like languages require much more writing than those that use more compact symbolisms. Let class members familiar with HyperTalk (and perhaps Cobol) debate the pros and cons of English-like programming langauges with aficionados of such non-English-like languages as Basic.

TELECOMMUNICATIONS

INTRODUCTION

The term *telecommunications* refers, in general, to any form of electronic communication. When applied to computers, the term refers to transferring data from one computer to another via electronic links such as telephone lines or optical fibers; the term *data communications* is also used with the same meaning. Telecommunications offers for text and graphics the same near-instantaneous transmission that the telephone provides for verbal communications. Messages sent by computer have some advantages over telephone calls, however, since messages can be copied automatically and routed by the computer system, and the computer will store messages until the recipient is ready to accept them. In the future, computers are likely to be used as much for communication as for storing files and carrying out computations.

WIDE AREA NETWORKS

Any facility for electronic communication among computers is known as a *network*. We distinguish between *local area networks* and *wide area networks*. A local area network provides communications within a limited area, such as a single building. A wide area network provides communications within a larger area, such as a city, a country, or the entire world.

A local area network is usually owned and operated by the organization whose computers communicate over the network. A wide area network, in contrast, usually makes use of facilities provided by another company. In the past, wide area communication was almost invariably provided by "the" telephone company serving the area in question. Now, after the breakup of the Bell system, communications services are offered by a variety of companies, including long-distance carriers, local telephone companies, and *value-added networks* that enhance the basic services offered by the telephone companies. We will often not distinguish between the different companies in the now-complex communications marketplace, but will instead just refer to them all as *communications companies*.

Telecommunications with a portable terminal and an acoustic coupler for a telephone handset.

The Telephone Network

The telephone network consists of the lines and equipment used for ordinary telephone communications. We can think of it as a single entity even though it is no longer the sole province of a single company. The telephone network, as it exists today, was designed for voice communications; in using it for data communications, we are pressing it into a service for which it was never designed. Not surprisingly, the results are sometimes less than satisfactory.

A *dial-up line* is one obtained by dialing a telephone number in the usual way. As every telephone user knows, one takes pot luck on the quality of a dial-up line. Sometimes the other party can be heard loud and clear, but other times the connection is plagued with weak signals, noise,

A computer terminal in an automobile communicates with a remote computer via radio.

and distortion. The reliability of data communications over dial-up lines likewise varies with the quality of each particular connection.

A *leased line* is a permanent connection between two computers. A leased line does not pass through telephone office switching equipment, which is where much noise and other problems originate. The reliability of a leased line—its freedom from noise and distortion—is about ten times that of a dial-up line. On the other hand, a leased line is much more expensive than the usual telephone service, and it can be used only for communications between the two machines to which it is connected. Leased lines are widely used for communications between mainframe computers or between a mainframe and remote terminals. Microcomputers, on the other hand, usually use dial-up lines.

Modems

The existing telephone network is designed to handle the analog signals that carry speech between telephones, not the digital signals (0s and 1s) that computers send to one another. Digital signals must be converted to analog form before they can be sent over telephone lines. The process of converting a digital signal to an analog signal suitable for telephone transmission is called *modulation*; the reverse process, of converting an incoming analog signal to a digital signal a computer can use, is called *demodulation*. A device for doing both conversions is called a modulator-demodulator, or *modem*. A modem serves as an interface between a computer and the telephone network.

The signal that a modem transmits has the form of a tone, which is called a *carrier* since it serves to carry the digital signal over the telephone line. Some modems feature a signal light that is on whenever a carrier is being received. When this light goes out, the carrier has been lost, either due to a bad connection or because the other computer has "hung up the phone." In this situation, the modem or communications program may display the message "no carrier" or "carrier lost" on the computer screen.

Usually, one tone is used to carry information in one direction (say from computer A to computer B) and another tone is used to carry information in the opposite direction (from computer B to computer A). The two tones are far enough apart in pitch so that they do not interfere with each other.

A modem is in either the *answer mode* or *originate mode* depending on which tone it uses for transmission and which it uses for reception. In the answer mode, a modem uses the higher-pitched tone for transmission and the lower-pitched tone for reception; in the originate mode, it uses the lower-pitched tone for transmission and the higher-pitched tone for reception. A modem in the answer mode can only communicate with one in the originate mode, and vice versa. Two modems in the same mode cannot communicate. Answer or originate mode can be set with a switch on the modem or by a command from the computer. As the names imply, originate mode is normally used when placing a call, and answer mode is used when accepting a call.

The speed of data transmission is measured by the number of bits that are sent each second. The transmission rate is given in *bits per second (bps)*. Commonly used transmission speeds are 300, 1200, 2400, and 9600 bps. Normally, each character is transmitted as 10 bits (one byte plus two control bits), so at 300 bps we can transmit 30 characters a second, at 1200 bps we can transmit 120 characters a second, and so on.

For an example of transmission times for a large file, consider the text of this book (illustrations excluded), which occupies about one megabyte. The following table shows the time required to transmit one megabyte at each of the four transmission speeds:

Speed	Time
300 bps	9 hr. 16 min.
1200 bps	2 hr. 19 min.
2400 bps	1 hr. 10 min.
9600 bps	18 min.

The following are some additional remarks about each speed:

■ **300 bps** This speed is satisfactory if you are typing at the keyboard and reading text as it appears on the screen. No one can type 30 characters a second, and text coming in at higher speeds may appear too fast to be read comfortably. On the other hand, as the table shows, transmitting large files is exceedingly slow at this speed. Also, rewriting the entire screen, which is necessary for some applications, is painfully slow. Most commercial information and communication services support 300 bps (that is, you can access these services with a 300-bps modem).

1200 bps Currently, 1200 bps is the most popular speed among business users. As the table shows, file transmission is dramatically faster than at 300 bps, and the same is true of screen rewrites. Most information and communications services also support 1200 bps.

2400 bps This speed is rapidly becoming popular where large amounts of data have to be transmitted. However, it is not as widely supported by information and communications services as are 300 and 1200 bps.

9600 bps As the table shows, 9600 bps allows a large amount of data to be transmitted in a reasonably short time. Unfortunately, there are currently some drawbacks to using 9600 bps: (1) the modems are expensive; (2) owing to lack of agreement on transmission standards, modems made by different manufacturers may not be able to communicate with one another; (3) 9600-bps transmission pushes the telephone network to its limits with the result that the slightest problem with the telephone connection can disrupt communication; and (4) most information and communications services do not support 9600 bps.

In computer publications, you will sometimes see the word *baud* used to mean bits per second. This usage is not correct. *Baud* refers to the rate at which signals are transmitted over the telephone line. If each signal represents one bit, the number of baud will equal the number of bits per second. If, however, each signal represents more than one bit, the number of baud will be a fraction of the number of bits per second.* Therefore, avoid the term *baud*; if you see it used in a computer publication, however, you can assume it is being misused to mean bits per second.

Computers are finding ever increasing use in radio-dispatched vehicles such as police cars. Even when no one is in the car, the dispatcher can access information stored in the computer (such as the status of a patrol unit) and store new information (such as assignments to be carried out).

---

*A 300-bps modem transmits at 300 baud, with each transmitted signal representing one bit. A 1200-bps modem and a 2400-bps modem both transmit at 600 baud; each signal represents two bits in the case of the 1200-bps modem and four bits in the case of the 2400-bps modem. Standards for 9600-bps transmission vary; however, one type of 9600-bps modem transmits at 2400 baud with each signal representing four bits.

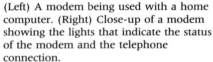

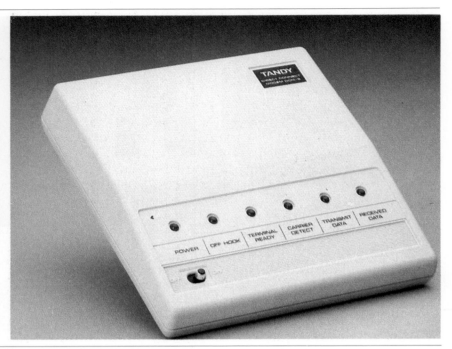

(Left) A modem being used with a home computer. (Right) Close-up of a modem showing the lights that indicate the status of the modem and the telephone connection.

There are three ways of providing a computer with a modem:

1 The modem can be permanently built into the computer. This is common for portable computers, which are frequently used for entry and temporary storage of information that later will be transmitted to another computer.

2 The modem can be on an expansion board, which is installed in one of the computer's expansion slots. This approach is widely used with computers that provide expansion slots.

3 The modem can be external to the computer, installed in its own separate box. The computer must have a *serial* port*, a connector on the back of the computer through which data can be sent and received. A cable connects the serial port to the modem. A serial port is often referred to as an RS-232 or RS-232C port; RS-232 and RS-232C refer to a particular standard for transmitting data between computers and modems.

Most modern modems are of the *direct connect* type: the modem is connected to the phone line by a telephone cord that plugs into a standard telephone jack. If a telephone is already plugged into the jack, it is unplugged and the modem is plugged in. The telephone can be plugged into the modem for use in placing calls and conversing with operators.

An alternative approach is to connect the modem to an *acoustic coupler*, a special cradle into which a telephone handset can be placed. The acoustic coupler converts signals from the modem into tones that can be

---

*The term *serial* means that data is sent one bit at a time; in contrast, a parallel port usually sends eight bits at once, with each bit on a separate wire.

picked up by the handset; tones produced by the handset are picked up by the acoustic coupler and converted into electrical signals for the modem. Both the handset and the acoustic coupler can pick up room noises, which may interfere with data transmission. Acoustic couplers are usually used only with phones that do not plug into phone jacks, such as those in phone booths and motel rooms.

You may occasionally encounter the term *null modem*, which refers not to a modem but to a special cable. Computers that are not too far apart—in the same room, say—can be connected directly by means of their RS-232 ports. No modems are needed, the telephone network is not used, and data transmission speeds of 9600 bps or more are possible. There is only one problem. In connecting the two computers, certain wires must be crossed so that, for example, the wire on which one computer *transmits* data is connected to the wire on which the other computer *receives* data, and vice versa. A cable in which the necessary wires are crossed is called a null modem, modem eliminator, or modem bypass.

Figure 9-1 illustrates various possibilities for connecting a computer to a telephone line or directly to another computer.

Modems are classified as *dumb* and *smart*. A dumb modem performs only the signal conversion previously described. A standard telephone set must be used to place and answer calls. A smart modem, on the other hand, performs all the functions of a telephone set. On command from the computer, it will do the electrical equivalent of taking the phone off the hook, wait for a dial tone, and dial a number supplied by the computer. For incoming calls, the modem will inform the computer when a ringing signal is received and will answer the call at the computer's request. With a smart modem, a standard telephone set is needed only if one must go through an operator or otherwise mix voice and data communication.

Most smart modems are controlled by *AT commands*, so called because each command begins with AT, which stands for *attention*. For example, the command

    ATDT5556193

instructs the modem to dial the number 555-6193. The AT indicates a modem command, the D instructs the modem to dial a number, and the T specifies tone dialing (as with a push-button phone); the remainder of the command gives the number to be dialed. Users can type AT commands directly. Most people, however, use communications programs that request dialing instructions in a user-friendly manner and then automatically generate the somewhat cryptic AT commands.

Synchronous and Asynchronous Communication

In *asynchronous communication*, each character is transmitted individually as soon as it is typed. Since each character is handled individually, there is no problem if the user of the transmitting computer types at an irregular rate. To help the receiving computer cope with the irregular rate of transmission, however, the code for each character must be preceded by a *start bit* and followed by at least one *stop bit*. The start bit warns the receiving computer that transmission of a character is about to begin; the

FIGURE 9-1 Possibilities for connecting a computer to a telephone line or directly to another computer.

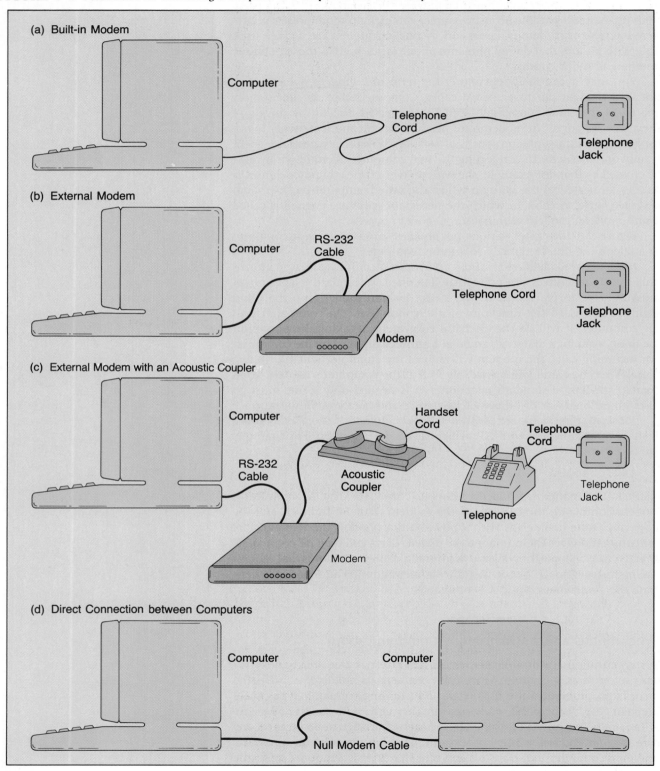

Acoustic coupler.

stop bit assures the receiving computer that transmission of a character has been completed.

For asynchronous communication, the bit transmission rate refers only to the rate at which bits are sent during transmission of a character. Between the transmission of two successive characters there may be an arbitrarily long interval in which no information at all is sent. This is the usual situation when the characters are being sent as they are typed on a keyboard.

When a block of data, such as a disk file, is transmitted under computer control, characters are transmitted one after another with no intervening intervals. In this situation bits are transmitted steadily at the specified transmission rate. In figuring the rate at which characters are being sent, however, the start and stop bits that frame each character must be taken into account. For example if each character is represented by an eight-bit code, and there is one start bit and one stop bit, then ten bits must be sent for each character. Hence the rate at which characters are transmitted is one tenth the rate in bits per second.

In *synchronous communication*, characters are not transmitted individually but are accumulated and transmitted in blocks called *packets*. During transmission of a packet, characters are sent at a steady rate, allowing the sending and receiving computers to operate in synchronism, or lockstep, with each other. No start and stop bits are required to signal the beginning and end of each character; this allows characters to be sent more rapidly for a given bit transmission rate. Synchronizing bits may have to be sent periodically to keep the two computers in step with one another; sending these, however, takes up much less time than sending a start and a stop bit for each character.

The computer terminal is connected to a modem having a built-in acoustic coupler.

Most microcomputers use asynchronous communication. Synchronous communication is used mainly in two situations. First, some large mainframes employ synchronous communication with remote terminals. If a microcomputer is used in place of such a terminal, it too must employ synchronous communication. Second, *packet switched networks*, which are discussed further later, employ synchronous communication to allow a number of computers to share the same communications line.

The user usually does not have to worry about the details of synchronous communication, which are handled by special hardware and software intended for a particular purpose, such as emulating a particular kind of terminal or interfacing to a particular network. On the other hand, the user frequently does have to worry about the details of asynchronous communication, which are apt to be different for different computers with which one might wish to communicate.

Asynchronous Communications Protocols

The exact details of how data is transmitted over a communications channel are referred to as a *protocol*. Two computers can communicate only if they use the same protocol. To communicate with an existing computer system, such as one operated by an information service, you must adjust your hardware and software to use the same protocol as the system with which you wish to communicate. This means that before you can call another computer system you must determine what communications protocol it uses and provide this information to your communications software. The following are some of the details that must be provided.

Transmission Speed   For communication via modem, the usual choices are 300, 1200, 2400, and 9600 bps. You can only choose rates that both your modem and the one at the other end of the line are prepared to handle.

Number of Data Bits   This is the number of bits used to represent each character. The usual choices are seven and eight bits. Seven bits are sufficient for the ASCII character code and leave room for a parity bit (see below) to be included for error checking. Eight bits allow the transmission of arbitrary bytes that do not necessarily represent characters. (For example, they might be the codes of a machine-language program.) Usually, no parity bit is included when eight bits are used for data.

Parity Bit   As illustrated in Figure 9-2, a *parity bit* is used for error checking. The user can choose to transmit characters with either *even parity* or *odd parity*. For even parity, the parity bit is chosen so that an even number of 1s occur in the parity and data bits. For odd parity, the parity bit is chosen so that an odd number of 1s occur in the parity and data bits. If a character is transmitted with even parity and received with odd parity, or vice versa, the computer at the receiving end knows that one of the bits in the received character is incorrect, and hence a transmission error has occurred.

To meet the needs of some systems that do not use the parity bit for error checking, we also can specify the parity bit to be always 0 or always 1.

Usually, a parity bit is used with seven data bits but not with eight. Either even or odd parity can be selected for the transmitted characters; the same parity option must be selected for both the transmitting and receiving computers. You can specify whether your software will check

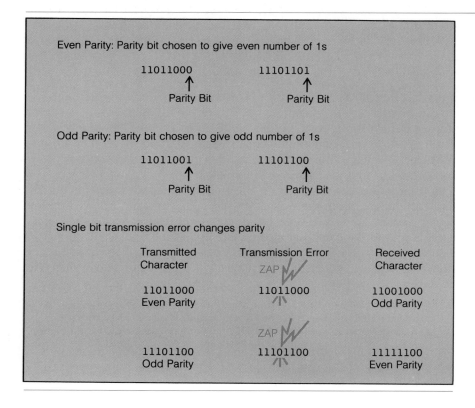

FIGURE 9-2
Using a parity bit for error checking. The transmitting computer can send all characters with even parity (even number of 1s) or odd parity (odd number of 1s). If a character arrives with a parity different from the one being used by the transmitting computer, the receiving computer knows that a transmission error occurred.

Combined computer terminal and telephone

the parity of incoming characters and inform you when errors are detected. During interactive sessions, transmission errors usually make themselves obvious in the form of garbled text on the screen, so parity checking by the communications software may be more of an annoyance than a help.

Number of Stop Bits   Either one or two stop bits may be used after each character; with today's equipment, the choice is normally one. Teletype machines, which were widely used in the past but are now obsolete, require two stop bits.

Figure 9-3 illustrates the start, parity, data, and stop bits and shows the choices available for each.

Full-Duplex and Half-Duplex Transmission   In full-duplex transmission, data can be transmitted and received simultaneously. In half-duplex transmission, on the other hand, each computer must take turns sending and receiving; simultaneous transmission and reception are impossible.* Asynchronous communication is usually full duplex; synchronous communication is usually half duplex.

As far as the user is concerned, the main difference between full duplex and half duplex lies in the way characters are *echoed* or displayed on the screen as they are typed. With full-duplex transmission, each typed character is sent to the computer at the other end of the line. Upon receipt of a character, the other computer "echos" it or sends it back to the computer that originated it, where it is displayed on the screen. Thus when the characters you type appear on your own screen, they have made a complete

---

*Full-duplex transmission is like an ordinary telephone call, in which both parties can talk at the same time if they wish. Half-duplex transmission is like that of a two-way radio for which a button must be held down to transmit and released to receive. Since the transmit button is always either up or down, simultaneous transmission and reception are impossible.

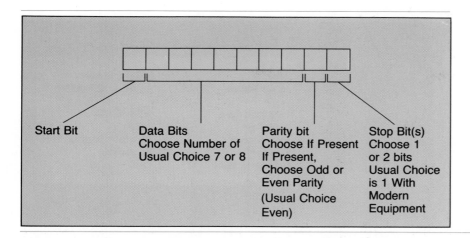

Start Bit

Data Bits
Choose Number of
Usual Choice 7 or 8

Parity bit
Choose If Present
If Present,
Choose Odd or
Even Parity
(Usual Choice
Even)

Stop Bit(s)
Choose 1
or 2 bits
Usual Choice
is 1 With
Modern
Equipment

FIGURE 9-3
Start, data, parity, and stop bits, with the
usual choices for each.

round trip to the other computer and back. If the characters on your screen are correct, you can be sure that what you typed was received correctly by the other computer.

In half-duplex transmission, the other computer cannot echo the characters you type since simultaneous transmission and reception are not allowed. Therefore, your communications software must display on your screen the characters that you type so that you can see what you are typing. The typed characters will always be displayed correctly on your screen, but this tells you nothing about how they are being received by the other computer.

Asynchronous communications can be either half duplex or full duplex provided the software in both computers is informed of the desired mode of operation. In general, full-duplex operation is best and should be used whenever the hardware permits. Note that if your computer is in half-duplex mode and the other computer is in full-duplex mode, then each typed character may appear on your screen twice—echoed once by your communications software and once by the other computer.

Packet-Switched Networks

Packet switching is a technique by which a number of computers can share a communications network. The data sent by each computer is broken down into blocks called packets. Packet sizes vary, but about a thousand bytes per packet is typical. Each computer using a packet-switched network is identified by a unique address. Each packet has a header, which contains the address of the computer to which the packet is directed. Thus, like letters moving through the postal system, packets from different sources and with different destinations can move together through the communications channels of a packet-switched network. At each distribution point, the destination address of the packet is examined and the packet is sent along a channel that takes it closer to its destination. Packets that are part of the same message may travel along different routes. The header of

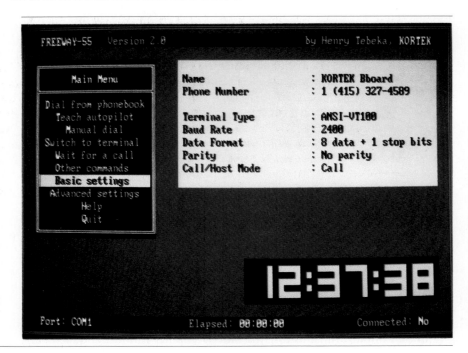

A communications program prompts the user to specify the telephone number to be called, the type of computer terminal the program is to emulate, and the communications parameters to be used.

each packet also contains a serial number so that the packets can be reassembled in the proper order even if the order at which they arrive at their destination is different from the order in which they were transmitted.

Wide area packet-switched networks are usually operated by communications companies. Your computer communicates via modem over a dial-up line with the local office of the communications company. Data transmitted by your computer is placed on the network in the form of packets addressed to the computer with which you are communicating. When packets addressed to your computer are received at the local office of the communications company, the information in them is sent to your computer over the dial-up line.

A wide area packet-switched network is an example of a value-added network; the operator of the packet-switched network leases communications channels from long-distance carriers, then "adds value" to the leased channels by implementing packet-switched digital communications.

ISDN

We have seen that the existing analog telephone network is far from ideal for carrying digital data. To attain even moderately high speeds, we must use expensive modems, and the speed is still often not as high as we need. Also, line noise and poor transmission quality can cause errors or even disrupt communication entirely. Fortunately, the telephone industry is planning to switch to an all-digital telephone network, a switch that might be completed by the end of this century. This *Integrated Services Digital Network (ISDN)* will offer transmission about nine times faster than that obtainable with a 9600-bps modem, and several independent signals can be transmitted at the same time. Reliability should be ten times greater than for analog leased lines and hundred times greater than for analog dial-up lines.

ISDN provides two kinds of channels, called *B channels* and *D channels*. The B channel can carry either voice or high-speed data. The D channel is used for call-control and signaling information, allowing all such information to be removed from the B channels and making their full capacity available for data transmission. Since a D channel is not fully occupied with control information, it can also serve as a slow-speed, packet-switched data channel. Basic ISDN service, which would be used by residences and small-to-medium-size businesses, provides two B channels and one D channel. Large businesses could use primary service, which provides twenty-three B channels and one D channel. In each case, the D channel handles all the control and switching information for all the B channels.

The B channel provides full-duplex digital communication at about 64,000 bps. If each character is transmitted as one byte, about 8000 characters per second can be sent. To use our previous example, one megabyte can be sent over an ISDN B channel in about two minutes, in contrast to eighteen minutes for an analog line using a 9600-bps modem.

Voice communication also takes place over B channels. Analog voice signals must be digitized—converted to digital form—at the transmitting end and converted back to analog form at the receiving end—jobs that will be done automatically by telephones designed for use with ISDN. This situation is just the opposite of the one for analog networks, where data rather than voice signals have to be converted at both ends of the connection.

Basic ISDN services might cost about twice as much as an analog business line (which, in turn, costs more than an analog residence line). Time estimates for the widespread availability of ISDN vary; but in view of the billions of dollars of analog telephone equipment that would have to be replaced, at least five to ten years will be required.

ISDN will arrive faster and cost less if residence subscribers can be interested in home applications such as access to information services, home shopping via data terminals, and home banking. Such services are already obtained (via modem) by telecommunications enthusiasts; so far, however, little interest has been shown in them by the average person. One service that ISDN can supply to everyone, however, is to display the name and number of the calling party when the telephone rings; the name and number would be part of the control information transmitted over the D channel.

Telephone industry visionaries look forward to a Universal Information Service (UIS) that could carry live television pictures as well as voice and data. In addition to supporting teleconferencing—conducting conferences via television hookups—UIS would allow cable television as well as voice and data communication to be supplied through a single cable and a single set of wall jacks.

ISDN allows telephone subscribers to access databases via a computer terminal connected to the telephone.

APPLICATIONS OF WIDE AREA DATA COMMUNICATIONS

Microcomputer owners who engage in telecommunications today are pioneers, like those who drove cars when horses were still the most practical mode of transportation, or those who listened to the radio when programs could be heard only faintly through earphones. Out of their pioneering efforts, and those of the companies that serve them, is likely to arise an important and powerful data communications industry that will have features in common with today's telephone, broadcasting, and publishing industries.

Electronic Mail

Electronic mail, which refers to transmitting letters and other messages via electronic communications channels, combines features of both telephone calls and conventional mail. Like a telephone call, an electronic message reaches its destination almost instantly. But unlike a telephone call, an electronic message does not interrupt the recipient since the message can be stored in a computer until the recipient is ready to read it. Electronic messages are also easily duplicated and routed by computers. Several of the forms of data communication described below provide for electronic mail.

Communication Between Personal Computers

Microcomputer owners can exchange data and programs via telecommunications. Microcomputers in the same room can be connected directly via their serial ports. More widely separated machines can communicate over the telephone via a modem at each of the line.

Often telecommunications provides the only way to transfer information from one computer to another. Different kinds of computers store data on disks in different formats, so a disk written by one kind of computer often cannot be read by another kind. However, such otherwise incompatible machines usually can transfer information via a communications link, provided each has a serial port or built-in modem, and the users agree on a common communications protocol. Some portable computers do not even have disk drives; they are intended only for storing information temporarily until it can be communicated to another computer for permanent storage.

Communication with Mainframes

Most large organizations store their business data in a database maintained by a mainframe computer. An organization's microcomputers will be much more useful if they can access the data stored in the mainframe. One way to accomplish this is to provide the microcomputer with hardware and

Wide-area communication often takes place at least partially by satellite.

software that allow it to emulate a computer terminal of the type normally used to access the mainframe. Unlike a terminal, however, a microcomputer can store and process the data it receives from the mainframe.

Two problems can arise. First, frequent access by microcomputers can take up much of the mainframe's time, interfering with its use for other purposes. This is particularly true if the microcomputers request time-consuming operations, such as a search for all records satisfying some complex condition. Second, microcomputer users may inadvertently change the contents of the database, destroying its validity. One solution is to transfer periodically a copy of the database to another computer whose sole purpose is to handle communication with microcomputers. The microcomputers can access the copy of the database but they cannot corrupt the original or take up excessive amounts of the mainframe's time.

A mainframe can provide other services for microcomputers, such as routing, storing, and duplicating electronic mail, running programs that are too large for microcomputers, and providing access to the high-speed or high-quality printers usually attached to mainframes.

Bulletin Board Systems

Like a conventional bulletin board, a computer bulletin board system allows users to post messages and read messages posted by others. Private messages, which can be read only by the person to whom each is addressed, also can be posted, thus providing an electronic mail service. In contrast to a conventional bulletin board, large data files, such as computer programs, can be stored on and retrieved from computer bulletin boards.

A computer bulletin board system is implemented on a microcomputer; the minimum system requirements are a microcomputer, a modem, a hard disk, and bulletin board software. Most computer bulletin boards are operated by individuals as a hobby and public service; however, a few computer-oriented businesses, such as computer stores and computer magazines, also operate bulletin boards. Each bulletin board is usually devoted to a particular subject, such as a particular kind of computer, computer gaming, rock music, or science fiction. There are now bulletin boards devoted to almost every conceivable subject in which people are interested.

Telephone numbers of bulletin boards are sometimes listed in computer magazines and in publications devoted to the subject area in which the bulletin boards specialize. Usually there is no charge for using a computer bulletin board. In the past, you were free to use any bulletin board whose phone number you knew. Now, in an effort to prevent certain abuses, such as posting of illegally obtained information, some bulletin-board operators require prospective users to register and obtain a password before using a bulletin board.

Computer bulletin boards have suffered from some adverse publicity in recent times. Some bulletin boards have been found to contain stolen credit-card numbers and instructions for gaining illegal access to computer systems and networks. Some bulletin boards provide information on how to make unauthorized copies of commercial software; others feature X-rated material. And some of the software available on bulletin boards has been found to contain *viruses*—programs maliciously designed to spread from one computer system to another and to damage the systems they infect.

Information Services

Unlike most bulletin boards, *information services* (also called *information utilities*) are businesses operated for a profit. You must register with the information service before using it, and you will be billed for the services you use. Charges generally include a fee for *connect time* (the time you spend in contact with the information service's computers), fees for the specific services you use, and a minimum monthly fee (not all services charge a minimum fee). Rates are usually higher during normal business hours; nonbusiness users generally confine their use to evening hours and weekends when rates are lower. Individuals are usually required to pay by credit card, by electronic funds transfer, or in advance so that the information service will not have to bother sending and trying to collect bills; billing may be available for companies.

You also must pay the cost of communicating with the information service's computers. The cost of long-distance telephone calls can far exceed the charges made by the information service. Fortunately, the larger information services have arrangements with packet-switched networks that make it easy for subscribers to use this lower-cost form of communication; you just call the local number of the network and enter a code for the service you wish to contact; communications charges are added to your account with the information service, so you do not need to have a separate account with the network.

One packet-switched network allows you to contact bulletin boards and smaller information services that have not made any arrangements with the network. The network places a local telephone call to the information service in the city in which it is located; communication between your city and that of the information service takes place over the network. You must have an account with the network and pay it a monthly fee to use this form of communication.

The following are some of the services provided by information utilities.

Access to Databases   Information services provide access to databases, each of which contains information useful in some specialized field, such as law, medicine, business, or finance. Many information services exist only to provide access to a particular database. Any other services are provided only to facilitate use of the database. Less specialized information services provide access to a number of databases in addition to their other services. There are over a thousand *on-line databases*—databases accessible by computer over the telephone network.

News   Some of an information service's databases are usually devoted to news. One database might contain stories from a major wire service, for example, whereas another might contain an electronic version of a major newspaper, such as *The Washington Post*. Still other databases contain more specialized news such as sports scores and stock prices.

Electronic Mail   Each registered user of an information service is assigned an electronic mailbox. One user can communicate with another by entering a message and instructing the system to store it in the other person's mailbox. Every time you log on,* the system informs you if there is any mail in your box. With appropriate commands to the system, you can have each message displayed. After you read a message, the system will prompt you to enter a reply; if you enter your reply at this time, the system will automatically route it to the sender of the message you just read.

Conversation   Some information services provide the means whereby users can chat with one another via their keyboards and terminals. This service is often referred to as CB, since it is analogous to the Citizen's Band (CB) radio with which many people are familiar. As with actual CB radio, a number of independent CB channels are provided. By informal agreement among users, certain channels are reserved for particular topics of conversation. A user selects the channel that most nearly coincides with his or her interests and conversational preferences.

Computer Conferencing   A computer conference is an ongoing discussion devoted to a particular subject. Users can leave public messages for all other members of the conference and can direct private messages to particular members. Users who are on line (participating in the conference) at the same time may be able to chat in CB fashion. A computer conference, then, is an ongoing discussion in which each member can

---

*To log on is to identify yourself to the information service's computer, something you must do at the beginning of each session. You must usually provide an account number and a password when logging on.

Using a videotex terminal.

participate at whatever times and for whatever lengths of time that are convenient. Computer bulletin boards and information services often provide a large number of computer conferences devoted to a variety subjects.

Videotex   Videotex (also spelled "videotext") is an information service for persons who are not trained computer users. Typically, information is displayed on the screen of an ordinary television set. An attachment to the television set communicates with the information utility over the telephone network or a television cable system. The user specifies the information desired by selecting items from a menu. Selections are made by pushing buttons on a box similar to a television remote control unit. Often the user must work through a long series of menus before obtaining the desired information. For the sake of an attractive presentation, the screen displays involve both text and graphics; special techniques are used to allow graphics to be transmitted with reasonable speed over narrowband channels such as telephone lines. A videotex service intended for home users might provide generally useful information, such as airline schedules and theater listings, together with advertisements classified according to the product or service offered.

Videotex has not been tried on a major scale in the United States. It has, however, been tried and well received in some other countries, including England. Some information services provide what they call videotex service, but it is provided to owners of personal computers, not the public at large. By providing data channels on telephone lines, ISDN would simplify the provision of videotex services; likewise, widespread interest in videotex would promote a more rapid changeover to ISDN. It remains to be seen, however, whether the general public will develop any interest in videotex.

Electronic Shopping   An electronic catalog provides information about a company's products and allows users to place orders electronically. Orders are charged automatically to the user's credit card; the merchandise is shipped by mail or by a parcel delivery service.

Securities Trading   Stocks, bonds, and other securities can be traded electronically by users who have opened accounts with a brokerage firm associated with the information utility. In addition to placing orders to buy or sell securities, an account holder can obtain the status of his or her brokerage account as well as financial information such as stock market quotations.

COMMUNICATIONS SOFTWARE

Communications software aids the computer user with such tasks as transferring files between computers and communicating with computer bulletin boards and information services. A communications program may be a stand-alone program or it may be part of an integrated software package that also offers such functions as word processing, spreadsheet analysis, and database management. The communications program and the modem must be compatible since the program must be able to send commands to the modem and receive status reports from it. Most microcomputer communications programs are designed for modems that use the AT command set.

Terminal Emulation

The simplest function a communications program can carry out is to allow the microcomputer to be used as a *dumb terminal*. A dumb terminal is so called because it carries out no data storage or processing of its own. Characters typed on the keyboard are immediately sent to the computer at the other end of the line. Characters from the other computer are displayed as they are received. In half-duplex mode, characters typed on the keyboard are echoed on the screen by the communications program. In full-duplex mode, it is left up to the other computer to echo the typed characters.

Most communications programs will also emulate one or two of the most common types of *smart terminal*. A smart terminal will respond to special command codes arriving over the communications line. Such command codes may instruct the terminal to erase all or part of the screen, for example, or to move the cursor to a particular point on the screen. An information service may be able to position information on your screen more rapidly if your communications program is set to emulate a smart terminal.

Uploading and Downloading

Transmitting a disk file to another computer is known as *uploading*; receiving a file from another computer and storing the file on disk is known as *downloading*. A communications program must be able to transmit the contents of a designated disk file and store received information in a disk file designated by the user.

Line noise can introduce errors into the material being uploaded or downloaded. When the file contains only text, often no attempt is made to detect and correct transmission errors. Thus the uploaded or downloaded text may contain occasional typographical errors, which will usually cause the reader little trouble since the necessary corrections will be obvious.

Disregarding errors is unacceptable for binary files—files containing binary codes that do not represent text. Errors in binary files are almost impossible to find and correct manually, and they can have serious consequences. If the file contains a machine-language program, errors will cause the program to crash or malfunction when it is executed. If the file is to be used by another program, such as a word processor* or spreadsheet program, errors may cause that program to crash or malfunction when it attempts to process the file.

---

*The formatted text files produced by word processors contain binary formatting codes in addition to text and so are classified as binary files.

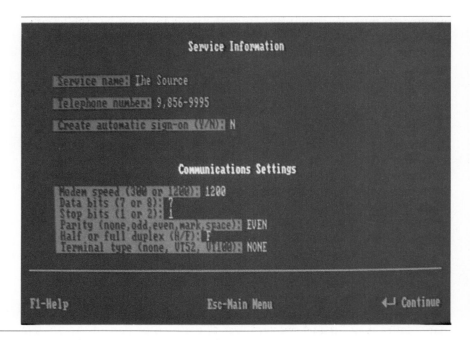

Screen display produced by a communications program. The user has entered the communications parameters in response to prompts by the program.

To upload or download binary files, we must use an *error-correcting protocol*. With such a protocol, the file being transferred is broken down into small blocks, and a special *error-detecting code* is transmitted along with each block. The computer receiving the file uses the error-detecting codes to determine which blocks contain errors; when an erroneous block is detected, the computer receiving the file requests the other computer to retransmit the erroneous block.

Error-correcting protocols do not absolutely guarantee against errors—there's a small chance of errors slipping past the error-detecting codes—but the likelihood of errors is much less than if no error-correcting protocol was used. Uploading and downloading is substantially slower when an error-correcting protocol is used, which is why such protocols are often not used for text files. The most popular error-correcting protocol is *XMODEM*, which is widely supported by information services and communications programs.

Automatic Dialing and Log On

A communications program can maintain on disk a small telephone directory containing information about frequently used information services. For each service the directory lists the phone number to be called, the communications protocol required by that service, and the information that must be transmitted to log on. (The log-on information normally consists of an account number and password plus perhaps some details about communications protocol, such as whether half-duplex or full-duplex mode is to be used.) When the user enters the name of a particular service, the program will look up the name in the directory, adjust the modem for the required communications protocol, and dial the specified number. If contact is established, the communications program will transmit the specified log-on information before returning control to the user. The user can begin communicating immediately without having to bother with such tedious preliminaries as setting communications protocols, dialing, and logging on.

Automatic Answering

Microcomputers are used far more frequently to place calls than to answer them. Occasionally, however, it is convenient to have the computer automatically answer calls and receive messages. For example, if you have a portable computer, you may wish to call your main computer from a remote location and transmit information to it from the portable. Thus communications programs often provide an unattended mode of operation in which the computer will automatically answer incoming calls and store any information received in a separate disk file for each call.

LOCAL AREA NETWORKS

A local area network (LAN) is a network that extends over a limited area such as a single building. A local area network can interconnect microcomputers and mainframes as well as peripheral devices such as disk drives and high-speed or high-quality printers. Computers connected to the network can exchange information with one another and can share the use of the peripherals.

In the past, all the business data at a particular company installation was stored in and processed by a single mainframe computer. With the

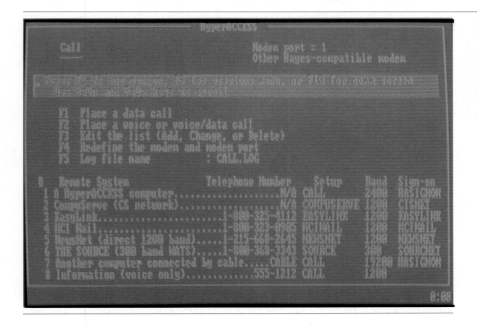

Screen display produced by the communications program HyperAccess. If the user selects one of the information services listed at the bottom of the screen, the program will set the communications parameters, place the telephone call, and log onto the information service's computer.

advent of microcomputers, it became necessary to provide many different microcomputer users with access to the same data. Local area networks are one approach to sharing the same data among a variety of computers. Alternate approaches are microcomputer-mainframe communication, which provides many microcomputers with access to a common mainframe, and multiuser systems—microcomputers or minicomputers that can be used by more than one person at a time by means of attached computer terminals.

Transmission Media

The computer equipment in a local area network communicate by means of *twisted pairs*, *coaxial cables*, or *optical fibers*.

Twisted Pairs   The wires used for telephone communications within a building are known as twisted pairs. Twisted pairs also can be used for data communications; data transmission rates of 50 thousand bps or greater are possible. Twisted-pair wiring is inexpensive and, most important of all, is already installed in most buildings as part of the existing telephone system.

Coaxial Cables   Coaxial cables are most familiar as the cables used in cable television systems. Coaxial cables allow data transmission rates of up to 50 million bps, about a thousand times faster than is possible with twisted pairs. Because of this extremely high transmission rate, a single coaxial cable can be shared easily by a large number of computing devices via the packet-switching technique discussed earlier.

A coaxial cable can be used in baseband or broadband mode. In baseband mode, the cable provides a single, high-speed data communications

Computers and peripheral devices connected by a local area network.

channel. In broadband mode, the cable provides a number of channels that can be used for data communication, voice communication, television transmission, and for other forms of electronic communication, such as facsimile. A baseband network can be used for data communications only. A broadband network provides a general-purpose local communications facility. Note that a cable television system is a broadband network.

Optical Fibers   Information can be carried by laser beams traveling over thin, transparent fibers. The information-carrying capacity of optical fibers far exceeds that of coaxial cables; higher data transmission rates are possible, and the number of channels in a broadband network can be far greater. Currently, optical fibers are not as widely used as coaxial cables. Their use may well increase in the future, however, as greater demands are placed on the information-carrying capacity of local area networks.

Circuit-Switched Networks

In a circuit-switched network, switching equipment establishes a connection between each pair of devices that wish to communicate. The telephone network is an example of a circuit-switched network; when you dial a number, a connection is established between your telephone and the one you are calling.

Telephone calls within a building are carried over twisted pairs. Connections are made by a central switching unit known as a *private branch exchange*, or *PBX*. (The term *private automatic branch exchange*, or *PABX*, is also used. The "automatic" excludes manually operated switchboards.) Many existing PBXs are designed for voice communications only; to transmit data through them, a modem must be used at each end of the line, just as with the public telephone network. Some modern PBXs, however, can be used for both voice and digital communication. ISDN can be implemented on PBXs; thus companies can choose to use ISDN for their local area networks even before it becomes available for wide area communications. On the other hand, when ISDN does become widely available for wide area communications, companies may find it advantageous to choose the same technique for their local area networks.

Packet-Switched Networks

A packet-switched network does not establish a separate connection for each data exchange. Rather, blocks of data—packets—are routed through a fixed network that is shared by all communicating devices. We can think of a packet-switched network as a highway system through which different packets follow different paths as needed to reach their individual destinations. Currently, the most popular transmission medium for packet-switched local area networks is the coaxial cable.

Each computer or other device attached to a network is called a *node*. Most nodes are microcomputer workstations, but mainframe computers, printers, and hard disk drives can also serve as nodes. Each node has a unique network address that is used for designating that node as the originator or recipient of a particular packet.

Each node is connected to the local area network cable via a network interface. The network interface can be mounted in its own box, or it can be on a circuit board that plugs into one of a computer's expansion slots. The interface usually has the responsibility of intercepting packets addressed to a particular node and ignoring or passing on packets addressed to other nodes.

The configuration of connecting cables is known as the *network topology*. Figure 9-4 shows three popular topologies: the *star*, the *bus*, and the *ring*.

Star Topology   In the star topology, all packets are sent to a central switching point that forwards each packet to its proper destination. The main advantage of this toplogy is that a break in any cable or the malfunction of any device other than the central switch will not bring down the entire network. The main disadvantage is that each node must be connected to the central switch by a separate cable.

A network in which a number of microcomputers or computer terminals communicate with a central computer (a mainframe, minicomputer, or multiuser microcomputer) has a star topology. The central computer is at the center of the star and the other computers or terminals are at the points. The central computer serves not only as a message forwarding device but as a repository for data and a source of computing services. Circuit-switched networks also have a star topology, since central switching equipment is needed to establish connections between different devices. Normally, topologies other than the star are preferred for packet-switched networks.

Bus Topology   In the bus topology, all nodes are connected to a common cable called the bus.* A packet transmitted by one node is received by all other nodes connected to the bus. Only the node to which the packet is addressed accepts and processes it. Only one node can transmit at a time; if two or more nodes transmit at the same time, all the transmissions will be garbled.

The nodes share the bus in same way that radio operators share a common channel such as a CB channel. Before transmitting, each operator listens to make sure that the channel is not in use. Each transmission is received by everyone else that is listening to the channel, but only the operator to whom the message is addressed pays attention to it. If two or more operators happen to transmit at the same time, all transmissions will be garbled and all will have to try again at a later time.

The computer version of this protocol goes by the formidable name of *Carrier Sense Multiple Access with Collision Detection (CSMA/CD)*. Before transmitting, each node checks whether the bus is in use, which it does by *sensing* the *carrier* signal that will be present if another node is transmitting. A *collision* occurs when two or more nodes happen to begin transmitting at the same time. Each of the simultaneously transmitting

---

*Not to be confused with the internal bus found in most computers and discussed in Chapter 3.

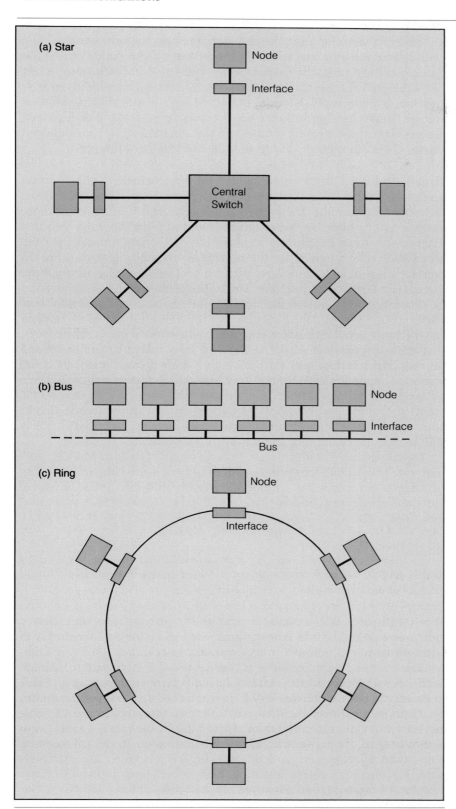

FIGURE 9-4
The star, bus, and ring network topologies. The small boxes represent the network interfaces and the larger boxes represent the nodes. For the star topology, the large central box represents the central switching device.

nodes can *detect* that a collision has occurred. Each node waits for a randomly chosen length of time and then attempts to transmit again. The waiting time must be randomly chosen because if the nodes waited the same amount of time, they would again interfere with each other when they attempted another transmission. After each failed attempt to transmit a packet, a node waits a longer period of time before making another attempt. Thus when traffic on the bus becomes congested, the nodes transmit less frequently, helping to alleviate the situation. In a well-designed system, collisions are rare and have little effect on performance.

Ring Topology   In the ring topology, packets circulate in one direction around a circular cable that passes through the interface of each node. Each interface monitors the packets passing through it and accepts those addressed to its node. A packet can be removed from the ring when it is accepted, or it can be allowed to make one full circuit around the ring, after which it is removed by the node that originally sent it. Since an interface must be able to remove packets, packets must pass through the internal circuitry of each interface. The failure of one interface will interrupt the flow of packets around the ring and thus bring down the entire network.

The most popular protocol governing transmission on a ring network is called *token passing*. A special code, called a *token*, circulates around the ring. An interface can transmit only when it has the token in its possession. A node that does not have a packet to transmit simply passes the token on to the next node. A node that does have a packet to transmit retains the token and transmits its packet. It then transmits the token, either immediately after sending its packet or after its packet has made a complete circuit of the ring and has been removed.

Token passing is a much more orderly protocol than CSMA/CD; collisions are impossible, for example, since only one node—the one that has the token—can transmit at a time. One pays for this orderliness, however, with data transfer rate, which is typically about a quarter of that achievable with CSMA/CD.

Nodes

In this section we look briefly at the kinds of nodes that might be found on a local area network.

Workstations   Microcomputers attached to a network are often referred to as *workstations*. Office workstations, used in businesses, are similar to other office microcomputers. They may, however, lack hardware components that can be accessed over the network. A workstation may not need a printer if access to a printer is available through the network. Some workstations do not even have disk drives; all the data and programs they need are obtained over the network. A diskless workstation must be able to "boot from the network"—that is, to load its operating system automatically from the network each time it is turned on. Technical workstations, used by engineers and other technical personnel, are extremely powerful microcomputers featuring high speed microprocessors, large amounts of memory, and advanced graphics capabilities.

Optical fibers are finding ever increasing use in both wide area and local area networks.

File Servers   A *server* is a dedicated microcomputer that acts as an interface between the network and one or more peripheral devices. A file server provides access to one or more disk drives. Workstations transfer data files to and from the disks by exchanging appropriate messages with the file server.

Printer Servers   A printer server provides access to one or more printers. Workstations generate printout by sending appropriate messages to the printer server.

Utility Servers   A utility server provides access to miscellaneous peripherals such as a modem or plotter.

Mainframes   A mainframe can be a node on a local area network, providing computational services to workstations and allowing them access to its files.

Gateways   A gateway allows messages to be sent to and received from another local area network. For example, local area networks in different buildings may be joined by gateways. Via gateways, local area networks can function as nodes in a wide area network.

Summary

Telecommunications and data communications refer to the electronic transfer of data between computers. Any facility for communication among computers is known as a network. In a circuit-switched network, a connection is established between each pair of communicating computers. A packet-switched network, in contrast, serves as a fixed highway system over which blocks of data, or packets, are routed as needed to reach their individual destinations. A wide area network allows communication between widely separated computers, such as those in different cities or countries. The telephone network is often pressed into service for wide area data communications, a function that it was not designed for and does not always perform well. A modem serves as an interface between a computer and the telephone network. In the future, the telephone industry is expected to convert to an Integrated Services Digital Network (ISDN), which promises faster and more reliable digital communication.

Computer bulletin board systems and information services offer a variety of services to the public via the telephone network. Communications software helps microcomputer users communicate with information services and transfer files between computers. A local area network (LAN) extends over a limited area such as a single building. Businesses are increasingly using local area networks to link microcomputer workstations, peripherals such as printers and disk drives, and perhaps mainframe computers as well. A gateway allows messages to be exchanged between local area networks; with the aid of a gateway, a local area network can be a node a wide area network.

Vocabulary Review

acoustic coupler
answer mode
asynchronous
  communication
AT commands
carrier
circuit-switched
  network
coaxial cable
collision
communications
  protocol
dial-up line
direct connect modem
downloading
dumb terminal
echoing
electronic mail
error-correcting
  protocol
error-detecting code

even parity
information service
Integrated Services
  Digital Network
  (ISDN)
leased line
local area network
  (LAN)
modem
network
node
null modem
odd parity
on-line database
optical fiber
originate mode
packet
packet-switched
  network
parity bit

private branch
  exchange (PBX)
serial port
server
smart modem
smart terminal
star topology
start bit
stop bit
synchronous
  communication
technical workstation
token
token passing
twisted pair
uploading
value-added network
wide area network
workstation
XMODEM protocol

For Further Reading

Bartee, Thomas C., ed. *Digital Communications*. Indianapolis: Howard W. Sams, 1986.

King, Stephen S. "Network Complexity" (a survey of LAN technology). *PC Tech Journal*, June 1988, pp. 44–52.

Tannenbaum, Andrew S. *Computer Networks*. Englewood Cliffs, NJ: Prentice-Hall, 1981.

Review Questions

1 Distinguish between wide area networks and local area networks.

2 Contrast dial-up and leased lines.

3 What is the function of a modem?

4 Distinguish between answer and originate modes.

5 What four transmission speeds are most commonly used on dial-up lines?

6 Describe four methods by which a computer can be connected to a telephone line or directly to another computer.

7 Distinguish between synchronous and asynchronous communication. Which is usually employed by microcomputer users?

8 Describe the details that must be fixed to establish a protocol for asynchronous communication.

9 What is packet switching? Describe how a microcomputer might communicate over a packet-switched network operated by a communications company.

10 Describe the difficulties of digital communication over the existing telephone network. How will these difficulties be alleviated by ISDN?

11 Why must data files often be transferred between computers over a communications channel rather than by carrying disks from one computer to the other?

12 What two problems can arise when microcomputers are given access to files stored on a mainframe?

13 What services are provided by computer bulletin board systems? How have these systems sometimes been misused?

14 Describe some of the kinds of information provided by an information service.

15 Describe typical functions of a communications program.

16 Describe three transmission media used for local area networks. Which is the most economical and why? Which is most widely used for packet-switched networks?

17 What is a PBX? How can a circuit-switched local area network be implemented with a PBX?

18 What is a node on a network? What is a node's network address?

19 Describe the three network topologies commonly used for local area networks. Which topology is used for circuit-switched networks?

20 Contrast the CSMA/CD and token-passing protocols. For which network topology is each protocol normally used?

21 Describe six types of nodes commonly found on local area networks.

22 What does it mean to say that a workstation can "boot from the network?"

Topics for Discussion

1 Discuss the likelihood that the general public will ever become interested in using computerized information and ordering services such as videotex. Note that such services are popular when they do not involve computers, as evidenced by the popularity of home-shopping television channels, which show products that viewers can order over the telephone.

2 Some have suggested that computer conferences provide ideal forums for debating highly controversial topics. Because participants have as long as they wish to consider and compose their remarks, tempers might remain cooler and the remarks might be more thoughtful. Discuss; if possible, include in the discussion someone who has participated in computer conferences on electronic bulletin boards or information services.

PART FOUR

PUTTING COMPUTERS TO WORK

COMPUTERS IN HEALTH CARE

INTRODUCTION

Information processing plays a central role in the practice of medicine. Medical workers must take into account all the information relevant to a patient's problem before deciding on the proper course of action. This involves coordinating the patient's complaints, the results of examinations and laboratory tests, the patient's previous medical history, and the known symptoms and treatments for many thousands of diseases. Computers are becoming more and more important in helping medical workers cope with the massive amounts of information that may have to be taken into account in making even the simplest medical decision.

Both the hospital and the private doctor's office are businesses that must keep ordinary business records such as accounts receivable, accounts payable, inventories, and payroll records. Record keeping is more complicated than for many other businesses because much medical care is paid for by insurance companies or government agencies, each of which may have its own special requirements. Computers are now standard in hospitals, and they are making their way into private doctor's offices as well.

Computers are playing ever increasing roles in medical training and research. Some of the most recent diagnostic techniques developed by medical researchers would be impossible without computers.

HOSPITAL AND MEDICAL OFFICE ADMINISTRATION

A hospital has most of the same administrative requirements as any other business: ordering and paying for supplies, collecting payments for services rendered, paying employees, and controlling inventories. This is particularly true since many hospitals today are profit-making corporations rather than public institutions, a controversial development but one that seems to be a permanent feature of American medical practice. The payment rules and the reporting and record-keeping requirements of insurance companies and government agencies greatly increase the complexity of payment collection.

Hospital Information Systems

A *hospital information system* maintains a database containing each patient's medical record. The information stored for each patient includes vital signs, examination results, laboratory test results, diagnoses, treatments ranging from drugs to surgery, and dietary requirements.

When a patient is admitted, his or her personal data is entered into the system along with insurance information. Newly admitted patients or their relatives are asked to fill out a questionnaire concerning allergies and other problems that might affect treatment; this information, along with medical information transmitted by the patient's doctor, also goes into the system. During the patient's stay, the doctor's orders are entered into the system along with records of all treatments administered and the results of all tests that were carried out. This information can be displayed im-

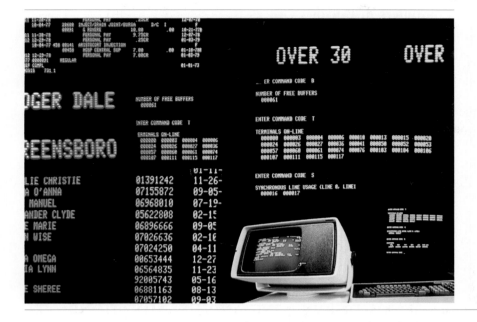

Hospital accounting via computer.

mediately when needed by nurses and doctors. All tests and other procedures ordered by the doctor are scheduled by the computer system.

The system is responsible for communicating medical information between the central database and the points where the information originates and where it is used. This is done via a local area network that connects the central computer to video display terminals and printers at such points as the patients' bedsides, nurses' stations, doctors' offices, operating rooms, laboratories, and the dietician's office. At each terminal it is possible to view a patient's records and to enter new information. The system may also communicate directly with automated medical equipment.

When new information is entered, the computer compares it with information already in the database and alerts medical workers to any situation that needs immediate attention. For example, a blood test might indicate a low potassium level; in this situation certain drugs, such as the heart drug digoxin, are dangerous. If the laboratory entered blood test results showing a low potassium level, and the database indicated that the patient was receiving digoxin, the system would immediately alert nurses to the danger.

A hospital information system can collect statistical information on patients and the conditions from which they suffer. This information is useful for medical research, and it can help hospital administrators set charges and make decisions about staffing, equipment purchases, and construction of new buildings.

Future hospital information systems probably will be able to store medical images (such as X rays) in the central database and transmit them to terminals wherever they are needed. This is well within the capabilities of current technology; the problem is the high cost of the necessary high-resolution graphics terminals, wideband communications links, and substantially greater storage capacity in the central database.

Computers in Doctor's Offices

The private doctor's office faces many of the same problems as the hospital, although on a smaller scale. Microcomputers have begun to appear in private doctors' offices; however, their adoption has been slow, because until now it was up to individual doctors to collect the necessary hardware and software to implement an office computer system, something likely to be done only by the technologically adventuresome. But now more and more vendors are concentrating on *vertical markets*—markets in particular application areas, such as medical office systems. Doctors are likely to find the complete hardware and software systems offered by these vendors increasingly hard to resist.

Currently most computers in doctors' offices are used for managing business and financial information. But other applications are emerging, such as on-line medical databases and advice systems that the doctor can access over the telephone with the aid of a computer and a modem.

PATIENT INTERVIEWING AND EXAMINATIONS

Collecting medical information through examinations and patient interviews occupies a large part of the time of trained medical workers, many of whom would be more effective working at other tasks. Although neither interviews nor examinations can be completely turned over to computers, both can be considerably automated.

In computerized *patient interviewing*, questions for the patient appear on a video display terminal. For each question, the patient is given a menu of possible responses. The patient selects the proper response using a light-pen, mouse, or touch-sensitive screen. The screen may show a diagram of the human body, with the patient asked to point out the locations of pains and other difficulties. Typing is often avoided because many patients may not have typing skills or may be prevented from typing by the nature of their disorders.

Patients seem happy with automated interviews and may even prefer them to being interviewed by a medical worker. One reason is that the computer is infinitely patient; the subject of the interview has all the time needed to consider each question without pressure from a medical worker anxious to get through with the interview and get on to the next patient. In certain emotionally charged areas, such as sex-related disorders, patients may feel much more comfortable interacting with an emotionless computer than with a possibly judgemental medical worker.

For this reason, computerized interviews are proving particularly useful in psychology, where patients are often reluctant to discuss their problems with human therapists. Also, some psychologists are finding that their patients benefit from playing computer games that challenge the players to solve typical problems in such areas as dating, marriage, and family life.

Automated multiphasic health testing, a highly automated approach to physical examinations, is becoming increasingly popular. On reporting to the testing center, the patient's personal data is entered into the computer and the patient is given a computer-generated identification card that can

Computer in doctor's office.

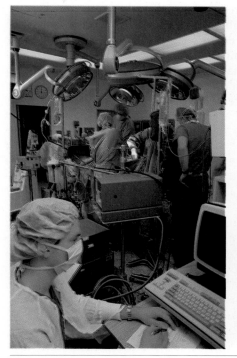

Computer terminals at nurses' station (top), in an operating room (bottom left), and at patient's bedside (bottom right) provide access to the hospital information system.

be used to locate his or her records on subsequent visits. The computer schedules the patient's tests and produces any needed printed copy, such as labels for specimen containers. The actual tests are administered by medical workers and the analyses are performed by laboratory technicians using highly automated equipment. Whenever possible, the results of tests are transmitted directly to the computer from medical and laboratory instruments. When all tests have been completed, a computer-printed report containing the results is sent to the patient's physician.

Automatic equipment now makes it possible to carry out more tests in the doctor's office rather than at a laboratory or testing center. For example, a recently developed machine, the Vision blood analyzer, tests blood samples in the doctor's office. The $18,500 machine, which is about the size of a microwave oven, takes 10 to 15 minutes to perform 10 common blood tests.

MEDICAL DATABASES AND ADVICE SYSTEMS

Medical workers are burdened with the need to retain and assimilate enormous amounts of information. A doctor may need to be familiar with the treatments and symptoms of thousands of diseases. New results crucial to a doctor's practice appear almost daily in the more than 5000 medical journals. The medical community has responded to this problem by creating narrower and narrower specialties, but so complex is the situation that it may be difficult for a general practitioner to determine the specialist to which a patient should be referred.

Computers are being pressed into service to help doctors deal with this deluge of information. Some doctors resist this form of computerization, which they see as encroaching on their professional responsibilities. But so serious is the medical information explosion that doctors who resist the use of computers may be as out of step with the development of their profession as were those who once resisted washing their hands before administering to patients.

Doctor consulting medical database via computer terminal.

Medical Databases

A straightforward attack on the problem is the creation of on-line *medical databases* containing the latest results in a particular branch of medicine. Doctors and researchers can access the databases from their offices through computer terminals or microcomputers. A database can be searched automatically using criteria meaningful to medical workers; for example, a doctor might search for all discussions of a particular set of symptoms or a particular method of treatment.

One medical database contains the case histories of around 3000 heart patients. When the physician enters the details of a patient's condition, the computer system retrieves the most closely matching case history. The physician may then use the course of treatment described in the case history as a guide in treating his or her current patient.

Another well-known medical database is PDQ (Physician Data Query), which is operated jointly by the National Cancer Institute and the National Medical Library. PDQ provides information on cancer-treatment protocols: detailed descriptions of new treatments being tested in ongoing clinical trials. PDQ helps a doctor locate those experimental treatments that might be beneficial for a particular patient. Also, the doctor can obtain the names and addresses of the researchers studying a particular treatment, thereby enabling the doctor to consult the researchers or refer the patient to them.

Advice Systems

An *advice system* can be viewed as a special approach to storing and retrieving medical knowledge. Instead of merely displaying stored information on request, the system uses the stored knowledge to advise physicians on the diagnosis and treatment of individual cases. Advice systems are based on the techniques of artificial intelligence, particularly the branch of artificial intelligence that studies expert systems. Expert systems use stored knowledge to emulate a human expert's ability to solve problems, answer questions, and make judgements. More about expert systems can be found in Chapter 15, which is devoted to artificial intelligence.

Advice systems can be divided into consultation systems and critiquing systems. With a *consultation system*, the physician enters the patient's symptoms and the results of examinations and tests; the system suggests possible diagnoses and treatments. With a *critiquing system*, the physician enters a proposed diagnosis and treatment along with the symptoms and test results. The system critiques the diagnosis and treatment by suggesting alternatives to the physician's decisions, thus alerting the physician to possibilities that might have otherwise been overlooked. Either kind of system will, on request, display the details of the reasoning behind any of its proposals.

Some well-known advice systems are DXplain and QMR (Quick Medical Reference), which consult on diagnoses, ONCOCIN, which consults on the management of cancer treatment, and ROUNDSMAN, which critiques the management of breast-cancer treatment. Advice systems are still largely experimental, but some are becoming available to physicians for routine use. For example, DXplain is available on the American Medical Association's AMA/NET computer network, and can be consulted by any physician with a personal computer and modem.

No computer system can have the breadth and depth of knowledge and experience that a physician brings to a case. Thus a doctor may be able to eliminate quickly as unrealistic many of the proposals made by an advice system. On the other hand, such systems can alert physicians to possible diagnoses and treatments they may have overlooked because the doctor either lacked experience with the disease in question or was not familiar with the latest research in a particular area.

For perhaps understandable reasons, many physicians show little enthusiasm for sharing their diagnostic responsibilities with computers. Yet others feel that medical databases and advice systems may herald fundamental changes in the way physicians are trained. Because of the massive amounts of information that physicians must master, medical education currently emphasizes rote memory rather than mastery of fundamentals. If computers can be used to keep track of the facts that must be at a physician's disposal, medical students can concentrate more on acquiring the judgement, wisdom, and understanding that no one has yet succeeded in incorporating in any computer program.

MEDICAL IMAGING

Some modern medical examination procedures would be completely impractical without computers. These procedures require extensive computations to get the desired results from the data collected. Without the computer, the calculations would take months or years, and the results would come too late to be of any use. Into this category fall *medical imaging* techniques, which use extensive computations to extract meaningful images from masses of data recorded by medical instruments.

The most widely used imaging technique is *computer-aided tomography (CAT)*. *Tomography* comes from a Greek word meaning "slice." This name was chosen because tomography presents the physician with a picture of a cross-sectional slice of the human body.

Tomography uses X rays to look inside the body, but it differs from conventional X-ray methods in several ways. A conventional X-ray picture is just a collection of shadows, since X rays cannot be focused with lenses. An X-ray picture is related to a true picture of the inside of your body much as your shadow is related to your photograph.

The internal organs of the body do not stand out well in conventional X-ray pictures because the organs differ only slightly from the surrounding tissues in their ability to absorb X rays. (To make them stand out better, patients may have to endure unpleasant procedures, such as having their internal organs inflated with air.) In conventional X-ray pictures, the shadows of several organs may overlap, obscuring details.

In tomography, an X-ray source rotates around the patient, sending a beam of X rays through the slice to be observed. An X-ray detector also rotates around the patient in such a way that it is always on the opposite

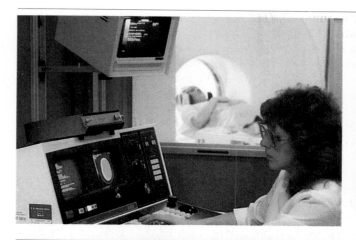

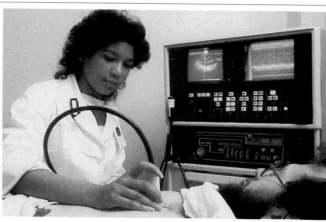

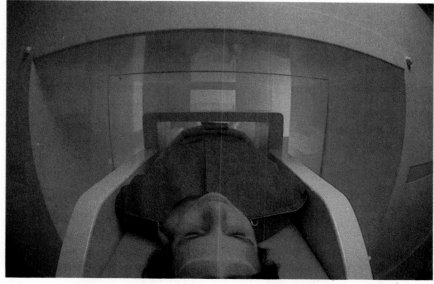

Patients receiving CAT scan (top left), ultrasound scan (top right), and NMR (nuclear magnetic resonance) scan (bottom).

side of the patient from the X-ray source. The detector records the intensity of the X-ray beam after it has passed through the patient.

From the recorded data, it is easy to determine the degree to which the X-ray beam is absorbed as it passes through the patient in different directions. But without further processing, this information is useless. This is because each X-ray beam passes through many different organs as it travels through the patient's body; part of the beam is absorbed by each organ it travels through. Thus the degree to which the beam is absorbed as it passes through the patient's body tells us nothing about any particular organ.

Here is where the computer comes in. Starting with the absorption data for beams passing through a slice of the body in many different directions, the computer can calculate the degree to which the beam must

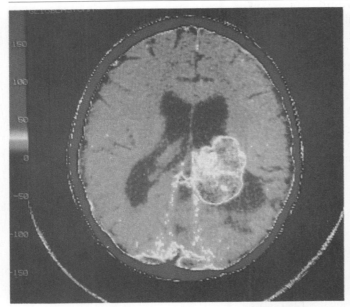
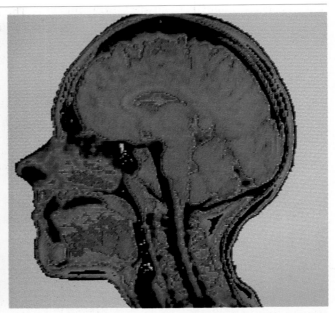

CAT scan of brain tumor (top left) and NMR scans (top right and bottom).

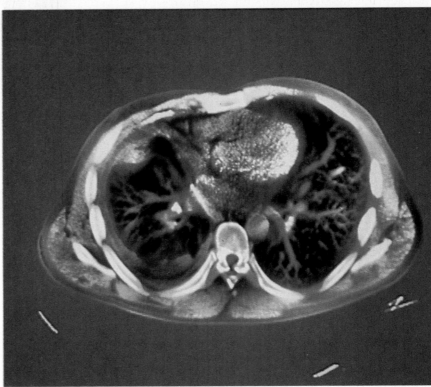

have been absorbed at each point inside the slice. The result is presented as a picture in which different colors correspond to different degrees of absorption. The internal organs stand out vividly in this picture.

X rays are not the only physical effect that can be used to obtain images of internal organs. Two other important techniques are *ultrasound*, which uses sound waves pitched beyond the range of human hearing, and *nuclear magnetic resonance (NMR)*, which uses radio waves. Just as a scene may appear different when illuminated by different colored lights, so different aspects of the human body are seen when it is investigated with X rays, sound waves, and radio waves. In each case, a computer is essential for creating an image from the data collected by the medical instrument.

PATIENT MONITORING

Computers are widely used for *patient monitoring* in intensive-care units. The computer can monitor such variables as heart rate, temperature, blood pressure, and the gaseous components of the patient's breath. An alarm is sounded if any variable goes outside of a predetermined range or if a life-threatening event, such as abnormal heartbeat, occurs. A single central computer can monitor many different patients via connections to medical instruments installed in each patient's room.

Microprocessors have made possible portable medical monitors that can be carried easily by seriously ill patients. A heart patient, for example, can wear a portable computerized monitor that continually analyzes the electrical signals generated by the heart. When the computer detects an abnormality, it can warn the patient to lie down and rest, to take a certain medicine, or to consult a doctor immediately. If despite all precautions an attack does occur, the monitor can sound an alarm to alert bystanders.

Portable medical monitors can also aid diagnosis by collecting and recording details of important but rare events. For example, people with heart disease suffer from arrhythmias—irregular heartbeats. Data on arrhythmias provide valuable information about the condition of the heart. The difficulty is that only a few of the hundred thousand heartbeats in a 24-hour period are likely to be arrhythmias. Thus a 12- to 24-hour electrocardiogram (recording of the electrical activity of the heart) may be needed to find any arrhythmias at all. Even then, the task of finding arrhythmias is tedious, as each is buried among many normal heartbeats.

The solution to this problem lies in the use of a portable monitor. A microprocessor inside the monitor analyzes the electrical signals generated by the heart. It ignores the signals for normal heartbeats but stores those for arrhythmias. The patient can wear the portable monitor through a normal day's activities. At the end of the day, the patient telephones the hospital's computer and connects the monitor to the telephone line through a modem. The data for the day is sent over the telephone to the hospital computer, where it is stored for analysis.

Detecting arrhythmias is an application of *pattern recognition*, an important concept in artificial intelligence. The monitor must be able to distinguish arrhythmias from normal heartbeats; that is, it must recognize the patterns of electrical events that signal an arrhythmia. It must be able

Medical monitor attached to a baby.

to do this in spite of electrical interference that the monitor might pick up. Also, the pattern-recognition program must be adaptable, since what is an arrhythmia to one patient may be a normal heartbeat to another.

APPLICATIONS TO PHARMACY

Prescribing drugs is fraught with dangers. Some patients are allergic to some drugs. Although a drug is prescribed for a particular beneficial effect, such as combatting an infection, most drugs have additional side effects that can be harmful to some patients. Drugs that are safe when taken by themselves can, when taken together, interact in ways harmful to the patient. This problem is particularly severe when a patient sees several physicians, each of whom knows nothing of what the others are prescribing.

To aid physicians and pharmacists in dealing with this problem, a number of databases have been constructed to deal with drugs and drug interactions. The entry in the database for each drug gives the approved use for the drug, its recommended dosages, possible side effects, and possible interactions with other drugs.

Systems that automatically alert pharmacists to improper medication are coming into increasingly wider use. Each prescription that a patient has filled is entered into the computer system. The computer maintains a drug profile for each patient showing what drugs the patient is currently taking. If a newly prescribed drug would interact adversely with a drug the patient is already taking, the pharmacist is notified. If the computer system contains additional information about the patient's health and the conditions for which the patient is being treated, it can alert the pharmacist to allergies, side effects, and improper therapy.

Computer systems can also be used to construct drug-prescribing profiles for physicians. These profiles show how a particular physician's use of each drug compares with national averages. After reviewing such profiles, physicians may wish to modify their drug-prescribing habits to bring them into closer conformity with the practice of other physicians. On the other hand, it would be unfortunate if the use of such systems tended to suppress legitimate differences of opinion among physicians as to how certain drugs should be used.

MEDICAL RESEARCH

Computers now play a fundamental role in almost all forms of scientific research. Medical research is no exception. The following are some of the most common applications of computers in medical research.

- **Controlling Laboratory Apparatus and Collecting Data** The computer allows experiments to be run for long periods of time without human intervention.

- **Statistical Analysis of Experimental Results** Statistical analysis helps scientists arrive at valid conclusions in spite of the unavoidable errors in experimental data.

- **Statistical Analysis of Medical Records** Statistical analysis of hospital and other medical records yields valuable information as to the prevalence of various diseases and the geographical patterns in which they occur. This information can be used to alert medical workers to threats of epidemics, to focus the efforts of medical researchers where they are most needed, and to aid the medical community in allocating such resources as people, equipment, and buildings.

Pharmacist using a computer.

■ **Reducing Experimental Data to Useful Form** Readings obtained from laboratory apparatus are seldom the results actually sought in the experiment. Computations usually have to be performed to extract useful information from the raw data. Imaging systems provide one of the best examples of this.

■ **Simulating Real Systems** A computer can be programmed to mimic or *simulate* the behavior of some real system such as the human body or the population of a city. The purpose of a simulation can be (a) to do experiments that would be impractical with the real system, (b) to test our knowledge of the real system by incorporating our ideas into a computer model and comparing the model's behavior with that of the actual system, or (c) training students to deal with the actual system.

■ **Collecting and Analyzing Data from Portable Medical Monitors** Portable medical monitors carried by research subjects allow data to be gathered under the conditions of everyday life rather than under those prevailing in hospitals and laboratories.

TRAINING OF MEDICAL STUDENTS

Computer simulations allow medical students to experiment with various courses of treatment without endangering the lives of real patients. The simulation program presents medical data for a hypothetical patient and invites the student to choose a treatment. After the student makes a choice, the program displays the response of the hypothetical patient. If the response is unsatisfactory, the student chooses another treatment, to which

Computer in a medical laboratory.

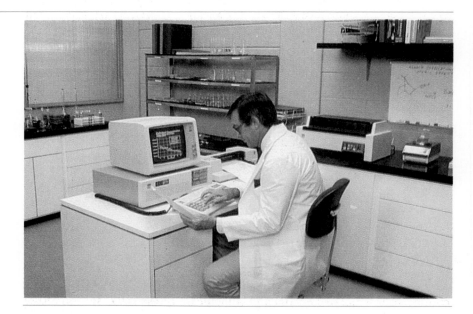

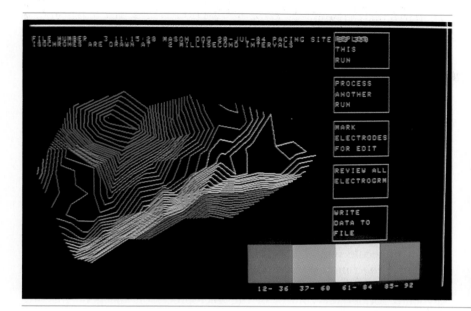

Map generated from electrocardiogram data reveals the size and shape of the heart and the condition of heart tissues.

the program again displays the patient's response, and so on. If the hypothetical patient dies, the program produces an autopsy report.

For practice in emergency procedures, a computer can be connected to a lifelike mannequin whose temperature, blood pressure, respiration, heartbeat, and so on are controlled by the computer. Under the control of the computer, the mannequin can suffer such difficulties as respiratory failure and cardiac arrest. The computer determines the mannequin's responses to such emergency procedures as the administration of oxygen and drugs.

Many of the educational applications of computers described in Chapter 11 apply also to medical education. For example, a computer-controlled optical-disc player can present the student with the sounds heard through a stethoscope, pictures of various parts of the patient's body, X rays, the output from medical imaging systems, and the sight and sound of the patient explaining his or her symptoms.

Many computer games are now available that challenge medical students and practicing physicians in such areas as diagnosis, treatment, emergency procedures, and interacting with patients. One such game program, called CYBERLOG, presents physicians with simulated case problems involving such topics as high blood pressure, fluid balance, and diabetes. The program is provided on a diskette for use in the physician's personal computer.

BIOTECHNOLOGY

All living organisms, from bacteria to human beings, are constructed according to instructions encoded in a molecule called *DNA*. By modifying these instructions, *biotechnology (genetic engineering)* can create new forms of life and modify existing ones. The immediate goal is to create bacteria that will produce useful compounds called proteins. Important proteins include insulin for diabetics, hormones for persons with glandular disorders, the experimental virus-fighting agent interferon, the heart-attack drug TPA, and enzymes—special proteins that help bring about important chemical reactions such as those that change milk into cheese.

The study of the message carried by the DNA molecule and the errors that can occur in the message may yield insight into many hitherto incurable diseases. For example, the discovery that particular genes (segments of the DNA message) are responsible for some forms of cancer is considered to be an important advance in the fight against the disease.

The message carried by the DNA molecule is encoded in a series of compounds called bases. The four possible bases serve as letters in the genetic alphabet. To compose a particular genetic message, one must create a DNA molecule with a particular sequence of bases. This can be done with *gene machines*, microprocessor-controlled devices for synthesizing DNA. To use a gene machine, the operator enters a genetic message on a keyboard. Under the control of the microprocessor, the gene machine carries out all the chemical steps necessary to synthesize the corresponding strand of DNA. Currently, gene machines can synthesize only short segments of DNA. However, the short segments can be inserted into much longer segments obtained from living organisms, thereby modifying their genetic messages.

Computer-controlled machines are also used for sequencing DNA—for determining the sequence of bases in a naturally occurring strand of DNA, thereby allowing the genetic message to be read. Scientists are now preparing to embark on the *Human Genome Initiative*, a project designed to sequence the strands of DNA that make up the human genome—the genetic blueprint from which all human beings are constructed. Since the human genome contains some 3 billion bases, the project is a major one,

Computer graphics display of DNA, the molecule that carries the genetic message.

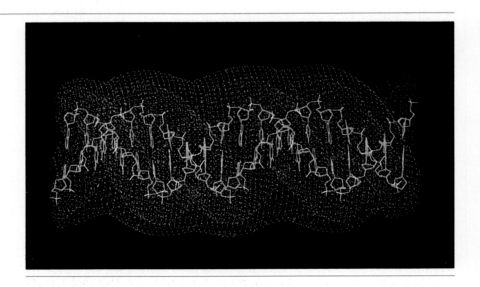

expected to cost about $3 billion and take over ten years to complete. The results, however, are expected to be of enormous importance to medical research. Computers will be essential not only for controlling the machines that sequence DNA strands, but also for maintaining and accessing the large databases in which the results will be stored.

Computers also play an important role in designing the proteins that are synthesized with genetic techniques. Computer models of proteins and other chemical molecules have largely replaced the stick-and-ball models that chemists previously used (and were often photographed holding). Computer models help chemists to determine the structure that a protein must have in order to serve a particular purpose. This information is then used to genetically program bacteria to synthesize the desired protein. High-quality computer graphics are essential for displaying the molecules being modeled.

◥ AIDING THE HANDICAPPED

The brain receives information from sense organs and directs the movement of the limbs via electrical messages carried by nerves. Handicaps result when nerve pathways are damaged and when natural limbs and sense organs must be replaced by prosthetic devices. Computer-based electronic systems offer the possibility of bypassing damaged nerve pathways and allowing the brain to directly perceive and control prosthetic devices. Research in this area of *bioengineering* (designing aids for the handicapped) is in its infancy, but the results obtained so far are encouraging.

For example, a recently developed system combats deafness by stimulating the auditory nerve endings in the inner ear when sound is picked up by a microphone. At present the fidelity of sound perception leaves much to be desired, but the patient can at least detect when certain kinds of sounds are present and thus be able to respond to, say, a ringing telephone or a crying baby.

In one well-publicized experiment, a computer system was used to give a paralyzed person some control over her legs by bypassing destroyed nerve connections. Nerve impulses picked up from the patient's shoulder muscles were processed by the computer and transmitted to the leg muscles. By flexing her shoulder muscles, the patient was able to control her leg muscles and so walk in a limited way.

Computers can translate the information usually perceived by a sense that has failed into a form that can be perceived by a sense that is working. For example, a computer can read printed words and pronounce them for a blind person. In another approach to the same problem, images picked up by a television camera are converted into tactile (touch) sensations that a blind person can perceive.

◥ RELIABILITY AND SAFETY

Hardware and software failures in medical computer systems can have tragic consequences and lead to enormous legal liabilities. One major man-

Machine for reading printed text to the blind.

ufacturer of microprocessors specifies that they are not intended for use in medical equipment; the reason is not that the microprocessors are particularly unsuited for medical applications, but because the manufacturer fears the lawsuits that would surely result if a microprocessor malfunction or design flaw caused injury or death.

Software presents even greater possibilities for catastrophe than hardware. Failure of a hardware component often renders the computer system inoperative or at least produces effects that warn the operators of the problem. On the other hand, a software bug can cause a system to appear to be working properly but to do something quite different from what was intended, with tragic consequences.

Such tragedies have occurred with the Therac 25, a computer-controlled machine for administering radiation therapy. Due to a bug in the control program, a routine correction of an operator's typing error could cause the radiation delivered by the machine to be thousands of times more intense than intended. The problem was not discovered until several patients had been severely injured; two of the injured patients died.

The problem was hard to pin down because the machine usually worked correctly; only a particular sequence of keystrokes, used to correct an operator error, would trigger the bug. The machine actually displayed a cryptic error message after it had malfunctioned. But because it seemed to be working properly otherwise, operators initially ignored the error message as well as complaints of excruciating pain from the patients on whom the machine malfunctioned.

After the problem was discovered, the machine's manufacturer recommended removing the upward-arrow key from the computer's keyboard, since it was the use of this key during error correction that triggered the bug. With this modification, Therac 25s were certified for continued use. Sadly, however, not all the bugs had been found: later a completely different software bug caused a Therac 25 to deliver radiation 45 times more intense than desired, killing another patient.

After the second software bug was discovered, the manufacturer installed so-called fail-safe circuitry, which is supposed to bypass the computer and assure that the machine can never deliver excessive radiation. With this modification, Therac 25s once again have been certified for use, although the hospital at which the original two deaths occurred does not plan to resume use of its Therac 25. Lawsuits have been filed on behalf of the dead and injured; their outcome may set precedents for cases in which people are injured or killed by malfunctioning software.

In 1988, the Food and Drug Administration (FDA) announced its intention to regulate software incorporated in medical devices (such as the Therac 25). Software whose output is interpreted by medical professionals, such as medical database and advice systems, will probably be exempt from regulation. The question can be raised, however, whether the FDA will be any more successful than anyone else in finding rarely occurring software bugs.

Summary

Medical workers must cope with enormous amounts of information in the form of business records, patient records, laboratory reports, and the ever increasing body of medical knowledge and procedures. To cope with this deluge of information, medical workers are increasingly turning to computers, which are now standard in hospitals (hospital information systems) and are becoming more and more widely used in other places, such as independent laboratories and private doctor's offices.

Computers are being used for patient interviewing and managing physical examinations. Most patients seem satisfied with computer-conducted interviews and some even prefer them to interviews conducted by medical workers.

Medical databases provide doctors with the latest information on diagnoses and treatments. Advice systems diagnose illnesses and recommend treatments based on the patient's symptoms, the results of tests, and medical knowledge stored in a database. Understandably, many doctors are reluctant to turn any part of their diagnostic and prescriptive responsibilities over to a computer. On the other hand, some see in such systems the promise that medical training can one day emphasize mastery of fundamental principles rather than rote learning of symptoms and treatments for particular disorders.

Computers are being applied in a number of areas related to health care, such as medical imaging, patient monitoring, pharmacy, medical research, medical training, biotechnolgy (genetic engineering), and bioengineering (designing aids for the handicapped).

The more computers are used in medicine, the greater are the chances that malfunctioning hardware or software will have tragic consequences. Such tragedies have already occurred with a computer-controlled radiation-therapy machine; a software bug caused the machine to deliver intense doses of radiation that killed or injured several patients.

Vocabulary Review

advice system
automated
  multiphasic health
  testing
bioengineering
biotechnology
computer-aided
  tomography (CAT)
consultation system

critiquing system
DNA
gene machine
genetic engineering
hospital information
  system
Human Genome
  Initiative
medical database

medical imaging
nuclear magnetic
  resonance (NMR)
patient interviewing
patient monitoring
pattern recognition
ultrasound
vertical market

For Further Reading

Gordon, Richard, et al. "Image Reconstruction from Projections." *Scientific American*, October 1975, pp. 56−68.

Hastings, Susan. "Psychiatric Assessment via Computer." *Creative Computing*, July-August 1977, p. 34.

Redington, Rowland W. and Walter H. Berninger. "Medical Imaging Systems." *Physics Today*, August 1981, pp. 36−44.

Rennels, Glenn D. and Edward H. Shortliffe. "Advanced Computing for Medicine." *Scientific American*, October 1987, pp. 154−161.

Sochurek, Howard. "Medicine's New Vision." *National Geographic*, January 1987, pp. 2−41.

Swindell, William and Harrison H. Barrett. "Computerized Tomography." *Physics Today*, December 1977, pp. 32−41.

Ubell, Earl. "How Computers are Helping Doctors Treat You Better." *Parade Magazine*, 13 March 1988, pp. 4−7.

Wingerson, Lois. "A Window on the Body." *Discover*, April 1982, pp. 84−88.

Review Questions

1 Why does information processing play such a vital role in the practice of medicine?

2 Why is collection of payments for services rendered often more complex in medicine than in other businesses?

3 Describe the structure and operation of a hospital information system.

4 Describe how a computer can be used to collect a patient's medical history.

5 Characterize the attitudes of most patients toward computerized medical interviews.

6 Describe how computers can aid in the management of physical examinations.

7 Describe some applications for medical databases.

8 How do advice systems help physicians arrive at diagnoses and treatments?

9 Distinguish between consultation systems and critiquing systems.

10 What may be the eventual impact of medical databases and advice systems on medical education?

11 What is the advantage of tomography over conventional X-ray pictures?

12 Describe briefly how computer-aided tomography works. Why is a computer essential for this technique to be practical?

13 Describe how computers can monitor the conditions of patients both in and out of the hospital.

14 Describe some ways in which computers are used in medical research.

15 Describe some applications of computers to medical training. What is simulation and why is it important in both research and training?

16 How can computers help physicians avoid prescribing drugs with undesirable side effects and interactions?

17 Describe some applications of computers in biotechnology.

18 What roles will computers play in the Human Genome Initiative?

19 How can computer-based electronic systems aid the handicapped?

20 How are computer games being used in (a) psychology and (b) medical training?

Topics for Discussion

1 Many physicians are reluctant to adopt computerized techniques such as consulting on-line databases and advice systems. Why are people often hesitant to replace existing techniques with new, computer-based methods?

2 Computers are sometimes criticized for being inhuman and impersonal. Yet the reason many patients prefer them for medical and psychological interviews is that the patient can count on the computer to be impersonal and nonjudgemental. Discuss.

3 Discuss how liability should be apportioned when malfunctioning hardware and software cause injury or death. Should the liability fall on the manufacturer of a malfunctioning chip or on the programmer who wrote a malfunctioning program? Or should it fall on the company that manufactured the entire instrument or system that failed? To what extent should the doctor or hospital that used the instrument or system (perhaps failing to notice its malfunctions) bear responsibility?

4 Patients often complain that doctors have grown remote and impersonal, having lost their traditional bedside manner. Are the developments discussed in this chapter likely increase the impersonality of modern medicine? Or might they give physicians more time for considering the emotional needs of their patients?

5 It is a paradox of modern medicine that while technology has greatly increased the ability of doctors to detect and correct medical problems, it has also increased the cost of medical care to the point where many people (particularly those not covered by insurance) cannot afford it. Critics have pointed out medical imaging systems as expensive technologies that increase the cost of medical care. Discuss.

CHAPTER 11

COMPUTERS IN EDUCATION

INTRODUCTION

Modern public schools strive to provide education for everyone rather than letting it be reserved, as it once was, for the privileged few whose parents could afford private tutors. Attempting to educate large numbers of students with a limited number of teachers and on a limited budget, however, can give rise to the following problems.

- Students do not receive enough individual attention. Classroom lectures and exercises must be based on the abilities of a typical student. Students who are ahead of their class become bored; those who are behind become lost.

- Students who have grown up with electronic information sources and entertainment—radio, television, video games, and perhaps home computers—are bored with traditional textbooks and classroom lectures. Can education be provided in forms more nearly resembling the ones in which modern students are accustomed to receiving information? And can the education be made entertaining enough to compete with the many sophisticated forms of entertainment available at the touch of a switch?

- Can the productivity of teachers be increased so that one teacher can reach more students? This is particularly important for teachers with specialized skills, such as music, art, science, and computing. To be sure, most teachers would probably prefer to go in the opposite direction, and allow each teacher to work with fewer students. But practical considerations of availability of teachers and the funds to pay them often militate against small classes. Today, teachers are often given larger classes than they can handle, aggravating the problem of lack of individual attention.

Skilled, dedicated, and creative teachers can go a long way toward overcoming these problems, but sometimes they work against overwhelming odds. Over the years, various forms of technology have been brought to bear on the problem. Phonograph records, motion pictures, audio tapes, slides and overhead-projector transparencies, educational television, and video tapes all make their contributions, but none has provided a technological fix for the problems facing mass education.

The computer is the latest product of technology to make its way into the classroom. *Computer-assisted instruction (CAI)* is the technique of using computers to aid teaching. While some teachers see the computer as one more gadget that will gather dust in the supply closet after its novelty has worn off, others feel that computer-assisted instruction has the potential of alleviating or eliminating many of the problems of mass education. So far this potential has not been realized. Lack of suitable equipment, lack of instructional software, and lack of teacher training in the use of computers have caused computers to have relatively little impact on education.

In addition to using computers to teach other subjects, many schools are giving courses in computer use and programming. Courses in computer literacy attempt to provide students with the skills they will need to function in a computer-oriented world. Controversy has arisen over whether

More and more college students are purchasing their own computers; some colleges require students to buy computers, which may be available at a discount through the college book store.

all students should study computer literacy and just what topics such courses should include.

◤ DRILL AND PRACTICE

The purpose of *drill and practice* is to help students memorize facts and acquire skills. The computer presents the student with problems to solve or questions to answer; it accepts the student's answers and informs the student whether each answer is right or wrong. If the student fails to get the right answer, the program displays the correct answer and goes on to the next problem. To aid the teacher, the computer can collect statistics on how well each student is doing and what kinds of problems are giving the most trouble.

A drill-and-practice program can follow a number of strategies when the student fails to give the correct answer. The following are some of the most frequently used possibilities.

■ **Simple Refusal** The program informs the student that the answer is wrong and asks him or her to try again. If the student repeatedly gives the wrong answer, the program will eventually give the right answer and go on to the next question.

■ **Dead-key Refusal** The student is not allowed to type any answer other than the correct one. For example, suppose the correct answer is "zebra." If the student types anything other than *z* for the first letter of the answer, the program ignores the keystroke and perhaps causes the computer to beep. Likewise, the program will only accept *e* for the second letter, *b* for the third, and so on.

A student does her homework with the aid of the lowest-cost computer in the IBM PS/2 line.

■ **Wrong-key Correction** If the student types the wrong key, the program displays the character that should have been typed. For example, suppose the correct answer is "zebra" and the student tries to type "horse." When the student strikes *h*, the program displays *z*; when the student strikes *o*, the program displays *e*, and so on.

■ **Graded Hints** When the student misses a question, the program provides a hint as to the correct answer. If the student misses again, a stronger hint is provided. Only after several increasingly explicit hints does the program give up and provide the correct answer.

■ **Additional Information** When the student misses an answer, the program provides additional information that should help the student arrive at the correct result. This type of CAI program lies on the borderline between drill-and-practice programs and the tutorial programs described in the next section.

Drill-and-practice programs are the most popular educational programs for microcomputers. These programs are currently available for such subjects as elementary arithmetic, algebra, geometry, personal finance, physics, chemistry, astronomy, history, spelling, alphabetizing words, parts of speech, sentence diagramming, and typing.

The authors of drill-and-practice programs use the full capabilities of the computer to make the practice interesting. The computer screen can display amusing figures, such as a smiling face for a right answer and a frowning one for a wrong answer. Or it may play a sprightly tune to reward a right answer and make a raucous noise for a wrong one. Many drill-and-practice programs are organized as games in which players earn points by giving correct answers.

TUTORIALS

A tutorial program program teaches new material rather than merely providing practice for material previously studied. Most *tutorial CAI* is based on *programmed instruction*, which in turn is based on the work of the well-known psychologist B. F. Skinner. The two fundamental ideas of programmed learning are:

- **Active Responding** The student must respond to each piece of information presented by taking some action, such as answering a question about the information just presented.

- **Immediate Confirmation** The student must be informed immediately whether each response is correct or incorrect.

A lesson designed for programmed instruction is called a *learning program*. This should not be confused with a computer program; although a learning program can be implemented by means of a computer program, the two are not the same. A learning program presents the student with a series of *frames*. Each frame either introduces a new piece of information or reinforces an old one. Each frame ends with a question that the student must answer before going on to the next frame.

Proponents of programmed learning disagree on how the frames should be arranged. Skinner and his followers advocate *linear programs*—programs in which the frames come one after another, just like the pages of a book. Each student who uses the program works through every frame. The frames are constructed so that students will make as few errors as possible, thus preventing them from inadvertently learning wrong answers.

Although experiments show that linear programs are effective, students often find them unappealing. Since every student has to work through every frame, linear programs contribute little to individualized instruction.

Screen display produced by a drill-and-practice program.

And because no one is supposed to make any mistakes, the program must be geared to the poorest students. Average and better-than-average students have to suffer through many frames reinforcing concepts that they have long since learned.

Fortunately, there is another kind of learning program—the *branching program*—in which the answer to the question in one frame determines which frame the student goes to next. Different students work through different sequences of frames, the sequence for each student depending on how that student answers the questions. Thus a good student who masters a fact quickly can proceed immediately to more advanced material. The student who gives a wrong answer is directed to additional frames that cover the troublesome concept in more detail. These frames may also review concepts covered previously if the student's answers indicate that he or she does not understand the concepts or is not applying them properly.

What is the best physical form for learning programs? For linear programs, all we need is a conventional book with the pages divided into frames. Linear programs are also easy to adapt to simple teaching machines that present the lesson one frame at a time. Simplicity of implementation, then, is the best thing that can be said about linear programs.

The more flexible branching programs are far more difficult to present through conventional media such as books. One approach is to use what is called a scrambled book. Each frame is on a separate page of the book.

Screen display produced by a drill-and-practice program.

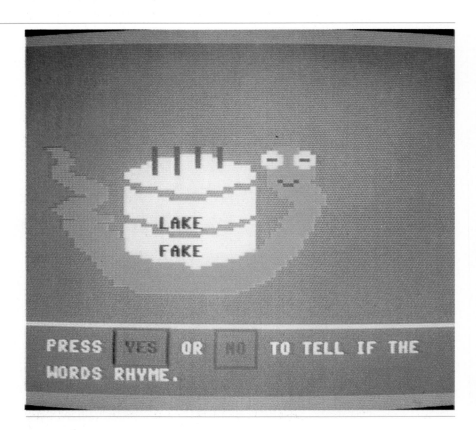

Eskimo students in Alaska learn math with the aid of a computer tutor.

At the end of each frame is a multiple choice question. For each possible choice, the student is told to turn to a particular page and continue the lesson. Needless to say, thumbing through the book to find the proper page quickly becomes tiresome.

Computers are ideal for implementing learning programs. The computer program displays, one at a time, the facts and explanations the student is to learn. The program asks frequent questions and, depending on the student's answers, it can review material the student has not grasped, explain previously covered material in more detail, or skip over material the student seems to understand. The student does not have to worry about these details; the program makes all the decisions about what material to present.

Conventional programmed-instruction materials, although effective, can be dull. Students quickly become bored with working through seemingly endless numbers of similar frames. With the aid of pictures, sound effects, jokes, comments on the student's progress, and responsiveness to the student, computers can make learning programs not only interesting but exciting. Programmed learning becomes not a straitjacket into which a lesson must be forced but a broad framework that allows program authors enormous room for individual creativity.

A number of programming languages have been developed to help authors write learning programs. These *authoring languages* allow the writer to forget about the technicalities of computer programming and concentrate on the information the student is to receive, the questions that are to be asked, and the responses the student is to make. One of the most popular authoring languages is called Pilot.

A learning program requires the computer to store large amounts of information, such as explanations, questions, and comments. As a result, complex learning programs are likely to exceed the main and auxiliary

Engineering student using an Apple Macintosh.

memory capacities of the low-cost microcomputers currently found in schools. Some of the most recently developed microcomputers do have enough main and auxiliary memory for learning programs, but these machines are more costly than the more limited computers still found in many classrooms.

One promising solution to the storage-capacity problem is to use a microcomputer to control an optical disc player. All the actual lesson material is stored on the optical disc; the program running on the microcomputer sends commands to the optical disc player to cause the stored material to be displayed as needed. Optical discs can hold enormous amounts of information, including text, computer programs, sounds, and still or moving television pictures. Pictures and sounds stored on the optical disc can be used to illustrate the lesson. A program on music can show (and present the sounds of) a concert; a program on science can show a laboratory experiment or a field trip; a program on geography can show scenes from a foreign country.

Some researchers are trying to apply the techniques of artificial intelligence and expert systems to tutorial and other forms of CAI. An expert system analyzes the student's responses, attempts to determine precisely which concepts the student seems not to understand, and provides suggestions or remedial material precisely tailored to the student's weaknesses. If the student is solving a problem, the system can determine from the student's attempts what possibilities the student may be overlooking and provide appropriate hints.

SIMULATION

A *simulation* is a computerized model of a real-life system, such as an airplane, a segment of the economy, or a laboratory experiment. A description of the current state of the real-life system is stored in the computer's memory. Also stored are rules specifying how the system will change if left to itself and how it will respond to external events, such as a movement of the controls of a simulated airplane or a change in policy affecting a simulated segment of the economy. The user enters the external events as they occur and the computer calculates and displays the responses of the simulated system.

The methods by which students interact with the simulated system vary considerably. For an economic simulation, the user might just type in a description of the policies to be followed and the computer would print the economic data representing the system's response. But much more highly interactive simulations are common. In a simulation of an airplane, the screen might display the pilot's instruments and the view out the front of the cockpit. Joysticks, game paddles, or keys on the keyboard simulate the pilot's controls. As the user manipulates the simulated controls, the view of the terrain below and the readings on the instruments change to represent the motions of the airplane. In the flight simulators actually used for pilot training, the student pilot sits in a mock-up of an actual cockpit that, under the control of the computer, is turned, tilted, and twisted to simulate the motions that an actual airplane would undergo under the same circumstances.

Simulations are important in both education and scientific research because many real-life systems cannot be studied conveniently, particularly in the classroom. The real system may be too fast (a speeding bullet), too slow (continental drift), too large (the solar system), or too small (a microorganism). The system may be too expensive to be used for training purposes, and its operation by untrained persons may be dangerous (airliner, nuclear power plant).

Educational simulations fall into three broad categories: using a machine (flight simulator), making decisions (economic or business simulation), and studying a process (simulation of population growth).

Student computer laboratory.

For students who know a programming language, such as Basic, writing simulation programs can be even more enlightening than using them. Writing a simulation requires the programmer to make a detailed study of the system to be simulated and to give considerable thought to its inner workings. Any failure to understand the system will show up as a failure of the simulation program to mimic the behavior of the real-life system. Frequently, one starts with a crude simulation and improves it in steps. Each improvement is based on further study of the real system and a deeper understanding of its operation.

Computer simulations can sometimes provide a kind of mathematical leverage. Many important systems, such as moving objects in physics or animal populations in ecology, are described by so-called differential equations that can be solved only with the aid of calculus and other branches of advanced mathematics. On the other hand, computer simulations of these systems can be written and understood using only elementary algebra. High school students, for example, can simulate systems that would require college-level mathematics to study by any other means.

COMPUTER GAMES

Just about every game demands that the players develop certain skills. If the skills developed are also useful in everyday life, the game is classified as "educational." Computer games are popular with young people and can be far more educational than conventional games. Some educators argue that almost all CAI programs should, to some degree, be formulated as games. Most educational computer games either provide drill and prac-

Screen display produced by a program that simulates the dissection of a frog.

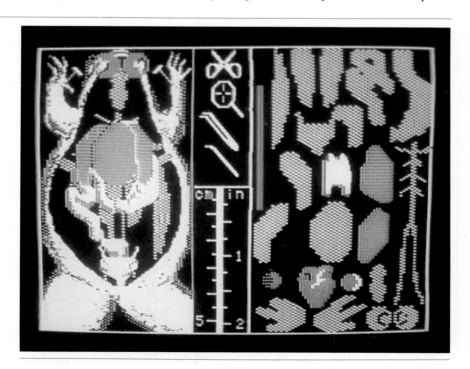

Student using Apple II computer; note mouse and disk drive in foreground.

tice in a particular topic or simulate a real-life system for the student to explore, experiment with, and eventually understand.

Three reasons why educational games are popular with students and teachers alike are:

- **Challenge and Competition** Students respond to the challenge of obtaining high scores in a game. Competition between classmates inspires students to strive for the best score in the class or at least for better scores than the persons with whom they normally play.

- **Fantasy and Role Playing** Simulation games allow students to fly a plane, operate a nuclear power plant, rule a country, or conduct an elaborate scientific experiment—activities that few if any young people can experience in real life.

- **Curiosity** Interesting games capture students' attention and inspire them to seek the underlying principles by which the game can be mastered. If the game is well designed, these underlying principles will be precisely the information that is to be taught.

◣ COMPUTER LITERACY

Computer Literacy courses attempt to provide students with the knowledge and understanding needed to function in a computer-oriented world. They do not attempt to provide specific job skills, such as programming or using a word processor; rather they strive to convey an appreciation of the computer and its role in society. The book you are now reading is a computer literacy textbook, and you are probably reading it in connection with a computer literacy course.

Some educators have called for eliminating computer literacy courses or at least for reevaluating their content and their place in the curriculum.

(Left) Computer bus brings computer literacy to schools that cannot afford extensive computer equipment; (right) student workstation in computer bus.

These critics argue that few students will go on to technical or managerial positions that call for detailed knowledge of computers. Indeed, the bulk of future job openings are expected to be in personal service areas such as retail sales and fast food service. If workers in these areas interact with computers, they will do so in simple, straightforward ways, such as by pushing buttons on a computerized cash register. Also, with computers in about fifteen percent of all homes, and with computers often featured in the news media, some students can pick up all the computer literacy they need through casual encounters with computers. Courses in computer literacy make just as much sense, the critics argue, as would courses in "automobile literacy."

In response, we might begin by asking whether it is proper to educate students on the assumption that they will only be employed in certain restricted areas. The assumption may be true for many students, but it will not be true for all, and some will be cheated out of education from which they could benefit. It has been suggested that computer literacy courses be made elective instead of being taught to all students. Yet elementary and high school students often have little idea as to what career they wish to pursue. A computer literacy course might spark the interest of some in computer-oriented careers, while convincing others that they are best suited for careers not involving computers. And if courses are to be chosen only on the basis of job training, the value of history, geography, and literature, to say nothing of art and music, would also seem to be put in question.

We must bear in mind, too, that economically or socially disadvantaged students may have much less previous contact with computers than those brought up in more affluent circumstances. Males and females also often differ in their interest in and involvement with computers, a difference that may disappear in time but has not done so yet. In judging the need for education in computer literacy, we must not base our considerations purely on the needs of affluent males.

Perhaps the most potent argument for computer literacy courses is the widespread occurrence of *computerphobia*—the unreasoning fear of computers. Some people become uncomfortable, nervous, or even physically ill when forced to use a computer. Some have resigned from otherwise excellent positions rather than work with computers. Managers and executives often refuse to use computers that could give them substantial help in doing their jobs. Computer literacy courses can help people to feel comfortable with computers, to understand that their complications are more an annoyance than an impassible barrier and that almost all computer systems can be mastered with reasonable effort by any intelligent person. Most important of all, prospective computer users can be reassured that difficulties such as unreliable operation and unmasterable complexity are deficiencies of the computer system, not of the person who is trying to learn to use it.

◤ TEACHING PROGRAMMING

An important application of computers in education is teaching courses in programming and computer science. A programming course often focuses on a particular programming language; the details of the language are taught along with basic concepts of program construction and problem solving. Computer science courses focus more on underlying concepts that are independent of any particular programming language or computer system. The two most widely taught programming languages are Basic and Pascal. Basic, which is easy for beginners to learn and use, is often favored for introductory programming courses. Pascal, which embodies more advanced concepts of program and data structuring, is favored for computer science courses. Business programming languages, such as Cobol and the fourth-generation language RPG (Report Program Generator), are often taught to business students. Logo, discussed later in this chapter, is becoming increasingly popular in the public schools.

People can use computers without being able to program them, so programming courses are not for everyone. Yet they need not be restricted to only those who plan to be professional programmers. Students of mathematics and the sciences will find it helpful to know how to write simple programs. Anyone planning to work with computers extensively will un-

Instructing students in computer-generated business graphics.

derstand their strengths and weaknesses all the better for knowing how they are programmed. A computer user who almost never programs may occasionally find that a simple program of only a few lines can solve an otherwise vexing problem.

Educators differ as to whether programming should be taught in computer literacy courses. Since computer literacy courses are intended to explain concepts rather than to provide job training, any instruction in programming should focus on the underlying principles of the programmer's art rather than on training in the use of a particular programming language.

COMPUTER-MANAGED INSTRUCTION

Rather than teaching students directly, a computer can oversee their instruction but direct them elsewhere for actual learning experiences. For example, the computer can ask students to read certain books, listen to certain tapes, see certain films, and so on. When the students complete their assignments, they return to the computer for testing and further assignments. This process is called *computer-managed instruction (CMI)*.

Because each student is managed individually by the computer, each can proceed at his or her own pace. Yet students are not limited to materials that can be presented on a computer display. They can read books; see movies, television shows, and works of art; perform laboratory experiments; and go on field trips. The computer does all the testing and keeps the necessary records that allow the teacher to judge the student's progress.

Such completely automated management of instruction is unlikely except in special circumstances. Even in traditional classrooms, however, computers can help the teacher with such routine chores as compiling tests from a bank of test questions, test grading, and maintaining student records.

NEW DIRECTIONS: HYPERTEXT AND LOGO

Programmed instruction is sometimes criticized because the computer, and not the student, determines what material will be covered. To be sure, the student's answers to the computer's questions determine what will be covered. But the student does not have the option of asking for one topic or another or of requesting that an explanation be summarized or presented in greater detail.

Can computers help students explore the world of knowledge, let them experience the delight of browsing in a library or the thrill of personal discovery? Good simulation programs can serve this purpose. We shall examine two other attempts in this direction: Theodor H. Nelson's hypertext and Seymour Papert's Logo programming language.

Hypertext

Hypertext was introduced in Chapter 8 as a means of text and graphics storage that stores not only individual documents but links between different documents and between different parts of the same document. Readers of hypertext are being constantly invited to explore related subjects by following hypertext links. In this respect, hypertext is in sharp contrast to programmed instruction. A learning program maintains tight control over the lesson, choosing which frames will be presented to the student and their order of presentation. Hypertext, on the other hand, invites the student to roam freely through a vast network of interrelated topics.

Programmed instruction and hypertext are likely to appeal to different kinds of students. Lower-ability students may well prefer their information delivered in small doses and in an order guaranteed to lead to mastery of the subject. But higher-ability students, who are often impatient with the slow pace of programmed instruction, may prefer to discover their own paths through a hypertext network.

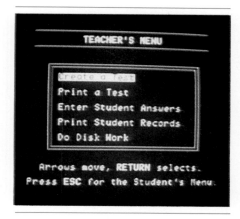

Screen display produced by a program for computer-managed instruction.

Logo

Some skills convey immediate and obvious rewards to those who acquire them. Motivated by the rewards, children pick up such skills on their own without formal training. Thus children learn their native language so as to be better able to make their needs and wants known to their friends and family. They learn to play popular games both for the enjoyment of the games and for the ability to participate in their friends' activities.

But skills in some subjects, such as mathematics, do not reward a child with any immediate advantages. As a result, such subjects are "school subjects" that children almost never acquire spontaneously. With little motivation to study these subjects, children often do poorly in them, develop a distaste for them, and become convinced that they have little skill in them.

Home and classroom computers can reward children for learning abstract subjects. If children enjoy using computers, they will acquire the skills needed to use computers more effectively. They will learn the computer's language to make the computer obey their wishes, just as they learn their native language to make their wants known to their friends and families. Mathematics and computer programming will no longer be just "school subjects" because they will offer immediate rewards to children who master them.

Logo is a programming language designed to make mathematics and computer programming attractive to children. Although the language is powerful in terms of what can be accomplished with it, it is very easy for children to use. The language also makes it easy to program a computer to do things that children find interesting and attractive, such as controlling robots and drawing pictures.

One of the most popular ways of using Logo is to control a so-called *turtle.* The original turtle was a computer-controlled robot that could roll about on a sheet of paper, drawing pictures with a pen attached to its underside. In most modern versions of Logo, the cumbersome mechanical turtle has been replaced by an electronic one that moves about on a video screen. The movements of the turtle are governed by a Logo program. Since the turtle can be made to draw a line as it moves, we can draw pictures by writing programs that make the turtle follow a particular path. This method of drawing pictures is often referred to as *turtle graphics.*

Mechanical turtle drawing a pattern. Today it is more common to simulate the turtle by an arrow on a video display than it is to use an actual robot.

As children play with the turtle—trying to make it move in a particular way to draw interesting pictures and designs—they pick up important principles of computer programming, mathematics, geometry, and physics. Because Logo is a powerful programming language (despite its simplicity and attractiveness), children who have become interested in programming from manipulating turtles can easily explore more advanced techniques and applications.

Logo language processors are available for a number of popular microcomputers, and Logo is being taught in some schools. However, Logo is most frequently used just to introduce students to computer programming, rather than (as its designer envisioned) getting them involved with such otherwise abstract subjects as mathematics, geometry, and physics.

THE OUTLOOK FOR CAI

The following are some of the considerations that will determine the future of computer-assisted instruction.

Cost

For many years computers were simply too expensive for classroom use. Although the microprocessor revolution has made computers affordable, financially pressed schools must still weigh the cost of computers and programs against other possible uses of their money. If computer-assisted instruction is to become widely used, it must prove itself cost-effective compared with other methods of teaching. Many of the arguments for and against computers in the classroom boil down to debates over the best way to spend limited funds.

Pattern traced out by a video-display turtle in response to a student's program. The turtle is the small triangle at bottom left.

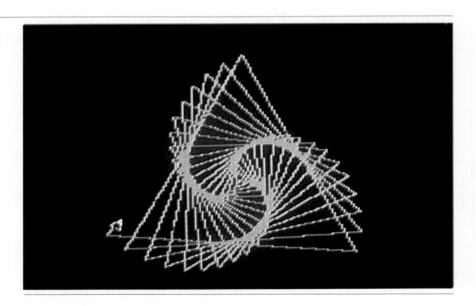

Proper use of available funds can also present problems. Many manufacturers are aggressively marketing their wares to the schools, and most educators have little training or experience to guide them in making reasonable selections. Rapid technological obsolescence is another problem; the computer most widely used in the public schools was probably the best choice several years ago but is now obsolete, with insufficient memory capacity for large simulations, tutorials, and sophisticated programming languages.

Computer manufacturers sometimes donate their products to the schools in hopes of building loyalty to their brand among students and teachers. Even these donations may be counterproductive, however, if the equipment is not suitable for educational use or is not compatible with equipment the school already owns.

Will Computers "Depersonalize" Students?

Some fear that students who learn from computers will develop rigid, machine-like behavior in place of human personalities. But there is no reason to think that computers will be any more depersonalizing than movie projectors, record players, or television sets. The computer is simply a machine that allows the programmer to communicate with the student in a much more flexible manner than is possible with conventional media. The best learning programs reflect the fact that they are written by human beings. They are replete with congratulations, admonitions, asides, and jokes. In short, any kind of communication can be personal or impersonal. The same is true of computer-assisted instruction.

Of course, it would be as undesirable for children to spend all their time with a computer as it would be for them to spend all their time with a record player, movie projector, or a television set. But no one suggests

Using a computer terminal to check out library books.

Children using Apple II computer.

More and more libraries are replacing the traditional card catalog with a computerized catalog that both librarians and patrons access via computer terminals.

doing away with human teachers and classrooms. The students need not lack human contact just because a computer has assumed part of the task of providing them with information and testing their performance.

Teacher Resistance

Although many teachers are enthusiastic about classroom computers, others refuse to become involved with them and even actively oppose their use. Why? Many teachers have never seen computer-assisted instruction in use and so are skeptical of its value. Like many other professionals, teachers are reluctant to set aside years of hard-won experience for new and unfamiliar ways of doing their job. Lack of appropriate training leaves many teachers unsure of their ability to cope with computers. Some teachers see computers as threats to their jobs, fearing that teaching staffs will be reduced if computer-assisted instruction increases the number of students that each teacher can handle.

This resistance is lessening as computers become more widely used in schools and teachers have greater opportunity to see them used effectively. Better instructional software and better training in computers for teachers will increase the acceptance of computers by the educational community. In a recent survey, 82 percent of the teachers questioned said that they thought the use of computers could improve teaching. Many, however, found computers difficult to use and expressed the need for more computer training.

Instructional Software

High quality instructional software (sometimes called *courseware*) is essential to the success of computer-assisted instruction. Drill-and-practice programs and educational games are now commonplace, although teachers complain that such programs are often not coordinated in any way with existing textbooks or school curricula. Educationally useful simulations and tutorials are rarer, in part due to the memory limitations of microcomputers, but also due to the difficulty of writing these programs. Advances in hardware capabilities, such as the use of optical discs, will make software production even more complex. The ultimate limit on computer-assisted instruction may well be set by the ability of educational publishers to produce suitable courseware.

◤ Summary

Computers have the potential of providing individualized instruction in interesting, exciting, and entertaining forms well suited to students who are more accustomed to electronic media than to conventional textbooks and lectures. Although many school systems have purchased computer equipment, problems such as equipment cost, lack of teacher training, and lack of good instructional software have prevented computers from having a noticeable impact on education. The lack of training can be attacked by conventional means such as computer courses for education students and computer workshops for in-service teachers. However, the difficulty of producing high quality courseware at affordable prices is likely to be a continuing problem.

◤ Vocabulary Review

active responding
authoring language
branching program
computer literacy
computer-assisted
 instruction (CAI)
computer-managed
 instruction (CMI)
computerphobia
courseware

dead-key refusal
drill and practice
frame
graded hints
hypertext
immediate
 confirmation
learning program
linear program

Logo
programmed
 instruction
simple refusal
simulation
turtle
turtle graphics
tutorial CAI
wrong-key correction

◤ For Further Reading

Educational Computing (special section). *Byte*, February 1987, pp. 146–206.

Haber, Ralph Norman. "Flight Simulation." *Scientific American*, July 1986, pp. 96–103.

Lang, Sylvia. "Computers Get High Marks From Educators." *USA Today*, 24 June 1985, p. 1D.

Marchionini, Gary and Ben Shneiderman. "Finding Facts vs. Browsing Knowledge in Hypertext Systems." *Computer*, January 1988, pp. 70–80.

Nold, Ellen. "Writing CAI." *People's Computers*, July-August 1977, pp. 36-37.

_____ and Sallie Cannom. "Pilot." *People's Computers*, July-August 1977, pp. 11–15.

Papert, Seymour. *Mindstorms*. New York: Basic Books, 1980.

Sadler, Lynn Veach and Wendy Tibbetts Greene. "Computer Applications for Writing: The Computer-Assisted Composition Movement." *Abacus*, Spring 1988, pp. 22–33.

Skinner, B. F. "Teaching Machines." *Scientific American*, November 1961.

Van Dyke, Carolynn. "Taking 'Computer Literacy' Literally." *Communications of the ACM*, May 1987, pp. 366–374.

Review Questions

1 What are some of the problems with traditional methods of mass education?

2 Describe five techniques used by drill-and-practice programs.

3 What are the two fundamental ideas of programmed learning?

4 Distinguish between computer programs and learning programs.

5 Describe linear programs.

6 Describe branching programs.

7 What are the advantages and disadvantages of linear and branching programs?

8 Give three methods of implementing learning programs.

9 What advantages does a computer have over other methods of implementing learning programs?

10 Describe some ways that computer simulations can be used in education.

11 Give three reasons why students are attracted to educational computer games.

12 Distinguish between computer-assisted instruction and computer-managed instruction.

13 What are some criticisms of programmed instruction?

14 Contrast hypertext and programmed instruction.

15 Why do children pick up some subjects without formal instruction?

16 What characteristics of Logo are designed to make mathematical and programming concepts meaningful to children?

17 Describe the role of the turtle in Logo.

18 What are some of the factors involved in teacher resistance to educational computing.

19 What kind of instructional software is most readily available? From what major problem does it often suffer? What kinds of instruction software are much more difficult to obtain?

20 Why has computer-assisted instruction had little impact on public education despite widespread purchases of computers by schools?

◥ Topics for Discussion

1 What topics do you think should be included in a course in computer literacy?

2 Mathematics teachers have long debated whether students should be allowed to use calculators or should be required to become skilled in pencil-and-paper arithmetic. Now students are using word processors (with such aids as spelling checkers and grammar checkers) for composition, spreadsheets for business and scientific calculations, and databases for organizing research notes. Discuss whether students learn more by using such high-tech aids or by mastering the traditional ways of accomplishing the same ends.

3 We have seen that computer simulation provides students with experiences that would be impossible or impractical in real life. Yet some educators warn against the overuse of simulation for fear that students will spend more time studying a computer-created fantasy world than studying the real world outside the computer. Discuss.

4 Discuss the fear that students who learn extensively from computers may be "depersonalized"—that the development of their human personalities may be adversely affected by their use of computers.

5 Just as psychological patients often prefer being interviewed by an impersonal computer, so students may prefer that their errors be corrected by an impersonal computer rather than a judgemental teacher. Discuss.

6 School officials often face the difficult decision of whether to spend the limited funds available on computer hardware and software, whose benefits may be difficult to predict, rather than on more traditional equipment and resources (movie projectors and films, phonographs and records, video equipment and tapes, and library books) whose benefits are better understood and accepted. Discuss.

COMPUTERS IN ART AND ENTERTAINMENT

INTRODUCTION

The ability of computers to manipulate pictures, sounds, and text and to control mechanical devices opens up applications in art, music, and literature. Computers are finding ever increasing use in television and motion picture production for generation and manipulation of images and for control of camera motion. Much of the music that we hear every day on radio, television, and recordings is generated by computer-controlled electronic music synthesizers. And interactive fiction turns a novel or play into a role-playing game in which the reader or viewer can make decisions for the characters.

COMPUTER GRAPHICS

Computer graphics is the technology of generating images with a computer. Applications of computer graphics include business charts and graphs, engineering drawings, artwork for producing computer chips and printed circuit boards, cockpit-window views for flight simulators, and artificial realities: computer-generated scenes for motion pictures.

We will concentrate here on flight-simulator and motion-picture applications, both of which involve computer animation—computer generation of moving images. For flight simulators, the animation must take place in real time—the view through the window of the simulated cockpit must change at the same rate as the view from the cockpit of a real airplane. On the other hand, the computer can take as long as needed (within reason) to produce each frame of movie film, since the speed at which the film is eventually shown is unrelated to the speed with which it was produced. Because the computer has more time to work on each frame, motion-picture graphics can be more detailed than graphics for flight simulators.

Economically, flight-simulator applications are of major importance because of their central role in training military and civilian pilots. Motion-picture applications are much less important economically but provide some of the most spectacular and readily accessible illustrations of computer graphics.

Graphics Hardware

The standard output device for computer graphics is the video display; most computer-generated images are created and edited with the aid of a video display even though some other device may be used for the final output. Projection displays are used in flight simulators, where the computer-generated images must be projected on a screen that partially surrounds the cockpit mock-up. A special laser-scanner film-recorder is used to transfer images to movie film with greater resolution than could be obtained by photographing a video display. Plotters are used to produce engineering drawings and artwork for integrated circuits and printed circuit boards. A dot-matrix printer can print images in color or black and white

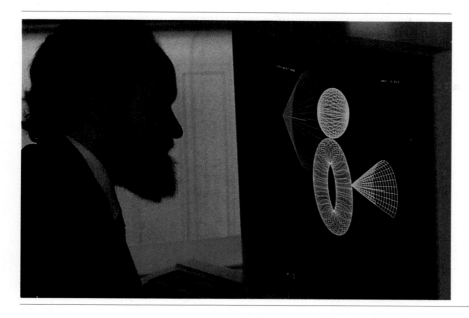

Artist using graphics display.

with fair to moderate resolution; a laser printer can produce black-and-white images with moderate to high resolution.

In this chapter we will focus our attention on the all important video display. Video displays were discussed in detail in Chapter 3; here we will briefly review some of their properties with emphasis on the needs of advanced graphics systems.

An image on a video screen is produced by a beam of electrons that causes the screen to glow at the point struck by the beam. The brightness of each point is controlled by adjusting the intensity of the beam. For a color display, the color of each point can also be set. Since a point will continue glowing for only a short time after the beam has left it, the entire image has to be repeatedly redrawn anew or *refreshed*. Each redrawing of the image is called a *frame* and is analogous to a frame of movie film. The information needed to redraw a frame is stored in a block of RAM memory known as a *frame buffer*.

There are two fundamentally different approaches to generating and refreshing the display. In *vector graphics*, each line of the image is drawn individually by the electron beam just as one might draw the image with pen or pencil. In *raster graphics*, the electron beam methodically scans the entire screen from left to right and top to bottom; the color and brightness of each point is set as the beam comes to it. The motion of the beam is independent of the image being displayed.

The main advantage of vector graphics is that less memory is required for the frame buffer. The reason is easy to see. In vector graphics, a single instruction could tell the display device to draw a line having a certain position, length, and orientation; in raster graphics, the brightness and color of every point along the line—indeed of every point on the entire screen—must be specified. The disadvantage of vector graphics is that it is suitable only for line drawings; large shaded areas are not possible. For this reason, raster graphics is overwhelmingly more popular than vector graphics. Applications requiring realistic images, such as flight simulation and motion picture production, always use raster graphics (at least for final output).

We recall that the resolution of a display is stated by giving the number of distinct dots, or *pixels*, in the horizontal and vertical directions. The total number of pixels in the display is the product of the numbers in the horizontal and vertical directions. Thus a microcomputer display might have a resolution of 640 pixels horizontally by 200 pixels vertically for a total of 640 × 200 or 128,000 pixels overall. High-quality graphics requires a resolution of at least 1000 by 1000 or one million pixels. A typical resolution for motion-picture graphics is 6000 by 4000 or 24 million pixels. High-quality graphics, then, requires millions of pixels for each frame. Since the color and brightness of each pixel must be computed and stored individually, increasing the number of pixels increases both the time required to compute a frame and the memory capacity required to store it.

Time requirements are most stringent for flight simulation, where the computer must be fast enough to keep up with the maneuvering of the simulated airplane. Although time requirements are not as strict for motion picture production, the computations for each scene must be completed in some reasonable time. Considerations of computation time often dictate the use of supercomputers, special purpose graphics chips, and special purpose computers designed for computer graphics.

If 8 bits are used to specify the brightness of each of the three primary colors, then 24 bits are required to store each pixel. For a resolution of 1000 by 1000, the frame buffer must have a capacity of 24 × 1,000,000 bits or 3MB. A resolution of 6000 by 4000 requires 72MB, which is greater than the main memory capacity of many mainframes. The problem of storage capacity becomes even more severe when storing many frames, such as a scene from a motion picture. A mainframe-type multiplatter disk

Graphics workstation.

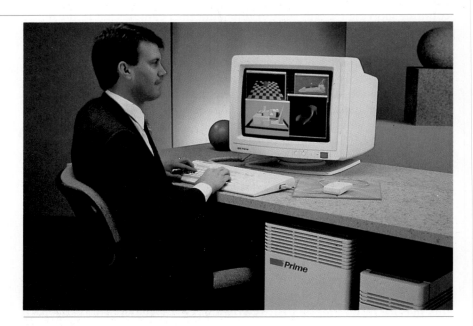

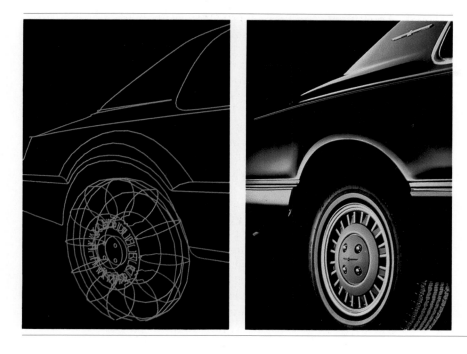

So called stick figures or wire-frame models such as the one at left are often the first step in constructing realistic solid images.

pack can store only a few seconds of screen action. Optical disc technology must be used to store a substantial number of high-resolution frames.

Three-Dimensional Models

It is possible to use a computer display as just an electronic canvas; the computer has no knowledge of what it is displaying but merely remembers the colors and intensities specified by a human artist. But for most advanced applications, such as animation, the computer needs an internal, *three-dimensional model* of the object it is to display. The model allows the computer to work out what the object would look like at different positions in the scene, with different sizes and orientations, and as seen from different viewpoints and with different kinds of illumination.

There are several methods for providing the computer with the information it needs for its internal model.

■ **Front, Side, and Top Views** By drawing on the screen with a light-pen or by using a graphics scanner to enter conventional drawings into the computer, we can provide the computer with front, side, and top views of the object. From these views the computer can construct a three-dimensional model.

■ **Combinations of Simple Geometrical Shapes** Objects can be specified as combinations of simple geometrical shapes such as blocks, spheres, cylinders, cones, and football-shaped ellipsoids. Shapes can be subtracted from an object as well as added to it, allowing holes of various shapes to be created. This method is convenient for constructing objects interactively on a display, since various shapes can be easily

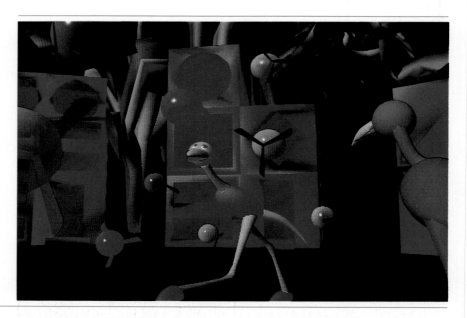

A frame from a computer-animated film titled *Snoot and Muttly*.

picked out with a light-pen or mouse, moved to the desired positions, and added to or subtracted from the object.

■ **Procedural Models** In a procedural model the image is generated by a computer program, which is usually based on some simple mathematical concept. Procedural models are often used for objects such as spheres and cones that are described by simple mathematical formulas. However, a recently developed technique based on fractals (which are described below) allows computers to generate realistic images of such natural objects as mountains, coastlines, and trees.

Computer Animation

Although still images are satisfactory for some applications, such as business graphics and engineering drawings, applications such as flight simulation and artificial realities for motion pictures require moving images. Moving images can be achieved with *computer animation*, which provides some the most spectacular demonstrations of computer graphics.

A motion picture or television of image is made up of a series of frames—24 frames per second for motion pictures and 30 frames per second for television. The computer must calculate the intensities of the three primary colors for each of the millions of pixels in each of the 24 or 30 frames required for each second of action.

The animator creates frames from objects whose models are stored in the computer memory. In one approach, the objects can be displayed on a vector graphics display called a vectorscope. The objects appear on the vectorscope as skeletal frameworks rather than solid objects. With the aid of controls on the vectorscope, the animator can magnify, reduce, position, and orient the various objects to obtain the desired frame. Once the first frame of a scene has been constructed, succeeding frames are produced by changing the positions of objects that are to move, such as the lips of a person who is talking.

We can reduce the labor of animation considerably by telling the computer how the various objects will move, allowing it to generate many of the thousands of frames needed for even a few minutes of screen action. One approach is to let the computer simulate the motion of the objects in the frame. For example, a computer simulation of an airplane or spaceship will allow the computer to determine the position and orientation of the object in each frame. Researchers are working to construct models that will allow the computer to simulate the motions of the human body.

Another approach is for the animator to outline the action with a series of key frames. The computer then generates the intermediate frames needed to get from one key frame to another. In the intermediate frames, the paths of moving objects are determined by mathematical functions called *splines*, which are named after and serve the same purpose as a drafting instrument used to draw a smooth curve through a series of points. Animation-oriented computer languages, called *animation languages*, provide a simple way of describing objects and their motions to the computer.

Computer animation is used extensively in producing television cartoons, such as those shown on Saturday mornings. Animated figures in early television cartoons usually moved in a stiff and unnatural manner, since time and budget restrictions prevented using the classical Disney technique of completely redrawing each figure for each frame. Computer animation allows the animated figures to move much more smoothly and naturally, although not as much so as when the Disney technique is used.

This computer-generated image illustrates three difficult areas of computer graphics: shadows, reflections, and transparent objects.

Perspective, Hidden Lines and Surfaces, and Illumination

When animation is complete, the computer knows the size, position, and orientation of every object in every frame. The next step is *rendering*—converting the stick figures seen on the vectorscope into realistic images of solid objects.

The objects in the scene are viewed from a particular vantage point, which we may think of as an imaginary camera photographing the scene. As with ordinary photographs, the objects must be seen in perspective—objects close to the imaginary camera must be larger than identical objects that are further away

Only lines and surfaces that can be seen by the imaginary camera may be present in the rendered image. Lines and surfaces present in the model but not actually visible from the selected viewpoint are said to be *hidden* and must be eliminated by the computer.

The color and brightness of each point on the surface of an object depends not only on the properties of the surface (which are specified in the model) but also on the color and intensity of the illumination falling on the surface. This includes not only the illumination that comes directly from light sources but also that reflected from nearby objects. For example, a neutrally colored object placed next to a strongly colored object is likely to reflect some of the color of the latter.

Just as the camera is frequently moved while photographing a live action scene, so we may want to move the imaginary camera through which a computer-generated scene is observed. The computer must keep track of the motion of the imaginary camera so that the proper viewpoint will be used in carrying out the calculations for each frame.

The most general method of handling problems of perspective, hidden surfaces, and illumination is *ray tracing*. The computer follows the path of each light ray as it leaves the source of illumination, bounces off or passes through various surfaces, and finally arrives at the imaginary camera. Each encounter with a surface affects the color, brightness, and direction of the ray; the cumulative effect of all such encounters determines the color and brightness seen by the imaginary camera.

Millions of rays must be traced to work out the appearance of an entire scene. This is usually too time consuming, particularly for computer animation, where the calculations must be repeated for thousands of frames. Researchers are working on ways to simplify ray tracing. Instead of tracing individual rays, for example, we might trace beams—bundles of adjacent rays that follow similar paths.

A flight simulator for a jet fighter.

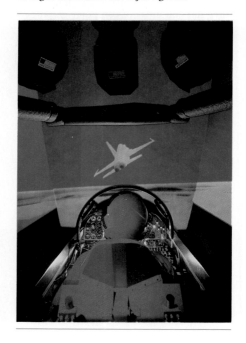

Textures

The surfaces of real objects are often rough and uneven; the nature of the surface and its coloring may exhibit a characteristic pattern. Examples of such patterns can be seen on a brick wall, a fur-covered animal, a straw basket, and a wooden cabinet. These surface patterns are called *textures*; any computer graphics system that is to display realistic-looking objects must be able to handle textures.

One approach is to enter the surface pattern for each object into the computer separately. The patterns are always entered as if the surface were flat. The computer then performs a mathematical transformation that wraps

An abstract computer-generated image.

each surface pattern around the corresponding object. If we apply this technique to simple geometrical objects, for example, we can create spheres, cylinders, and cones that appear to be woven from straw or covered with fur.

The texture patterns may be created by artists or taken from photographs. Although using photographs may seem like cheating to some artists, it is often the most practical solution, particularly for complex natural textures such as tree bark or animal fur.

Fractals

Computers can readily generate images of human-made objects, such as automobiles and airplanes, which are constructed from simple geometrical shapes. Generating images of natural objects, such as mountains and trees, is more difficult because of their complex, irregular shapes.

The mathematician Benoit Mandelbrot discovered an important principle underlying the complexity of nature. Consider, for example, a coastline, which appears smooth when viewed from afar—say by an astronaut in orbit. If we examine it more carefully, however, we will find that it is made up of many inlets and points. If we examine an inlet or point in detail, we find that it contains smaller inlets and points, which themselves contain still smaller inlets and points, and so on.

Mandelbrot found a mathematical description for curves and surfaces whose individual features exhibit the same structure as the curve or surface as a whole. Such a curve or surface shows the same structure no matter how much any part of it is magnified. Mandelbrot coined the adjective *fractal* to refer to such curves and surfaces, since they can be shown to be not one- or two-dimensional, like ordinary curves and surfaces, but to have fractional dimensions. *Fractal curves and surfaces* can be generated by computers and have been used to model such natural objects as coastlines, landscapes, mountains, and trees. Some of the most realistic-looking computer-generated images have been produced with fractal surfaces.

Nebulous Objects

Smoke, fire, and clouds are made up of innumerable tiny particles. It would be far too complex to have the computer simulate the motion of each particle. Fortunately, researchers have been able to devise models that give the same visual appearance as the actual object although the number of particles is far fewer and their motions are far simpler. Success in computer graphics often results from greatly simplifying a natural object while retaining its visual appearance.

Aliasing

In the real world, quantities such as the brightness of a point change smoothly both as we move from one position to another and with the passage of time; recall that we use the word *analog* to characterize such smoothly varying quantities. For computer processing, such analog quantities must be represented digitally, that is, by discrete numerical codes. Digital quantities can never vary smoothly because there is always a gap between the value represented by a given whole number and the values represented by the whole numbers just below and just above it. These gaps introduce a form of distortion called *aliasing*, which must be dealt with whenever analog quantities are represented digitally. Aliasing occurs when an analog quantity changes more rapidly than the system of digital representation can handle; the solution is to smooth out, or blur, sharp changes.

Because a slanting or curved line is made up of individual pixels, it may appear as a staircase rather than a smooth curve. Because smooth lines and edges are turned into jagged ones, such aliasing effects are often referred to as *jaggies*. To eliminate jaggies, each sharp edge, such as a sharp transition from one color to another, must be blurred slightly so as to make it several pixels wide. Pixels inside a blurred edge are given colors intermediate between the colors of pixels on either side of the edge. After blurring, there is no sharp change in color from one pixel to the next, and the jagged edge disappears.

A similar aliasing affect, but involving time rather than space, can occur for moving objects. An animated image may appear not as a motion picture but rather as a series of still pictures seen in rapid succession. This effect is called a *strobing* because objects appear as if viewed under a strobe light, a bright, flashing light used for entertainment effects as well as for scientific studies of motion. The solution is to blur the moving parts of a scene so that they appear to flow smoothly from one position to the next. Indeed such blurring occurs when live action is photographed. If you use the "freeze frame" feature of a movie projector or VCR to view a single live-action frame, you will see that rapidly moving parts of the image—such as an athlete's hands and feet—are blurred.

◣ OTHER APPLICATIONS TO MOTION PICTURES AND TELEVISION

Aside from cartoons, computer animation still finds only occasional use in motion picture and television production. In the near future, at least, computer applications that augment traditional production techniques will probably have a greater impact on the entertainment industry.

Film Editing

When shooting for a movie is completed, the result is a large number of pieces of film showing individual scenes. The amount of film actually shot is far greater than will appear in the final print that is seen in movie theaters. Usually each scene is shot from several different camera angles, and some scenes may be shot in several different versions. To tighten the pace of the film, some scenes will need to be shortened and others will need to be eliminated entirely. Sometimes a film will be reedited after its initial release if audiences complain that it is too long or or that the story does not develop fast enough.

Film editing is the art of creating the final print out of the many pieces of film shot on the set and on location. Traditionally, the film is cut into short segments, which are spliced together in the desired order. But cutting and splicing is slow and tedious, which makes film editing time-consuming and restricts the editor's ability to experiment with various sequences of shots to see which produces the best effect.

Computer-controlled editing machines are freeing film editors from the tedium of cutting and splicing. The images on each piece of film are stored on an optical disc along with identifying information that will allow

Computer generated image; note the realistic appearance of airplanes and terrain.

the original piece of film to be located. With a computer keyboard, the editor creates a trial version of the final print by having the computer select various segments of film and display them in the order specified. The editor can modify the trial version by inserting or deleting frames at any point or by moving frames from one point to another. The film editor can manipulate the frames of the film in much the same way that a writer manipulates text with a word processor.

When all concerned parties (editor, director, producer, studio executives) are satisfied with the editing, the computer generates instructions for cutting and splicing the original pieces of film to produce the final print. The reason one must return to the original film to produce the final print is that conventional video cameras and recorders cannot provide the high-quality images required for filmmaking. *High-definition television*, a video technology with sufficient resolution for filmmaking, is now available but is not yet widely used. High-definition television will allow video technology to be used for all phases of moviemaking, with images being transferred to film only to produce the final prints that are sent out to theaters.

Editing the sound track of a film can be even more complex that editing the visual action because each segment of the sound track may contain sound from such diverse sources as sounds recorded on the set, sound effects, and music. As with film editing, the task of editing the sound track can be greatly simplified with a computerized editing machine. Because digital sound recording techniques are completely adequate for movie production, the final sound track can be created directly from sounds stored in the editing machine. It is never necessary to cut and splice the tapes on which the sounds were originally recorded.

Special Effects

The special effects department of a movie studio is responsible for producing images of objects that cannot be photographed conveniently. The objects may be imaginary ones, such as starships, dragons, and giant sandworms. Or they may be just too costly to construct and photograph, such as a fleet of sailing ships, an ancient temple, or the interior of a large cavern. Although computer animation is one approach to creating special effects, computers are also used widely as aids in producing special effects by more traditional techniques.

Traditionally, special effects are created through a process known as matte, in which different objects are photographed separately and the films are combined in the darkroom to give a composite image. For example, if the script calls for an actor to face a fire-breathing dragon, the actor is photographed normally in the studio and a model dragon is photographed by the special effects department. The actor and the dragon are photographed in such a way that, when the images are combined, the dragon will appear much larger than the actor, although in reality the reverse is true.

Computers can play a vital role in this process by controlling the movements of cameras and models. If several films are to be combined, the camera movements must be coordinated. In the actor-dragon scene, for example, if the camera photographing the actor moves to show a

Computerized equipment plays a central role in videotape editing.

different view of the scene, the camera photographing the dragon must do likewise. Computer-controlled camera movements are also used to simulate moving objects. When a maneuvering spaceship appears on the screen, for example, in reality the spaceship is stationary and the camera is moving.

Computers are now widely used to control the movements of movie cameras. The director of photography specifies key camera positions and the computer automatically moves the camera smoothly from one position to another. What's more, once the movements have been programmed, they can be duplicated exactly, either for retakes of the same scene or for photographing different scenes to be combined later.

Although a moving spaceship can be simulated with a stationary space-ship and a moving camera, living objects such as dragons and giant gorillas have to do some of their own moving. The traditional way of doing this is to photograph the model one frame at a time. Between frames, the model is manually adjusted to a new position. Tedious calculations are needed to determines what adjustments will make the model move most naturally. Now, however, the model can be moved under computer con-trol, with the camera photographing the movements. The motion appears smoother and more fluid than with frame-by-frame techniques because images of the moving parts of the model are slightly blurred, which helps avoid strobing.

Production Planning

The scenes of a motion picture are not shot in the order in which they will appear on the screen. The story action often shifts back and forth between different settings such as a character's home and office. But prac-tical considerations require the production crew to shoot all scenes that take place in one location, then move on to the next location and shoot all scenes that take place there, and so on.

This approach calls for detailed preproduction planning. In what order should the scenes be shot to make the best use of available facilities? What sound stage needs to be reserved for each day's shooting? What sets need to be constructed and when? When can each set be torn down? What performers, technicians, and equipment will be needed on the set each day? These questions suggest only a few of the enormous logistical problems that arise in producing a movie.

Because movie production is a business, cost estimates are needed for each step of production. And all the personnel have to be paid for the work they do, including extras and bit players who may work in only a single scene. This job is made more difficult by the extensive unionization of the film industry. The people working on a film belong to many different unions and must be paid according to rules spelled out in many different union contracts.

Computers are ideal for the kind of detail work required to plan production, estimate costs, and produce payrolls. Although some of the major studios still use armies of pencil pushers to perform these tasks, many of the smaller production companies are turning to computers.

Colorization

Colorization is the process of adding color to films that were originally photographed in black and white. The role of the computer in colorization is similar to its role in animation: the human operator specifies the colors for a small number of key frames, and the computer uses this information to color the remaining frames. In doing so, the computer must adapt to the changes from frame to frame that result from the movements of cast members and other moving objects.

The main technical challenge of colorization is to prevent the computer from confusing distinct objects. For example, if an actor sits down in a chair, the computer may have trouble telling where the actor leaves off and the chair begins. It might accidentally give part of the chair a color specified for the actor's clothing, or give part of the actor's clothing a color specified for the chair. To help prevent such confusion, each scene is broken down into layers, as if the objects in the scene were drawn on transparent plastic sheets that were stacked atop one another. Objects in the background go in the bottom layer; objects in the foreground go in the top layer; and objects at intermediate distances go in the middle layers. The computer follows the objects in different layers separately, so that it is less likely to become confused when, for example, an object in the top layer moves in front of an object in the bottom layer.

The actual colors to be used are chosen by a human art director, not by the computer. Considerable research is done to determine the actual colors of the sets, costumes, recognizable landmarks, and cast members' hair and eyes. When, as is often the case, the actual color of an object cannot be determined, then the art director must make a reasonable, but otherwise arbitrary, choice.

Inevitably, mistakes are sometimes made. For example, Frank Sinatra appeared in one colorized movie with brown eyes; apparently the art director was unacquainted with Sinatra's well-deserved nickname, Ol' Blue Eyes. Another source of error arises when different groups of people work on the colorization of different scenes. If two groups inadvertently choose different colors for the same object (such as a car), the object appears to change color during the course of the movie.

Colorization is the subject of a bitter controversy that has led to lawsuits and congressional action. On one side, directors, actors, and other motion picture artists maintain that a black-and-white film is a work of art that should not be tampered with. They argue that one has no more business colorizing a black-and-white movie than one would have coloring a black-and-white drawing by a famous artist. On the other side, broadcasters and videocassette distributors point to viewing and sales figures that show strong viewer preference for colorized movies over the black-and-white originals. Those who would profit from showing or selling colorized movies argue for giving the public what it wants.

In mid-1988, the House of Representatives approved legislation that would discourage, but not ban, colorization of classic black-and-white movies such as "Casablanca" and "The Maltese Falcon." A thirteen-member National Film Preservation Board would designate movies for inclusion in a National Film Registry. A registered film would be given a special seal, which could be used to promote any version that had not been altered through colorization or extensive editing. Altered versions would have to be labeled as such in their advertising and on the boxes in which videocassettes are sold. At the time of this writing, it is unclear how this colorization legislation will fare in the Senate.

ELECTRONIC MUSIC

Many of the instrumental sounds heard on radio, television, and recordings are generated electronically. This greatly simplifies and reduces the cost of the recording process, since a single keyboard player can replace most or all of a band. On the other hand, many talented musicians are finding it more and more difficult to get work because the sounds of their instruments can be easily synthesized—that is, created electronically.

Digital and Analog Recording

Music synthesis creates music in a form suitable for recording, and techniques used for recording music also play a major role in music synthesis. Before turning to synthesis, then, let us look briefly at the analog and digital techniques for recording music.

In analog recording, a microphone converts the sounds it picks up into an analog electrical signal that is amplified and recorded, in analog form, on disc or tape. On playback, the analog signal from the disc or tape is amplified and sent to a loudspeaker, which reproduces the sounds picked up by the microphone.

Digital recording is similar except that before the signal is recorded, an *analog-to-digital converter* changes the analog signal to digital codes. On playback, a *digital-to-analog converter* changes the digital codes back into an analog signal that is amplified and sent to a loudspeaker. Digital recordings are much more impervious to noise and distortion than analog recordings, since small imperfections in the recording and manufacturing processes affect analog signals more than digital codes. Also, error-correcting codes allow the playback equipment to correct errors that were introduced during recording and manufacturing. Many recording studios now use digital recording for making master tapes, although the digital codes must be converted to analog signals before being transferred to conventional discs and tapes.

Digital recordings are available to the public in the form of compact discs (CDs), the principles of which were discussed in Chapter 3. In some countries, including Japan, consumers can purchase digital audio tape (DAT) recorders for home use. In the United States, record companies have fought—so far successfully—against the introduction of DAT recorders. They fear that home users would deprive the record companies of income by using DAT recorders to make (in violation of the copyright law) high-quality tape copies of records, cassette tapes, and compact discs.

Music Synthesis

Music can be synthesized by electronically generating the corresponding electrical signal rather than picking it up with a microphone. In *analog synthesis*, electronic components such as oscillators (which generate signals) and filters (which modify signals) are connected to produce the analog signal directly. In *digital synthesis*, the music originates as computer-gen-

Experimental computer music center at MIT.

erated digital codes, which must be converted to an analog signal before they can be amplified and sent to a loudspeaker.

For both analog and digital synthesis, a computer is needed to place the synthesis process under the control of the musician. The sounds produced by early analog synthesizers were controlled by a bewildering array of knobs and by a maze of connections made by patch cords, which resemble the connecting cords of an old-fashioned telephone switchboard. Although the setup for a synthesizer is to this day called a *patch*, actual patch cords have joined telephone switchboards in oblivion.

Keyboard Synthesizers

A *keyboard synthesizer* is a convenient device for generating electronic music both for recording and for live performance. Notes are produced by pressing keys on a pianolike keyboard. The simplest keyboards can turn a note on and off but cannot affect its loudness. With a velocity-sensitive keyboard, the loudness of a note depends on how forcefully the key is struck; with a *pressure-sensitive keyboard*, the loudness of the note depends on how firmly the key is pressed down. A *pitch-bending* control allows the pitch of a note to be changed while the note is sounding. Many synthesizers allow sequences of notes to be entered on the keyboard and stored in the machine's memory; each sequence can be played back at the touch of a button.

Switches just above the keyboard control the nature of the sound that the synthesizer produces. Many synthesizers feature preset sounds that the musician can select by pressing a few buttons instead of having to set each characteristic of the sound separately. The switch settings for the preset sounds are stored in ROM chips; many synthesizers allow the musician to enlarge the machine's repertoire of preset sounds by purchasing and installing additional ROM chips. Some synthesizers allow the switch settings, or patches, to be stored on cassette tapes or diskettes and to be reloaded into the synthesizer when needed. Others store patches in RAM memory, the contents of which are maintained by a battery when the synthesizer is turned off.

Synthesizer programming—creating patches for new sounds—is now a recognized specialty. Depending upon the synthesizer, programmers deliver their patches on ROM chips, cassette tapes, or diskettes. Many musicians rarely if ever program their own sounds, relying instead on the preset sounds provided with the synthesizer and on patches purchased from synthesizer programmers.

Digital Sampling

A keyboard synthesizer creates notes from scratch according to a recipe determined by the settings of the synthesizer's controls. On the other hand, a digital-sampling keyboard, which looks like and is played like a keyboard synthesizer, produces notes by playing back short digital recordings (called *samples*) that have been previously stored in its memory. The recorded samples may be modified in certain ways on playback; for example, a sample can be played back at different pitches, allowing a single sample to serve for a number of different notes. Musicians can record their own samples, but they do not have to do so. A number of prerecorded samples are built into the keyboard, and additional samples can be purchased on such media as ROM chips, cassette tapes, and diskettes.

Digital sampling is not restricted to musical sounds. Barking dogs, honking horns, and other sounds can be recorded by digital-sampling keyboards and played back when the appropriate key is pressed. In recording sessions, keyboard players may find themselves responsible for sound effects as well as music.

Digital sampling is also used in electronic instruments that are intended to mimic a particular acoustic (nonelectronic) instrument. Specifically, electronic pianos and organs, which in the past were not very faithful to the sounds of their acoustic counterparts, now often use digital sampling to provide excellent imitations of acoustic pianos and pipe organs.

Digital sampling is extremely convenient for recording sessions, since a single keyboard player can imitate a wide variety of acoustic instruments. On the other hand, electronic music enthusiasts criticize digital sampling because it merely plays back the recorded sounds of acoustic instruments instead of exploiting the freedom that electronic music offers for creating entirely new sounds. And we must not forget the plights of players of acoustic instruments, whose services can be (and often are) dispensed with once the sounds of their instruments have been recorded for digital-sampling keyboards.

Drum Machines

Although some keyboard synthesizers will also produce percussion sounds, these are usually the province of special electronic instruments called *drum machines*. Digitally sampled recordings of common percussion instruments, such as bass drums, snare drums, tom-toms, and high hats, are stored in the drum machine. Sounds can be triggered manually via drum pads, which can be struck with conventional drumsticks or with the player's hands. More importantly, rhythm patterns can be programmed into the drum machine and played back with far more precise timing than most human drummers can achieve. This rhythmic precision makes drum machines highly valued for creating the underlying rhythms of dance music. Drum machines are used extensively in pop and rock recordings; the drummer we see pounding away in videos and at concerts may well have to give way to a drum machine in the recording studio.

The MIDI Connection

MIDI (Musical Instrument Digital Interface) is a standard system for interconnecting electronic musical instruments. Most electronic instruments now on the market are compatible with the MIDI standard. MIDI-compatible expansion cards can be purchased for microcomputers, allowing

Well-known keyboardist Herbie Hancock surrounded by keyboard synthesizers and other electronic music equipment.

them to control electronic instruments. "MIDI" has become a standard term in the musician's vocabulary; electronic instruments are not connected, they are "MIDIed together."

The MIDI interface provides sixteen control channels. The channels can be used to control different instruments or different voices (simultaneously sounding notes) on the same instrument. The signals on a MIDI channel represent events, such as the pressing of a key and the release of a key. Information about how forcefully a key was struck can be transmitted for controlling velocity-sensitive instruments. Pitch-bending information can be sent to change the pitch of a note while it is sounding. Via MIDI, a musician can control several instruments from a single keyboard. Musicians sometimes now carry portable keyboards, which are strapped on and held somewhat like a guitar, and which control one or more remote synthesizers via a MIDI connection.

Sequencers

A *sequencer* is a master control device for a set of electronic instruments. Sequences of notes up to and including entire compositions can be stored in the sequencer and sent out to the instruments over the MIDI channels. There is generally some provision for editing—for making changes in the stored sequences.

There are two kinds of sequencers. A hardware sequencer is a special purpose machine that may be a separate device or may be built into a keyboard. A software sequencer is a program that runs on a widely used microcomputer, such as a Macintosh, an Atari ST, or an IBM PC. (The Atari ST is notable for including a MIDI interface as standard equipment.) Sequencer programs offer the greatest flexibility; note sequences can be displayed on the screen in a variety of notations and edited in word-

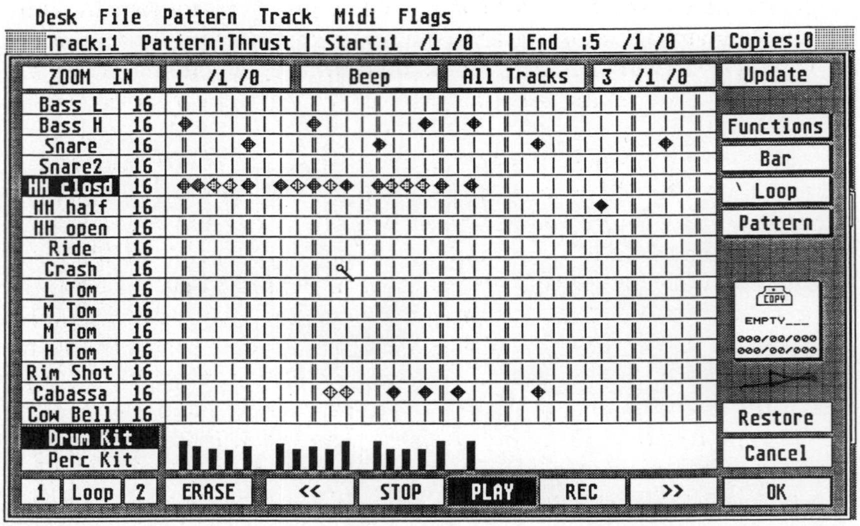

Sequencer programs often display a grid on which the user places marks indicating the times at which various musical events (such as starting or stopping a note) occur. The grid shown here is used for sequencing drum sounds.

processor fashion by moving a cursor to the point at which changes are to be made. Hardware sequencers, however, may be more convenient for musicians who do not wish to become involved with the technicalities of computer hardware and software.

Other Ways of Controlling Electronic Instruments

When electronic instruments are played manually, rather than under the control of a sequencer, the musician usually controls the instrument by playing on a pianolike keyboard. However, other forms of control are available for musicians whose training is with nonkeyboard instruments. A *MIDI guitar* is a special kind of electric guitar that does not produce sounds directly, but rather produces MIDI codes that can be used to control any MIDI-compatible electronic instrument. One kind of *breath controller* looks like and can be played like a woodwind instrument such as a clarinet; breath pressure, lip pressure, and the depressions of keys are all converted into MIDI codes, which can be used as desired for controlling electronic instruments. Converters are available that will pick up the sounds of any instrument and convert them into MIDI codes.

Other Music Software

A number of programs are intended to help composers, arrangers, and copyists with the complex task of writing musical scores. These programs may be thought of as "word processors for music": they provide services for a composer, arranger, or copyist similar to those a word processor provides for a writer. Scores are created by using a mouse to select musical symbols from a menu and to position them on the musical staff. Some programs enable the user to hear what has just been written by automatically playing the music described in the score on a built-in synthesizer or, via a MIDI interface, on an external electronic instrument. When satisfied with the score, the user can have it printed out with a dot-matrix or laser printer.

Some recent music-writing programs allow the user to simply play the music on a MIDI keyboard and send the MIDI codes to the computer. The music-writing program interprets the MIDI codes and writes out the music that was played. Some manual editing may be required to correct misinterpretations or to put some passages into a form that will be easier for other musicians to read. The program can be set to correct small timing errors made by the musician. For example, if the user specifies that the smallest time division is to be a sixteenth note, then the time value of every note will be rounded off to a whole number of sixteenth notes.

The controls of a keyboard synthesizer are often quite inconvenient for creating complex patches. There may be only a small calculator-like display for showing the values of parameters, and a few buttons for selecting parameters and changing their values. Programming such a synthesizer can be as tedious as setting a digital watch or programming a VCR. Computer programs for creating patches provide such conveniences as a full-screen display of all the parameters affecting a patch; to change the value of a parameter, the user has only to move the cursor to the part of the screen reserved for that parameter and type in a new value. Commands to the program can be selected with a mouse from convenient menus, and the program will display diagrams and graphs that help the musician visualize the structure of the sounds being created. Patches created with such a program can be transmitted to the musical instrument via its MIDI interface.

The musician at left, holding a MIDI breath controller, is preparing to preform with well-known saxophonist David Sanborn (right).

COMPUTER COMPOSITION

Computers can be programmed not only to play music but to compose it as well. The computer uses a pseudorandom-number generator to produce a series of numbers representing the pitches and durations of the notes. The output of the pseudorandom-number generator is rejected when it does not conform to certain rules of composition based on the principles of harmony and melody. The final composition is random except for the constraints imposed by the rules.

This kind of random composing was practiced long before computers came along. Schemes for composing music by rolling dice date back to the seventeenth century; one such method was published by Mozart. Such schemes can produce pleasant music and even music in the style of a particular composer; however, the compositions are bland and uninteresting. Still, experiments in computer composition are interesting, if not for the music they produce then for the insight they may yield into the methods used by human composers.

COMPUTER POETRY AND FICTION

Computers have been programmed to write poetry by stringing together randomly selected poetic-sounding phrases, sometimes constrained by poetic rules, sometimes not. The result sometimes sounds like modern poetry, although some might prefer to say that some modern poetry sounds like it was written by a computer.

The computer does not understand the poem it writes; it merely strings together phrases at random. Any sense that the poems make is purely accidental. The only reason we do not immediately reject such poetry (as

A tone-editor or patch-editor program is used to design the sounds produced by a synthesizer. The graphics help the musician understand the structure of the sound being created.

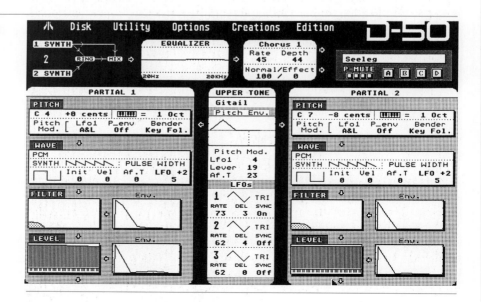

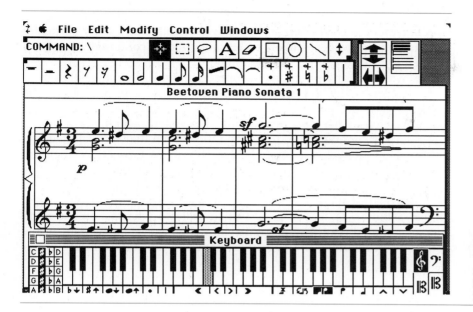

Screen display produced by the NoteWriter music-writing program for the Apple Macintosh. The musical symbols at top can be selected with a mouse and positioned on the musical score. The pitches of the notes can be entered on the piano keyboard at bottom.

we would reject nonsensical prose) is that we grant a poet the license to be inconsistent or illogical on the surface in the hope that some deeper meaning will emerge out of the apparent nonsense. If there is no deeper meaning, our imagination may be willing to supply one.

No computer has ever composed a traditional poem that tells a story, laments a lost love, appreciates some aspect of nature, or otherwise addresses a significant human idea or emotion. This does not mean that computers will never be programmed to compose meaningful poetry. But we should not expect it to happen soon, and we must be wary of false claims that it has already been done.

Computers have also been used to write fiction. If the computer composes the work from scratch, rather than merely stringing together scenes written by the programmer, then the story line is quite rudimentary. Although the resulting fiction has little value except as a novelty, the experiments themselves, like other experiments in computer composition, are interesting.

◣ INTERACTIVE FICTION

An interactive story is one in which the reader can make certain decisions for one of the characters. The outcome of the story depends on the particular decisions the reader makes. *Interactive fiction* is similar to role-playing games in that the reader takes the role of one of the characters and attempts to make decisions that will realize that character's aims.

An interactive story is like a learning program in that both have a branching structure. Different readers will follow different branches depending on the choices they make at the decision points. Like learning programs, interactive stories can be presented in books. The story cannot be very long, however, since so much space in the book is taken up by alternate branches, only one of which will be followed by any particular reader. And the reader is likely to become tired of continually being instructed to turn to another part of the book.

As with learning programs, computers provide a simple solution to these problems. The computer displays the text and illustrations of the story. At each decision point the computer provides the reader with a menu of actions that a character can take. When the reader makes a choice, the computer continues the story along the branch that was selected.

Interactive fiction is now available both in book form and in the form of computer programs. Some video games also incorporate interactive fiction. An animated adventure is recorded on an optical disc and displayed on the screen of the game machine. At each decision point, the player presses a button or moves a joystick to indicate what action the main character should take. The game machine then moves to the part of the optical disc containing the particular branch of the story that the player selected.

LITERARY RESEARCH

Computers have proved extremely valuable to researchers in languages and literature. For example, a powerful research tool for studying any written work is a concordance, an index of every occurrence of every word in the work. Preparing such an index manually is pure tedium, but a computer can do the job in a fraction of the time with a fraction of the labor. And the result is likely to be more accurate than if it had been done by hand.

Concordances are constantly needed for literary research, and a computer is almost always the proper tool for the job. The main obstacle to using a computer is converting the text to be studied into a form the machine can read. In the past the text often had to be punched on cards; now it may have to be typed at a terminal or typed with a special typeface that an optical character reader can recognize. If the work was originally produced using word processing or computer typesetting, however, it may be possible to obtain a machine-readable version of the work from the author or publisher.

It is possible to characterize the style of an author by certain statistics—the average length of sentences and paragraphs, the percentage of words having a certain number of syllables, and so on. A comparison of the statistics of two different works can determine whether they were written by the same person. Several cases of disputed authorship have been settled in this way. Statistics can also be used to gauge reading difficulty of a work. Schools sometimes use such statistics in selecting books appropriate for a particular grade level.

DANCE NOTATION

Dance notation describes a dance just as musical notation describes a musical composition. There are, in fact, two such systems of notation, each with its own adherents. Unfortunately, both notations are so complex that it can take a year or more to write out a complex dance. This time can be shortened considerably, however, by entering the notation into a computer and editing the copy stored in the computer's memory. After editing, the computer prints out a perfect copy of the score.

The computer can also check for common errors in dance scores. For instance, the writer may put in a symbol that places the dancer in a bent-over position but forget to put in a symbol to straighten the dancer up again. The computer can point out such places at which the score seems unreasonable. Also, when a sequence of movements is to be repeated, the user has to enter it only once and instruct the computer to repeat it the required number of times in the score.

It would be even more helpful if a performance could be recorded directly, instead of the dance notation being laboriously entered by a human observer. One suggestion that has been made is that dancers wear sensors that transmit the positions of their bodies to the computer as they dance. The computer would automatically translate the motions picked up by the sensors into dance notation.

Dancers are used to learning a new dance by seeing it demonstrated rather than by reading a written score. Therefore, work is being done on computer systems that will accept dance notation as input and display animated figures executing the dance.

Some of the problems that arise in applying computers to dance also arise in computer animation. In both cases, we want to convey bodily movements to the computer and have the computer manipulate animated figures in accordance with those movements. The technical problem in each case is how to represent the positions of the human body inside the computer and how to get the computer to generate natural motions.

An Apple II computer aids in teaching a children's dance class.

Summary

The ability of computers to manipulate images, sounds, and words leads to applications in the arts and in the entertainment industry. Computer graphics and computer animation have been applied to creative art and to artificial realities for motion pictures as well as to such practical endeavors as engineering drawing and flight simulation. Computers have also been applied to film editing, controlling cameras and models for special effects, and managing the logistical and financial problems of producing a movie.

Computerized electronic musical instruments, such as keyboard synthesizers, digital-sampling keyboards, and drum machines, are now standard equipment for popular music groups and are widely used in making recordings. A standard interface known as MIDI provides a flexible means for interconnecting different instruments. Electronic musical instruments can be controlled manually from keyboards and drum pads or automatically with a sequencer, or with a general purpose microcomputer running sequencer software. Other control devices, such as MIDI guitars and breath controllers, enable musicians who are not keyboard players to play synthesized music. Other music software helps musicians write music and create patches—the settings that govern the sounds produced by synthesizers.

Computers have also been used to compose music, poetry, and even fiction. Although experiments in computer composition are interesting, computers have a long way to go before the can equal human composers, poets, and authors.

Interactive fiction, in which the reader's decisions determine the outcome of the story, is available as books, computer programs, and video games. In literary research, computers have been used to compile concordances and collect statistics for resolving cases of disputed authorship. Similar statistics are often used to gauge the level of reading difficulty of a work.

Computers are being used to help record dances for posterity in standard dance notations. Since both dance and computer animation are concerned with natural-looking motions of the human body, there is some overlap between these two computer applications.

Vocabulary Review

aliasing
analog synthesis
analog-to-digital
  converter
animation language
breath controller
colorization
computer animation
computer graphics
digital sampling
digital-sampling
  keyboard
digital synthesis
digital-to-analog
  converter
drum machine

fractal curves
  and surfaces
frame
frame buffer
hidden lines
  and surfaces
high-definition
  television
interactive fiction
jaggies
keyboard synthesizer
MIDI (Musical
  Instrument Digital
  Interface)
MIDI guitar
patch

pitch bending
pixel
pressure-sensitive
  keyboard
raster graphics
ray tracing
rendering
sequencer
spline
strobing
texture
three-dimensional
  model
vector graphics
velocity-sensitive
  keyboard

For Further Reading

Brody, Herb. ''Kurzweil's Keyboard.'' *High Technology*, February 1985, pp. 26–32

Gannes, Stuart. ''Lights, Cameras...Computers.'' *Discover*, August 1984, pp. 76–79.

Keyboard Magazine (special issue on the basics of electronic music technology). June 1988.

"Microcomputers Enhance the Arts." *Infoworld*, 5 April 1982, pp. 20–27.

Moorer, James Anderson. "Music and Computer Composition." *Communications of the ACM*, February 1972, pp. 104–113.

Nelson, Ted. "Smoothers of the Lost Arc." *Creative Computing*, March 1982, pp. 86–110.

Press, Larry. "What You See Is What Your Hear." *Abacus*, Fall 1984, pp. 61–64.

Schneider, Ben Ross, Jr. *Travels in Computerland*. Reading, MA: Addison-Wesley, 1974.

Tucker, Jonathan B. "Computer Graphics Achieves New Realism." *High Technology*, June 1984, pp. 40–53.

_____. "Visual Simulation Takes Flight." *High Technology*, December 1984, pp. 35–47

West, Susan. "The New Realism." *Science 84*, August 1984, pp. 31–39.

◤ **Review Questions**

1 List several applications of computer graphics.

2 Why does high-quality graphics require a large storage capacity for the frame buffer?

3 Describe three kinds of three-dimensional models for objects that are to be depicted with computer graphics.

4 Describe the process by which the animator creates the frames for a computer-animation sequence.

5 Describe the problems presented by perspective, hidden lines and surfaces, and illumination. Describe the method of ray tracing.

6 How can surfaces in computer-generated images be given realistic textures?

7 What are fractal surfaces and how are they used in computer graphics?

8 How can nebulous objects such as clouds and smoke be modeled?

9 Describe two aliasing effects and describe the way in which each is eliminated.

10 Describe the use of computers in film editing. How may this application be simplified by the use of high-definition television?

11 Describe two uses for computers in special effects.

12 Describe how computers can help with the logistical and financial problems of producing a motion picture.

13 Describe three electronic musical instruments now widely used by musicians.

14 Why are some proponents of electronic music less than enthusiastic about digital sampling?

15 In what respect do drum machines usually surpass human drummers?

16 Describe some of the devices that have been introduced to allow musicians who are not keyboard players to play electronic musical instruments.

17 To what degree have computers been successful in composing music, poetry, and fiction?

18 What is interactive fiction?

19 Describe two applications of computers to literary research.

20 How are computers being used to preserve dances for posterity?

Topics for Discussion

1 Discuss the colorization controversy. When the question of altering a work of art arises, whose opinions should be given the most weight: those of the artists who created the work, or those of the members of the public who feel that the alteration would increase their enjoyment of the work?

2 Discuss the conflict between electronic music enthusiasts, who use electronics to create completely new musical sounds, and many practicing musicians, who use digital sampling as a convenient way of imitating acoustic instruments with an electronic keyboard.

3 It has been suggested that when a musician's playing is used to create digital samples, then the musician should receive a royalty whenever those samples are used for profit (as in making a record). Today this is almost never done; instead, the musician receives a flat fee for the session in which the samples are recorded. Discuss.

4 Some keyboard players have been known to take their samples from other musician's recordings without permission. For example, the distinctive drum sounds of the pioneering heavy-metal group Led Zeppelin are reputed to have turned up on many other rock recordings. Although the copyright laws do not specifically address this form of copying, many authorities in copyright law feel that it would be ruled illegal in court. On the other hand, it would probably be very difficult to prove that an instrumental sound (as opposed to a melody or lyric) was copied from a particular record. Discuss the morality of this form of copying.

COMPUTERS IN INDUSTRY

INTRODUCTION

The industrial revolution replaced the power of human muscles and the dexterity of human fingers by machines that could achieve the same or better results faster and at lower cost. Yet as cleverly designed as these machines were, they still required human operators to load and unload workpieces* and supplies, to initiate various operations at the appropriate times, to make adjustments, to replace worn or broken tools, and to intervene when the machine malfunctioned. Modern technology promises— or threatens, depending on your point of view—a second industrial revolution in which the human operators will be replaced by computers. The use of such computer-controlled machines is known as *automation*.

Automation promises to increase worker productivity and lower the costs of producing many products. On the other hand, it threatens to eliminate many if not most unskilled and semiskilled jobs, a prospect that may be welcome in the long run (boring, repetitive jobs are better done by machines than by people) but threatens economic and social turmoil in the short run. In this chapter we will focus on the uses to which computers can be put in industry and manufacturing. The social and economic implications of replacing people by computers will be addressed in Chapter 17.

COMPUTER-AIDED DESIGN

Computers can contribute to both the design and the manufacture of a product. The former application is known as *computer-aided design (CAD)*, the latter as *computer-aided manufacturing (CAM)*. The two are often referred to in combination as *computer-aided design and manufacturing (CAD/CAM)*.

Drafting

One of the earliest applications of computer-aided design was to drafting: producing the detailed drawings that describe a product and guide its manufacture and assembly.

With *computer-aided drafting*, the designer makes a drawing by repeatedly designating points on the screen and instructing the computer to draw the line or curve defined by the points. For example, the designer may designate two points and instruct the drafting program to draw a straight line between them. To specify a particular circle for the program to draw, the designer can designate the center of the circle and one point through which the circle must pass. Points can be designated with a mouse,

---

*The workpiece is the object that is being machined, and the tool is the part of the machine that actually cuts or bores into the workpiece. For example, if holes are being drilled into a metal panel, then the panel is the workpiece and the drill bit is the tool.

Computer-aided drafting: creating a drawing with a graphics tablet.

light-pen, or other graphics input device; alternatively, the designer can use the keyboard to enter the numerical coordinates of each point.

With appropriate commands to the drafting program, the designer can make any part of the drawing larger or smaller, rotate it about any point and through any angle, move it from one part of the drawing to another, make any number of copies of it, or create a mirror image of it. The copying feature is used often since drawings frequently contain many repetitions of a single feature. The mirror-image feature sometimes makes it possible to do just half a drawing, then create the other half as the mirror image of the half that was drawn.

Entering a complete drawing into the computer may take as much time as drawing it on paper. But when changes are needed, as they always are when a product is being designed, they are made much more easily on the drawing stored in the computer than on one that has been committed to paper. As with many other computer applications, such as word processing and spreadsheet analysis, much of the computer's utility derives from the speed and convenience with which changes can be made to the information stored in memory.

Solid Modeling

A situation similar to the one described for computer animation also prevails for computerized drafting. We can use the computer as just an electronic drawing board that preserves the lines and other symbols entered by a human operator. But the computer can be of much greater service if it has a three-dimensional, or *solid*, model of the object to be drawn. It can then automatically generate drawings from different viewpoints, cross sections, exploded views, drawings with particular details enlarged, and so on. Such three-dimensional models are even more important when we

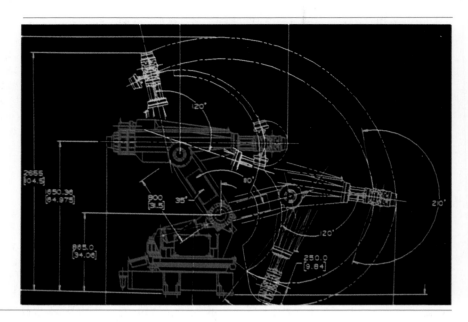

Drawing created with computer-aided drafting.

wish to go beyond mere drafting and have the computer analyze and simulate the operation of the device represented by the drawing. Creating and using such three-dimensional models is known as *solid modeling*.

In solid modeling, the designer constructs an object, such as a machine part, by adding and subtracting basic geometrical shapes such as boxes, cylinders, and spheres. For example, a complex machine part might be constructed by joining together solid boxes with various dimensions and orientations. To make a round hole in the part, the designer would first define a solid cylinder with the same diameter and depth as the desired hole. Then the designer would position the cylinder where the hole was required and instruct the computer to "subtract" the cylinder from the rest of the object—that is, to make a hole in the object with the same size, shape, and location as the cylinder.

Feature-Based Design

A recent development called *feature-based design* allows designers to work with typical features of mechanical parts rather than with basic geometrical shapes. The designer can specify directly such features as holes, grooves, bevels, slots, notches, balls, and sockets rather than having to construct them from boxes, cylinders, and spheres. For example, since the program already knows the shape of a round hole, the designer need only tell the program where the holes should go and how large each should be.

Of even more significance, the program knows the important properties of holes, such as that holes are actually made with drills. Thus the program can warn the designer if the specified hole would call for a non-standard drill size. If the tolerance (allowable error) specified for the diameter of the hole is very small, the program can warn the designer that the hole will require reaming in addition to drilling; the designer then might wish to consider whether a larger tolerance would suffice, thereby allowing the extra machining step to be avoided. Only a single command would be needed to have the program countersink all the holes in a part—to create about each hole a depression for a screwhead. A single command suffices because the program knows which parts of the model represent holes, and one of things it knows about holes is how to countersink them.

Analysis and Simulation

Although the first step in designing a product is usually to sketch a drawing of it, the design must be validated by extensive mathematical calculations. No matter how good the drawing looks, the product will be useless if it breaks due to excessive stress or strain, burns up due to inadequate heat dissipation, blows out due to excessive voltage or current, or tears itself apart due to excessive vibration. Many of the drawings filed with patent applications depict machines that if actually built would fail to work for one or more of these reasons.

Once a model for an object has been entered into the computer, an engineering analysis program can automatically calculate such quantities as stress, strain, temperature, current, and voltage at every point of interest. The program can point up difficulties, informing the engineer where stresses exceed the limits that the material can withstand, for example. When the engineer makes a change in the design, the analysis can be redone automatically, much as values on a spreadsheet are recalculated when one or more items of input data are changed.

The computer model of a product can be a full working model, in which case the operation of the product can be simulated before the product

Computer-aided design: engineer designing a turbine.

is ever built. The computer model can be subjected to extensive testing designed to reveal weak points in the design. A new airplane or spacecraft, for example, can be extensively "flown" while still on its computerized drawing board.

Applications to Electronics

The electronics industry itself makes extensive use of computer-aided design. Modern computer chips containing tens or hundreds of thousands of components could not be designed in any reasonable time without the aid of computers.

Computers can be used for circuit designs in much the same way as for mechanical designs. A circuit is diagrammed on the computer screen with a drafting program. The computer does the calculations necessary to validate the design, and simulates the operation of the circuit.

Nowadays, electronic circuits are usually realized on either silicon chips or printed circuit boards. Although the technologies of chips and circuit boards are different, the design problems are similar. In each case, components must be positioned on the chip or board in such a way as to minimize the complexity of the interconnecting wiring, and then the wiring itself must be designed. The design process must yield artwork from which the actual chips or boards will be produced by a photographic process. Computer programs can remove much of the labor of laying out chips and boards; when the layout is satisfactory, they can (with the aid of a plotter) automatically produce the necessary artwork.

A recent development is a program called a *silicon compiler*. An ordinary compiler translates a program from an easy-to-work-with higher-level language into the more complex and technical machine language

Screen display produced by CAD program shows a robot arm in two different positions.

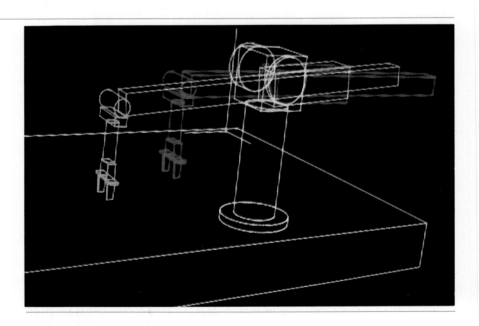

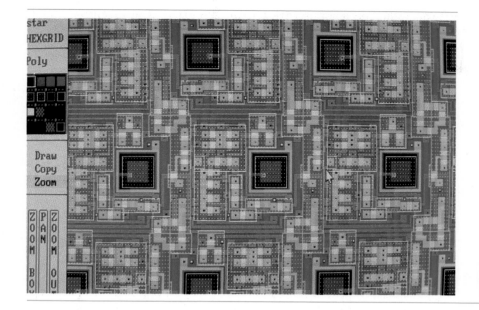

Screen display produced by CAD program shows design for a computer chip. Note the command menu at left.

required by a computer. A silicon compiler accepts a description of the structure and operation of a silicon chip in a form similar to a program written in a higher-level programming language; it translates this high-level specification into a detailed description of the chip's circuitry. The circuit description produced by the silicon compiler is passed on to other programs that simulate the chip's operation (allowing the design to be tested), create the layout that shows how components and connections are actually positioned on the chip, and generate the artwork that will be used to manufacture the chip.

◣ COMPUTER-AIDED MANUFACTURING

In computer-aided manufacturing, the machines that manufacture a product are controlled by a computer. The instructions for the controlling computer are usually generated automatically by computer-aided design programs.

Numerically Controlled Machines

In conventional machining, a skilled machinist manipulates manual controls to guide a cutting tool over the workpiece. After each pass over the workpiece, the machinist must make careful measurements to determine how much more material must be cut away to achieve the required shape and dimensions. Some parts are almost impossible to machine manually, such as those whose shapes are defined by complex mathematical formulas.

In a *numerically controlled machine*, numerical codes rather than adjustments by a human operator guide the cutting tool over the work-

A numerically controlled machine.

piece. Numerically controlled machines can cut complex shapes with errors of less than one ten-thousandth of an inch. The machine can automatically select tools from a carousel, allowing it to switch rapidly from one machining task to another.

Originally, the codes for numerical machine tools were punched into paper tape by programmers working from engineering drawings. Later, computers were employed to aid in producing the punched tape. Today, the codes may be generated automatically by computer-aided design programs, stored on magnetic tape or disk until needed, and conveyed to the numerically controlled machine over a local area network that connects all numerically controlled machines to the factory's central computer.

Robots

In the most general sense of the word, a *robot* is any computer-controlled machine. The word is usually reserved, however, for general-purpose machines that handle parts and tools, as opposed to machines with more specialized functions, such as a numerically controlled drill press. Many robots mimic in some form the functions of the human hand and arm.

The robots of science fiction are mechanical parodies of the human form that play the roles of menacing monsters, servile slaves, or cute companions. An industrial robot is more likely to consist of a single hand and arm mounted on a stationary base. The hand can grasp and release objects and rotate about its mechanical wrist. The arm can tilt up, down, left, and right, and can extend or retract the mechanical hand. One writer pictured a group of industrial robots as pelicans that lowered and stretched out their necks (the mechanical arms) to "peck" at each piece of work that came by.

Technician inserting a circuit board in the industrial computer that controls the computerized milling machine at left. Note the heavy-duty cabinet in which the computer is installed; each circuit board is individually protected by a heavy-duty case.

Many current robots merely go through preprogrammed motions without actually sensing the objects they work with. A paint-spraying robot, for example, always moves the sprayer along a fixed path. If an item to be painted is not in the correct place, the robot will paint the floor and walls instead. If the item is not positioned correctly with respect to the robot, it will not be painted properly; for example, only part of it might be painted.

More advanced robots depend on sensory feedback from their surroundings to control their movements. For example, the hand may contain embedded sensors that allow the robot to feel the object it is grasping. Touch allows a robot to determine not only the size and shape of the object, but such things as temperature, vibration, and the force needed to move the object in a particular direction.

Touch also allows robots to assemble objects by feel. Suppose that a robot is trying to insert a rod into a hole, but the rod is not precisely aligned with the hole. By noting the resistance that it encounters when it tries to insert the rod, the robot can determine the nature and degree of the misalignment. Using this feedback, the robot adjusts the position of the rod and attempts once again to insert it. If the rod still will not go in, the resistance to insertion provides the robot with information for still further adjustments, and so on.

Some robots can sense their surroundings in ways that no human can. For example, a laser beam can be used to locate objects. For objects close to the robot, the brightness of the reflected beam can be used to gauge the distance to the object. For more distant objects, a technique similar to radar can be used. A pulse of laser light is directed toward the object; the time required for the reflected pulse to return is proportional to the distance of the object. Sonar, which applies the principles of radar to sound waves, can be used in the same way.

Technician adjusting automated machine.

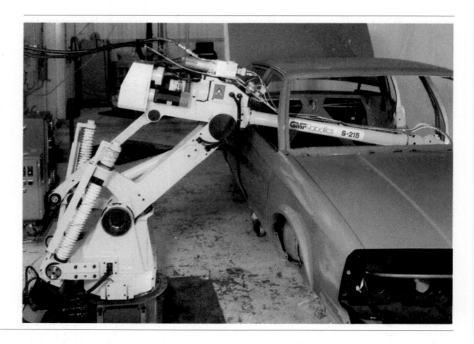

Robot working on automobile.

Robot arm removing automobile hood from rack.

Ultimately, however, there is no substitute for having robots *see* what they are doing. Television cameras can serve well as a robot's eyes, but there is a problem in analyzing the image picked up by the camera. Objects may be viewed from unusual angles, and the images of different objects may overlap one another. Highlights, shadows, and reflections may obscure the outlines of objects. The computer controlling the robot must analyze this complex image and identify the various objects in it—a process known as image analysis. Although much remains to be done, image analysis is making progress, and robot vision systems are starting to appear on the market.

An outstanding challenge for robot sensing and control systems is assembly from randomly oriented parts. We would like robots to be able to select parts from bins, position and orient them as required, and fit them together to form larger assemblies, such as motors or compressors; robots with these capabilities are called *bin-picking robots*. The main obstacle to the development of bin-picking robots is the robot-vision problem of getting the robot to recognize a part regardless of its orientation in the bin; a secondary problem is getting the robot to pick up a part it has recognized and to orient the part as needed for the assembly the robot is working on. As with robot vision, progress is being made with bin-picking robots, although much remains to be done.

The biggest customer for U.S. robot makers has long been the automobile industry, where robots are used extensively for painting, welding, cutting, and parts handling. In 1987, however, spending cutbacks in the automobile industry, particularly at General Motors, cast a pall over the U.S. robot industry. Some companies failed, and others withdrew from robot manufacturing. Chrysler Motors, however, still plans to increase its use of robots substantially, thereby holding out some hope for U.S. robot makers. Meanwhile, some robot manufacturers are concentrating on parts-handling and parts-assembly robots that are used to assemble such products as electronic circuit boards and small appliances.

One reason for the shifting fortunes of robot makers is changing perceptions as to how robots are best used. In the past it was believed that human workers should be replaced directly with robots, whose purchase and operating costs would be less than the wages that would have been paid to the replaced workers. But experience has shown that robots serve best not as direct replacements for existing human workers but as components of carefully designed automated factories. Also, the economic justification for robots seems to lie less in saved labor costs than in more subtle benefits such as more consistent product quality and less time needed to prepare for production of a new product.

The leading user of robots is Japan, where completely automatic factories are becoming more and more common, and where robots are often manufactured by other robots.

Flexible Factories

Flexible manufacturing systems that can process a number of dissimilar products at the same time provide an alternative to the traditional production line and job shop. Before considering flexible manufacturing systems, we look briefly at the strengths and weaknesses of the two traditional approaches.

Production Lines　　Most industries use the technique of mass production made famous by Henry Ford. The item being manufactured moves down a production line. At each station on the line, a worker performs some operation on the item—a part is installed, a weld is made, paint is applied, and so on. Each worker does the same small job on each item that passes his or her station.

Although production lines are highly efficient, they are hardly the answer to every production problem. For one thing, a production line requires many special machines, each designed to do just one job at one station on the production line. Each has to be foolproof, as it will be operated by a semiskilled or unskilled worker, not a skilled machinist. Many items must be produced and sold to recover the costs of these special tools; production lines are not economical for small production runs. What's more, changing the design of the product is expensive because the special tools have to be changed. The retooling necessary to produce a new model car, for example, significantly increases the cost of the car.

The products coming off a production line are uniform. The customer's options consist mainly of specifying whether certain parts will be included or omitted. There is no possibility of ordering customized versions that the manufacturer did not originally anticipate. We cannot give special instructions to a production line as we can do to an individual artisan.

A production-line worker has to do the same job over and over again, possibly at high speed to keep up with the conveyor that brings workpieces to his or her station. People are asked to keep up with (and, to a certain extent, behave like) machines. Such jobs are often unfit for human beings.

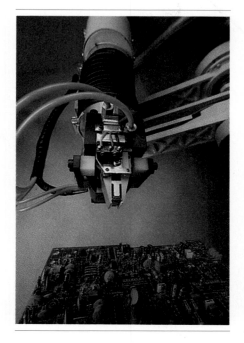

Robot arm inserting integrated circuit into printed circuit board.

Job Shops   Small numbers of items are made in a job shop using general-purpose machines operated by skilled machinists. This approach is more expensive than that of a production line for two reasons. First, the skilled machinists command higher salaries than production-line workers. Second, and more important, the general-purpose machines spend only about six percent of their time doing useful work. The rest of the time they stand idle while machinists insert and remove workpieces, change cutting tools, and make adjustments. Because of the higher labor cost and the lower productivity of the machines, a part produced by a job shop can be hundreds of times more expensive than an identical part produced by a production line.

Flexible Manufacturing Systems   *Flexible manufacturing systems* combine the advantages of production lines and job shops. Machine utilization is high as on a production line, yet jobs calling for only a small number of parts can be accommodated as in a job shop. At their simplest, flexible manufacturing systems provide versatile automated machine shops for conventional factories. At their most elaborate, they hold out the possibility of automatic factories that will work unattended except for a small contingent of human supervisors. The technology of flexible manufacturing systems is also referred to as *computer-integrated manufacturing (CIM)*.

Each machine in a flexible manufacturing system is controlled by its own computer, either a microprocessor or a minicomputer. The computers controlling the individual machines communicate with a central computer via a local area network. The central computer keeps track of the flow of workpieces through the system. As each workpiece arrives at a machine, the central computer sends the machine instructions for processing the part. Operating under the control of its own computer, which is in turn

Robot arm holding carburetor. Designing robots to handle and assemble small parts is a major challenge for robot engineering.

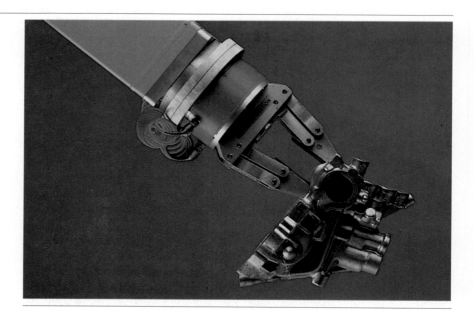

Automated assembly line.

following the instructions downloaded from the central computer, the machine carries out the requested cutting operations, selecting tools from an adjoining carousel as needed. When its work is complete and the workpiece has been removed, instructions for machining the next workpiece are received from the central computer. Workpieces are inserted into machines, removed from them, and transported between them by robots or by an automated conveyor system.

A flexible manufacturing system is analogous in some ways to a time-sharing computer system. We have seen that it is inefficient to grant a single person sole use of a large computer system, since one person cannot fully utilize the system. The system will stand idle while input and output devices operate and the person is thinking of what to do next. Similarly, if a machine can be used for only one job at a time, it will stand idle while being set up for each new job. But if the machine can be switched quickly from one job to another under computer control, then it can handle a steady stream of workpieces belonging to a variety of jobs, adapting itself automatically to the particular machining operations needed for each workpiece. The factory can be working on many jobs at the same time just as a time-sharing computer system works on many users' programs at the same time.

Flexible systems raise the prospect of completely automatic factories. Under the control of a central computer, automated vehicles would transport materials from an automated warehouse to the factory floor, where they would be loaded into machines by robots. Robots would also unload finished work from machines and, with the aid of an automated conveyor system, transport pieces between machines. Robots would assemble parts into finished products, which would be automatically transported back to the automated warehouse. A small contingent of human supervisors—perhaps only one—would oversee the operation of the factory with the

Automated product distribution center.

Checking the operation of an automated fabricating machine.

aid of television displays and computer readouts. The human supervisor would be present mainly to handle emergencies, such as fires, burst pipes, and broken machines.

Although human intervention will probably always be required for extraordinary emergencies, the machines need to be able to handle routine problems themselves. Such a problem is worn and broken tools. All tools eventually wear out; the machine must monitor wear and determine when it is time to change the tool. Since wear is gradual, a worn tool is not an emergency—the change usually can be deferred until operations on the current workpiece have been completed. A broken tool, on the other hand, must be changed immediately to prevent damage both to the workpiece and, more importantly, to the very expensive automated machine.

Researchers are still working to improve methods of detecting worn and broken tools. Methods under study include monitoring the forces the tool exerts on the workpiece and detecting the sounds produced by a breaking tool. Because of the limitations of current techniques, it sometimes has been necessary to provide automated machines with human operators whose sole duties are to detect and replace worn and broken tools.

PLANNING AND CONTROL

The operations of both conventional and automated factories need to be scheduled so as to produce products as they are needed without building up excessively large inventories of finished products. *Management resource planning (MRP)* works from current inventories, promised delivery dates, and sales forecasts to determine what products must be finished at what times. Deliveries of material and manufacturing operations are scheduled so as to assure that products are ready when needed.

Control of an automated factory is organized into a hierarchy of levels. The highest level is concerned with long-term planning while the lowest levels deal with the detailed operations of individual machines. Intermediate levels focus on such matters as the flow of workpieces through the factory. Levels concerned with more than one machine are handled by one or more central computers, while those that apply only to a particular machine are handled by that machine's built-in computer. All the computers in the factory communicate over a local area network.

◣ Summary

Computer-aided design employs computers for drafting, engineering analysis, and simulation. In the electronics industry, computers are used to design, analyze, and simulate the operation of circuits, to lay out chips and printed-circuit boards, and to produce the artwork from which chips and boards are manufactured. Researchers are working on silicon compilers that would translate a higher-level-language description of the chip's operation into a detailed design.

Computer-aided manufacturing is based on two technologies: numerically controlled machines, which are guided by numerical codes generated by computer-aided design programs, and robots, which are general-purpose machines for handling products and tools. Computer-aided manufacturing seems to be moving in the direction of flexible manufacturing systems in which computer-controlled machines could quickly switch from one job to another, thus combining the efficiency of a production line with the flexibility of a job shop. The most advanced versions of these systems would be automatic factories that would function with little human supervision.

Computers also play an important role in managing the operations of a factory. Management resource planning (MRP) systems schedule deliveries of raw materials and manufacturing operations to produce products as fast as, but hopefully not faster than, they are needed.

◣ Vocabulary Review

automation
bin-picking robot
computer-aided design (CAD)
computer-aided design and manufacturing (CAD/CAM)
computer-aided drafting

computer-aided manufacturing (CAM)
computer-integrated manufacturing (CIM)
feature-based design
flexible manufacturing system

management resource planning (MRP)
numerically controlled machine
robot
silicon compiler
solid modeling

For Further Reading

Bairstow, Jeffery N. "Chip Design Made Easy." *High Technology*, June 1985, pp. 18–25.

Brody, Herb. "CAD meets CAM." *High Technology*, May 1987, pp. 12–18.

——————. "U.S. Robot Makers Try to Bounce Back." *High Technology Business*, October 1987, pp. 18–24.

Edson, Daniel. "Bin-Picking Robots Punch In." *High Technology*, June 1984, pp. 57–60.

Horn, Berthold K. P. and Katsushi Ikeuchi. "The Mechanical Manipulation of Randomly Oriented parts." *Scientific American*. August 1984, pp. 100–111.

Nevins, James L. and Daniel F. Whitney. "Computer-Controlled Assembly." *Scientific American*, February 1978, pp. 62–74.

Raia, Ernest. "Helping Machine Tools Help Themselves." *High Technology*, June 1985, pp. 44–48.

Scientific American (special issue on mechanization of work), September 1982.

Review Questions

1 Contrast the first and second industrial revolutions.

2 The first industrial revolution introduced *mechanization*—the use of machines controlled by human operators. Distinguish between automation and mechanization.

3 Give the meanings of the acronyms CAD, CAM, and CAD/CAM.

4 Describe some of the facilities provided by computer-aided drafting.

5 Describe solid modeling.

6 Contrast feature-based design with conventional solid modeling.

7 Describe the use of computers in analysis and simulation of engineering designs.

8 Describe the applications of computer-aided design to the electronics industry.

9 Contrast a silicon compiler with a compiler for a programming language.

10 Describe computer-aided manufacturing.

11 Contrast conventional and numerically controlled machines.

12 Contrast science-fictional robots with those actually used in industry.

13 Describe some of the sensing systems that allow robots to perceive the objects they are manipulating.

14 Discuss the changing perceptions as to how robots are best used.

15 Contrast a production line, a job shop, and a flexible manufacturing system.

16 In what way is a flexible manufacturing system like a time-shared computer system?

17 Describe the operation of an automatic factory.

18 Describe the obstacles to unattended machine operation presented by broken and worn tools.

19 Describe management resource planning.

20 Describe the organization of the planning and control system for an automatic factory.

◣ Topics for Discussion

1 The first industrial revolution made low-cost manufactured goods commonplace and provided employment for large numbers of people. Yet it also led to child labor, sweatshops, and "dark, satanic mills"—abuses that were corrected only with the advent of organized labor. Discuss the possible benefits and pitfalls of the second industrial revolution. What social forces might act (as organized labor did) to curb abuses brought about by the second industrial revolution.

2 The first industrial revolution led to rioting in which workers tried to smash or sabotage the machines that were replacing them. Indeed, the very word *sabotage* comes from shoes, called *sabots*, that were thrown into machines to damage them. So far, no such widespread rioting has resulted from the second industrial revolution. Why the difference?

3 Many production line jobs are so dull and monotonous, yet must be executed at such high speed, that they have been described as unfit for human beings. Yet the people who now hold these jobs might be unable or unwilling to get others. Discuss the morality of eliminating jobs that are unfit for human beings, yet human beings depend upon for their livelihoods.

COMPUTERS IN BUSINESS AND FINANCE

INTRODUCTION

The term *business* encompasses the planning, organization, direction, and control of profit-making activities. In many ways business is a particularly human activity, for it involves investors, managers, employees, and customers cooperating for their mutual benefit. Yet planning and supervising these human activities requires coordinating massive amounts of information, which computers are admirably suited to handle.

Financial institutions such as banks and brokerage houses are businesses that deal in money itself and in such financial instruments as stocks and bonds. Only a small portion of the money supply is represented by currency. The remainder is represented by entries in the records of various financial institutions. Transferring funds from one account to another involves exchanging messages authorizing the records of each account to be altered to reflect the transfer. Careful control must be maintained to assure that all transfers are in accordance with the many laws and regulations governing financial transactions. Here, too, computers are well suited to handling the required information processing.

In fact, computers are now so widely used in business and finance that a complete coverage of their uses is impractical. Instead, we will concentrate on five important and typical applications: management information systems, point-of-sale equipment, office automation, electronic funds transfer, and financial trading.

MANAGEMENT INFORMATION SYSTEMS

Automation of business data processing began with the punch-card sorting and tabulating machines developed by Herman Hollerith. Processing with electromechanical punch-card machines was known as Automatic Data

Computers are becoming increasingly popular in small businesses such as this automobile repair shop.

Processing (ADP). Replacing punch-card machines with electronic computers gave us Electronic Data Processing (EDP). Today the "electronic" is taken for granted and we just refer to *data processing (DP)*.

The more sophisticated processing available with computers allowed data processing systems to be used not only for handling routine transactions but also for generating information to aid managers plan and control the company's operations; such systems are known as *management information systems (MIS)*. Perhaps because *management information system* sounds more important than *data processing*, the former term is often applied to the entire data processing operation, including the part that handles routine transactions.

Management and control of a company's operations takes place on four levels, each of which has its own data processing and management information requirements:

- **Transaction processing** handles such routine transactions as orders, shipments, and payments.

- **Operational control** refers to control of day-to-day operations such as assuring that factory workers meet their daily quotas.

- **Tactical planning** involves such short- and intermediate-range planning as adjusting production levels in response to changes in demand for a product, to excessively low or high inventory levels, or to moves by the competition.

- **Strategic planning** focuses on such long-range decisions as building new plants, closing those that are no longer needed, introducing and discontinuing products, and purchasing, selling out to, or merging with other companies.

The most massive data processing occurs at the transaction-processing level, where every order, shipment, invoice, and paycheck is processed. Operational control requires summaries of daily or weekly operations. Tactical and strategic planning requires summaries of the overall operation of the company and forecasts of its future operations for each plan or policy that is under consideration.

Central to every management information system is the corporate database and the database management system that maintains it. A crucial feature of the database management system is data independence, whereby the form in which the data is viewed by programs and interactive users is independent of the way it is stored on media such as disks. This assures that changes in storage techniques, as might be required by changes in the operation of the company or in the regulations that govern it, will not invalidate existing programs that use the data. Data independence also ensures that the data can be retrieved and used in ways that were not envisioned when the data storage format was originally designed.

TRANSACTION PROCESSING, BOOKKEEPING, AND ACCOUNTING

A management information system is composed of a number of subsystems, each of which consists of one or more programs and data files. In this section we will look at those systems that underlie the routine order processing, bookkeeping, and accounting operations of a company.

Order Entry, Shipping, and Billing

The *order entry system* accepts orders and sees that they are filled. Orders received by mail or phone are entered at a display terminal. The order entry system checks that the customer's credit is good and that the ordered items are in stock. If no problems are found, the order entry system prints the packing slips and other paperwork needed to get the merchandise shipped. The system keeps track of the status of each order so that customer inquiries can be answered easily.

The order entry system passes the order to the billing system, which prints and mails an invoice for the merchandise sold. The *billing system*, in turn, passes the invoice to the accounts receivable system, which keeps track of the invoice until it is paid.

Inventory Control

The *inventory control system* keeps track of the merchandise that is on hand for shipment. It automatically updates inventory records when merchandise is sold and when new merchandise arrives from the factory. Controlling inventory can be tricky. Too large an inventory results in excessive storage costs and taxes, yet too small an inventory will result in running out of items and, hence, lost sales. The inventory control system generates periodic reports showing the quantity on hand for each item, the number sold in the preceding period (month, quarter, year), and the dollar volume—the amount resulting from those sales. Based on such reports, managers may decide to increase production for a popular item, place an item on sale if the quantity on hand is too high, or discontinue an item whose dollar volume is too low.

The inventory control system is a primary source of input to the manufacturing resource planning system, which schedules manufacturing operations.

Using a spreadsheet on construction site.

Accounts Receivable

The *accounts receivable system* keeps track of money owed to the company. Monthly statements and past due notices are routinely mailed to customers. Information concerning amounts that are too long overdue is passed to the credit and collection system. The credit and collection system may send some demands for payment routinely. If payment is not forthcoming, however, the account must ultimately be brought to the attention of a person, who will investigate the reason for nonpayment and determine what action to take.

An important management report produced by the accounts receivable system is the aged trial balance. This report shows the current purchases, current payments, and outstanding balance for each customer. The report also shows how much of the outstanding balance is current, how much is one month old, two months old, and so on. If too much of the money owed the company is one or more months past due, the company may have to adjust its credit and collection policies.

Accounts Payable

Invoices received from suppliers and approved for payment are entered into the *accounts payable system*, which prints and mails the necessary checks. Payments are made as close as possible to the due dates to conserve cash, avoid penalties for late payment, and preserve the company's credit rating. Routine repetitive payments, such as rent, are made automatically. The accounts payable system generates such reports as the cash requirements report, which shows the amount of cash needed to handle upcoming payments, and the check register, which gives information on every check that has been issued.

Payroll

The *payroll system* is one of the most complex transaction-processing systems, so much so that many companies with their own data processing systems have their payrolls done by outside service bureaus that specialize in payroll processing. One outstanding requirement for the payroll system is its reliability. Although invoices may occasionally be paid late, missing a payroll date by even a single day is likely to result in enormous employee-relations problems.

One source of complexity is the different ways in which employees are paid. Some are paid fixed wages, some are paid by the hour (with different hourly rates for regular and overtime hours), some are paid by the number of pieces of work produced, and some are paid commissions.

Another source of complexity is the many deductions that must be taken from paychecks. These include withholding taxes, employee contributions to fringe benefits such as retirement plans and health insurance, and union dues. The amount of each deduction depends not only on the status of the employee and the options he or she chooses, but also on continually changing laws, regulations, and union contracts.

General Ledger

The *general ledger system* is responsible for bookkeeping and accounting—tracking the flow of cash throughout the company and generating reports summarizing the company's financial status. Most of the other systems described interact with the general ledger system to get all charges and payments posted to the proper accounts.

Reports produced by the general ledger system include the chart of accounts, the profit and loss statement, and the balance sheet. The chart of accounts lists all the categories in which charges and payments are

```
MENU

                 GENERAL LEDGER AND FINANCIAL REPORTING SYSTEM       MENU 00

                                  MAIN MENU

        _  MENU 01        ACCOUNT MASTER DATA DISPLAY
        _  MENU 02        ACCOUNT ANALYSIS
        _  MENU 03        RELATIONSHIPS, ALLOCATIONS, REPORT INQUIRY

        _  MENU 04        JOURNAL ENTRY COLLECTION
        _  MENU 05        COLLECTED JOURNAL MAINTENANCE
        _  MENU 06        COLLECTED JOURNAL INQUIRY

        _  MENU 07        STATISTICAL, BUDGET AND USER SCREENS

        _  MENU 08        USER SCREEN GENERATOR
        _  MENU 09        SECURITY FUNCTIONS

        _  MENU 10        IMMEDIATE UPDATE FUNCTIONS

        _  END            EXIT GENERAL LEDGER SYSTEM


     POSITION CURSOR AND PRESS ENTER
```

Screen display produced by a general ledger program.

recorded. The profit and loss statement summarizes income and expenses for each category. The balance sheet summarizes what the company owns (its assets) and what it owes (its liabilities).

Auditing

The financial records of a company need to be verified by *auditing* for two reasons. First, the company wants to make sure that employees are not misusing its funds and inventory, such as by issuing checks to fictitious suppliers, shipping merchandise to fictitious customers, or tampering with the books to cover embezzlement. Second, investors, lenders, and regulatory agencies need to be assured that financial statements such as the profit and loss statement and the balance sheet present a fair picture of the company's financial status.

Auditors use special software to follow transactions through the computer system. To aid auditors, the system must maintain audit trails by which account entries can be traced back to supporting documents such as invoices and checks.

MANAGEMENT REPORTS

The reports produced by a management information system can be classified as scheduled listings, exception reports, demand reports, and predictive reports.

Scheduled Listings

Scheduled listings are produced every week or month and are distributed to those who might need the information they contain. Although scheduled listings are the most common kind of report, they are also the least helpful; much of the information in them is likely to be irrelevant to a manager's immediate needs. Scheduled listings are more likely to be useful for operational control and short-range tactical planning than for long-range strategic planning.

Exception Reports

Exception reports contain information that needs to be brought to managers' attention—customers whose accounts are overdue, orders that have not arrived from suppliers, districts in which sales have been particularly good or bad, and products that are selling particularly well or poorly. Exception reports are usually more useful than scheduled listings because instead of reporting all transactions, the management information system selects those that are of special interest or require special handling.

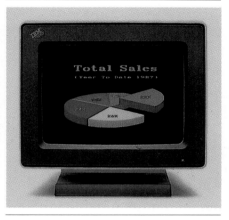

Computer-generated graphics can help managers understand business data.

Demand Reports

Demand reports supply specific information that managers have requested. Because demand reports are produced in direct response to the needs of management, they are more likely to be useful than either scheduled listings or exception reports. Generating demand reports can place a heavy burden on data processing personnel. Ideally, managers could request such reports from desktop computer terminals; in many cases the requested information could be presented on the screen, so that no paper report need be printed at all. Unfortunately, the top-level managers for whom demand reports are more useful often resist personally using computer equipment.

Predictive Reports

Predictive reports attempt to extrapolate current data to predict such things as future costs, sales, and profits. Spreadsheet programs are often used as tools for generating predictive reports. Increasingly, however, predictive reports are becoming the province of a specialized component of the management information system, the decision support system.

◣ DECISION SUPPORT SYSTEMS

Computers contribute to tactical and strategic planning by aiding managers anticipate the effects of decisions. Spreadsheet programs have often been used for this purpose, but there is a trend toward *decision support systems* that provide more powerful computational capabilities, more powerful modeling facilities, and are more closely integrated with the database management system and other components of the management information system. Like spreadsheet programs, decision support systems must be user-friendly as they are often used by managers with little background in computing.

Modeling

To anticipate the effects of decisions, the decision support system needs a model of the company, its market, and its financial environment. Such a model might be used, for example, to determine how sales volume would vary with the price of a product, the amount spent on advertising, and the staffing level of the sales force. As circumstances change, models must be adjusted accordingly, a process known as calibration. Decision support systems provide the means for constructing, calibrating, and using models.

Analysis

Decision support systems provide a variety of means of analyzing the consequences of decisions and policies. The following are some of the most common kinds of analysis provided by decision support systems.

- **What-If Analysis** The user can explore the effects of various assumptions, such as an increase in interest rates, a decrease in the demand for a product, or a shortage of raw materials. Two special forms of what-if analysis are impact analysis and sensitivity analysis.

- **Impact Analysis** The user can gauge the damage that might result from a specific event, such as the bankruptcy of a supplier, a strike, or a contract cancellation.

- **Sensitivity Analysis** The user can determine how sensitive certain important quantities, such as sales and profits, are to such uncontrollable factors as changes in interest rates or in costs of supplies.

- **Goal Seeking** The system attempts to find ways of adjusting the parameters under the user's control (such as prices and production levels) so as to obtain a specific goal.

- **Monte Carlo Analysis** Some information, such as the number of people who will call a customer service department at the same time, are inherently unpredictable, The best we can do is collect statistical information such as the rate at which calls are received at each time of day. A Monte Carlo simulation would choose the times for simulated calls at random, subject only to the requirement that the rate at which calls were made conformed to the available statistical information. Based on the simulation, the system would determine such things as the number of customers who received busy signals when they called and the average and longest time a customer was kept waiting on the line before his or her request was processed. If the statistical information was accurate, the results of the Monte Carlo simulation should be typical of those that would be encountered with the real system.

- **Optimization Analysis** The system analyzes how parameters under the user's control can be adjusted to achieve the best operation. For example, it might determine production levels, pricing policies, and advertising expenditures should be adjusted to maximize profits.

OFFICE AUTOMATION

Since offices are devoted to information processing, it is hardly surprising that computers should find a place in them. It took the microprocessor revolution, however, to make computers small enough and inexpensive enough for office use. Now computing equipment is turning up on more and more desks in the form of computer terminals, personal computers, and computerized workstations. The extensive use of computers in offices is often referred to as *office automation (OA)*.

Word Processing

Word processing improves typists' productivity by allowing them to correct mistakes quickly without having to retype an entire page. Mistakes discovered after a document has been typed can be corrected as easily as those detected at the time they are made. (On some conventional typewriters, mistakes discovered as soon as they are made can be corrected, but mistakes discovered later may be impossible to correct since there is no way to move existing text to make room for additional characters or to close up the space left by deleted characters.)

Using a portable computer in the office. Portable and laptop computers are enjoying increasing popularity among business users.

Word processing also simplifies revision. Frequently a businessperson will dictate a letter or report, have a first draft typed, make corrections in pencil, have a revised draft typed, and so on, until he or she is satisfied with the result. These corrections can be entered easily into the word processor so that the entire document does not have to be retyped for each draft.

Other applications for word processing include generating form letters that appear to be individually typed and contain the name and address of the person to whom each is addressed. Standard text, known as boilerplate, can be stored on disk and inserted as needed in documents such as letters and contracts.

Electronic Mail

If we are going to use computers to create documents, we might as well use them to send the documents to their destinations electronically, instead of printing the documents and delivering them by conventional means. More generally, communication plays a crucial role in the office and in business generally. Office automation would have little value if it failed to improve the ability of people to communicate with one another.

A variation on electronic mail is *voice mail*, in which a spoken message is converted into digital form for computer processing. The digitized speech can be stored in a computer, duplicated, and routed over a computer network, just as with ordinary electronic mail. When the recipient is ready to receive the message, the digital codes are converted back into spoken words. Voice mail is attractive to businesspeople, who usually prefer oral over written communication.

Both electronic and voice mail can help avoid "telephone tag," in which person B is out when person A calls, person A is out when person B returns the call, person B is out when person A tries again, and so on.

Facsimile

Facsimile, also known as *fax*, transmits images of documents over telephone lines and other communications links. The user inserts the document to be transmitted into the fax machine and a copy emerges from the fax machine at the other end of the telephone connection. Thus a fax machine is used much like an office copier except that the copy is produced at a remote location; for this reason, facsimile is sometimes referred to as *telecopying*. Documents are scanned, digitized, and transmitted at 9600 bps using modems built into the fax machines; transmission time is less than 30 seconds per page. Resolution is 200 dpi, which is two-thirds the resolution of a laser printer.

With the aid of a special adapter, personal computers can send and receive facsimile images. Software can convert ASCII-coded text files (such as those produced by word processors) to graphics images for facsimile transmission. The reverse process of converting incoming graphics images to text files has turned out to be more difficult to implement. Optical character recognition must be used to convert the graphics images into

Automated office.

ASCII codes. Unfortunately, the limited resolution of facsimile systems obscures fine details that are needed for reliable optical character recognition.

Although facsimile has long been used for special purposes, such as transmitting news photographs, it has recently enjoyed a surge in popularity due to the compact, low-cost fax machines made possible by modern microelectronics. So popular has facsimile become that it is threatening the revenues of overnight delivery services such as Federal Express. Many find facsimile more convenient than electronic mail because printed documents, including graphics, are transmitted directly. Information does not have to be typed into a computer at the transmitting end or viewed on a screen at the receiving end. In the future "paperless office" envisioned by some, there might be little need for facsimile. But as long as paper documents are as widely used as they are today and are likely to be in the foreseeable future, facsimile transmission will be a strong competitor to electronic mail.

Personal Computers and Data Sharing

Personal computers are widely used in offices for office applications such as word processing and electronic mail as well as for management-oriented applications such as spreadsheet analysis and database management. A problem that remains to be solved satisfactorily in many offices is that of sharing data, of making data created on one personal computer available to users of other personal computers. All too often this is done by physically carrying diskettes from one computer to another, a form of communication jokingly referred to as the "Nike network" after the shoes presumably worn by the office assistants who carry the diskettes.

One approach to data sharing is multiuser systems, in which many users communicate via terminals with a single central microcomputer, minicomputer, or mainframe. Data stored on the central computer is available to all the users via their terminals. The terminals can be dumb terminals, in which case all processing must be done by the central computer, or they can be personal computers, in which case they may do their own processing and communicate with the central computer only to store and retrieve data. The drawback to this approach is the heavy load placed on the central computer, which must do far more work than any of the terminals or personal computers connected to it.

The best approach to data sharing is generally believed to be local area networks, which provide communication among personal computers, mainframes, workstations (essentially, personal computers designed for use with a network), and special-purpose equipment such as file servers (which provide disk storage) and print servers (which provide access to printers).

Local area networks are not nearly so widely used as they could be. Obstacles to their widespread use have included lack of support by some computer manufacturers and lack of industry-wide standards that would allow computers made by different manufacturers to communicate with each other. Now, however, the major computer manufacturers have joined in support of an international communications standard known as *Open Systems Interconnection (OSI)*; this industry-wide support of a single standard is expected to greatly increase the use of local area networks. The joining of individual computers and workstations by local area networks is the next major step in office automation.

Office Information Systems

Current trends seem to be toward *office information systems* in which many office functions will be performed with the aid of computers, eliminating much (but probably not all) paperwork. Future office information systems might, like one current prototype, be based on electronically stored and manipulated forms. These forms, when displayed on the screen of the workstation, look very much like paper forms. They can be filled in or modified by typing on the keyboard of the workstation. The screen serves as a kind of electronic desk on which a number of forms can appear at the same time, perhaps overlapping one another as on an actual desk.

The workstation maintains an electronic in-basket containing forms received from other workstations and an electronic out-basket containing forms that are to be sent to other workstations. Typically, one or more forms will be selected from the in-basket, filled in or modified as necessary, and then placed in the out-basket to be sent to other workstations. The workstation will also display a blank form of a particular type when a form needs to be filled in from scratch.

Some proposed office information systems use a model of office procedures to track forms from one workstation to another. Once a particular kind of form has been entered into the system, the system will see that it is routed to the first workstation that is to process it. If the form remains at that workstation too long, the system will send a reminder message to the user. After the form has been processed at one workstation, the system will see that it is routed to the next. If several forms are needed before action can be taken, the system will inform the user when all the needed forms have arrived at the workstation. If one of the needed forms is delayed or missing, the system will send a reminder message to the workstation responsible for the missing form.

Human Factors

Because so many people work in offices and because office computers have become so widely used, the office has become a major area of contact between people and computers. Not surprisingly, problems have arisen. People who suffer from computerphobia, an unreasoning fear of computers, have quit otherwise excellent office jobs to avoid having to work with computers. Training people to use computer hardware and software has become a major office expense. Office lighting and furniture are often not well suited to computers and terminals, with the result that some computer users suffer from eyestrain, muscle cramps, and perhaps even more serious disorders. Computerized performance monitoring, in which computers keep track of how rapidly workers carry out their tasks, has been criticized for dehumanizing workers, increasing job stress, and perhaps even violating workers' privacy. These and other human-factors questions are discussed in more detail in Chapter 18.

◣ BAR CODES AND THE PRICE-MARKING CONTROVERSY

The traditional cash register has given way to a variety of electronic terminals that serve many functions other than storing cash and totaling orders. These terminals are known as *point-of-sale (POS) equipment.*

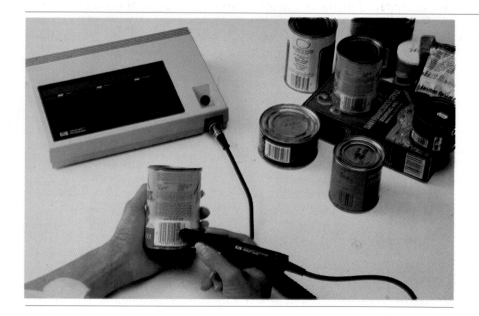

Portable bar code scanners are often used for taking inventory.

One of the most common uses of POS equipment is reading the *bar codes* printed on many products and using the code on each item to determine its price. The code, which represents a ten-digit identification number, is read with a hand-held scanning wand or, more commonly, with a scanner built into the counter top. The POS terminal transmits the identification number to a computer, which looks up the number in a price list and sends the price and description of the item back to the terminal. Both the description and the price are displayed to the customer and printed on the sales slip. In addition, the computer updates the store's records to reflect the sale of that particular item.

Bar codes allow stores to avoid the tedious chore of marking a price on each item of merchandise. In the 1970s, a controversy erupted over whether the elimination of individual price marking imposed a burden on the consumer. The stores pointed out that prices are still marked on shelves below the items being sold. And the sales tickets contain not only the prices, but also the descriptions of the items, making it easier for customers to determine what was charged for each item. Some stores made a scanner available to customers so they could check the prices of items after they had been removed from the shelves. Others offered an item free if the price printed on the sales ticket differed from that on the shelf.

In spite of these gestures, however, many consumer groups opposed the elimination of individual price marking, fearing this would make it more difficult for consumers to compare prices and suspecting that the price stored in the computer might not always be the same as the one on the shelf. They were joined by store employees' unions, who feared the loss of jobs that would result if individual price marking were eliminated. In some states this combination of special interests got laws passed requiring individual price marking.

The price-marking controversy delayed the widespread use of POS equipment. (The cost of changing over to POS equipment was also a factor

In many of today's stores, the cash register has given way to a computerized point-of-sale terminal.

in the delay.) Now that the fuss has died down, many stores have eliminated individual price marking with few objections from their customers. What organized consumer groups vigorously opposed in the 1970s is apparently of little concern to the individual consumers of the 1980s.

POS systems have many applications beyond the elimination of individual price marking. Because the system is aware of every item sold, it can keep track of the store's inventory. It can also keep track of the amount of cash in each cash register, so that excessive cash can be removed for deposit in a safe or bank. And as described in the next section, POS terminals play an important role in electronic funds transfer.

ELECTRONIC FUNDS TRANSFER

Electronic funds transfer (EFT) transfers funds by means of electronic messages rather than paper tokens such as cash, checks, and credit-card vouchers. EFT allows bankers and merchants to transfer funds more rapidly and at lower cost, and it offers customers more convenient access to their funds. Critics, however, have been quick to point out possible pitfalls of EFT, such as new possibilities for theft, embezzlement, and violation of customers' privacy.

Preauthorized Payments and Deposits

Preauthorized payments and deposits take place automatically according to standing agreements between banks and customers. With direct deposit, for example, monthly checks, such as paychecks, welfare payments, and Social Security checks, are deposited directly into the recipient's account without the recipient ever seeing the check or having to take it to the bank. The organization sending the checks saves the substantial cost of making out and mailing individual checks. For the recipient, the chance of loss or theft is eliminated, as is the need to carry the check to the bank. People who receive Social Security checks are constantly being urged to take advantage of direct deposit.

The same procedure can be used for recurrent payments, such as utility bills, house and car payments, and payments on charge accounts. In each case, the customer is sent a statement showing the amount of the bill, but the payment takes place automatically. Procedures are provided whereby a customer can prevent payment if a dispute arises over the amount of the bill.

Teller Terminals

Teller terminals allow tellers to enter transactions directly into the bank's computer. When you make a deposit or withdrawal, for instance, the teller will enter the details of the transaction on the teller terminal, causing the computer to increase or decrease the balance for your account by the appropriate amount. Teller terminals are also useful for verifying checks and for giving customers information about their accounts.

The computer system that supports these terminals can generate useful management information. For example, it can record the number of transactions that take place during each hour of the day at a particular teller station or branch office. Managers can use this information to plan banking hours and staff assignments for more efficient operation, while still providing satisfactory service to depositors.

Automatic Teller Machines

A number of banks now provide 24-hour banking with *automatic teller machines (ATMs)*, which are placed either just outside the bank or in convenient public places, such as shopping centers and malls.

To use an ATM, the customer inserts a card similar in appearance to a credit card and enters a personal-identification number (PIN) on a calculator-like keyboard. The bank's computer reads the identifying information recorded magnetically on the card and checks that it refers to the same person referred to by the identifying number entered manually. Once the user's identity has been established, the user can carry out most traditional banking activites—such as making deposits and withdrawals—by pressing keys on the ATM. The machine dispenses cash when withdrawals are made.

ATM Networks, Debit Cards, and POS Terminals

Automatic check processing.

It is impractical for every bank to place its own ATM machine in every desirable location, such as a supermarket, convenience store, or shopping mall. This problem is solved by *ATM networks*, which electronically route ATM transactions between banks, allowing customers to carry out ATM transactions with banks other than the one that owns the ATM machine. By joining such a network, a bank allows its customers to access their accounts from any ATM machine on the network, rather than from just the bank's own ATM machines. Some ATM machines on the network are owned by member banks; others are owned by the network, which may arrange with supermarket and convenience-store chains to place an ATM machine in every store. Some networks cover a limited region, such as a state, whereas others are nationwide. Customers are usually charged a fee for transactions that must be routed over an ATM network; banks differ on whether to charge for transactions that take place on their own ATM machines.

ATM networks are striving to expand the services that they offer. For example, some networks are planning to allow customers to use ATM machines to make airline, hotel, and rental-car reservations and to purchase airline and other tickets.

Another area into which ATM networks are trying to move is that of debit cards and POS terminals. A *debit card* allows a customer to pay for purchases with funds transferred electronically from the customer's bank account. POS terminals connected to an ATM network would allow cus-

Drive-up automatic teller machines (right) are becoming increasingly popular; walk-up automatic teller machines (left) are already common sights in banks, malls, and grocery stores.

tomers to use their ATM cards as debit cards and to pay for purchases from accounts in any bank on the ATM network. Currently, progress in this area is slow: merchants are waiting for customers to demand debit-card services before installing the required POS terminals, and customers will use debit cards only when they are accepted by most merchants. Also, there are still questions of who should pay who for POS terminals: ATM networks expect merchants to pay the network for the privilege of having the terminals in their stores, and the merchants expect the network to pay them for the privilege of installing the terminals.

Some have suggested that debit cards and other forms of electronic funds transfer would lead to a "cashless society" in which all funds transfers will be carried out electronically. But people use cash in such a wide variety of situations that its use is unlikely to be eliminated in the foreseeable future.

Smart Cards

A *smart card* is a credit or debit card containing a built-in microprocessor and memory. The memory stores a personal-identification number, the amount of funds available, and a record of all transactions carried out with the card. Because the stored information must be retained even when the card is not in use, the memory must be nonvolatile—its contents must not be lost when electrical power is removed. In use, the card is inserted in an ATM or a POS terminal, which supplies power to the built-in microprocessor and communicates with it via electrical contacts on the card. The user enters a personal-identification number, which is compared with the identification number stored in the card's memory. If the two identification numbers match, the user is allowed to carry out transactions, which are stored in the card's memory. The amount of funds available is adjusted

Magnetic stripe banking card.

to reflect transactions: it is increased for deposits or payments and decreased for withdrawals or purchases.

Smart cards can be viewed as an alternative to telecommunications-based EFT such as ATM networks and the telephone calls now used to authorize credit-card purchases. The card itself contains all the information needed to verify the user's identity and to assure that credit limits are not exceeded and accounts are not overdrawn. Because of the computational capabilities of the built-in microprocessor, elaborate coding techniques can be used to prevent tampering, counterfeiting, and fraud. Smart cards have been used successfully in France; they have been used only on an experimental basis in the United States.

Possible Pitfalls

Electronic funds transfer has been viewed with alarm in many quarters because of possible problems such as the following:

- **Equipment Failure** If all our funds are stored as computer records, what would be the effect of a major breakdown in the system, such as if a major computer center were destroyed by sabotage or natural disaster? Some people have predicted "credit blackouts" perhaps even more devastating than the electric power blackout that paralyzed the northeastern United States in 1965.

- **Theft and Embezzlement** Criminals have demonstrated the ability to manipulate computer files for their own benefit. Is it wise to trust our finances to computers until we are sure we know how to foil such criminals? Properly used, computers can probably provide far greater protection than can conventional methods, but whether we now know enough to take advantage of this potential is not clear.

- **Loss of Privacy** With all our financial records stored in computers, it would be possible for an intrusive government (or other interested party) to learn almost every detail of our finances, such as what political contributions we make and what causes we support. A less sinister intrusion, but one we may still consider an invasion of privacy, would be the use of EFT data to analyze our buying habits. The results could be used to compile mailing lists of people interested in particular products or services.

■ **Elimination of Float** The term *float* refers to the delay in processing paper checks, which allows checks to be written several days before the funds to cover them are deposited. Float provides depositors with short-term, interest-free loans; people who take advantage of float are apt to be unhappy with instantaneous EFT transactions. One French vendor of smart cards has gone so far as to build an artificial float into the system to satisfy customers.

■ **Computerphobia** Many people, particularly the elderly, are frightened and confused by computerized devices. Some existing ATM machines aggravate this problem by being distinctly user-unfriendly; the instructions they provide are terse and hard to understand, and they frequently refuse transactions for reasons that are not explained to the user.

EFT Legislation

In 1978, Congress passed the Financial Institutions Regulatory Act. Two parts of this legislation, the Fair Funds Transfer Act and the Right to Financial Privacy Act, regulate EFT systems.

The Fair Funds Transfer Act defines EFT as "any transfer of funds which is initiated through an electronic terminal, telephone instrument,

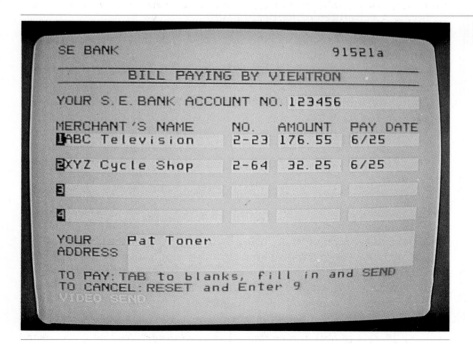

Screen display produced by a home banking program.

or computer magnetic tape.'' The act requires financial institutions to do the following:

- Notify customers of terms and conditions of EFT services.

- Provide written documentation of all EFT transactions at the time they take place.

- Provide periodic statements at least every three months.

The act limits the liability of a customer for an EFT transaction to $500. The burden of proof is on the financial institution to show that the customer authorized a disputed EFT transaction. (To help provide such proof, some EFT terminals take a picture of each customer.)

The Right to Financial Privacy Act details the procedures the government must follow in obtaining financial records. An individual must be notified that his or her financial records have been requested and must be advised of his or her rights to keep the records from the agency requesting them. Records requested by one agency cannot be provided to any other agency or department.

COMPUTERS AND FINANCIAL MARKETS

Computers are used extensively to carry out, record, and report the millions of transactions that take place each day in a financial market such as the stock market. However, the speed with which computers can trade large numbers of shares of stock without human intervention has been blamed for recent stock-market volatility—large fluctuations in stock prices.

Brokers, Exchanges, and Regulators

Brokers buy and sell securities (such as stocks) on behalf of their customers; almost all securities transactions take place through brokers. Brokerage firms use computers extensively; on every broker's desk is a computer terminal that is used to obtain market information (such as securities prices), to examine customers' accounts, and to enter orders for transactions. Brokers accomplish most of their work via telecommunications, using a telephone to communicate with customers and a computer terminal to communicate with the brokerage firm's mainframe computer.

The financial exchanges, the markets in which securities transactions are actually carried out, use computers extensively to record and report transactions. Most exchanges have not completely computerized, however; many transactions are still negotiated by traders on the exchange floor in the time-honored fashion.

Government regulators are using computers to help detect illegal stock-market activity. For example, computers can spot unusual trading activity that precedes a public announcement affecting a stock. This preannouncement activity possibly may be the result of inside trading, in which persons associated with a company illegally attempt to profit from inside information that has not yet been made public.

Computer displays at the New York Stock Exchange.

Using Personal Computers

Owners of personal computers can avail themselves of a variety of financial services. Users can access a wide variety of financial databases through general-interest information services such as CompuServe or through more specialized financial information services such as Dow Jones.

Some brokers allow their customers to obtain information and place orders with their personal computers. The customer's computer communicates with the broker's either directly or via an information service. Customers can examine their brokerage accounts, obtain financial data, and place orders for transactions. Orders entered with personal computers are examined by a human broker before being executed; the broker may telephone the customer if any questions arise concerning the order.

A number of programs are available to help users make investment decisions. Although such programs can undoubtedly be helpful, they do not work any miracles. Investors who use such programs are not notably more successful than those who rely on more traditional sources of investment advice.

Program Trading

By far the most controversial use of computers in financial markets is *program trading,* in which a computer program running on a brokerage-house computer makes trading decisions without human intervention. The program acts on its decisions by transmitting buy and sell orders directly to financial-exchange computers. These computer programs can trade millions of shares of stock in a very short time; such large sales and purchases can cause large fluctuations in stock prices.

Programmed trading is based on a trading technique called *arbitrage* (pronounced arby TRAZHE), which seeks to profit from price differences between equivalent investments traded in different markets. If two investments represent the same underlying value, but are priced differently, then it pays to sell the more expensive investment and purchase the less expensive one: you retain the same underlying value and also receive as profit the difference in price between the investment that you sold and the one that you bought. Computers can monitor the prices of such equivalent investments and act quickly to take advantage of any price differences that arise.

The most popular form of program trading involves stocks and *stock-index futures*. A future is a contract to deliver a certain package of stock on a given date, the expiration date of the future. A stock-index future is so called because the package contains stocks whose values are used to compute a widely reported stock-market index. Stocks are traded on stock exchanges and futures are traded on commodity exchanges; because of differences in these markets, the price of a future may differ from the price of the stocks it represents, presenting an opportunity for arbitrage.

When many trading programs act on the same opportunity, the stock and future prices may change dramatically. Large price fluctuations are common in commodity markets but not in the stock market. Program trading is thus accused of bringing to the stock market much of the risk and uncertainty that has long been associated with commodity markets. Sales of stock by trading programs contributed greatly to the severity of the stock-market crash on October 19, 1987 (Black Monday).

Options, which convey the right to purchase certain stock at a given price on a given expiration date, can also be used for arbitrage. Fluctuations in stock prices due to program trading are particularly severe four times a

Computer in stockbroker's office. The computerized display near the ceiling simulates the traditional ticker tape.

year when stock-index futures, stock-index options, and options on individual stocks all expire at the same time. Stock traders have come to refer to these times as "triple-witching hours."

Most observers agree that program trading presents a severe threat to the stability of stock prices. They differ, however, on whether the problem lies with the use of computers for automatic trading, or whether it is the very existence of stock-index futures and options that threatens stock-market stability. Various trading restrictions called "collars" and "circuit breakers" are being considered to interrupt program trading when stock-market stability is threatened. At the time of this writing, a fifty-point collar is in effect: program trading is suspended whenever the Dow Jones industrial average moves up or down by more than fifty points. The fifty-point collar does not seem to be very effective and is expected to be discontinued and replaced with some other restriction.

◣ Summary

Management information systems process transactions, keep records, and provide management with information for planning and control. Subsystems such as order entry, billing, inventory control, accounts receivable, accounts payable, payroll, and general ledger handle routine transactions, keep the company's books, and produce periodic and exception reports. Decision support systems aid managers to analyze the company's operations and explore the impacts of decisions, policies, and strategies.

Office automation refers to the increasing use of personal computers and workstations in the office. Although a completely paperless office will probably never arrive, the highly automated office information systems now on the drawing boards promise to eliminate much paperwork and increase substantially the speed with which information can move from one office worker to another. Office workers have not always been pleased with office automation, their complaints ranging from the difficulty of understanding and using the systems to eyestrain and muscle cramps resulting from long hours before display terminals. Finding ways to avoid such problems is the province of human-factors analysis, which is discussed in Chapter 18.

Bar codes and point-of-sale equipment allow stores to avoid the massive task of marking the price on each item of merchandise. These systems can collect useful management information such as the quantity sold and dollar volume for each item of merchandise. Opposition to the elimination of individual price marking, rampant in the seventies, seems to have largely subsided.

Electronic funds transfer (EFT) refers to the transfer of funds by electronically transmitted messages rather than by cash, check, or credit-card voucher. Although the cashless society may be even further off than the paperless office, the use of such forms of EFT as preauthorized payments and deposits, automatic teller machines (ATMs), ATM networks, and smart cards is likely to continue to increase. EFT raises concerns about possible invasion of privacy and the effects of equipment malfunctions and computer crime.

Computers are now widely used in financial markets such as the stock market. Program trading, a form of computerized trading, has been widely criticized for producing large fluctuations in stock prices.

Vocabulary Review

accounts payable system
accounts receivable system
arbitrage
ATM network
auditing
automatic teller machine (ATM)
bar code
billing system
data processing (DP)
debit card
decision support system
demand report
electronic funds transfer (EFT)
exception report

facsimile (fax)
general ledger system
inventory control system
management information system (MIS)
office automation (OA)
office information system
Open Systems Interconnection (OSI)
operational control
order entry system

payroll system
point-of-sale (POS) equipment
preauthorized payments and deposits
predictive report
program trading
scheduled listing
smart card
stock-index future
strategic planning
tactical planning
telecopying
transaction processing
voice mail

For Further Reading

Deitel, Harvey M. and Barbara Deitel. *Computers and Data Processing.* Orlando, FL: Academic Press, 1985, pp. 331–419.

"EFT Bill, Consumer Privacy Act Passed." *Communications of the ACM,* December 1978, p. 1093.

Ellis, Clarence A. and Gary J. Nutt. "Office Information Systems and Computer Science." *Computing Surveys,* March 1980, pp. 27–60.

Ernst, Marvin L. "The Mechanization of Commerce." *Scientific American,* September 1982, pp. 133–145.

Gilchrist, Bruce and Artaana Shenkin. "The Impact of Scanners on Employment in Supermarkets." *Communications of the ACM,* July 1982, pp. 441–445.

Giuliano, Vincent E. "The Mechanization of Office Work." *Scientific American*, September 1982, pp. 149–164.

McIvor, Robert. "Smart Cards." *Scientific American,* November 1985.

Reimann, Bernard C. and Allan D. Waren. "User-Oriented Criteria for the Selection of DSS Software." *Communications of the ACM,* February 1985, pp. 166–179.

◣ Review Questions

1 Give the four levels of management and control of a company's operations.

2 Describe the data processing associated with order entry, shipping, and billing.

3 Describe the inventory control system.

4 Describe the accounts receivable system.

5 Describe the accounts payable system.

6 Describe the payroll system.

7 Describe the general ledger system.

8 Describe four kinds of reports produced by a management information system.

9 Describe decision support systems.

10 How are word processing and electronic mail used in the office. What is voice mail?

11 Why is facsimile sometimes referred to as telecopying?

12 What is the Open Systems Interconnection? What obstacles to the widespread use of local area networks does it help overcome?

13 Describe how the advanced office information systems of the future might work.

14 List some of the human-factors problems that have arisen in automated offices.

15 How are bar codes used? Describe the price-marking controversy.

16 Describe each of the forms of electronic funds transfer discussed in this chapter.

17 Contrast ATM networks and smart cards as alternative approaches to verifying cardholders' identities and authorizing transactions.

18 Give four possible pitfalls of electronic funds transfer.

19 Describe two pieces of legislation affecting electronic funds transfer.

20 What is program trading and why is it controversial?

◣ Topics for Discussion

1 Although computers were originally developed for scientific applications, business applications now dominate the computer field. Hardware and software vendors design their products and programs to appeal to business users, and many computer magazines devote themselves to business-oriented topics. Discuss the reasons for the dominant role of business applications in the computer industry.

2 Discuss the price-marking controversy. Why has an issue that caused such controversy in the 1970s been largely ignored by the consumers and consumerists of the 1980s?

3 Some have predicted a cashless society in which all financial transactions are carried out by electronic funds transfer. Discuss reasons why it may or may not be possible to do away with cash in the foreseeable future.

4 Discuss the advantages and disadvantages of electronic funds transfer. Does the added convenience for consumers and the lower cost for banks and merchants outweigh possible drawbacks? Is additional EFT legislation possibly needed?

5 Discuss why facsimile, which transmits paper documents, is often more popular than electronic mail, in which documents are maintained in electronic form. What does this popularity say about the likelihood of the paperless office arriving any time in the foreseeable future?

CHAPTER 15

ARTIFICIAL INTELLIGENCE

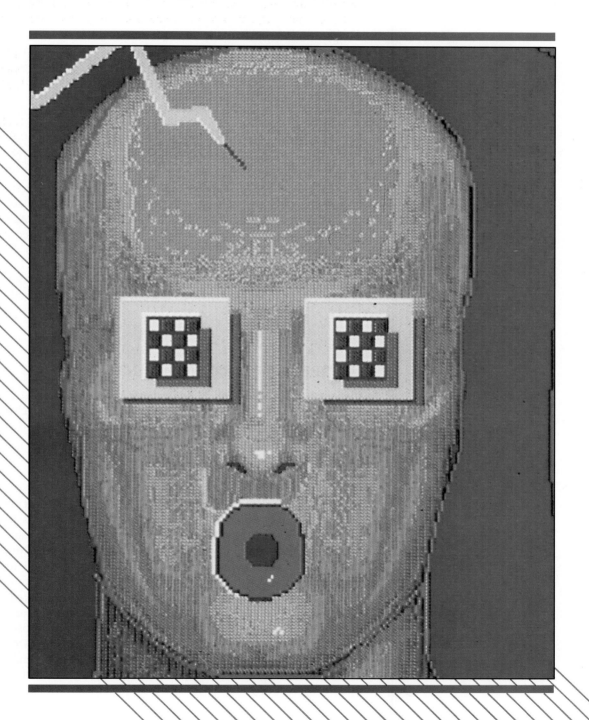

INTRODUCTION

Artificial intelligence (AI) research seeks to understand the principles of human intelligence and apply those principles to the creation of smarter computer programs. The original goal of AI research was to create programs with humanlike intelligence and capabilities; after many years of research, little progress has been made toward this goal. As a result of years of fruitless effort toward a controversial goal, artificial intelligence has long been the subject of scorn and ridicule, particularly from those who were not sympathetic to its ultimate goal or who felt that funding for AI research could better be spent in other areas, such as the critics' own disciplines. Like comedian Rodney Dangerfield, AI researchers could justifiably lament that they got no respect.

In recent years, however, AI researchers have pursued much more modest goals with much greater success. Programs based on AI techniques are playing increasingly important roles in such down-to-earth areas as medicine, education, recreation, business, and industry. Such programs come nowhere near to achieving human levels of intelligence, but they often have capabilities that are not easily achieved with non-AI programs. A number of companies have been formed to market AI-based programs; like many companies in new high-tech fields, the fortunes of these enterprises will undoubtedly have their ups and downs. But this much seems certain: artificial intelligence is getting a lot more respect now that it is providing the basis for marketable products and entrepreneurial ventures.

PRINCIPLES OF ARTIFICIAL INTELLIGENCE

In this section we will look at some basic principles that AI researchers have gleaned from their studies of human intelligence and have successfully applied to AI programs.

Search

When we have no idea how to solve a problem, we resort to trial and error, whereby we *search* for a solution among the various possibilities that come to mind. Early AI researchers hoped that the high speed of computers would allow most problems to be solved by searching through all logically possible solutions. This hope was not realized in practice. Unless special rules of thumb called *heuristics* are used to limit the scope of the search, so many possible solutions have to be considered that even the fastest computer cannot complete the search in any reasonable time.

The most successful programs based on search are those that play games such as chess, which has long been a challenge to AI researchers. Faced with a chess position, the program considers possible lines of play—sequences of moves by the computer and its opponent. If the computer could follow each line of play to its logical conclusion, in which the game is won or lost, the computer could play perfect chess. But except for very near the end of a game, there are far too many lines of play for the computer to explore in any reasonable time. Instead, the computer must use heuristics to estimate the value of each line of play and to discard unprofitable lines of play as quickly as possible.

With the aid of efficient search techniques, clever heuristics, fast computers, and computer hardware specially designed for chess playing, AI researchers have programmed computers to play chess at the expert and master levels. These programs are far better chess players than the vast majority of people, though they have yet to defeat consistently the very best human chess players, the grandmasters.

Rules

We would be in trouble if we had to use trial and error or any other problem-solving technique for the many minor problems of everyday life, such as how to get dressed in the morning or how to order a meal in a restaurant. Fortunately, we need expend little if any thought on such routine problems because we can draw on our knowledge and experience for ready-made solutions.

In AI programs, knowledge about what actions to take in particular circumstances is stored as *rules*. Each rule has the form

IF situation THEN action-or-conclusion

The part of the rule following IF describes the situation in which the rule can be applied. The part following THEN specifies an action to be taken or a conclusion to be drawn.

For example, a program that diagnoses automobile malfunctions might include rules such as

Computer-assisted instruction using speech recognition; saying the correct word ("elephant") will make the bear smile.

```
IF    the engine will not turn over and
      the lights do not work
THEN  the battery may be dead
```

and

```
IF    the engine will not turn over and
      the lights work
THEN  the starter may be defective
```

The IF-part of each rule describes a particular combination of symptoms that might be observed; the THEN-part gives a conclusion that can be drawn from those symptoms. The conclusions could also be formulated as actions for the program to carry out, such as "tell the user to check the battery" or "tell the user to check the starter." An actual program would contain hundreds or thousands of such rules to cover the many possible combinations of symptoms that are likely to occur.

Programs that draw on substantial amounts of stored knowledge are called *knowledge-based*; those for which the knowledge is in the form of rules are called *rule-based*. The most successful rule-based programs are the expert systems that are discussed in detail later in the chapter.

Reasoning

Programs can use *reasoning* to draw conclusions from the facts and rules available to the program. AI programs use two kinds of reasoning. *Forward chaining* discovers conclusions that follow from a given set of facts. *Backward chaining* tries to discover arguments that support a given conclusion. For example, a detective faced with the facts of a crime may use forward chaining to draw conclusions about the motive for the crime, the time it was committed, the means by which it was carried out, and who might

Programming Belle, a special purpose chess computer that has won a number of computer-chess tournaments.

have committed it. After a suspect has been arrested for the crime, the prosecuting attorney would use backward chaining to try to construct arguments that prove the defendant guilty. Forward and backward chaining can complement one another: after forward chaining has suggested a possible culprit, the detective may use backward chaining to see how strong a case can be constructed against the tentative suspect.

Planning

People make extensive use of plans—step-by-step descriptions of the actions to be taken in certain situations. Organizations such as businesses, schools, police and fire departments, and military units develop many plans to guide their actions in particular situations. Plans often need to be revised to meet changing circumstances. For example, we may plan an automobile trip by deciding what roads we will take and what cities we will pass through. If one of the roads turns out to be closed, however, we must revise our plan to detour around the closed section. We can then continue according to the revised plan until some new obstacle arises.

In artificial intelligence, *planning* is most widely used in robot control. The control program plans the actions a robot must take to accomplish a particular goal, then modifies the plan if the robot encounters unexpected obstacles.

Computer chess player with a robot arm to move the pieces.

Pattern Recognition

People are extremely good at spotting significant patterns in the vast amount of information that bombards their senses. Normally we have no difficulty recognizing objects in a photograph, comprehending a printed sentence, or recognizing spoken words. A particular pattern of symptoms may immediately suggest a disease and a course of treatment to a doctor, although the same pattern would be meaningless to a person with no medical training.

The importance of *pattern recognition* is obvious for programs that read printed text, understand spoken words, or analyze the images picked up by a robot's television-camera eye. But pattern recognition is also important for rule-based systems: the IF-part of a rule specifies a particular pattern of facts; the rule is to be applied when that pattern is recognized in the facts known to the program.

Knowledge Bases

A *knowledge base* stores the facts and rules that govern the operation of an AI program. An AI program may use both a knowledge base and a database; the latter may be the same company database used by human workers. The knowledge base contains general concepts and principles, and the database contains specific details. For example, consider a program that selects securities for brokerage customers. Its knowledge base might include the characteristics of different kinds of securities and the principles

To avoid the complexities of image analysis, many robots use nonvisual means to perceive their surroundings. This robot vehicle is guided by sonar—reflected sound waves.

for choosing securities according to a customer's investment goals. The database might contain the prices and other current data on available securities as well as the investment goals of the firm's customers.

Human knowledge appears to be organized in collections of facts and rules that apply to particular situations. When we go in a restaurant, for example, the procedures for using the menu, placing an order, tipping the waiter, and paying the check all come effortlessly to mind; yet we never think of these when engaged in other activities. Driving on the freeway, playing baseball, or playing a musical instrument each calls forth its own collection of relevant facts and skills. AI researchers use the term *frame* for the collection of facts and rules relevant to a particular situation. The more advanced knowledge-based programs often use a knowledge base that is organized as a collection of frames.

We all have in our heads a model of the outside world that allows us to anticipate the consequences of our own actions and to better understand the actions of others. Likewise, the knowledge base of an AI program may contain computer models of the real-world systems with which the program is concerned, such a robot or the investment preferences of a brokerage customer. Such models allow the program to formulate, analyze, and compare plans "in its head" before attempting any of the contemplated actions.

EXPERT SYSTEMS

Expert systems, also called *knowledge-based systems*, are the most widely used and most commercially successful products of AI research. Sometimes called an "expert on a disk," an expert system captures the ability of a human expert to solve routine problems. Current expert systems cannot emulate the creativity and ingenuity that human experts bring to bear on new and challenging problems. But problems that do not call for such creativity and ingenuity often can be solved by an expert system faster, at less cost, and with far less labor than if a human expert had been used.

The simplest expert systems use only rules, which are applied to facts entered by the user as well as those previously deduced by the program. More advanced expert systems may combine rules with other techniques such as forward and backward chaining, frame-structured knowledge bases, and conventional computer programming.

Creating Expert Systems

An expert system is created by a *knowledge engineer* working with one or more experts in the field of interest. The knowledge engineer starts with an *expert-system shell*, which is an expert system without a knowledge base, and uses a *knowledge-acquisition system* to build a knowledge base out of information gleaned from the human experts. The knowledge engineer (but not the human experts) needs to be thoroughly conversant with the AI techniques used by the expert-system shell.

Creating an expert system is often expensive and time consuming. The problem is that human experts usually find it difficult to state exactly what rules they follow in solving a particular kind of problem. Thus a lengthy trial-and-error process is required to extract the needed rules from the human experts. The knowledge engineer begins by having extensive discussions with the experts and incorporating the information so obtained into a preliminary knowledge base. The resulting expert system is then given a series of test problems, and its performance is evaluated by the human experts. When the expert system solves a problem incorrectly, the human experts are asked to provide additional knowledge that will allow problems of the kind in question to be handled correctly. The expert system's failures often remind the human experts of exceptions to rules, special cases, and additional techniques they have not yet discussed with the knowledge engineer. As this process is repeated time and time again, the capabilities of the expert system gradually improve. This process of gradual improvement may need to be continued even after the expert system is in day-to-day use, until users feel that the system in its current state meets their needs.

In the remainder of this section we will look at some of the many applications that are emerging for expert systems.

Medical Advice Systems

In Chapter 10 we discussed medical advice systems that, given a patient's symptoms, either suggest diagnoses and treatments or critique those proposed by the physician. We can view such systems as an alternative approach to storing medical information. Instead of just putting the information in a database and hoping that physicians who need it will find it, we put it in the knowledge base of an expert system that can use the stored information to make suggestions or criticisms for the handling of specific cases.

Medical advice systems are examples of expert systems that serve as advisors to human experts. Such systems often serve best by reminding the human expert of possibilities he or she might otherwise have overlooked. Thus the expert system may suggest a number of possible solutions to the problem presented; it is left up to the human expert to evaluate the suggestions of the expert system. To aid in this evaluation, the expert system must be prepared to give its reasons for each suggestion that it makes.

Medical advice systems long have been a popular subject of AI research. Although such systems are still considered experimental, some have emerged from the laboratories and are seeing use in day-to-day medical practice.

Business and Financial Applications

Because of the large number of routine decisions that face business people every day, business and finance are fertile grounds for expert systems. As usual, we cannot expect expert systems to solve problems that call for creativity and ingenuity. For example, we cannot expect an expert system to create an advertising campaign for a new product. On the other hand, if the company's database contains information on the capabilities of products and the needs of customers, an expert system might suggest which customers might be interested in receiving advertising literature for which products.

Selecting Direct-Mail Prospects   Merchants, magazine publishers, and fund raisers wish to select from their mailing lists the names of the people most likely to respond favorably to a particular mailing. Such selections are based on analysis of the results of previous mailings and of test mailings designed to test the appeal of a particular offering or request.

An expert system called More/2 has been designed to perform this analysis. By analyzing previous mailings, More/2 tries to determine how response to a particular kind of mailing varies with such variables as age, sex, household income, and zip code. In tests, More/2 has shown it can select 50 percent of an existing mailing list in such a way as to achieve 70 to 80 percent of the responses obtained when the entire list was used. More/2 is now used routinely by some service bureaus that specialize in selecting names for direct mailings.

Telemarketing   When a customer telephones in an order, the salesperson may offer information on discounts, special promotions, and other products in hopes of inducing the customer to place a larger or a more profitable order. During the short time that the customer is on the telephone, the salesperson needs to be advised of specific offers that would be profitable for the company and might interest the customer in question.

The TOLAS-Telestream telemarketing system submits each incoming order or information request to six expert systems; these systems make suggestions that are displayed on the salesperson's terminal. Most suggestions, such as information about special promotions, are relayed directly to the customer. Others, such as a credit evaluation, determine how the salesperson handles the order. The six expert systems are as follows:

■ The *inventory/purchasing* expert is in charge of maintaining the company's inventory. It can tell the salesperson what parts of an order

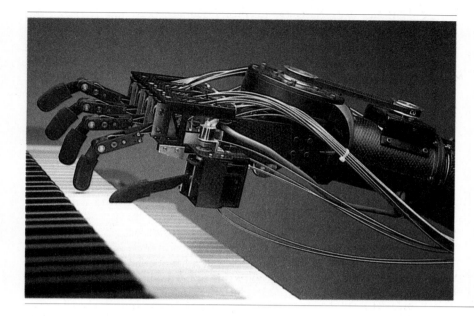

This robot hand has sufficient dexterity to play the organ.

can be shipped immediately and can give expected shipment dates for items that are currently out of stock.

- The *product-manager* expert can suggest substitutes for requested items that are not stocked. Such an expert can be particularly useful to parts supply houses, which often need to determine a generic replacement for a part carrying the label and part number of a particular equipment manufacturer.

- The *promotions* expert points out special offers that are relevant to a particular order. Such a discount, rebate, or other incentive may persuade a customer to increase the number of items ordered or to order additional items.

- The *pricing/discounts* expert is in charge of pricing and volume discounts. In many industries, the best discounts are reserved for a company's best customers. Thus the pricing/discounts expert may take into account a customer's previous purchases in deciding what volume discounts to offer.

- The *sales-director* expert tries to improve the company's profits by suggesting items that carry a high profit margin.

- The *customer-history* expert can alert the salesperson to important customers that the salesperson should take particular pains to keep satisfied. It can also warn of problem customers, such as those that do not pay their bills on time or who already have large unpaid balances.

Risk Assessment   A frequent problem in the financial-services industry is deciding whether to assume risk and how much to charge for doing so. For example, a loan officer must decide whether to grant a given loan and, if the loan is granted, decide how much interest to charge. An insurance underwriter needs to decide whether to write a particular policy and, if the policy is written, decide how much the premiums should be.

Often elaborate rules exist for making such decisions, but applying the rules consistently is time consuming and error prone. Situations that are already handled by formal rules are ideal applications for expert systems, and a number of expert-system vendors are concentrating on financial-services applications.

Everyone who has an American Express card may be affected by American Express's authorization assistant, an expert system that aids in the authorization of credit-card transactions. Most credit-card companies base transaction authorization on a fixed credit limit; a transaction is automatically authorized if the account is in good standing and the transaction does not cause the credit limit to be exceeded. American Express, however, imposes no fixed limit but authorizes each transaction individually according to its estimate of the cardholder's ability and willingness to pay. Little time is allowed for deliberation, since customer and merchant must wait while the authorization request is considered.

When a transaction is entered into the computer system, a non-AI program compares it with the cardholder's normal charging pattern. If the current transaction is consistent with this pattern, authorization is granted without human intervention. If the current transaction is a departure from the normal pattern, then information about the customer is retrieved from a database; that information and the details of the requested transaction are sent to the authorization assistant. This 800-rule expert system analyzes the data and sends its recommendations to a human authorizer, who makes the final decision.

Brokerage Applications   Expert systems are finding increasing use in helping with the many business, financial, and trading decisions that bro-

Screen display produced by an image-analysis program that recognizes geometrical shapes. The display shows the shapes being analyzed and the path that the computer follows in examining them.

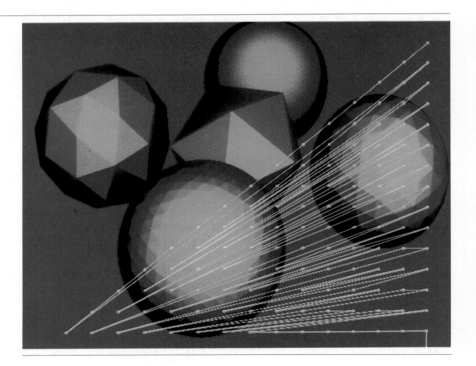

kerage houses must make every day. The following list briefly describes some common brokerage applications of expert systems.

- **Portfolio selection** The expert system constructs a portfolio—the collection of securities owned by a particular customer—based on the customer's investment profile and such characteristics of the securities as risk and profit potential.

- **Sales assistant** Similar to other telemarketing systems, this expert system uses a customer's investment profile and information about the customer's current holdings to collect information that may be of interest to the customer and to suggest transactions that may interest the customer and be profitable for the broker.

- **Intelligent quotation systems** Securities are traded in many different markets and the transactions are reported by different information services. As a result, trading rooms are often crammed with video monitors and ticker-tape displays corresponding to these diverse sources of information. An intelligent quotation system monitors these many sources of information and displays the particular information that a trader has requested. The trader can ask to be informed when particular events occur, such as when a stock reaches a certain price or when its price changes by a given amount. The system also can select securities that are best according to some given criterion. Intelligent quotation systems are examples of how an expert system can fit into a complex computer system with other, non-AI components. The expert system determines the best way to carry out the trader's requests. To actually act on those requests, however, the expert system must interact with other system components that handle telecommunications, databases, mathematical calculations, and monitoring for specific events.

- **Brokerage risk analysis** This expert system analyzes the risk resulting from the company's own holdings and warns management of any problems. In the past, brokerages and other financial institutions have lost large amounts of money because traders made very risky investments without the knowledge of management.

Industrial Applications

Process Planning   After a product has been designed, engineers must plan the exact details of how each part is to be produced. There may be several alternative techniques available for each machining operation, such as trimming a sheet-metal part to the desired shape. The planners must choose the particular combination of machining steps that will allow the part to be produced at the required cost and volume. For example, each of the ten thousand parts of a jet aircraft requires its own process plan, which a human planner may require up to twelve hours to complete. Still more time will be required if some of the plans contain errors that are not discovered until workers attempt to follow the plans on the shop floor.

At Northrop Aircraft Division, a 500-rule expert system is being used to generate process plans for certain types of parts in about five minutes. To verify the accuracy of the plan produced by the expert system, Northrop

Adjusting an industrial robot.

uses a simulation program that simulates the machinery on the shop floor. Any defects in the plan are discovered before any special tools are made and before any time, labor, or material is wasted.

Fault Diagnosis   Diagnosing problems with faulty equipment becomes increasingly difficult as business and industry adopts more complex equipment such as computers and robots. Fortunately, expert systems are well suited to fault diagnosis because it is usually possible to formulate a series of rules for narrowing down the location of the fault to a particular component. Applying such rules manually can be tedious and time consuming, however, so an expert system can greatly speed up the process of fault location. In this application, expert systems can be regarded as replacements for the repair manuals that were formally used to guide human repair technicians.

In many cases, sensors built into the equipment being repaired can provide automatically the data that the expert system needs to make its diagnosis. Some convenient means of acquiring this data is imperative. One diagnostic expert system failed because users found it easier to diagnose the fault manually than to type the necessary data into the computer.

System Configuration   Industrial equipment is often available in many different models and with many different optional features. A customer who is building a factory, for example, or constructing a power-distribution system needs to select the particular equipment models and options that will accomplish the task at hand. It usually falls on the equipment vendor to propose an appropriate configuration. Some vendors have found expert systems useful for this purpose. The expert systems are typically much faster and less error-prone than human engineers, who might have to spend hours leafing through component drawings and specifications to find the particular model or options appropriate for a particular application. Such expert systems are also being used by marketing departments to assure that they do not overlook any necessary pieces of equipment when preparing a bid.

NATURAL-LANGUAGE PROCESSING

Many more people would be encouraged to use computers if computers could communicate in natural languages such as English. Areas in which *natural-language processing* is particularly useful include information retrieval, computer-assisted instruction, and medical interviewing. *Automatic translation*, in which computers translate from one natural language to another, has long been a goal of AI research.

Natural Languages for Database Queries

The most successful applications of natural-language processing are systems that allow database queries to be stated in a natural language. Before

Using an experimental voice-operated word processor.

acting on a query, the computer may restate the query in its own words to confirm that it has understood the user's request. The results of the query can be stated in English or given in more mathematically oriented forms such as tables or graphs.

Natural-language interfaces for databases owe their success to the restricted nature of the sentences that they must process. These sentences fall into a small number of patterns because they are all questions about the contents of the database. Likewise, the words appearing in the queries refer only to the persons, places, and things covered by the database, to their properties, and to the relations between them. These limitations assure that the system has sufficient information to understand most queries. Also, a question-answering system has an advantage that some other systems (such as automatic translation systems) do not: if the system fails to understand some part of a query, it can ask the user for clarification, something that human beings also often find it necessary to do.

Automatic Translation

One of the first great failures of AI research was the attempt in the 1950s to design programs for translating from one natural language to another. (Russian and English were the languages of primary interest.) By looking up words and phrases in a Russian-English dictionary, and by applying simple syntactical (grammatical) rules, the computer could translate about 80 percent of the text presented to it. But there seemed no way to get it to translate the remaining 20 percent without greater understanding of the material being translated. After an advisory committee directed sharp criticism at the lack of progress in the field, funding for automatic translation projects largely evaporated. Some AI researchers feel that the loss of funding occurred at exactly the wrong time, when more powerful com-

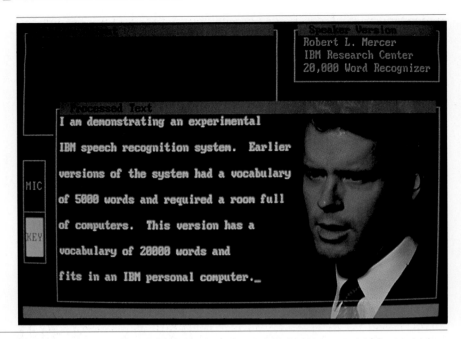

Image of the speaker is superimposed on the display produced by an experimental speech recognition program.

puters and more sophisticated techniques for sentence analysis were just starting to be utilized.

Despite this early failure, computer translation is still a subject of AI research, and systems that produce rough but useful translations have proved cost-effective in some applications. Recent research has focussed on determining and representing the meaning of sentences, on the theory that the computer must understand a sentence to be able to translate it correctly. (Translation without understanding has led to such famous computer-translation blunders as the translation of "out of sight, out of mind" into "blind and insane.") Interestingly, however, all current practical applications of computer translation use the earlier, more simplistic techniques; the more sophisticated meaning-oriented techniques have yet to emerge from the laboratory.

Speech Recognition

It would be enormously convenient for people to be able to direct their computers verbally, rather than having to use keyboards or other traditional input devices. Although keyboards might be preferable for some kinds of input, such as numerical data, most people would probably prefer speech for ordinary English text.

Unfortunately, the difficulties facing speech recognition are formidable. Different people use different pronunciations and speak with different accents, and we all tend to run together distinct words. Current experimental systems can understand disconnected speech, in which the speaker pauses between words. Some such systems are already in productive use, and this use may well increase in the not-too-distant future. Systems that understand normal, continuous speech have yet to emerge from the laboratories. Thus that old science-fiction standby, the typewriter that takes diction, seems unlikely to be realized in the near future.

IMAGE ANALYSIS

Image analysis is the process of isolating and identifying the various objects in a photograph or video image. The most important application of image analysis is robot vision: interpreting the images picked up by a robot's television-camera eye. Defense agencies have long been interested in image analysis because of such military applications as interpreting satellite-reconnaissance photographs and guiding cruise missles over enemy territory. Image analysis can also be applied to colorization, one of the problems of which is to keep the computer from confusing distinct objects that are to be given different colors.

An image-analysis program usually begins by trying to identify the regions in the scene that represent the surfaces of objects, such as the sides of a box or the top surface of a table. Generally, each such region appears in the image as an area of relatively uniform brightness, whereas the brightness changes abruptly where different surfaces meet at the edges of objects. Thus the program can try to pick out regions of uniform brightness (region analysis) or try to find lines at which the brightness changes abruptly (edge analysis). The two methods complement each other; region analysis can help fill in gaps in the edges separating the regions, and edge analysis can help locate the exact boundaries of each region.

The next problem is to determine the orientation of the surfaces represented by the regions. Is the camera looking at a particular surface straight

Conducting research on speech recognition; the screen displays voiceprints—graphical representations of speech sounds.

Robot vehicle guided by a computer vision system.

on or is it viewing the surface from an angle? One approach, which plays an important role in human vision, is to analyze how light falls on the various surfaces. If we assume that light is coming from a particular direction, we can determine what orientation would give each surface the apparent brightness that it has in the image. Through complex calculations, the image analysis program can try to find a direction of illumination and a set of surface orientations that are consistent with the observed brightnesses. Analysis of the shadows cast by objects is also important; analyzing an object and its shadow can give more information than could be obtained by analyzing either one separately.

Finally, the image-analysis program has to try to combine the surfaces and edges to form objects. If the objects are simple geometrical shapes, such as boxes, spheres, cones, and cylinders, then geometrical principles can be used to determine which surfaces belong to which object. More complex objects sometimes can be approximated as combinations of simple geometrical shapes; for example, a telephone can be approximated as a wedge and a Coke bottle as a generalized cylinder—a cylinder whose diameter varies with height.

An approach to object identification that humans seem to use routinely is knowing what objects should be present and looking for them. For example, in a fuzzy photograph of an office desk, we might identify a certain wedge-shaped object as a telephone, particularly if no other object on the desk looks more like a telephone. We expect to see a telephone on the desk, and we identify as a telephone the object that most closely meets our expectations. If the same not-very-clear object were in the middle of the floor or hanging from the ceiling, we would be much more hesitant to identify it as a telephone.

Progress continues to be made in image analysis, and some image-analysis programs are in routine use. In general, however, the capabilities of such programs fall far short of what we need for important applications such as robot vision.

ROBOT CONTROL

A *robot-control* program manipulates a robot in such a way that it accomplishes a useful task, such as selecting and assembling parts from a bin. Signals from sensors inform the program of the positions of the robot and its appendages and of the locations and positions of the parts with which it is to work. The program sends control signals to the robot to manipulate it as needed to accomplish the task.

As we saw in the section on image analysis, interpreting the images seen by television cameras can be complex. Other sensors, such as those that detect the position of a robot's hand or the pressure it is exerting on the object it is holding, present fewer problems of interpretation. In any event, we assume that the signals from the sensors can be interpreted and can provide the control program with the information that it needs about the robot and its surroundings.

Suppose the control program wants the robot to pick up an object whose position and orientation have been determined by sensors. The program plans the particular motions of the arm, hand, and fingers that will move the hand over the object, position the hand properly relative to the object, and grasp the object with the fingers. When the plan is complete, the program can start sending control signals to get the plan carried out.

Unfortunately, there is a good chance that difficulties will arise along the way, requiring the plan to be changed. For example, there are limitations on the accuracy with which the robot hand and arm can be positioned. At some point in the process, therefore, the sensors may report that the hand or arm is not in the position called for by the plan. The control program will have to either take steps to correct the error or else modify the rest of the plan to take the error into account. More seriously, the part might slip from the robot's grasp, requiring the control program to devise a plan for picking it up again.

Much work has been done on robot control, and programs have been demonstrated that can plan and carry out complex assembly operations. In addition to further improvements in such programs, the main requirement for assembly robots is adequate vision or other means of acquiring information about the robot and its surroundings.

AI PROGRAMMING LANGUAGES

AI programs can be written in any general-purpose programming language. However, AI programming is usually much simpler in a language that focuses on symbolic rather than numerical computation. Such a language provides symbolic names for representing real-world objects such as robots, and it provides a powerful means for representing and manipulating the properties of objects and the relations between different objects. The two most widely used symbolic programming languages are *Lisp* (List Processor) and *Prolog* (Programming in Logic). Lisp, which dates back to the late 1950s, is the most popular language for AI programming.

Lisp is valued for the ease with which real-world information can be represented. For example, experimental robot-control programs are often tested by having them manipulate children's blocks. The arrangement of the blocks at any time has to be represented inside the computer. Consider a very simple situation in which a red block is stacked atop a yellow block that rests on a table. In Lisp, the two blocks and the table are represented with symbolic names, say BLOCK-R for the red block, BLOCK-Y for the yellow block, and TABLE for the table.

Lisp associates with each symbol, such as BLOCK-R, a *property list* that lists all the needed properties of the object represented by the symbol. The property list for BLOCK-R might be

```
(IS-A             BLOCK
 COLOR            RED
 SUPPORTED-BY     BLOCK-Y
 DIRECTLY-SUPPORTS NIL)
```

The IS-A entry tells us that BLOCK-R belongs to the general class of blocks and inherits all the properties defined for the symbol BLOCK, which represents a generic block. The COLOR entry gives the color of the block, the

SUPPORTED-BY entry tells us that BLOCK-R rests on BLOCK-Y, and the DIRECTLY-SUPPORTS entry tells us that no block rests on BLOCK-R. (Lisp uses the symbol NIL to indicate the absence of an applicable value.) Likewise, the property list for BLOCK-Y would be

```
(IS-A            BLOCK
 COLOR           YELLOW
 SUPPORTED-BY    TABLE
 DIRECTLY-SUPPORTS BLOCK-R)
```

How would the two property lists change if the robot picked up the red block and placed it on the table, so that both blocks now rest directly on the table?

Prolog is a newcomer to AI programming, but one that has attracted much attention. Information is represented in Prolog by logical statements rather than by property lists. For example, the properties of our yellow block could be represented in Prolog by the following statements:

```
is_a(block_Y, block).
color(block_Y, yellow).
supported_by(block_Y, table).
directly_supports(block_Y, block_R).
```

These statements should be read as "block_Y is a block," "the color of block_Y is yellow," and so on.

Experimental robot arms.

The most important difference between Lisp and Prolog is the way in which programs are formulated. In this respect, Lisp is similar to most other programming languages: the programmer provides lists of instructions that specify step-by-step what operations to perform. With Prolog, on the other hand, the programmer specifies the logical restrictions that the program's results must satisfy. The Prolog system then searches for one or more sets of data values that satisfy the restrictions imposed by the programmer. In carrying out this search, the computer determines the sequence of operations that must be carried out to compute the results. The automatic search is particularly convenient for expert systems, which must search through lists of rules to determine which can be applied to the available data.

Convenient as this automatic search can be, however, it can also present difficulties: we have seen that searches must be carefully controlled if they are not to get out of hand and consume excessive amounts of time. Prolog provides the means for controlling the search, but their use can destroy the logical clarity of the programs, making them more like traditional programs that give step-by-step instructions.

Both Lisp and Prolog programs can be run on conventional computers; indeed, language processors for both Lisp and Prolog are available for personal computers. However, programs may run too slowly on conventional computers and require more memory than is available. For these reasons, special computers for symbolic processing have been designed. Most of these are intended for use with Lisp and are usually referred to as *Lisp machines*.

Many of the early commercial expert systems were designed to run on Lisp machines. However, prospective purchasers of expert systems generally prefer programs that will run on their existing computer equipment, rather than requiring expensive, specialized computers that have to be programmed in unfamiliar languages. For this reason, some recent expert-system products have been written to run on conventional computers, such as personal computers. This usually means that the programs have to be written in conventional programming languages such as Pascal and C. An alternate approach is to provide personal computers with a plug-in circuit board that gives them many of the capabilities of Lisp machines, allowing them to run Lisp programs efficiently.

This experimental robot arm has a pressure-sensitive hand that can feel the objects it grips, which are then described by the controlling computer.

◥ NEURAL NETWORKS

It was mentioned earlier that AI programs often imitate human reasoning processes. Some researchers would go even further and imitate not only human reasoning processes but the physical structure of the human brain. The brain is made up of billions of cells called *neurons*, which are connected by a complex network of nerve fibers. The individual neurons are very simple compared to computer components such as microprocessors. The computing power of the brain seems to lie not in the capabilities of the individual neurons but in the complex way they are interconnected. For this reason, the approach to AI that imitates the structure of the brain is known as *connectionism*.

A Lisp machine—a computer especially designed to run programs written in the AI programming language Lisp.

A *neural network* consists of many artificial neurons, which are simplified models of the neuron cells in the human brain. As in the brain, the neurons are joined by a complex array of interconnections. Each neuron receives many input signals from other neurons and produces a single output signal. The output signal is computed from the sum of the input signals using a simple mathematical relationship.

Each connection between artificial neurons has a *weight*, which determines how much the strength of a signal diminishes as the signal travels along that connection. For example, if a connection has a weight of 0.25, a signal that passes through that connection will be reduced to 25 percent of its original strength. The weights determine the behavior of a neural network; we program the network for a particular task by adjusting the weights. More importantly, the network can be trained for a particular task by supplying its input connections with a series of examples, such as patterns to be classified. During training, we increase those weights that lead to desired responses and decrease those that produced undesired responses.

Connectionism has had its ups and downs. Neural networks were studied extensively in the 1960s for pattern-recognition tasks. However, a mathematical analysis published in 1969 seemed to impose serious limits on the capabilities of neural networks, and they fell into disrepute for over a decade. Recently, ways around the earlier mathematical objections have been found, and interest in neural networks is again on the rise.

As has been true in so many other areas of computing, exaggerated claims have been made for neural networks. Some have touted them as the key to achieving humanlike intelligence. More realistically, neural networks have the advantage that computations are carried out simultaneously by the many neurons, rather than one after another by a single central processing unit. Thus neural networks have the potential for producing results much faster than a conventional computer executing a step-by-step program. This can be particularly important for complex pattern-recognition tasks, such as image analysis, where complex calculations have to be carried out for each of the thousands or millions of picture elements making up the image.

◣ Summary

Artificial intelligence (AI) seeks to make computers smarter, that is, to increase their capabilities and improve their ability to communicate with human beings. To this end, AI researchers study the principles of human intelligence and try to incorporate them into computer programs. Some principles that lie behind many current AI programs are search, the use of rules, reasoning, planning, pattern recognition, and the representation of knowledge in knowledge bases.

The most widely used and commercially successful products of AI research are expert systems, which emulate the problem-solving capabilities of human experts. Expert systems are becoming increasingly popular in such areas as business, industry, and medicine.

Natural-language processing tries to make computers more user-friendly by enabling them to communicate in human languages; the most successful application of natural-language processing is natural-language interfaces for database management systems. Image-analysis programs try to interpret photographs or video images, such as the images picked up by a robot's television-camera eye. Robot-control programs try to determine the sequence of movements that will enable a robot to carry out some useful task, such as assembling parts selected from a bin.

The two most popular languages for AI programming are Lisp and Prolog. Both are symbolic-programming languages in that both provide symbolic means for representing real-world entities, their properties, and the relations between them. Lisp, the older and more popular of the two, specifies programs as lists of step-by-step instructions, just like most other programming languages. A Prolog program, on the other hand, specifies the logical restrictions that relate the desired results to the input data; the Prolog system searches automatically for results that satisfy the given restrictions.

Instead of emulating the principles of human reasoning, neural networks mimic the structure of the human brain. Because the capabilities of such networks lie not so much in the individual computing elements (called neurons) but in the connections between them, the neural-network approach to artificial intelligence is known as connectionism. A possible advantage of neural networks is that they can be trained (rather than programmed) to perform particular tasks. Another possible advantage is that, because many neurons carry out their computations simultaneously, neural networks may be able to carry out some computations faster than would be possible with conventional computers.

Vocabulary Review

artificial intelligence
(AI)
automatic translation
backward chaining
connectionism
expert system
expert-system shell
forward chaining
frame
heuristics
image analysis

knowledge base
knowledge engineer
knowledge-
acquisition system
knowledge-based
system
Lisp
Lisp machine
natural-language
processing
neural network

neuron
pattern recognition
planning
Prolog
property list
reasoning
robot control
rule-based system
rules
search
weight

For Further Reading

AI Expert (special issue on natural language interfaces), July 1988.

AI Expert (special issue on neural networks), August 1988.

Davis, Dwight B. "Artificial Intelligence Goes to Work." *High Technology*, April 1987, pp. 16—27.

Feigenbaum, Edward A. and Pamela McCorduck. *The Fifth Generation.* Reading, MA: Addison-Wesley, 1983.

Hofstadter, Douglas. *Göedel, Escher, Bach: An Eternal Golden Braid.* New York: Basic Books, 1979.

Kinnucan, Paul. "Software Tools Speed Expert System Development." *High Technology*, March 1985, pp. 16—21.

McCorduck, Pamela. *Machines Who Think.* San Francisco: W.H. Freeman and Co., 1979.

Peat, David F. *Artificial Intelligence: How Machines Think.* New York: Baen Enterprises (distributed by Simon and Schuster), 1985.

Waldrop, M. Mitchell. "The Machinations of Thought." *Science 85*, March 1985, pp. 38—45.

Review Questions

1 What is artificial intelligence? Why was it often criticized and ridiculed in the past? Why is it now getting more respect?

2 Describe the most successful kind of AI program that is based mainly on search.

3 Describe how rules are used in AI. What is the most successful kind of rule-based program?

4 Give examples of forward and backward chaining.

5 In what area of AI is planning particularly important?

6 Give some examples of pattern recognition by humans and by AI programs.

7 What is a knowledge base? What characteristic of human knowledge suggests organizing a knowledge base into frames? Why does an AI program often need models of the real-world systems with which it interacts?

8 What kinds of problems can be solved by an expert system? What kinds are likely to be beyond its ability?

9 Describe the procedure by which expert systems are created.

10 How can expert systems help assure that doctors are using the latest results of medical research to make diagnoses and determine treatments?

11 Describe some business and financial applications of expert systems.

12 Describe some industrial applications of expert systems.

13 Give some applications in which it would be particularly useful for a computer to be able to communicate in a natural language.

14 Describe one reasonably successful application for natural language processing, and one that has achieved only very limited success.

15 Give several applications for image analysis.

16 Describe some of the techniques of image analysis.

17 Contrast the AI programming languages Lisp and Prolog.

18 Why may a robot-control program have to modify a plan several times in the course of carrying it out?

19 Why are some recent AI programs written in conventional programming languages rather than in Lisp or Prolog?

20 What is the motivation for using neural networks? What are some possible advantages of neural networks over conventional computers?

Topics for Discussion

1 People have long debated the question of whether computers can ever achieve human (or more than human) levels of intelligence. Certainly this is unlikely to be achieved any time soon; progress toward this goal has been very slow despite much effort by AI researchers. But can it ever be achieved? No, say some people who argue that human intelligence is something unique that can never be imitated by any machine, no matter how advanced. Discuss.

2 Artificial intelligence has long been the subject of unrelenting criticism and ridicule. Should a field of scientific research be disparaged because progress toward its stated goal is slow? Because some people do not feel the goal can be reached or would prefer that it not be? Should research have to yield commercially successful products in order to get respect?

PART FIVE

Computers and Society

COMPUTER CRIME AND SECURITY

INTRODUCTION

Crimes involving computers cost American businesses and financial institutions $3 to $5 billion annually. For example, dishonest employees may discover how to use a company's computer to divert funds and merchandise to themselves and their accomplices. Disgruntled employees may take revenge by sabotaging vital programs and data files. Some computer enthusiasts delight in bypassing the security provisions designed to prevent unauthorized use of computer systems; others labor to perfect malicious programs that will damage the programs and data stored in other people's computers. Employees may make unauthorized copies of copyrighted or licensed software, thereby defrauding the publishers of the software and exposing their own employers to lawsuits. *Computer security refers* to any means of protection against these threats as well as against natural disasters, such as fire, flood, and power or communications failure.

FRAUD, EMBEZZLEMENT, AND SABOTAGE

Computer fraud and embezzlement are most commonly committed by employees who use the computer system as part of their work. The culprits need not be computer experts: they accomplish their ends not by tampering with the internal workings of the computer but by entering false information, such as fraudulent orders for transferring funds and shipping merchandise.

Electronic sabotage consists of erasing or otherwise damaging program and data files; conventional sabotage, in which the computer hardware is physically damaged, has occurred but is much rarer than electronic sabotage. This crime requires more computer expertise than fraud or embezzlement and is usually perpetrated by disgruntled or fired programmers or other data-processing personnel. A fired programmer may leave behind a "time bomb," a program that will wreak havoc at some designated time in the future, long after its author has departed. Other programmers have installed programs that would do their dirty work if the programmer's name were ever deleted from the employee file (which would occur if the programmer were fired).

The following cases from the annals of computer crime illustrate fraud, embezzlement, and sabotage.

Although computers provide new opportunities for criminals, they also provide law enforcement officials with new weapons for fighting crime.

False Invoices and Claims

A terminal operator in the accounts-payable department of a computer manufacturer entered fraudulent invoices payable to a company formed by her and her boyfriend. After the computer had issued checks totaling $155,000, the operator and her boyfriend left for parts unknown.

An insurance company employee used the computer terminal in a claims office to defraud the company of $206,000 by entering fraudulent claims. She made the claims payable to fictitious individuals, but used the addresses of herself, her father, and her boyfriend. The insurance com-

Computer technology is providing more sophisticated locks for protecting our property. The punch-card-operated lock at left is often used on hotel rooms; the push-button lock at right is designed to protect rooms containing computer equipment.

pany's security department eventually became suspicious at the occurrence of the same addresses on many different claims.

The Gambling Teller

The head teller of a New York bank, who was addicted to gambling and hoped to win enough to pay back previous embezzlements, used his bank's computer to steal $1.4 million. The money itself he simply took from the bank's vault. To hide the thefts, he used teller terminals to reduce the balances in certain accounts. For these accounts, the figures stored in the computer showed a smaller balance than the depositor thought he or she had.

When a depositor detected the discrepancy and complained, the head teller would apologize for a "computer error" and then would use a teller terminal to transfer money from some other account to that of the complaining customer. Such errors occurred frequently at the head teller's branch, but he blamed them on mistakes made by the tellers under his supervision. He was finally caught when police raided his bookie and became suspicious on finding that a bank teller was betting $30 thousand a day.

Pacific Telephone

In this case, an eighteen-year-old college student learned how to direct Pacific Telephone's computers to deliver equipment to designated locations. He then picked up the equipment and sold it through his own company, Creative Telephone. The culprit was not an employee of the telephone company; instead he used a variety of schemes to obtain the

An FBI-sponsored class on detecting and preventing computer crime.

information and access codes needed to order the equipment through Pacific Telephone's computer. He obtained operation manuals for the computer system from company trash cans. By posing as a magazine reporter writing an article about the computerized ordering system, he was able to ask questions about the system and get demonstrations of its operation. Posing as a company employee, he telephoned to request current access codes, which were always provided.

Security Pacific

In 1979, Security Pacific National Bank was robbed of $10.2 million by a computer consultant and former college professor. While working for the bank as a consultant, he visited the bank's wire room and learned the procedures and authorization codes for transferring funds by computer. Telephoning the bank later, he posed as a branch manager and used the codes to order that funds be transferred to a New York bank. After ordering the New York bank to transfer the funds to Switzerland, he withdrew the funds and bought diamonds. He was caught only after he bragged about his crime. While awaiting trial, he used similar techniques in an attempt to steal $50 million from another bank.

Equity Funding

Usually computer crimes are committed by fairly low-level employees, such as tellers, data-entry clerks, and programmers. In the Equity Funding case, however, the company's management used computers to perpetrate a $2 billion dollar fraud. The fraud involved an accepted practice whereby an insurance company that issues a policy can sell the policy to another insurance company. The company that buys the policy receives the premiums paid by the policyholder and pays off any claims. Equity Funding used its computers to create over 60 thousand bogus insurance policies, which were then sold to other companies. Because no premiums were being paid on the bogus policies, Equity Funding had to pay the premiums itself; to get the money to pay the premiums, it created and sold still more phony insurance policies.

Turning Back the Clock

In Australia, a computer operator at a state-run horse betting agency set the computer's clock three minutes slow; as a result, the computer would continue to accept bets three minutes after a race had been run. Immediately after a race, the computer operator would telephone the results to his girlfriend, an input clerk, who would enter bets for winning horses.

Sabotage

Two days after he had been fired, a former employee of a securities trading firm entered the firm's headquarters and planted a time-bomb program that once each month would wipe out all records of sales commissions. The firm lost 168,000 records before disabling the program. Two former employees of a food corporation were charged with planting a time-bomb program that would erase inventory and payroll information for 400 retail franchise operations, then erase all traces of itself. A fired employee of a software company continued to access the company's computer from her home using her personal computer and a modem. She was charged with damaging files and downloading copies of the company's proprietary software.

UNAUTHORIZED ACCESS

Access to many computer systems is restricted to authorized users; these could be members of the organization the computer is intended to serve, for example, or they could be people who have paid a fee for the right to use the computer system. Passwords and other means are used to prevent unauthorized access. Unfortunately, many computer enthusiasts see such access restrictions as challenges and try to find ways to get around them, an enterprise at which they are all too often successful.

Unauthorized access is often the work of hackers, enthusiastic and compulsive computer users and programmers. Most hackers are dedicated hobbyists who engage in no illegal activities; in the community of programmers the designation *hacker* is a term of admiration and respect. Unfortunately, a small minority of hackers specialize in unauthorized access, thereby giving themselves and their fellow enthusiasts a bad name: to the public and most of the press, a hacker is someone who uses computers to commit illegal acts.

Although a few of these irresponsible hackers use their skills to commit petty crimes (such as charging purchases with other people's credit-card numbers), most are interested only in the challenge of exploring a computer system and circumventing its security provisions. But even the most well-intentioned intruder can accidentally destroy important data and perhaps even crash (interrupt the operation of) the system. And the ability of hackers to access files containing sensitive information makes a mockery of privacy legislation.

Modern telecommunications increases the exposure of computer systems to unauthorized access. If a system is connected to the public telephone network, anyone with a personal computer and a modem can call it up and have a try at penetrating its defenses. If a system is part of a computer network, then a hacker who penetrates the system may also gain access to all the other systems on the network. International computer and telecommunications networks make it easy for unauthorized access to cross national borders. In recent cases, West German hackers penetrated NASA computers and U.S. military networks, and another West German hacker spent two years accessing unclassified data in U.S. Defense Department computers.

Some hackers are highly skilled in working their way past the security provisions intended to prevent unauthorized access. But much unauthorized access is achieved in more obvious ways that involve little technical skill. People entrusted with telephone numbers and passwords of computer

Hackers have managed to access unclassified data in Pentagon computers such as the one shown here.

systems are often careless as to whom they provide this information (as in the Pacific Telephone case). Telephone numbers and passwords are often posted near computer terminals for the convenience of authorized users, a practice that is all too convenient for those contemplating unauthorized access. Authorized users are often allowed to choose their own passwords; unfortunately, many choose passwords that are easily guessed, such as common personal names. Some computer systems will accept passwords such as "test" that were used during system installation and (through oversight) were never removed from the list of valid passwords. Hackers can obtain the phone numbers of computer systems by writing programs that systematically dial different phone numbers and note which calls are answered with data signals.

Electronic bulletin boards are sometimes used to aid unauthorized access and other computer crimes. Just as most hackers are honest, most electronic bulletin boards are used only for legitimate purposes. Some, however, have been used to post illegally obtained information, such as credit card numbers and computer system passwords. A hacker who learns how to access a computer system (perhaps through the carelessness of an authorized user) may post the information on a bulletin board, making it available to the entire hacker community. In a celebrated case, an attempt was made to prosecute a bulletin board operator whose bulletin board was found to contain a telephone credit-card number, the disclosure of which was prohibited by state law. Charges were eventually dropped, however, because it was questionable whether the bulletin board operator could be held responsible for information posted by others. To avoid this kind of problem, many legitimate bulletin board operators now require users to register with the operator and obtain account numbers, which they must supply to gain access to the bulletin board. The account numbers identify the users and so allow any illegal information to be traced to the person who posted it.

Persons guilty of unauthorized access are being prosecuted under various computer crime laws. But unauthorized access is one of those crimes,

The memory of this call-back security modem holds a directory containing the identification codes and telephone numbers of authorized users. When a user calls, the modem requests the user's identification code, then hangs up and places a return call to the number obtained from the directory.

like car theft, in which prevention may be more effective than prosecution. If you leave the keys in your car, this does not lessen the guilt of the thief who steals it, but it leaves you looking stupid for not taking the most elementary precautions to protect your property. Many computer systems are as exposed as a car with the keys left in the switch. Improving computer security is the most important step in preventing unauthorized access.

◥ TROJAN HORSES, VIRUSES, WORMS, AND BACTERIA

Instead of personally penetrating other computer systems, some irresponsible hackers specialize in writing programs that will do the job for them. Some such programs merely commit minor pranks that show off their author's cleverness; others, however, take far more serious actions such as destroying data, tieing up networks, and violating security restrictions.

Trojan Horses

A *Trojan horse* is a malicious program that performs some useful task, such as sorting a disk directory, while at the same time carrying out some secret activity, such as introducing errors in data files, erasing files, or erasing the entire hard disk. The ostensible task that the program performs is made as useful as possible so as to increase the number of people who use the program and hence fall prey to its hidden activities. Such programs are named after the legendary wooden horse that the Greek army left at the gates of the enemy city of Troy. After the Trojans unwisely took the horse inside the city walls, Greek soldiers hidden inside emerged at night and prepared the way for a Greek invasion.

The most dramatic Trojan horse programs erase all accessible programs and data, then display a taunting message such as "Gotcha!" or "Arf! Arf!" All copies of the program may wreak their destruction on the same date (the program can determine the date from the computer's built-in calendar/ clock); this allows time for the program to be circulated widely before its destructive nature becomes apparent. If users have made backup copies of their data files, as they should have, then there may be no permanent damage. The lost data can be restored from the backup copies and the Trojan horse, having shown its true colors, can be eliminated from the system.

Much more insidious is a Trojan horse that, over a period of time, performs its useful function but at the same time introduces hard-to-trace errors in the users' data files. The errors cause continuing problems for the users, who will have great difficulty finding out what is going wrong. On multiuser systems, Trojan horses can carry out other harmful activities: the program might pass secret data from a user authorized to access the data to an unauthorized user, or it could install a so-called trap door that would allow unauthorized users to gain access to the system.

On a multiuser system, one user writes a Trojan horse program and then makes it available to other users. The more useful the ostensible function of the program, the more widely it will be used and the more harm it will be able to do. If a program becomes used widely enough, it may be installed as a system program, available to everyone, so that individual users will not have to store their own private copies. Nothing could please the author of the Trojan horse program more because the greater privileges accorded to a system program would greatly expand the program's opportunities for nefarious activities.

Trojan horses for microcomputers are usually so-called public-domain programs, which their authors make available to users free of charge and which are passed from user to user via electronic bulletin boards, information services, and computer networks. When such a program is found to be a Trojan horse, it is deleted from bulletin boards and information services, and users are warned of its insidious nature. Because of the widespread circulation of the program, however, the warning may not reach everyone who has a copy of the program. The lesson for users is clear: beware of programmers bearing gifts, particularly when the donor is unknown and the gift is distributed by electronic means.

Viruses

A *virus* is a segment of code that, when inserted in an otherwise harmless program, converts the program into a Trojan horse. Worse yet, a program containing virus code can "infect" other programs by inserting the virus code into them.

When an infected program is executed, the virus code is executed first, after which control is passed to the harmless program that carries the infection. Whenever the virus is executed, it searches the hard disk for uninfected programs and infects one or more of them. Eventually, all the programs on the hard disk will become infected. If any one of those programs is transferred to another system, it will carry the infection with it, and eventually all the programs on the other system will become infected too. Ultimately, each infected program will carry out some malicious act, such as erasing the hard disk. A virus, however, bides its time, trying to infect as many other programs as possible before revealing its own destructive nature.

To aid in combatting viruses, a number of *antiviral* or *vaccine programs* have appeared on the market. These programs work in several ways. One approach is to examine a suspected program for signs of infection; one sure sign is the presence of such messages as "Gotcha!" Another approach is to try to detect the change in a program when it becomes infected. The antiviral program computes a so-called signature for each program file; signatures are similar to the error-detecting codes used in telecommunications. After a program is infected, its signature will probably change, enabling the antiviral program to detect the infection. Still another approach is for the antiviral program to monitor all disk activity and try to catch the virus in the act of infecting other programs.

Each antiviral program has to make some assumptions about where a virus is stored and how it does its work; thus no antiviral program can detect all viruses. Authors of viruses will endeavor to use techniques that cannot be detected by any of the popular antiviral programs. This seems likely to lead to a technological competition in which every advance in antiviral programs is offset by a corresponding advance in viruses.

To avoid viral infections, users are being urged to practice "safe computing" by avoiding programs of unknown origin, such as those downloaded from bulletin boards or information services. Many companies now forbid computer users to run programs brought from home or downloaded from outside sources. Yet even confining yourself to programs from reputable software manufacturers may not be sufficient. In one case, a dealer put a software package back on the shelf after it had been returned by a customer; when the package was purchased a second time, the program disk was found to harbor a virus. Users can check that manufacturers' seals on software packages are unbroken, but even that may not be enough. A well-known software manufacturer inadvertently sold infected programs after a virus had invaded its own computer systems.

Worms and Bacteria

Worms and *bacteria* are names given to programs that infect computer networks. Although not as destructive as Trojan horses and viruses, they can force a network to be shut down until all copies of the hostile program have been removed.

A worm program takes over and disables idle workstations on a computer network. Like the tapeworm after which it is named, a worm program is made up of many segments, each of which occupies a workstation. The segments propagate by finding uninfected workstations and starting new segments running on them. If a workstation is disinfected by deleting its segment, it soon will be reinfected by another segment. To get rid of the worm, the entire network has to be shut down while all segments are deleted.

Bacteria programs simply multiply themselves until they clog the network. In December, 1987, for example, a West German law student sent a program for displaying a Christmas greeting into an IBM network. When the program was run, it sent copies of itself to everyone on the user's electronic-mail distribution list. Soon the network was clogged with copies of the program and had to be shut down while all copies were deleted.

SOFTWARE PIRACY

We seem to be moving inexorably into an information age in which information will be bought, sold, and traded just like such traditional commodities as oil, steel, and grain. A problem with information as a commodity, however, is that it can be duplicated without loss of or damage to the original. People who purchase information can make as many copies as they wish to give away or to sell. Laws and licensing agreements intended to prevent such piracy (unauthorized copying) are difficult to enforce.

Microcomputer software is a case in point. Programs for microcomputers are usually delivered on diskettes. Most microcomputer operating

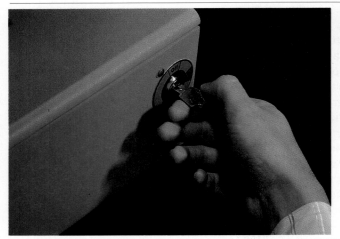

Many personal computers have locks that prevent the computer from being operated (left). A keyboard lock (right) disables the keyboard but allows the computer to remain on to receive messages sent to it over a network.

systems have a command to copy the contents of one disk onto another without in any way harming the original. A person who purchases a program can easily make copies for his or her friends. Sometimes one purchased program is used to make copies for all interested persons in a company, school, or computer club. Pirated copies of software are sometimes stored on electronic bulletin boards, from where they can be downloaded to users' computers. Professional software pirates copy software for resale; this practice is particularly common in some foreign countries. Software producers have estimated that more than half of the existing copies of some programs are pirated.

The initial response of the software industry was *copy protection*, which prevents disks from being copied with the standard operating system copy commands. The operating system expects the data stored on the disk to be organized according to a standard format. Copy-protected programs use a nonstandard disk format that the operating system's copying program cannot handle.

Unfortunately, copy protection imposes a severe burden on the user. Diskettes are easily damaged: a fingerprint on the exposed disk surface or the magnetic field from a ringing telephone are enough to render a disk unusable. Even if disks are protected from damage, they eventually wear out. For this reason, computer users are normally advised to make backup copies of all important programs and store the backup copies in a safe place. Copy protection prevents users from making backup copies. It also prevents users from copying programs to their hard disks; this, however, negates one of the major conveniences of a hard disk: the ability to execute any program merely by entering its name, without having to find and insert the diskette on which it is stored. Still another problem is that copy-protection schemes are often dependent on particular hardware, such as a particular disk-controller chip. A copy-protected program written for one computer might not run on another that uses different hardware, even if the two machines are designed to be compatible at the software level.

In an effort to alleviate these problems, software producers turned to copy-protection schemes based on the use of a key. The user could make as many backup copies of the program as desired and could copy it onto a hard disk. But the program would work only if the user provided a special key, the form of which varied from one copy-protection scheme to another. One approach required the user to insert a special *key disk* in a diskette drive. Another required the user to attach a special hardware device (informally known as a *dongle*) to one of the computer's communications ports. In another variation, the key was a special hidden file that was stored along with the program on the hard disk. Users remained dissatisfied, however. Nobody wanted to have to bother with key disks and dongles, and programs that used key files sometimes would not work after the contents of the hard disk had been lost due to a malfunction and then restored from a backup copy.

In response to the need for backup copies, several companies deciphered the most popular copy-protection schemes and put out programs that could make copies of copy-protected disks. Other anti-copy-protection programs would modify protected programs so that they would work without the presence of key files, key disks, or dongles. The software industry responded by inventing new copy-protection schemes, but these were quickly broken by the manufacturers of anti-copy-protection programs. At one time, software makers attempted to pressure computer magazines into not advertising anti-copy-protection programs, but these attempts enjoyed only limited success.

By the mid-1980s, copy protection was facing serious problems. Users hated copy protection; therefore, any software producer who abandoned copy protection could gain an advantage over competitors who retained it. Some copy-protected programs for the IBM-PC family would not run on some compatible machines from other manufacturers, thereby limiting the market for the programs. The more advanced operating systems that are emerging in the late 1980s do not allow the direct access to hardware components that is needed to implement copy protection. Every advance in copy-protection techniques was offset by a corresponding advance in anti-copy-protection programs, so that any user who wanted to defeat copy protection could buy an anti-copy-protection program that would do the job. As a result of these problems, almost all producers of business programs have abandoned copy protection. Many programs for home use are still copy protected, however, as are some programs used in specialized areas such as computer-aided design. Also copy protection may be retained for versions of a program sold outside the U.S. (where software piracy is sometimes rampant) even if copy protection has been removed from versions sold inside the U.S.

To protect their rights in the absence of copy protection, software producers have sued several companies for unauthorized copying (usually done by employees without the knowledge of the company's management). To avoid such lawsuits, companies have clamored for site licenses, in which the company pays a substantial fee for the right to make as many copies of a program as it needs. Major software vendors have resisted the movement toward site licensing; rather, they often offer volume purchase agreements by which large numbers of program diskettes can be purchased at reduced costs. These agreements sometimes include provisions that protect the company from lawsuits for copying that is done by employees in spite of management's reasonable efforts to prevent it.

In short, software producers seem to have reached a reasonable accommodation with business users: the annoyance of copy protection has been removed from business programs, and businesses, fearful of lawsuits, are taking steps to prevent unauthorized copying by their employees. Unfortunately, no one has yet come up with a complete solution to the problem of unauthorized copying. In some nonbusiness areas, particularly education, unauthorized copying and copy protection remain unresolved issues.

COMPUTER SECURITY

Computer security is concerned with protecting the data stored in computers. Positive identifications of users, access controls, and secure operating systems guard against unauthorized access. Encryption protects data during both storage and transmission. Backup copies protect data from accidental or malicious destruction.

Positive Identification of Users

Security is impossible without positive identification to prevent unauthorized users from impersonating authorized ones. Traditionally, a user is identified by an account number, a password, or both. But users are often careless in guarding this information. Allowed to choose their own passwords, users pick words that are easy to remember but also easy to guess, such as the name of a spouse or child. If the computer system generates hard-to-remember passwords, then users are likely to write them down in places that will be as convenient for intruders as they are for legitimate users. For examples, account numbers and passwords all too often have been posted near the computers or terminals with which they are to be used.

Some of these problems can be avoided if access codes are read from cards similar to credit cards. Because the user does not have to remember the access codes, they can be more complex and so harder to guess. The access card can be stolen, but the access codes will be changed when the authorized user reports the theft. To help guard against stolen cards, the user can be required to enter a personal identification number in addition to the information stored on the card.

Another approach to positive identification is a *callback system*. When a user telephones the computer system and supplies his or her access codes, the system hangs up and then places a call to the person authorized to use those codes. The return call goes to the authorized user, not to an unauthorized person calling from a different location. There are two problems with callback systems. First, they do not allow a user to call the computer from different locations, as when calling from both home and office or calling from hotel rooms while traveling. Second, hackers may be able to use the call-forwarding features of some PBXs (office telephone systems) to route the return call to the hacker instead of the authorized user.

A desktop computer (left) and a laptop computer (right) are attached to the furniture with steel cables to prevent theft.

Biometric devices identify users through personal characteristics such as size and shape of hands, fingerprints, patterns on the retinas of the eyes, voice inflections, typing habits, and pen motions as users sign their names. Drawbacks to biometric devices are the complexity and expense of the hardware needed to measure a particular characteristic and the software needed to interpret the measurements.

All efforts at identification will be for naught if an authorized user can be tricked into taking actions on behalf of someone who is not authorized to use the system or who is entitled to fewer privileges. One way this can be accomplished is with a Trojan horse program: the program enjoys all the privileges of the authorized user who runs it, but it takes secret actions on behalf of its author, who may not even be authorized to use the system. Another approach involves certain kinds of intelligent terminals that can be programmed to transmit a lengthy message automatically when the user presses a certain key. The programming commands can be hidden in any text that is sent to the terminal. Thus by sending electronic mail to a privileged user, the sender can program the recipient's terminal to take actions on behalf of the sender without the recipient's knowledge.

Access Controls

Once a user has been identified, it is the responsibility of the operating system and the database management system to control access to data. The system maintains a table showing what access rights each user has to each file. Generally three access rights are considered: read, write, and execute. *Read access* means that the user can read the information in a file but cannot change it. *Write access* conveys the right to change the contents of the file. *Execute access* conveys the right to execute a program but not the rights to read or change the program code. The operating system and the database management system consult the access-rights table for each requested data access and denies those requests for which the user does not have the proper rights.

Although access rights are most commonly applied to files, they can also be applied to individual fields within a record. For example, clerical employees at a company might have read and write access to all fields of an employee record except the salary field, access to which would be limited to the payroll department. Even most employees in the payroll department might have only read access to the salary field; only a few trusted employees might have write access, the right to change someone's salary.

Secure Software

User identification and access rights will go for naught if software and hardware access controls can be bypassed. In current systems, security is almost entirely the responsibility of software, with little or no support from the hardware. Operating systems and database management systems are so complex that loopholes are sometimes inadvertently left in their security systems. All too often clever hackers have found ways to do such things as print out a list of users' passwords or give themselves access rights to which they are not entitled.

It is essential that the system software be protected from modification by hostile users. Hackers are clever at installing *trap doors*, modifications

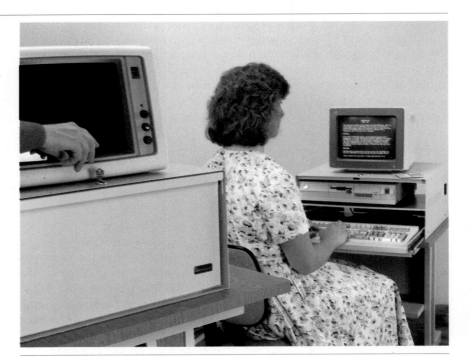

This steel cabinet protects the computer when it is not in use (left) but allows the computer to be used immediately when the cabinet is unlocked (right). The cabinet also has room to store a tray of 3½-inch diskette cartridges.

to system software that simplify bypassing security provisions in the future. For example, a Trojan horse program might install a trap door that will allow the author of the program to access the computer system from a remote terminal. A common target for the installation of trap doors is the program that checks users' passwords and determines what privileges each user is to be accorded. After it has been surreptitiously modified, the password program will not demand a password from the person who installed the trap door and will accord that person whatever privileges he or she may desire.

Current microcomputer systems provide little if any security. A hostile user can easily run programs that will bypass any security restrictions imposed by the operating system or a database management system. Utility programs intended for recovering data from damaged disks often can be used for bypassing security restrictions. The following are the only security options available to most microcomputer users:

■ Store sensitive data on floppy disks, which can be locked up in conventional filing cabinets and safes when not in use.

■ Store data on the computer's hard disk and keep the computer system locked when not in use; some computers are provided with a key-operated switch for this purpose. All bets are off if the entire computer is stolen, since any key-operated switch is easily bypassed by anyone with the opportunity to work on the machine unobserved.

■ Use data encryption to store data in a scrambled form meaningless to anyone not having the proper key.

Data Encryption

Encryption stores data in a scrambled form that can be unscrambled only by those having a special data item called the key. An encryption algorithm converts the plaintext—the data to be protected—into scrambled ciphertext. The scrambling is controlled by the key. Only someone who has the key can use the encryption algorithm in reverse to convert the ciphertext back into plaintext. As with passwords, it is often difficult to keep keys from being stolen or to prevent people from carelessly letting them fall into the wrong hands. Encryption can protect data stored in files as well as protect against wiretapping during telecommunications.

Backup Copies and Standby Equipment

Stored data can be lost through fire, theft, malicious destruction, or, more commonly, through failure of storage media such as disks and tapes. Most large computer installations periodically copy all their stored data on magnetic tapes and store the tapes in a remote location to prevent their loss in a fire or other disaster. Some organizations maintain (at a different location than the main system) a standby computer system to which they can turn if the primary system is destroyed. Organizations that do not maintain their own standby systems often have contracts with organizations that specialize in supplying computer facilities on short notice.

Wise microcomputer users make backup copies of all disks containing important programs or data. The backup copies protect not only against disk failure but against accidental erasure of files due to operator errors. Copy-protection techniques that do not allow backup copies of programs to be made present serious risks to users.

Although hard disks are reasonably reliable, they do fail occasionally, so data stored on hard disks needs to be backed up on floppy disks; many users are failing to do this. Hidden away inside the computer, the hard disk is out of sight and out of mind; many users are probably unaware that it can fail. Also, backing up all the data on a hard disk is cumbersome and time consuming, because many boxes of floppy disks are usually needed to store the data from one hard disk.

Power failure can interrupt processing, lose data, and damage equipment. These problems can be avoided by installing an *uninterruptable power source* (*UPS*, not to be confused with the delivery service with the same initials). When the power goes off, the UPS automatically switches the system to battery power; while the system is running on batteries, it can be shut down without damage to the hardware or loss of data, or local generators can be started up to permit continued operation.

Communications failures can have serious consequences for systems that depend heavily on telecommunications, such as airline reservation systems and brokerage-house trading rooms. Computer users who rely on the telephone system were alarmed by a recent fire in a telephone office that disabled service in a Chicago suburb for several days. Some users may need to provide themselves with alternative communications channels, such as a microwave links, for use when telephone and other communications services fail.

Summary

Computers have given rise to new forms of crime as well as to new variations on old forms of crime. Traditional crimes such as embezzlement may be even easier with computers, since computer systems will accept any transactions that obey certain formal rules even though the same transactions would look suspicious to a human auditor.

Unauthorized access to computer systems has become much more common since the microcomputers and modems needed to commit this crime have become widely available. Most unauthorized accesses result not from the cleverness of the perpetrators but from poor or nonexistent security. Although persons guilty of unauthorized access are being arrested and prosecuted, improved security techniques are likely to be far more effective than prosecution of offenders.

Malicious programs are one of the most recent threats to computer security. A Trojan horse performs a desirable service for its user while carrying out secret actions on behalf of its author. Viruses infect otherwise harmless programs, turning them into Trojan horses. Worms and bacteria can shut down a computer network.

Users have demonstrated that they will make unauthorized copies of software if not somehow prevented from doing so; unauthorized copying has been particularly prevalent in corporations, schools, and computer clubs. Copy protection presents problems for honest users and is not always successful in deterring copying. User hostility and other factors have forced the removal of copy protection from business software. Lawsuits have forced businesses to enforce policies against unauthorized copying. Unfortunately, there is still no general solution to the underlying problem of preventing unauthorized copying of programs and data.

Computer security is concerned with protecting data from loss and from unauthorized access or changes. Positive identification of users, access rights, and secure software help control access to data. Encryption can protect stored data as well as that being sent over communications links. Security is poor or nonexistent for most micrcomputer systems; measures such as locking up disks in filing cabinets or locking the computer system may be needed to prevent unauthorized access. Backup copies of computer files, preferably kept at a different location than the originals, are essential to guard against data loss due to disaster or failure of data storage media.

◣ Vocabulary Review

antiviral program	encryption	uninterruptable
bacteria	execute access	power source
biometric devices	hacker	vaccine program
callback system	key disk	virus
computer security	read access	worm
copy protection	trap door	write access
dongle	Trojan horse	

◣ For Further Reading

Denning, Peter J. "Computer Viruses." *American Scientist*, May–June 1988, pp. 236–238.

Freedman, David H. "Foiling Corporate Software Pirates." *High Technology*, July 1985, pp. 62–64.

Frenkel, Karen A. "Computers in Court." *Technology Review*, April 1982.

Hafner, Katherine M., et al. "Is Your Computer Secure?" *Business Week*, 1 August 1988, pp. 64–72.

Hutt, Arthur E., et al. *Computer Security Handbook*, 2nd ed. New York: Macmillan Publishing Co., 1988.

Levy, Steven. *Hackers: Heroes of the Computer Revolution*. Garden City, NY: Doubleday, 1984. (This book describes some of the worthwhile contributions of the much-maligned hackers.)

Parker, Donn B. *Crime by Computer*. New York: Charles Scribner's Sons, 1976.

_____, et al. "Computers, Crime, and Privacy: A National Dilemma." *Communications of the ACM*, May 1984, pp. 312–321.

Stoll, Clifford. "Stalking the Wily Hacker." *Communications of the ACM,* May 1988, pp. 484–497.

Witten, Ian H. "Computer (In)security: Infiltrating Open Systems." *Abacus,* Summer 1987, pp. 7–25.

Review Questions

1 Describe some of the techniques that have been used to commit fraud, embezzlement, and sabotage.

2 How has a small minority of hackers given a bad name to these dedicated and mostly law-abiding computer enthusiasts.

3 Describe some poor security practices that open the door to unauthorized access.

4 Compare the problem of preventing unauthorized access with that of preventing car theft.

5 How have a small number of electronic bulletin boards been used to aid unauthorized access?

6 Describe Trojan horse programs. Why are these programs so named?

7 Describe viruses.

8 Describe worms and bacteria.

9 Describe several approaches to copy protection. What are the advantages and disadvantages of each method?

10 Give the reasons why software producers have abandoned copy protection for business programs.

11 Give the advantages and disadvantages of simple, easy-to-remember passwords for identifying users.

12 Describe several other approaches to identifying users.

13 Describe read, write, and execute access rights.

14 Give examples of how access rights may be applied to (1) entire files and (2) individual fields within a record.

15 What software programs are responsible for enforcing access rights?

16 What is a trap door and how is it used?

17 What security options are generally available to microcomputer owners?

18 What is encryption? Give two situations in which data can be protected by encryption.

19 Discuss some measures that can be taken to protect data from loss due to theft, fire, malicious destruction, and failure of storage media such as disks and tapes.

20 What steps can be taken to protect against power and communications failure?

Topics for Discussion

1 For each of the computer crimes described in this chapter, discuss security measures that might have prevented the crime or permitted its early detection.

2 Discuss how employees might be prevented from being careless with computer access codes.

3 It has been suggested that unauthorized access might be reduced by setting up an on-line computer system for hackers to experiment with. The system would present various security hurdles that the hackers would be challenged to overcome. The winners would be given suitable recognition. Discuss.

4 Discuss the conflict between the need for software users to make backup copies and the need for software vendors to prevent unauthorized copying of their products.

5 Fingerprints seem to be one promising method of identifying users, although some of the technical problems of automatically taking and analyzing fingerprints remain to be solved. A possible human problem is that many people associate fingerprinting with being arrested and might resist having their fingerprints taken to authorize computer access. Discuss.

CHAPTER 17

COMPUTERS AND EMPLOYMENT

INTRODUCTION

Computers and computer-controlled machines are increasingly taking over jobs that were once done by people. As the capabilities of robots and other computer-controlled machines increase, so does their ability to replace human workers. Automatic factories run by only a few supervisory personnel are coming ever closer to reality. In the printing industry many Linotype operators lost their jobs when Linotype machines were replaced by computerized typesetting systems. Office automation may greatly reduce the number of office workers. Expert systems may reduce the need for human professionals in a variety of fields. Teachers worry about the impact of computer-assisted instruction on their profession.

Widespread replacement of people by machines will not take place overnight, of course. In many areas the necessary technology is not yet perfected. Even when it is technologically possible to replace people with machines, it may not be economically feasible. Because of investments in existing equipment and the cost of new equipment, a new method of doing a job must improve productivity or reduce costs by a factor of ten to justify the change. Opposition by labor unions and in some cases by customers will slow the pace of automation. Yet gradual automation will produce problems of its own. As long as the majority of people have jobs, the needs of the minority that do not may not be adequately addressed.

Looking to the future, we can envision a time in which most routine jobs have been taken over by computers. The only people with jobs will be those with extraordinary capabilities or those lucky enough to hold the few routine jobs that, for one reason or another, proved impractical to automate. Although this future is not just around the corner, it is by no means too early to start thinking about the challenges posed by a highly

Soldering components on a printed circuit board. This photo and the remaining ones in this chapter illustrate jobs that were created or changed by computer technology.

automated society. How will the wealth created by the machines be distributed to the people? Without work, how will people spend their time? How can the necessary political and economic changes be brought about? Will automation create a new Garden of Eden or a hell of unemployed souls who have long since abandoned all hope of meaningful lives.

◥ THE IMPACT OF COMPUTERS ON EMPLOYMENT

Historically, technological innovation has benefited workers. The industrial revolution relieved 70 percent of the workforce from the backbreaking, dawn-to-dusk agricultural work that once occupied almost everyone. Early industrial workers were badly exploited, but such exploitation was countered not only by social forces (child labor laws, the rise of labor unions) but by the realization that more affluent workers would provide better markets for the products the factories were turning out. Henry Ford once doubled the wages of his workers so that they could afford his automobiles! Continuing technological innovation has brought about enormous increases in employment, income, and standard of living.

Although technological innovation has improved the lot of workers as a whole, it has sometimes spelled disaster for particular groups of workers whose jobs were eliminated. The earliest labor unrest due to automation occurred at the very beginning of the industrial revolution when traditional weaving equipment was replaced by mechanized devices that required far fewer workers to operate. The operators of the new machines would (eventually, at least) have easier jobs and make better wages than those who worked with the manual equipment. But none of this was any comfort to the workers who had been displaced and who, in an age devoid of public assistance, were left to starve. Little wonder that they sometimes rioted and smashed the offending machinery.

So far, automation has created as many jobs as it has eliminated. If automated equipment eliminated jobs in a factory, new jobs were created to design, manufacture, sell, install, and service the automated equipment. As late as 1981 a study showed no net loss of jobs due to automation. Yet it is far from clear how long this situation will continue. As more and more jobs are taken over by machines, a crossover point must be reached at which jobs are being lost faster than they can be created.

Even if the net number of jobs remains the same, the nature of the job market is changing in ways that are already producing social problems. Unskilled workers are usually the first to be replaced by machines, since their jobs are the easiest for the machines to accomplish. The machines, however, are complex, high-tech devices that require substantial skill to manufacture, install, operate, and maintain. The net result is that there are fewer positions for unskilled workers and more positions for skilled workers. The affluent and the educated have little trouble getting jobs, but unemployment is high among the poor and uneducated. Precisely such employment patterns are observed today, and the situation is likely to get steadily worse in the future.

Purifying the silicon used to make computer chips.

Computers play a central role in weather forecasting.

To date, then, involuntary technological unemployment has not been a major public issue. The total number of jobs and the affluence of workers has continued to increase. Workers whose jobs were eliminated have rarely been fired; rather they were either retrained for other jobs or allowed to remain on their old jobs until normal attrition and retirement reduced their numbers to the desired levels. Economic forces such as recession and foreign competition have resulted in more workers being discharged than has automation. Yet we cannot be complacent about the future. We cannot turn our back on increasing unemployment among the educationally dis-

Working in an automated office.

advantaged or in certain segments of the economy, such as manufacturing. As more and more jobs are taken over by computers, increasing numbers of people will find their education and skills inadequate for the needs of the job market.

STOPGAP MEASURES

In the sections that follow it is suggested that radical social and economic changes will be needed to counter the threats of automation and to realize its benefits. Such changes will not come about easily. No matter how badly the existing system may be working, people are likely to prefer its known faults to the uncertainties of some radically new proposal. Such attitudes have changed little in the five hundred years since Machiavelli wrote, "There is nothing more difficult to take in hand, more perilous to conduct, or more uncertain in its success, than to take the lead in the introduction of a new order of things." Politicians who wish to keep their jobs do not take the lead in the introduction of a new order of things, but rather propose stopgap measures that will alleviate the problem of the moment while offending as few people as possible. The following are some of the measures that may be taken to combat the problems of automation as well as some naturally occurring changes that may work to alleviate those problems.

Changes in Population Makeup

One way of looking at unemployment is that there are too many workers for the available jobs. Thus some governments have advocated increased birth control as a means of reducing unemployment and achieving other

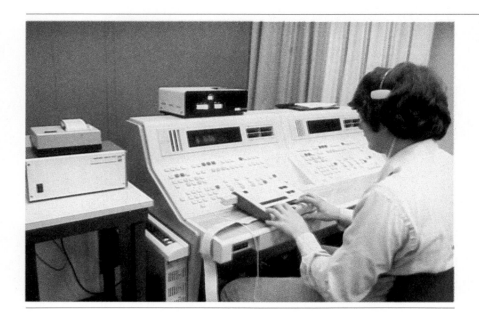

Today's telephone operators work at computerized consoles instead of switchboards.

Testing communications terminals.

social goals. Such an approach is probably not politically acceptable in the United States, but if existing trends continue, the makeup of the population may of itself change in ways that will lessen the adverse effects of automation. As the children of the baby boom move into retirement, the working population is expected to decrease and the retired population to increase correspondingly.

Of course, we will still be faced with the problem of providing for many nonworking individuals, but it is probably easier politically to provide for the elderly than for the unemployed. Retired individuals are considered both by themselves and by others to have made their contributions to society and to have earned whatever assistance they may need in their declining years.

A shift in job preference away from manufacturing and toward service industries is likely to reduce the working population in the industries that are likely to automate first. Indeed, some industries may be forced to automate because of a lack of qualified workers.

Reducing the Work Week

In the mid-nineteenth century the average work week was 70 hours. Over the years this figure has dropped to its present value of around 40 hours, which was realized around the end of World War II. Since then, little change has taken place. Further reductions in the work week would increase the demand for workers and so combat unemployment. If, in addition, workers' hourly wages were increased so that their take-home pay remained the same (or increased) as the work week decreased, this would provide a means by which some of the income generated by automated equipment could be passed on to the workers who were displaced. Since

The work of accountants and auditors has been dramatically changed by computerized bookkeeping and accounting systems.

Preparing the negative from which computer chips will be produced.

wages and working hours are often negotiated by employers and unions, this would seem to be a promising area for creative collective bargaining.

Increased Investment

Increased investment is often seen as a means of creating jobs and thus combatting unemployment. The difficulty is that increased investment accelerates the rate at which labor-saving machinery is introduced. Advances in labor-saving technology have thus increased the amount of investment needed to create a given number of jobs. Twenty years ago an investment of $50,000 was needed for each new job; now $100,000 dollars are needed and in 20 years this figure will have probably risen to $500,000 (amounts adjusted for inflation). Under these circumstances increased investment can make only limited contributions to relieving technological unemployment.

Public Assistance

Public assistance programs currently provide income for the unemployed. Yet they present both social and economic problems. There is a social stigma attached to receiving public assistance, and the regulations governing such programs are often demeaning. For example, recipients may have to prove that they have applied and been rejected for a certain number of jobs each week. Money for public assistance programs comes from general tax revenues, that is, out of the wages of those who are working. Those who are working feel that they are being forced to support "freeloaders" who are not, thus increasing social tension between the two

Securities trading room.

groups. Further, as the number of nonworking individuals increases and the number of working individuals decreases, the income of the working will be insufficient to support the nonworking.

The Japanese Approach

Japanese industries are among the most highly automated in the world; yet until recently, automation has not caused labor problems in Japan. One reason is the traditional relationship between Japanese companies and their employees: the employees are loyal to the company, sing the company song, and usually spend their entire working lives at the same company. The company, in turn, assumes responsibility for the employees, making sure that there is a job available for each employee and providing any retraining required for an employee to move from one job to another. Given the traditions of Japanese society, this approach can cope with job displacements produced by moderate levels of automation. But it cannot help in extreme cases where most of a company's workers are no longer needed, nor can it help those who were never employed in the first place. Recognizing this, Japanese trade unions now are beginning to voice concern about the impact of automation on employment.

Taxes on Automated Equipment

It has been proposed that a tax be imposed on automated equipment, with the money collected going to the workers who were displaced. Distributing the proceeds of the tax fairly might prove difficult. If the money was distributed only to workers who had been discharged when their jobs were taken over by automated equipment, this would leave out those who were denied jobs because the available positions had been filled by machines. Yet the latter group may be difficult to identify; if money were being handed out we can be sure that anyone out of a job for any reason would claim technological unemployment and get in line for their share.

Restrictions on Automation

One approach that many may find attractive is to restrict the use of automated equipment. Aside from explicit legal restrictions, taxing and regulatory policies might be adjusted to encourage investment in labor-intensive industries. Taxes on automated equipment or union contracts preventing displaced workers from being discharged may also discourage automation by reducing the amount of money that it will save.

If carried out worldwide, restricting automation might be feasible, although of course the benefits of automation (greater leisure time, for example) would be thrown out along with its pitfalls. It would be economic suicide, however, for one country to restrict automation while its economic competitors did not, for with lower manufacturing costs the countries that did not restrict automation could sell their products at lower prices than the country that did.

DISTRIBUTION OF INCOME

Automated machinery creates wealth by producing products that are more valuable than the raw materials from which they were made. A portion of this wealth must be returned as profits to those whose investments purchased the machinery. The remainder needs to be distributed to those who would otherwise have done the jobs now carried out by the machines.

Inspecting printed circuit boards.

Those still fixated on the concept of work for pay may ask what right workers have to profits from machines that they neither invested in nor operated. Humanitarian considerations dictate, of course, that the unemployed not be left to starve; when the unemployed are a substantial segment of the voting public, political considerations dictate the same thing. But aside from humanitarian and political considerations we can find purely economic justifications for the distribution of wealth. When the late Walter Reuther, then president of the United Auto Workers, was shown an early industrial robot and told how many workers it could replace, his reply was, "Yes, but how many cars can it buy?" This is the crux of the matter. If consumers have no money to buy the output of the automatic factories, the economic system will collapse as surely as if some other essential, such as investment, were missing. From a purely economic viewpoint (ignoring, it is emphasized, humanitarian and political considerations) wealth must be distributed to unemployed workers not because of some right they have to it but to provide them with the means to play an essential role in the economic system—the role of consumer.

Here is another view of the matter. All past and present economic thinking has been based on an economy of scarcity. Phrases such as "the pie can only be sliced into so many parts" typifies the concept of a limited amount of goods and services for which individuals and organizations must compete. But automation may have the power to create an economy of plenty in which we will be less concerned with allocating scare resources to those who have in some sense earned them than in distributing abundant resources to those who need them. To the extent that money has a role in an economy of abundance, it will be not something that has to be earned by the sweat of one's brow but rather a means for assuring reasonably equitable distribution of goods and services. The role of money might be similar to that of ration coupons, a certain number of which are periodically

Operating a CAT scanner.

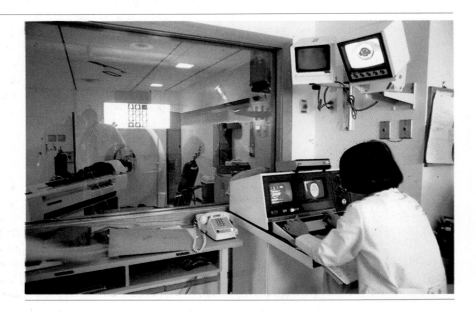

Teaching people to use computers is itself becoming a substantial industry.

issued free of charge to each individual. The emphasis here, however, would be not on restricting the consumption of scare resources but on preventing some individuals from wasting resources or consuming so much more than their fair share as to put a strain on even a reasonably abundant economy.

The question, then, is how can we gradually make the transition from our present economy of scarcity to one of abundance as technological innovations make the latter possible. The answer is that nobody knows. The desired transition will result in enormous social and economic changes, and no one ever has been very successful in predicting how such changes will take place. The science fiction writers of the 1930s and 1940s anticipated many of the technological innovations that have since come to pass, but their attempts to extrapolate social changes were much less successful: the future societies described in early science fiction stories bear little resemblance to the world in which we live today. Yet although we cannot hope to predict future social and economic changes in detail, it is worth looking at some of the directions such changes might take.

Because of people's preference for gradual rather than radical change, perhaps the most likely course is that future means of distributing wealth will grow out of existing mechanisms such as Social Security, medical insurance, unemployment benefits, and welfare payments. As mentioned earlier, the main drawback of such programs is the resentment by the employed of having to provide for the unemployed with their tax dollars. Anything that reduces the distinction between the unemployed and the employed is a step in the right direction. For example, in many European countries supplementary benefits are paid to anyone who works fewer than the normal number of hours per week.

A more radical suggestion has been put forth by robotics researcher James S. Albus, who proposes a National Mutual Fund (NMF). In stock

Using a laptop computer at a construction site.

market jargon a mutual fund is an organization that buys and sells stock and other securities, distributing the profits from this activity to its own shareholders. The NMF would work like this:

- Every citizen would be a shareholder in NMF by right of citizenship.

- NMF would borrow its investment capital from the Federal Reserve Bank. No contributions by shareholders would be required.

- NMF would concentrate its investments in highly automated industries; thus it would serve to distribute the wealth generated by automation.

- NMF would distribute its profits to all citizens over the age of 18. Each citizen would get the same amount. Because payments would be distributed to everyone regardless of income, no stigma would be attached to accepting them.

- Because NMF would use the normal investment process available in every capitalist society, it would achieve the necessary distribution of wealth with a minimum of social upheaval.

Not surprisingly, considering the arguments to which economic questions can give rise, many people have expressed doubts about NMF. Providing every citizen with unearned income might lead to rampant inflation, some say. Or the growth in industrial production needed to support the plan might have adverse effects on the environment. The people in charge of NMF (who Albus suggests should be publicly elected) would have enormous economic and political power. Similar questions, with the answers just as uncertain, can be raised about most plans for distributing wealth.

RETURN TO EDEN

According to tradition, Adam and Eve enjoyed a high standard of living with no work until they were expelled from the Garden of Eden to earn their bread by the sweat of their brows. For thousands of years mankind was condemned to the backbreaking, dawn-to-dusk labor of an agricultural economy. With the industrial revolution, however, we have begun gradually to work our way back toward the conditions that are supposed to have prevailed in Paradise. Suppose that this goal is achieved, that almost all work can be turned over to computers and robots, that such economic problems as the distribution of income have been solved or, more likely, have simply become irrelevant. How might people live in such a society?

Many people whose lives revolve around their jobs might deny that such a society could ever be satisfying or fulfilling. But those who feel this way may be making the mistake of assuming that the attitudes of contemporary, middle-class Americans necessarily apply to all people and all times. The ancient Greeks and the aristocrats of many ages have lived fulfilling, even glorious lives without stooping to routine labor, which was provided by a slave or servant class. At its best, automation can make us all aristocrats whose freedom is not gained at the expense of slaves or servants.

Computers are allowing increasing numbers of people to do all or part of their jobs at home.

Perhaps the question to ask is what rewards do we get from work? Students of the subject identify three:

■ Wages and other financial benefits

■ Personal relations with other workers

■ Satisfaction with doing the work itself

In the society we are considering, wages would no longer be necessary. More extensive social activities, for which people would have much more time, could provide the personal contacts that people once found in the workplace. The satisfaction that people once derived from work would have to be replaced with that provided by other challenging activities. The intellectually and artistically inclined might devote themselves to science, mathematics, music, literature, poetry, and the arts. The majority would probably be more inclined towards games, sports, hobbies, and the intricacies of social life. Some might wish to qualify for the few remaining jobs, because the jobs that had resisted all attempts at automation would probably be highly challenging and correspondingly prestigious.

◥ Summary

So far automation seems to have created at least as many jobs as it has eliminated. This situation is likely to change, however, as automation becomes much more extensive in the future. Also, the jobs created by automation usually require much higher skills than the jobs that were eliminated. The average level of skill required by the job market is thus steadily increased, producing extensive unemployment among the unskilled and poorly educated.

Because of reluctance on the part of the public and their elected leaders to accept the radical social and economic changes that automation demands, a number of stopgap measures are likely to be proposed for combatting unemployment. While many of these measures may be effective for moderate levels of automation, none seems able to cope with the ultimate situation in which almost all work is automated.

Eventually, ways must be found for distributing the wealth generated by the machines to the people that the machines replaced. More generally, we must make the transition from an economy of scarcity, in which all wealth has to be laboriously earned, to one of plenty in which the products of the automated industries will be freely distributed to those who need them, and in which money, if it exists at all, will serve mainly as a tool for allocating resources equitably and for discouraging wasteful or excessive consumption.

Unfortunately, no one knows what practical political and economic steps will get us from our present state to this Garden of Eden on earth. Debate over the proper course will undoubtedly be bitter; we can only hope that it is not also bloody. The Chinese have a curse that goes, "May you live in interesting times." The economic and political history of the next fifty to a hundred years may be very interesting indeed!

For Further Reading

Albus, James S. "The Economics of the Robot Revolution." *Analog Science Fiction/Science Fact*, April 1975, pp. 70–81. (For reader comments, see the issue of August 1975, pp. 171–176.)

Ginzberg, Eli. "The Mechanization of Work." *Scientific American*, September 1982, pp. 66–75.

Leontief, Wassily W. "The Distribution of Work and Income." *Scientific American*, September 1982, pp. 188–204.

Review Questions

1 Historically, what has been the effect of technological innovation on workers?

2 How has technological innovation sometimes spelled disaster for many current workers in an industry even as it was providing benefits for future workers in the same industry.?

3 How has automation affected so far the total number of available jobs. Is this situation likely to continue indefinitely?

4 How has automation affected the average level of skill required by the job market. What effect has this had on unemployment?

5 Why is taking a lead in the introduction of a new order of things so perilous to conduct and so uncertain of success?

6 How might changes in the makeup of the population affect employment?

7 What advantages would be gained by reducing the work week?

8 What limits the effectiveness of increased investment for reducing unemployment?

9 What are some of the problems of using public assistance programs, such as welfare, for distributing income to unemployed workers?

10 Describe the Japanese approach to providing workers with lifetime employment. Why, in spite of this approach, are some Japanese unions becoming concerned about the effects of automation?

11 What are the advantages and disadvantages of putting a tax on automated equipment and distributing the money collected to the technologically unemployed?

12 What would be the likely consequences of one country restricting the use of automation while its economic competitors did not?

13 Humanitarian and political considerations aside, what economic consideration demands that some of the income of automated machinery be distributed to the population at large?

14 Contrast the economies of scarcity and plenty.

15 Why is it perhaps likely that future systems for distributing income may grow out of existing public assistance programs such as Social Security and welfare?

16 Describe the proposed National Mutual Fund. How would it serve to distribute the wealth created by automated machines?

17 Give some objections that can be raised against the National Mutual Fund. Which of these objections might also apply to other methods of distributing wealth? What groups would be likely to oppose the National Mutual Fund should anyone attempt to put it into effect?

18 Describe some past societies in which people enjoyed a high standard of living without working.

19 Give three benefits that people derive from work. Which of these might still be needed and how might they be derived in a society in which work was not required?

20 List some of the activities in which people might engage in a society without mandatory work.

Topics for Discussion

1 It has been suggested that some jobs should be reserved for humans even though it might be technically feasible to automate them. List some jobs that might fall into this category. What distinguishes these jobs from the ones that should be automated?

2 What are some possible reactions to automation by management, labor, government, and the general public? Describe some of the societies to which particular combinations of reactions might lead.

3 Discuss the pros and cons of the National Mutual Fund.

4 Try to devise some other methods by which the wealth created by automation can be distributed to the people.

5 Describe what life might be like in a society in which most of the work is done by machines. Use your imagination! The attitudes and expectations of people in such a society might be quite different from yours, your friends', and your parents'. What are some of the activities that have been pursued in the past by members of economically privileged classes?

COMPUTERS AND PEOPLE

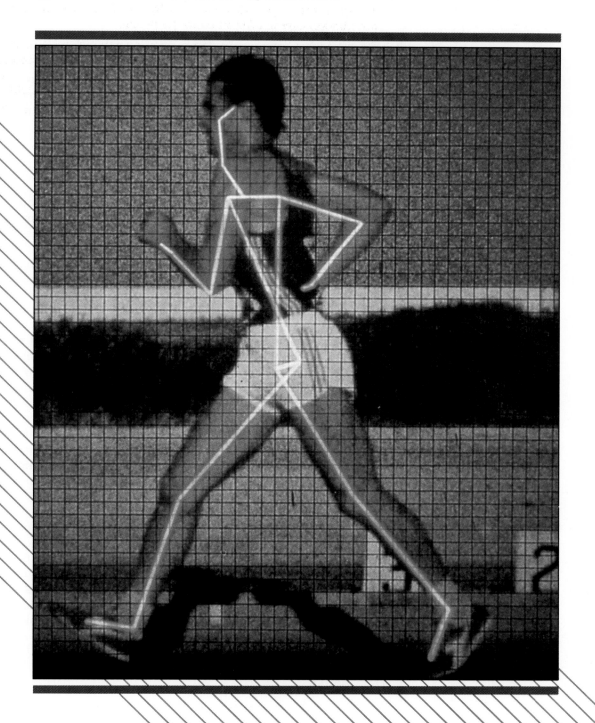

INTRODUCTION

This chapter focuses on several areas in which computers have a strong impact on our everyday lives. Many people fear that their privacy will be compromised by the many computerized files in existence; yet computers also can serve to protect our privacy. Office workers who use computers have complained of high job stress, vision difficulties, and back problems; some have quit otherwise desirable jobs rather than use computers. The reliability of computer systems is of growing concern as computers increasingly are used in ways that enable computer malfunctions to threaten human lives. The feasibility of certain computer systems has played a central role in the public debate over the Reagan administration's Star Wars program.

PRIVACY

Privacy is the ability to control the circulation of information about us. We wish to keep some facts to ourselves either to prevent tarnishing our public image or to prevent others from using the facts as excuses for denying us privileges and benefits. Often we wish to provide information to one person or organization, whom we hope will provide us benefits in return, yet conceal it from others, whom we fear will use it against us. Such selective disclosure of information could become ineffective if different organizations use a common database, or if they compare, merge, or exchange their computerized files.

Concerns about privacy are not unique to computerized systems; so far more misuse of information has occurred in noncomputerized systems than in computerized ones. But the use of computers increases our concerns because of the effectiveness with which computers can store, manipulate, and communicate information. With information about us hidden in many computer memories, we may have trouble determining who has information about us and what they are using it for. Information may be collected without our knowledge, such as by analyzing our financial transactions. Although people change, computers never forget, and thus they increase the chance that some youthful indiscretion will come back to haunt us in later life.

Yet if computers can be used to compromise privacy, they can also be used to protect it. For example, a computer system can keep track of who is allowed to see certain records, and demand passwords or other identification from those seeking access to restricted information. Even certain fields of a record, such as an employee's salary, can be restricted while allowing wider access to the remaining, less sensitive fields. Computer technology is often unique in presenting means for controlling the very problems that it creates. It is up to us to insist that the technology be used for our benefit rather than our detriment.

Data Banks

A *data bank* is any collection of information stored in a computer. The term *data bank* is used in discussing the impact of computers on society, whereas the equivalent term *database* is used in discussing the technical aspects of information storage and retrieval. Like a database, a data bank is made up of files, each of which contains information about a specific subject. The terms *data bank* and *files* are often used interchangeably.

Government Data Banks   The most extensive data banks are maintained by the federal government. The departments of Health, Education, and Human Services maintain files on over 1 billion people. The Internal Revenue Service maintains files on everyone who pays income taxes. Other government agencies that keep records on tens or hundreds of millions of individuals are the departments of Treasury, Commerce, Defense, Justice, State, Agriculture, Transportation, Housing and Urban Development, Labor, and Interior. State and local governments also maintain extensive files on citizens for such purposes as enforcing tax laws and administering public assistance programs. Law enforcement agencies maintain extensive files on people who have had some run-in with the law, many of whom were never convicted of any wrongdoing. Public and private educational institutions keep records on their students' behavior and academic achievements.

Private Data Banks   The private sector also maintains many data banks. Companies keep files on their employees and on the purchasing and payment activities of their customers. Financial institutions keep records from which our financial activities can be deduced; credit reporting agencies keep track of how promptly and diligently we pay our bills. Insurance companies not only keep records on their own policyholders, but they also share industry-wide data banks containing information, such as health and driving records, that may affect insurability. Information provided to one insurance company may be used by another company to deny you insurance. Insurance companies often obtain records from other sources, such as doctors, hospitals, and law enforcement agencies.

Government data banks are often stored in tape libraries such as the one shown here. Civilian data banks are usually stored on disks, allowing the data to be accessed instantly from remote terminals.

Law Enforcement Records　The records kept by law enforcement agencies are of enormous concern because they can focus suspicion on us and can be used to deny us employment, credit, and other benefits. Arrest records cause the most concern. People can be arrested because of mistaken identity, because they were in the wrong place at the wrong time, or because of charges made by someone with a grudge against them. If the person is acquitted, or if charges are dropped, then there should be no blemish on the person's record. Release of arrest records to employers, credit agencies, and the like surely contravenes the traditional assumption that a person is innocent until proven guilty.

How conviction records should be handled is less clear. Employers, credit agencies, and others have understandable reasons for wanting to know if a person has a criminal record. Yet after people who were convicted of crimes have paid their debts to society, should their convictions hang over their heads forever (Computers never forget!), denying them jobs and other benefits? Some maintain that after a person has gone straight for a certain time, the conviction record should be removed from law enforcement data banks or at least not released to outside organizations such as employers. Others go further and argue that such records should not be released even for recently freed prisoners, since it is when a person has just gotten out of prison and is trying to rebuild his or her life that conviction records can do the most harm.

Law enforcement agencies maintain data banks of unsolved crimes, wanted criminals, and stolen property. The most important of these is the *National Crime Information Center (NCIC)* maintained by the federal government. Police officers radio descriptions of suspected persons or property to headquarters, where the data bank is consulted via a computer terminal and the information obtained is radioed back to the officer. Such checks are often made routinely for persons and vehicles stopped for traffic violations. One benefit of such data banks is to alert police officers when they are dealing with dangerous criminals. But errors in such data banks can lead to false arrest and even tragedy. Records for stolen cars sometimes have not been deleted after the cars were recovered, causing the legitimate owners to be arrested for car theft. And several innocent people have been shot by nervous police officers who were erroneously informed that they were dealing with dangerous criminals.

Medical Data Banks　Patients might benefit (particularly in emergencies) if all their medical records were stored in a central data bank. Yet fears over the real possibilities of misuse of medical information will probably prevent such a data bank from being set up. One of the greatest dangers of misuse of medical information is that people will not seek proper medical care if they fear that the information they provide or their doctors' observations will be used against them.

The question is to whom, other than medical workers, should medical information be released? Insurance companies have a legitimate need for medical information on persons they are considering for life or health insurance, yet questions certainly can be raised as to how the information is collected and how it is used to determine insurability. Employers often discriminate against persons with handicaps or serious illnesses, even though these persons are perfectly able to do the jobs for which they are applying. Schools may refuse admittance to persons with certain diseases, even though the diseases are not contagious. The police can use medical information to identify and harass drug users. The right to medical privacy has become a hotly debated issue in connection with AIDS, the victims of which are subject to vicious discrimination.

Record Matching

One of the most frequently and hotly debated privacy questions is *record matching*—comparing records that refer to the same individual but are stored in files maintained by different government agencies. Record matching is usually carried out for law enforcement purposes; often the mere presence of records for the same individual in two different files, or the presence of a record in one file but not another, signals a possible violation of the law. The following are some typical examples of record matching.

- Medicare and Social Security files were compared to identify dead people to whom Social Security payments were still being sent, thus catching relatives and others who forge and cash Social Security checks after the intended recipient has died.

- Files of welfare recipients were compared with payroll files of federal agencies to identify government employees who were illegally receiving welfare payments.

- Social Security files were compared with Selective Service files to identify young men who had obtained Social Security cards but had not registered for the draft. Internal Revenue Service files were used to obtain the current addresses of those who had failed to register. The Selective Service proposed comparing its files with high school graduation lists and state driver's-license files.

- It was proposed that the government build a data bank of all people receiving public assistance. If records from this data bank were compared with those from files in other government agencies, many people who were receiving government payments illegally would be identified. The proposal was attacked on privacy grounds and not put into effect.

The arguments in favor of record matching are (1) the persons affected are breaking the law and should be brought to justice, and (2) when the lawbreakers are collecting government payments illegally, putting a stop to their activities saves the taxpayers money. Opposition focuses on the question of using information for purposes other than those for which it was collected. If people believe that any information they provide the government will be used against them, they may fail to take advantage of certain government programs, and they may provide false or misleading information to many government agencies, whose operations thereby will be impeded.

Universal Identifiers

Each record in a data bank contains an identifier, a data item that uniquely designates the person to whom the record refers. The most obvious iden-

To protect the privacy of their citizens, many countries are restricting the information that international corporations can send out of the country via telecommunications.

tifier is a person's name. Names are not satisfactory identifiers, however, because different people can have the same name and people sometimes spell their names in more than one way. Since names cannot serve as identifiers, each organization must assign identifiers to the people it deals with and insist that the identifiers be included in all communications with the organization. The result is the multitude of account numbers, customer numbers, credit-card numbers, and the like, that everybody has to keep track of.

It has been proposed that each person be assigned a *universal identifier* for use in all computer records. The universal identifier would be that person's "computer name," the unique code by which the person would be known to all computer systems. Each person would have to remember only a single identifier rather than many account and other identification numbers. Each organization would be relieved of the need to develop and administer its own system of assigning identifiers. And there would be less chance of confusing the records of persons with the same name.

Opposition to universal identifiers is strong, however, because they would simplify record matching. To match records belonging to different files, we need some way of determining when two records refer to the same individual. With universal identifiers, this is easy—two records match if they have the same universal identifier. If a separate system of identifiers is used for each file, however, matching is difficult or impossible, since there is no way of knowing when identifiers from different files refer to the same person.

The Social Security number is used as an identifier not only by the Social Security Administration but by the Internal Revenue Service and many other agencies. For years, the Social Security number has been on its way to becoming a universal identifier.

The Privacy Act of 1974 gave individuals the right to refuse to supply their Social Security numbers for any purpose not authorized by law. Later legislation, however, allowed exceptions to this prohibition, particularly for state government systems that were already organized around Social Security numbers when the Privacy Act was passed. As a result, the use of Social Security numbers by state and federal agencies is still widespread. As far as many branches of government are concerned, the Social Security number is a universal identifier.

Mailing Lists

Business, political, and charitable organizations use mailing lists that classify people according to their interests, their purchasing habits, the political causes they support, and the charities to which they contribute. Your name is likely to appear on lists compiled and sold by magazines you subscribe to, companies you trade with and perhaps even the one you work for, associations you belong to, and the causes you contribute to.

As long as mailing lists are used only to advertise products and appeal for contributions, it is hard to see what harm is done. Studies show that most people don't object to unsolicited mail. And those who do can have their names placed on a list maintained by the Direct Mail Marketing Association (DMMA). At least once a year, most large mailers remove from their lists any names that also appear on the DMMA list.

Yet it is also clear that information stored on mailing lists can be misused, particularly when it indicates a person's political preferences or the causes to which a person contributes. Some controls may be needed on how information about people's personal habits is collected and used. At a minimum, people should have the right to prohibit the organizations with which they deal from putting their names on a mailing list. Most professional organizations already offer their members this choice.

Electronic funds transfer (EFT) systems can be used to build extensive dossiers on the income we receive, the purchases we make, and the causes we contribute to. In the cashless society prophesied by some, few of our activities could escape the notice of such a system. As EFT becomes more widespread, citizens must be alert for possible misuses of the data stored in EFT systems.

Privacy Legislation

In response to concerns about privacy, Congress has passed several laws that address the issue. Many states have also passed privacy legislation. Like almost everything else about privacy, privacy laws are controversial. The organizations affected complain that the laws are too restrictive and complying with them is too expensive. Citizens' advocates, on the other hand, complain that current laws do not go far enough in protecting the rights of citizens.

The *Privacy Act of 1974* is the most important and comprehensive piece of privacy legislation. It applies to all federal agencies except for intelligence, law enforcement, and certain other sensitive government agencies. Its major provisions are as follows:

- Secret files are prohibited. Each agency must publish annually in the *Federal Register* a description of each file that it keeps and the kind of information that is stored in it.

- Individuals have the right to inspect the records kept on them and to demand that erroneous information be corrected. If an agency refuses to make a correction, it must give its reason in writing, and the refusal can be challenged in court.

- Information cannot be released without the written consent of the individual. For example, federal agencies cannot sell mailing lists containing the names and addresses of the people in their files.

- Information cannot be used for purposes other than those for which it was collected.

- Information cannot be released without the written consent of the individual. For example, federal agencies cannot sell mailing lists containing the names and addresses of the people in their files.

- Information cannot be used for purposes other than those for which it was collected.

- Information cannot be transferred from one federal agency to another without the individual's written consent.

- There are some exceptions to the restrictions on the release, misuse, and transfer of information. Information can be released to a law enforcement agency, to a congressional committee, in response to a court order, or to help someone with an urgent health problem. Statistical and historical information can also be released. The law also permits routine transfers, such as transferring payroll information to the Treasury Department so that employees' checks can be printed and mailed. Citizens' advocates charge that some agencies have misused this provision by defining possibly controversial transfers as routine. For example, the Internal Revenue Service defines transfers to all federal agencies as "routine."

- Individuals have the right to refuse to supply their Social Security number for any purpose not required by federal law. This provision, designed to prevent the Social Security number from becoming a universal identifier, was later weakened to allow other government agencies, such as state driver's-license bureaus, to require individuals to supply their Social Security numbers.

Several other acts of Congress also affect privacy and place restrictions on the collection and dissemination of information. The Fair Credit Reporting Act of 1970 governs the collection and reporting of credit information; persons who are denied credit must be given copies of the information that was used to make the decision. The Education Privacy Act of 1974 mandates the confidentiality of school records. The Right to Financial Privacy Act of 1978 spells out the procedures that federal agencies must follow to obtain an individual's banking or credit union records.

Adjustable workstation lamps can direct light on the user's papers and the computer keyboard while avoiding reflections and glare on the computer screen.

◣ HUMAN FACTORS IN THE WORKPLACE

As more and more jobs require people to use computers, questions have arisen about the impact of computers on employees, particularly office workers. Some employees are so terrified of computers that they will quit before they will try to learn to use a computer. The difficulty of learning to use computers is frustrating for employees and expensive for employers. Some users of video display terminals (VDTs) complain of physical ailments, such as eyestrain, back pains, and worse. The discipline that addresses these problems is known by two names: the cryptic *ergonomics* and the clumsy *human-factors analysis*.

The VDT Controversy

Many people spend their entire working day using video display terminals. Often such workers are telephone operators who use their terminals to enter information provided by callers (such as orders and requests for reservations) and to obtain information requested by callers (such as flight departure and arrival times). Other VDT workers enter information from paper forms such as insurance applications. Both kinds of VDT users are often under intense pressure to increase their productivity: to handle as many calls or forms as possible each day. Such pressure produces very high job stress for VDT workers.

Steady VDT users often complain of a variety of physical ailments, such as eyestrain and neck, back, and wrist pain. A study at the University of California at Berkeley indicates that regular work in front of a VDT screen may cause a premature loss of the ability to focus the eyes, thus requiring the use of glasses. This problem is not limited to VDT users, however; similar results have been found for people who read a lot, thus justifying the traditional image of a bookish person as someone who wears glasses. Apparently, large amounts of time spent looking at a surface a short distance away reduce the ability of the eyes to focus on objects at other distances.

By far the most serious complaint is that VDT use causes pregnant women to have miscarriages. Although long discounted by employers and VDT manufacturers, this complaint seems to have been given credence by a study published in 1988 by the Kaiser Permanente Medical Care Program. The study finds that pregnant women who use VDTs more than 20 hours a week are almost twice as likely to have miscarriages as other female office workers. Further research is under way to confirm these findings and, if they are confirmed, to determine the exact cause of the miscarriages.

Some people have sought to attribute these problems to radiation produced by the terminals. Repeated studies have shown that the only radiation from VDTs consists of low-level radio waves, a kind of radiation that is common in the environment because it is produced by every radio transmitter. There is no evidence that low-level radiation of this kind is harmful, although studies are still under way to determine any possible long-term effects. In short, radiation is not considered a likely cause of the problems suffered by VDT users. More likely causes are the rigid posture needed to view the screen and use the keyboard, the seeing difficulties resulting from reflections on the screen, the apparent loss of eye-focusing due to extensive reading, and the high job stress produced by the demand for high productivity.

This portable ergonomic workstation can be rolled to wherever a computer is needed, preventing users from having to place computers on desks or tables that may be at the wrong height.

Computerized Worker Monitoring

VDTs and other computerized equipment can keep track of workers' performance. For example, the computer to which a VDT is connected can record and report the number of transactions processed by the worker for each hour of the workday. A word-processing workstation can keep track of the number of keys that the operator strikes in any given time period.

Office workers' unions have criticized such monitoring on the grounds that it invades workers' privacy and increases job stress. Whether employers invade employees' privacy by monitoring their performance in the workplace is certainly a debatable question. But there seems little doubt that such monitoring can only increase the on-the-job tension that is a prime suspect in many of the medical problems of VDT users.

Ergonomic Office Equipment

The term *ergonomic* is used as an adjective to describe office equipment designed in accordance with the findings of human-factors research. Designers of ergonomic workstations, keyboards, displays, office furniture, and lighting fixtures strive to adapt the equipment to the needs of human workers rather than forcing the workers to adapt themselves to hard-to-use equipment.

What are some of the problems that ergonomics has addressed? Consider lighting. Many offices use overhead lights, but overhead lights in front of a workstation can get in the worker's eyes, and lights behind a workstation may wash out the terminal screen or even be reflected in it. On the other hand, the entire room cannot be darkened like a video-game arcade because most terminal users need to work with paper copy, which must be properly illuminated. Also, an overly dark room depresses workers and lowers morale. One solution is to provide an adjustable desk lamp for each worker, although care must be taken to see that a lamp at one workstation is not a source of glare for other workstations.

Video display terminals and the furniture used with them need to be adjustable to help users avoid neck pains, back pains, and fatigue. The height of the table on which the terminal rests should be adjustable, and it should be possible to tilt and rotate the display, both for operator comfort and as a means of avoiding glare. The keyboard should be separate from the display so the operator can position the keyboard anywhere on the worktable.

Another innovation is a lightweight keyboard attached to the rest of the terminal by a long cable; this allows the keyboard to be placed in the operator's lap. Typing with a keyboard in your lap might seem awkward at first, but its advantages quickly become obvious. Your hands and arms are in a relaxed position, so they tire less quickly. And you can place the copy you are typing from directly in front of you on the worktable, instead of placing it beside the terminal and turning you head to see it.

Adjustable, ergonomically designed chairs can help avoid the back pains that afflict many VDT users.

Learning to Use Computers

A typical software package contains one or more thick reference manuals. Unfortunately, busy users seldom have the time or inclination to study such manuals; indeed, persons not skilled at self-study may be unable to master so much information without assistance. Training courses are available for popular software packages; however, these are expensive for the employer not only because of the cost of the course but because of the time that workers are away from their jobs while attending. Major software producers provide telephone support in the form of hot lines that users can call with questions and problems. The expense of providing telephone support either reduces the profits of the software producer or, if the cost is passed on to the consumer, increases the cost of software; for this reason, some software producers charge separately for telephone support, thereby providing an additional expense for employers.

One approach to the training problem is to make the user interface sufficiently self-explanatory so that little training is needed. Instead of having to type commands, users can select them from menus. The computer displays a list of available options; the user makes a selection by pressing a key or manipulating a mouse. For complex commands, a series of menus may have to be used. Selecting an item from one menu causes the computer to display another menu. Selecting an item from this menu causes the computer to display still another menu, and so on.

Such interfaces often make extensive use of icons, small drawings that represent hardware and software components. By using a mouse to point to the icons and move them around on the screen, the user can carry out operations with the corresponding system components; for example, a user can erase a file by depositing a file-folder icon in a trash-can icon. The success of such interfaces usually hinges on the choice of a suitable metaphor; the metaphor enables the operation of the computer system to

The user can operate this graphics workstation by selecting commands from an input pad with a stylus (shown lying on the pad).

be presented in terms of actions with which the user is already familiar, such as working with papers on a desktop or files in a filing cabinet.

Novice and experienced users may prefer to interact with the system in different ways. Novices may prefer to be led by the hand with a series of menus. Experienced users, however, may prefer to give the computer a single, complex command that, once memorized, can be typed in more quickly that it is possible to work through a long sequence of menus. A well-designed system should cater to the needs of both novice and experienced users.

Documentation, the manuals that describe how to use a computer system, are often inadequate, poorly written, and directed to computer programmers instead of novice users. Although much can be done to improve manuals, much current work has focused on eliminating them altogether. Tutorial programs can lead users by the hand through the basic operations of a system; the tutorial programs provided by some major software manufacturers make excellent use of CAI techniques. Many systems feature a help key that causes the system to display information about the operation the user is currently attempting. In the future, artificial intelligence techniques might be used to analyze the user's mistakes and provide appropriate advice.

RELIABILITY AND FEASIBILITY

Hardware and software malfunctions were once just annoyances that might delay our paychecks or cause us to be presented with bills demanding the payment of $0.00. Now, however, with computers being used in more and more applications where malfunctions can threaten our safety, hardware and software reliability is of vital concern to everyone. When proposed computer applications go far beyond the current state of the art, we are justified in questioning whether the proposed applications are feasible, that is, whether they ever can be made to work reliably.

Reliability

Computer systems are playing increasingly vital roles in such areas as transportation, communication, and medicine. Malfunctions in such systems threaten us not only with inconvenience but with injury and death.

For example, when the Bay Area Rapid Transit System (BART) was first put into service in the San Francisco Bay Area, computer problems often caused trains to behave in unpredictable ways. Sometimes they would fail to stop at stations, sometimes they would stop between stations, and in one case the computer drove a train over a (fortunately small) embankment. The computer would imagine phantom trains that did not exist and, even worse, would forget about real trains. Fortunately, no one was seriously injured and the problems were eventually fixed. But while the bugs were being worked out, riding the system must have been an unwanted adventure.

Air traffic controllers have long complained of the unreliability of air-traffic-control computers, which often fail at critical times and sometimes exhibit other problems such as transposing the data associated with different airplanes. The current computer system is to be replaced by an entirely new one in the 1990s; the new system ultimately should be more reliable than the old, but we cannot help but wonder what problems will arise while the new hardware and software are being debugged.

Computers have long been used to control spacecraft and are increasingly being used for similar purposes in civilian aircraft. The latest airliners substitute computer displays for many conventional aircraft instruments and provide fly-by-wire capabilities in which the pilot controls the aircraft via the onboard computer. Yet there are frighteningly many examples of malfunctions of aerospace computers as well as their improper operation by flight crews. Gemini V, an early space mission, landed 100 miles off target because a programmer had forgotten to take into account the rotation of the earth. During the first moon landing, the computer in the lunar module failed due to software problems, and emergency intervention by the pilot was required to save the mission. The first launch of a space shuttle was delayed when—again due to a software problem—the onboard computers failed to synchronize with one another. In 1979, an Air New Zealand airliner crashed into a mountain because data in the navigational computer had been changed without the knowledge of the flight crew. It is believed that incorrect course data entered into a navigational computer caused Korean Airlines Flight 007 to fly into Russian airspace, where it was shot down.

In Chapter 10 we discussed the tragic deaths and injuries that resulted from software errors in the Therac 25 radiation therapy system. Now the FDA has announced plans to regulate software used in medical devices. But it is unclear how successful FDA-mandated testing will be in uncovering errors that manifest themselves only in unusual circumstances, as in the Therac-25 case in which correcting a particular operator error in a particular way triggered the software bug.

To improve reliability in critical applications, engineers have turned to *fault-tolerant computer systems*, which can operate reliably in spite of hardware failures and software bugs. Such systems are widely used in the aerospace industry and to control telephone switching equipment. Fault-tolerant systems are based on the concept of *redundancy*, of duplicating components that are subject to failure. For example, a calculation may be carried out independently by three or more computers; if their results disagree, a vote is taken to arrive at the correct result, and users are warned of malfunctions in those computers that disagree with the majority. Two computers can monitor one another; if either computer detects an error in the other, it raises an alarm that transfers control of the system to the computer that is functioning properly. Fault tolerance in software can be provided by doing the same calculation with several independently developed pieces of software and again using a majority vote to determine the correct results.

Unfortunately, the redundancy of fault-tolerant systems greatly increases the cost of such systems and the time required to develop them. Also, the use of fault-tolerant hardware increases the complexity of the

mined enemy may well devise ways to defeat the system that were not thought of by those who designed the testing programs.

It has been suggested that automatic program verification techniques could be used to prove the correctness of the SDI software. There are two problems with this. First, such techniques, which are still highly experimental, currently are capable of handling only the simplest programs; they cannot come anywhere near to verifying the millions of lines of code needed for SDI. Second, such techniques at best can check code against human-devised program specifications. Yet formulating the extremely complex specifications for the SDI software would be one of the major challenges of building the system, particularly since the requirements for the system would change with our estimates of Soviet military capabilities.

For these reasons and others, most computer scientists are highly skeptical of the feasibility of the software required by the Strategic Defense Initiative.

Summary

Privacy is our ability to control the use of information about us, to provide information to those who will use it to our benefit yet deny the same information to those who might use it against us. Many people fear that their privacy will be compromised by the numerous computerized data banks maintained by federal, state, and local governments as well as by a variety of private organizations. The public data banks maintained by law enforcement agencies are of particular concern, as are the private data banks maintained by insurance companies and credit reporting agencies.

Record matching refers to combining records about the same individual that are stored in different files. Often the mere presence of a record for a person in two different files, or its presence in one file but not another, is a cause for suspicion. While record matching sometimes can aid law enforcement activities, its use often violates the fundamental principle of privacy that information should not be used for purposes other than those for which it was collected.

It has been suggested that each person be assigned a unique universal identifier to replace the many account and identification numbers we all have to contend with now. Despite the convenience of universal identifiers to individuals and organizations, their proposed use has received little support and much criticism because they would greatly simplify the process of record matching. Despite legislation to restrict its use, the Social Security number is a de facto universal identifier for many federal, state, and local government agencies.

Many laws guaranteeing privacy have been passed by federal, state, and local governments. The following requirements are typical of most privacy legislation:

■ The existence of all files and data banks must be disclosed.

■ Individuals have the right to examine their own records and challenge mistakes.

■ Except by due process of law, information must not be released, transferred to other agencies, or used for purposes other than those for which it was collected.

As computers become more and more common in the workplace, employers and employees are becoming increasingly concerned with the impact of computer systems on the people who use them. Regular users of video display terminals suffer from vision problems; neck, back, and wrist pains; and possibly even miscarriages. Some of these problems may be alleviated by ergonomic computer equipment and office furniture, which are especially designed to minimize adverse effects on users. Electronic monitoring of workers' performance increases job stress, which may contribute to some of the aforementioned medical problems. The difficulty of training people to use computer systems is a burden on employees, employers, and software producers.

The reliability of computer systems becomes more and more crucial as computers play ever increasing roles in such vital activities as controlling trains and airplanes, routing telephone calls, delivering medical treatment, and defending our country against enemy attack. Both in our professions and as voters we may be called upon to decide whether a proposed computer system is feasible, that is, whether it is ever likely to work reliably, if it can be made to work at all. A case in point is the debate over the feasibility of the Strategic Defense Initiative, in which an enormously complex computer system would use futuristic weapons to destroy attacking ballistic missiles and warheads.

Vocabulary Review

data bank	identifier	redundancy
ergonomics	National Crime	Strategic Defense
fault-tolerant	Information Center	Initiative (SDI)
computer system	(NCIC)	universal identifier
human-factors	Privacy Act of 1974	
analysis	record matching	

For Further Reading

Borning, Alan. "Computer System Reliability and Nuclear War." *Communications of the ACM*, February 1987, pp. 112–131.

Dallaire, Gene, et al. "Computer Matching: Should It Be Banned?" *Communications of the ACM*, June 1984, pp. 537–545

Kling, Rob. "Value Conflicts and Social Choices in Electronic Funds Transfer Systems." *Communications of the ACM*, August 1978, pp. 642–656.

Ledgard, Henry. "Misconceptions in Human Factors." *Abacus*, Winter 1986, pp. 21–27.

Lin, Herbert. "The Development of Software for Ballistic-Missle Defense." *Scientific American*, December 1985, pp. 46–53.

Neier, Ayeh. *Dossier: The Secret Files They Keep on You.* New York: Stein and Day, 1975.

Nelson, Greg and David Redell. "The Star Wars Computer System." *Abacus*, Winter 1986, pp. 8–20.

Secretary's Advisory Committee on Automated Personal Data Systems. *Records, Computers, and the Rights of Citizens.* Cambridge: Massachusetts Institute of Technology, 1973.

Special Section on the Human Aspects of Computing. *Communications of the ACM*, July 1986, 593–647.

◥ Review Questions

1 In what contexts are the terms data bank and database used?

2 List some government agencies that maintain substantial data banks.

3 What fundamental human right is violated by the release of arrest records?

4 How might an offender's rehabilitation be retarded or prevented by the release of conviction records?

5 What are the advantages of law enforcement data banks of crimes, criminals, and stolen property? How have errors in such data banks resulted in innocent citizens being arrested or shot?

6 What would be the advantage of storing everyone's medical records in a central data bank? What are some ways that the information in such a data bank could be misused?

7 For what purposes do insurance companies and credit reporting agencies maintain data banks?

8 What is the purpose of record matching? What fundamental principle of privacy does record matching threaten?

9 What are universal identifiers? What would be the advantages of using them? What threats to privacy do they pose?

10 To what extent is the Social Security number a de facto universal identifier?

11 From what sources is data for mailing lists collected? What are some possible abuses of mailing lists?

12 What dangers to privacy are posed by EFT systems?

13 Give the major provisions of the Privacy Act of 1974.

14 Describe the medical problems experienced by regular VDT users.

15 What is electronic worker monitoring and why is it controversial?

16 Discuss some of the problems addressed by ergonomics.

17 Discuss the difficulty of training people to use computer systems and the problems this presents for employees, employers, and software producers.

18 Characterize the kinds of computer systems in which reliability is of greatest concern.

19 Why might FDA regulation do little to prevent the kind of tragic software error that occurred in the Therac 25?

20 Why are most computer scientists skeptical about the feasibility of the Strategic Defense Initiative?

Topics for Discussion

1 Discuss the pros and cons of combining all the files maintained by federal agencies into a single federal data bank.

2 Discuss the record matching controversy. Under what circumstances should people's privacy be sacrificed for the sake of law enforcement?

3 Discuss the attitudes of people toward universal identifiers. Ask some of your friends how they feel about the matter and discuss their responses. Are some of the attitudes based more on emotion than logic?

4 Should employers allow female VDT users to transfer to other jobs during pregnancy until such time as further investigation reveals the exact connection, if any, between VDT use and miscarriages?

5 What actions might ordinary people take if they feel that a computer system that affects them is dangerously unreliable?

6 Debate the feasibility of the Strategic Defense Initiative.

Buying a Personal Computer

INTRODUCTION

Buying your first computer can be a confusing and intimidating experience; prospective computer purchasers are faced with a bewildering variety of computers, hardware options, peripheral devices, and software packages. Fortunately, as a reader of *The Mind Tool,* you are far more knowledgeable about computer hardware and software than most first-time computer purchasers (the information in Chapters 1, 3–4, and 6–9 should be particularly helpful). If your study of computer literacy has provided you with hands-on experience with popular hardware and software, you are in an even better position to select your own system. This appendix provides some additional hints for individuals selecting computers for personal use.

DECIDE HOW YOU WILL USE YOUR COMPUTER

You should begin by thinking about how you intend to use your computer, since the intended application will have considerable influence on your choice of hardware and software. For example, a computer intended primarily for game playing needs color, graphics, and sound capabilities as well as game-playing accessories such as game-paddles and joysticks; however, it probably does not need a hard disk, a large memory, or a high-quality printer. On the other hand, a computer intended for word processing may not need color, graphics, or sound, but it would need a high-quality printer and (depending on the word-processing software used) may need a large memory and a hard disk.

Many home computers are purchased for young people.

You must select the proper hardware components and software packages to get a computer system that meets your needs.

If you have a specialized application, then publications in your field of interest can help you make a selection. For example, if wish to use your computer to compose music or control musical instruments, you can turn to articles in music technology magazines such as *Keyboard* and *Electronic Musician* for information on suitable hardware and software. Dealers that cater to your particular field might carry suitable computer systems; for example, some musical-instrument dealers carry computer hardware and software for musicians.

It is, of course, software that provides computers with their useful capabilities, so a good place to start is to see what software is available for your application. Trying out different software packages will help you determine how well available hardware and software will do the job you have in mind. You may be able to try out software at work, at school, or on friends' computers. Some computer dealers will allow you to try out software packages on showroom computers, particularly if you let it be known that you are contemplating a substantial purchase.

Software packages and advertisements generally give some information about the computer system needed to run the software; these system requirements include the kind of computer, the amount of memory needed, the kind of video display needed, and any needed peripherals such as a printer or a hard disk. Noting the system requirements for software packages that you examine can help considerably in selecting the hardware for your computer system.

◣ GETTING MORE INFORMATION

Clearly, the more information you have about the strengths and weaknesses of the systems you are considering, the better position you will be in to make your decision. Good sources of information are computer books and magazines, users groups and individual users, recommendations of

Software packages in a computer store.

salespeople, and (for persons who already have access to a computer and modem) on-line information services.

Magazines devoted to brands or kinds of computers can be found on magazine racks, in bookstores, and in computer stores. There are also magazines devoted to particular areas of application, such as desktop publishing. Computer magazines provide articles on various applications, reviews of new hardware and software, columns that answer reader questions, and tutorial articles on computing topics. Letters from readers often comment on the strengths and weaknesses of hardware and software, particularly that which has been reviewed in previous issues. Even the advertisements can be helpful by informing you of the range of hardware and software available for use with a particular computer system.

Most computer owners will be happy to discuss their systems with you and give you advice in selecting your own system. In many areas there are users groups that meet regularly to discuss computers and their applications; joining such a group will give you the opportunity seek advice and opinions from a wide variety of users.

When you visit computer stores, sales personnel will recommend hardware and software for your application. Such recommendations can be valuable. Realistically, however, you must keep in mind that salespeople often have their own objectives, such as selling the system that will yield the highest commission or getting rid of a system that is not selling well. The recommendations of computer salespeople must be received in the same way as recommendations from other sales representatives such as automobile dealers, real-estate agents, and stockbrokers: listen to what they have to say, but make your own decisions.

On-line information services, such as CompuServe and BIX (Byte Information Exchange) offer computer conferences devoted to different brands of computer, to different kinds of peripherals such as printers, and to different applications areas such as word processing. The merits of particular items of hardware and software are debated frequently, and questions placed in such conferences usually receive prompt answers from knowledgeable users. Of course, you must have a computer and modem to use these services, so they are not helpful to first-time purchasers. Once you have a computer, however, you may find them extremely helpful in choosing peripherals, software, and you next computer.

SELECTING A DEALER

Computer hardware and software are available through a variety of outlets including computer stores, mail-order houses, consumer-electronics stores, department stores, and discount stores; software is also sold in book stores. Your choice of a supplier will be influenced by three considerations: availability, price, and support.

Many stores specialize in one or two brands of merchandise, so the system you are interested in may not be available from all outlets. Also, systems from some major manufacturers, such as IBM and Apple, are almost never available through mail order because those manufacturers work hard to prevent their systems from reaching mail-order outlets.

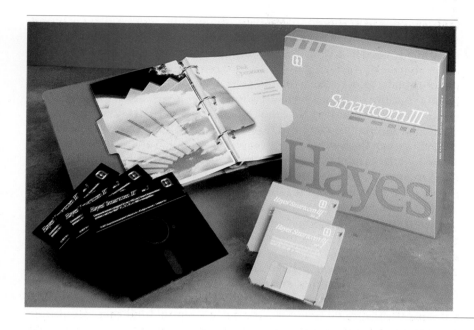

Software package for Smartcom III, a communications program for use with Hayes modems.

The actual selling price of a product, known as its street price, is often substantially less than the manufacturer's suggested retail price and may vary considerably from one vendor to another. Because of price fluctuations, mail-order vendors may ask you to telephone for the prices on some products, the street prices of which are likely to change during the several months that elapse between when an advertisement is submitted and when it actually appears in print. Generally, mail-order suppliers and discount houses will have lower prices than computer stores, but they may not provide the same level of support.

Support is the assistance that vendors provide to help customers get the best use out of their purchases. Support most often consists of answering customers' questions, either in person or by telephone. In some cases, however, it may consist of step-by-step demonstrations of procedures for using a particular piece of hardware or software. Support is particularly important to first-time purchasers, who easily can overlook some minor detail that will prevent their hardware or software from working properly. The need for support is no reflection on the user's intelligence; for example, a famous science writer, renown for the breadth and depth of his knowledge, reported that he needed repeated visits from a computer-company representative before he was able to use his newly acquired computer for word processing.

Generally, computer stores charge higher prices but provide more support than other outlets. However, computer stores can vary considerably in the degree of support that they are willing or able to provide. Some may be much less happy to talk to you after the sale than they were before; others may not be knowledgeable enough to provide you with the help you need. The latter situation is particularly common for software because it is difficult for store personnel to become adept at using all popular software packages. Thus before paying higher prices in anticipation of

To keep your computer working, you will need to purchase supplies such as printer paper, printer ribbons, and diskettes.

better service, you should try to talk to some of the store's other customers to see if the hoped-for support actually will be forthcoming. (A local users group is a good place to meet other customers of local dealers.) On the other hand, if you can find a knowledgeable dealer who is genuinely helpful both before and after the sale, then you may well be better off giving that dealer all your business in spite of lower prices elsewhere.

There is no question that mail-order prices are attractive; if price is a major consideration, then ordering by mail may let you get a substantially better system than would otherwise be possible. There are, of course, certain dangers to mail order. Some companies have been slow to deliver, have delivered defective merchandise, and have not lived up to warranties. There have even been some outright scams, in which a company collected money for as long as possible, then left town one step ahead of the police.

One step worth taking is to check back issues of computer magazines to see how long the mail-order dealer has been in business; those who have been advertising for a year or more are less likely to be fly-by-night operations than those that have recently appeared on the scene. You may wish to place a small order and see how it is handled before you trust the dealer with a large order. As with all kinds of dealers, discussions with satisfied or dissatisfied customers are the best way of finding out in advance what kind of service to expect.

Unless budget considerations are of paramount importance, the author suggests buying your first computer system from a local dealer with a reputation for good support. After you have gained some experience, however, you may well wish to consider mail-order dealers for expansion boards and peripherals (if you are confident of your ability to install them) and software (particularly if the software producer offers telephone support directly to customers).

Diskette file boxes can help you organize the large number of diskettes that most computer owners accumulate.

◣ WARRANTIES AND SERVICE CONTRACTS

As with most equipment purchased for the home or office, a computer is covered by a warranty, and a service contract often can be purchased to supplement and extend the warranty. A major point of difference among service contracts is how the faulty equipment will be delivered to and returned from the repair shop. The following list gives the usual options in order of increasing convenience and cost:

- **Mail-in Service** You must ship the equipment to the repair facility, which will ship it back to you when repairs are complete. This option is time consuming, expensive (you may have to pay shipping charges both ways), and inconvenient (computer equipment is often heavy and bulky, yet must be packed with great care to prevent damage). If you get stuck with this option, make sure that you obtain and retain the original cartons and packing materials in which your equipment was shipped from the factory.

- **Carry-in Service** You carry your equipment to the repair shop and pick it up when it has been repaired. If the repair shop is in the same city that you live in, this option is usually not too inconvenient. If you live in a small town, however, "carry-in" may mean carrying your system to a repair shop in the nearest major city.

- **Courier pickup** A courier picks up your equipment and returns it to you when it has been repaired. This option may be limited geographically to areas that are within reasonable distances of repair facilities.

- **On-site service** A service technician comes to your home or office and fixes your system. This is clearly the most convenient option, but

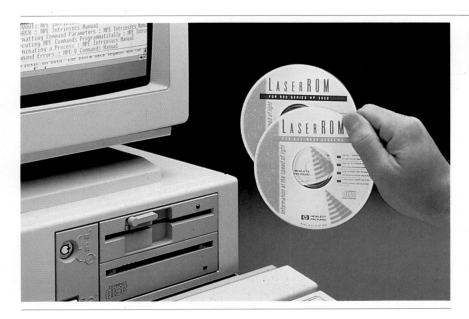

As time goes on, computer owners will be able to purchase more and more directories, reference manuals, and other information on CD-ROMs.

it is also the most expensive and may be even more limited geographically than courier pickup.

Usually, only mail-in and carry-in service are offered by standard warranties. The other options, if they are available at all, cost extra.

The majority of software carries little if any warranty. Most software producers will replace defective disks, and many will issue free updates (revised versions) when major bugs are discovered. In general, however, software is sold "as is" and you have no legal recourse if it does not perform as advertised.

As a result of public pressure and increasing competitiveness in the industry, some forward-looking software producers are offering better warranties. Some will warrant software to perform as advertised, and a few have even offered money-back guarantees of satisfaction. Software producers who offer reasonable warranties are far more deserving of your business than those who go to great lengths to disclaim all responsibility for the performance of their products.

acoustic coupler A device for sending and receiving data transmissions over a standard telephone set without connecting the modem directly to the telephone line. Acoustic couplers are used only when direct connection is impossible, as with pay phones, motel-room phones, and multiline business phones. See **direct-connect modem.**

active cell The cell of an electronic spreadsheet on which the cursor is positioned and on which the attention of the spreadsheet program is focused.

address A code that designates a particular memory location. If memory locations are analogous to post office boxes, then addresses are analogous to post office box numbers.

algorithm A set of step-by-step instructions guaranteed to solve a particular problem. An algorithm can be stated in any form, such as English, mathematical formulas, or diagrams. A program, on the other hand, must be written in a programming language that is suitable for computer processing. See **program.**

allocation table A table giving the location of all the unused space on a disk. The allocation table must be consulted and updated when storing new files on a disk, and it must be updated when files are deleted lest the space occupied by the deleted files be lost forever.

analog Refers to information representation by means of continuously varying quantities rather than by digital codes. An analog clock or watch, for example, represents the time by the continuously varying positions of the hands. See **digital.**

answer mode The mode in which a modem must be placed to receive calls from other computers. See **originate mode.**

arithmetic/logic unit The part of the central processing unit that carries out arithmetical and logical calculations. We can think of it as the computer's calculator.

artificial intelligence The study of how to make computers smarter by programming them to emulate human reasoning.

ASCII code The American Standard Code for Information Interchange, a character code almost universally used by microcomputers and minicomputers. See **EBCDIC code.**

assembler A language processor that translates programs from assembly language into machine language.

assembly language A low-level programming language similar to machine language but allowing convenient abbreviations for operation codes and addresses.

auxiliary memory The component of a computer system used for long-term storage of large amounts of data. Magnetic tape and magnetic disk are common forms of auxiliary memory. Other names for auxiliary memory are auxiliary storage and secondary storage.

backup copy An extra copy of a program or data file that is kept in a safe place for use in the event that the working copy is destroyed by computer malfunction, operator error, or failure of the magnetic tape or magnetic disk on which it is recorded.

Basic Beginner's all-purpose symbolic instruction code, an easy-to-learn programming language widely used by students, educators, hobbyists, and owners of personal computers.

baud A measure of the rate at which data is transmitted over a communications link. In computing (but not in communications engineering) baud is synonymous with bits per second, which is the preferred term.

binary code A coding scheme that represents information using only the two binary digits 0 and 1.

binary digit One of the two digits, 0 and 1, used to code information in a form suitable for computer processing.

binary notation A number system using only the two binary digits 0 and 1, which play the same roles as the decimal digits 0 through 9 do in the more familiar decimal notation.

bit A binary digit.

bit copier A program or hardware device designed to defeat copy protection schemes by copying the individual bits recorded on a disk, ignoring as far as possible the unorthodox formatting intended to prevent copying.

bit-mapped display A display for which the color and intensity of each dot or pixel can be controlled individually. It is in contrast to a text display on which only certain predefined patterns, such as the letters of the alphabet, can be displayed.

bits per second (bps) A measure of the rate at which data is transmitted over a communications link. This term is preferred to baud, which is often used inaccurately to mean bits per second. Microcomputers often send and receive data at 300, 1200, 2400, or 9600 bps.

Boolean algebra The algebra of logic, named after its inventor, the English mathematician George Boole.

boot To automatically load the operating system when a computer is first turned on.

bug An error in a program.

bulletin board A small-scale information service usually operated by an individual as a hobby. See **information service**.

bus A group of wires over which the components of a computer exchange data and control signals.

byte A group of eight bits. The information storage capacity of a memory device is usually measured in bytes.

cathode ray tube (CRT) The display tube used in television sets, video displays, radar sets, and laboratory instruments. A video display is sometimes called a CRT display, a CRT, or just a "tube."

CD ROM A form of optical disc that adheres to the same standards, and can be manufactured with the same equipment, as the compact discs used for sound recording.

cell One of the rectangular blocks composing a spreadsheet; the intersection of each row and column of the spreadsheet defines a cell. Each cell can hold a label, a value, or a formula. See **active cell**, **spreadsheet program**.

central processing unit (CPU) The part of a computer that carries out calculations and follows program instructions. See **arithmetic/logic unit**, **control unit**, **microprocessor**.

chip A tiny wafer of silicon containing a multitude of electronic components. Often each chip serves as a major component of a computer system, such as a microprocessor or a memory unit.

circuit board A thin fiberglass and resin board on which electronic components are mounted. The components are connected by one or more layers of copper-foil wiring. Also called a circuit card. See **expansion card**.

coaxial cable A cable similar to that used for cable television. Computers in a local area network are often connected by coaxial cables.

compiler A language processor that translates programs from a higher-level programming language into the machine language that the central processing unit can execute. See **interpreter**.

computer A machine that stores, manipulates, and communicates information in accordance with the step-by-step instructions contained in a program. See **algorithm, program.**

computer system All the hardware and software making up a computer installation.

control character A character code intended to control an output device or convey a command to a program rather than to produce a printed character. Examples of control characters are *carriage return*, which returns the printing head to the left margin, and *line feed*, which moves the printing head to a new line.

control key A key, usually marked Ctrl, that is held down to type control characters. For example, the control character *line feed* is often designated Ctrl-J because it can be typed by pressing J while the Ctrl key is held down.

control unit The part of the central processing unit that executes the user's program. The control unit sends control signals to other hardware components to get the program instructions carried out.

copy protection A method for preventing users from making unauthorized copies of software. Copy-protection schemes often employ unorthodox disk formatting to confuse copying programs.

core A now obsolete form of main memory made up of tiny magnetic rings called cores. Old-timers in the computing field still often refer to main memory as "core."

cursor An underline or highlighted block, often flashing, that indicates the part of the display that will be affected by a command.

cursor control keys Keys marked with arrows that can be used to move the cursor left, right, up, or down on the display.

daisy-wheel printer A letter-quality printer in which the type is mounted on bars that radiate from a central hub in the manner of the petals of a daisy. The printer's type font can be changed by changing the daisy wheel.

data 1. Information coded in a form suitable for computer processing. 2. The information needed to solve a problem or carry out a calculation. See **information.**

data communications Electronic transmission of data between computers. Also called telecommunications, which see.

data encryption Storing and transmitting data in scrambled form to prevent its unauthorized use.

data processing (DP) In principle, any manipulation of data by a computer can be referred to as data processing. In practice, the term is usually applied to the processing of large amounts of business data, as when printing paychecks or invoices. Formerly referred to as automatic data processing and electronic data processing.

data type A classification of data items according to their use and the operations that can be carried out on them. For example, in most programming languages, numbers belong to a different data type than character strings (text).

database A collection of related files.

database management system (DBMS) A program for creating and manipulating the files in a database. All access to and modification of the stored data is accomplished through commands to the database management system.

debugging Finding and correcting the errors in a program.

decimal notation The number system using the digits 0 through 9 that we all learned in school. People normally write numbers in decimal notation; computers, however, can process numbers more efficiently if they are first converted to binary notation.

de facto standard A standard that exists in practice even though it is not endorsed by any standards-setting organization.

default An action taken or assumption made by a program in the absence of instructions to the contrary from the user. A well-thought-out set of default actions and assumptions can greatly simplify the use of a program.

desktop metaphor An approach to understanding the operation of a computer system in which the display is pictured as a desktop on which one or more documents have been placed. Each "document" is actually a window through which can be seen the data that a particular program is processing.

desktop publishing Use of a computer to produce a single copy of a work to be printed. The copy produced by the computer is then reproduced using conventional printing technologies.

digital Refers to the representation of information by discrete symbols rather than continuously varying quantities. A digital clock, for example, represents the time by numbers that change abruptly from minute to minute. See **analog**.

digitize Convert an analog quantity into digital form. Most information picked up by sensing devices, such as cameras and microphones, is in analog form and must be digitized prior to computer processing.

direct access Another name for random access.

direct-connect modem A modem that is connected directly to the telephone line by plugging it into a telephone jack rather than using an acoustic coupler to send and receive signals through a standard telephone set. See **acoustic coupler**.

directory A table listing all the files stored on a disk. The directory is stored on the disk whose files it lists. For each file the directory includes the name of the file, its size, and its location on the disk. For the user's convenience, additional facts are often included, such as the date and time at which the file was created.

disk A plastic or metal disk coated with a magnetic material on which data can be recorded. Magnetic disks are the most widely used form of auxiliary memory.

disk drive The device into which a disk is inserted to store information on it or retrieve information from it.

disk operating system (DOS) An operating system whose major function is managing information stored on disks. DOS is sometimes used as an abbreviation for PC-DOS and MS-DOS, operating systems used on IBM and IBM-compatible personal computers.

diskette A miniature disk that can be readily carried about or stored in a filing cabinet. A diskette is either a descriptively named floppy disk or a pocket-sized hard plastic cartridge enclosing a hard plastic disk. See **floppy disk**.

distributed processing Computing with several processors, each with its own private memory. The processors can be in widely separated locations and exchange data over a communications link. Each processor can be the central processing unit of an independent computer system.

documentation Information on the use and operation of a program or computer system.

dot-matrix printer A printer for which each printed character is formed by an array of dots. Dot-matrix printers are compact, inexpensive, reliable, and reasonably fast, but the printing produced by some is ugly and hard to read. See **draft quality, letter quality**, and **near letter quality**.

draft quality The lowest quality printing produced by dot-matrix printers. Characters may be crudely formed, and the individual dots making them up are usually visible. Draft-quality printout is produced faster but is harder to read than higher-quality printout. See **letter quality, near letter quality**.

EBCDIC code Extended Binary Coded Decimal Interchange Code, a character code widely used on mainframes. See **ASCII code**.

editing keys Keys labeled with text editing operations such as Insert and Delete.

enter key The key used to terminate a typed line and enter the data on the line into the computer. The enter key is in the same position on a computer keyboard as the return key is on the keyboard of an electric typewriter.

execute Carry out the instructions in a program.

expansion card A circuit board that can be plugged into a computer to expand its capabilities. For example, the circuits that control peripherals such as video displays and printers are often on expansion cards. See **circuit board**.

field A part of a record reserved for a particular data item. For example, an employee record might have a field for the employee's name, a field for the hourly pay rate, and a field for the number of hours worked during the current week.

file In data processing, a collection of records. In general, any set of data stored on a disk and having an entry in the disk's directory. Thus a program stored on disk is also considered to be a file.

fixed disk See **hard disk**.

floppy disk A flexible, plastic film disk mounted in a protective jacket. See **diskette**.

formatting 1. Arranging text on pages with page numbers, headers, footers, and margins. 2. Preparing a disk for use by recording identifying information at the beginning of each sector and initializing the disk's directory and allocation table.

function keys Keys that a program can dedicate to particular functions or operations, so that pressing a key causes the corresponding operation to be carried out.

general purpose computer A computer whose program can be easily changed, thus allowing it to be used for a wide variety of purposes.

gigabyte (G or GB) Approximately a billion bytes; precisely 1,073,741,824 bytes.

graphics Images produced by a computer. Used as an adjective, as in graphics display and graphics printer, the term indicates the ability to produce arbitrary images rather than merely text.

hacker A dedicated, sometimes compulsive computer enthusiast. Hackers have been given a bad name by a small minority who attempt to gain unauthorized access to computer systems.

hard disk A high-capacity metal disk that usually is mounted permanently in its disk drive, from which it cannot be removed. Removable hard-disk cartridges are available but not nearly so widely used as permanently mounted hard disks. Also called a fixed disk.

hardware The computing machinery itself, as opposed to the software—the programs that control the hardware.

higher-level language A programming language that allows programs to be expressed in terms suitable for discussing a particular kind of problem rather than in those required to describe the internal operation of the computer.

information Facts, ideas, and knowledge. The terms *information* and *data* are often used almost interchangeably. The term *information* emphasizes the meaning or content of a message, whereas the term *data* emphasizes the concrete symbols (such as the letters of the alphabet) by which a message is transmitted, stored, and processed. See **data**.

information service A company that provides electronic access to information; electronic mail, computer conferences, and on-line databases are common offerings of information services.

ink-jet printer A printer that forms characters by spraying droplets of ink on the paper. Electrical forces control the paths of the droplets so that the desired characters are formed.

instruction set   The set of instructions that a computer can carry out; specifically, the instructions that can be understood and acted on by the control unit.

integrated circuit   An electronic circuit constructed on a computer chip. See **chip.**

integrated software   Software that combines into a single program several popular applications such as word processing, spreadsheet analysis, database management, and data communications.

interpreter   A language processor that executes a program written in a higher-level language. Unlike a compiler, which translates a program into machine language, an interpreter carries out the operations called for by the program without producing a translated version. See **compiler.**

interrupt   A signal to the central processing unit that a situation requiring immediate attention has arisen. An interrupt can be compared to an alarm sounding or a telephone ringing.

ISDN   Integrated Services Digital Network, a telephone network that provides high-speed digital transmission. Existing telephone lines can be used, but new equipment is required in the central office and in the customer's home or office.

key field   A field whose contents uniquely identifies the item or individual to which a particular record refers.

kilobit (K)   Approximately one thousand bits; precisely 1024 bits.

kilobyte (K or KB)   Approximately one thousand bytes; precisely 1024 bytes. Note that the abbreviation K can be used for both kilobyte and kilobit, so one must determine from the context whether bytes or bits are being referred to.

language processor   A program that allows a computer to execute programs written in a language other than machine language, even though the central processing unit can execute directly only programs written in machine language.

laptop computer   A compact, lightweight, battery-operated computer that can be used while resting on the operator's lap.

laser printer   A high-quality printer that operates in a manner similar to, and often looks like, an office copier.

LCD display   A compact display similar to that of a digital watch; its main drawback is that it can be difficult to read under less than ideal lighting conditions. Most laptop computers use LCD displays.

letter quality (LQ)   The print quality produced by a high-quality office typewriter. Letter-quality printout can be produced by daisy-wheel printers, laser printers, and the best dot-matrix printers. See **draft quality, near letter quality.**

light-pen   A device for designating a particular point on a video display. With the aid of appropriate software, one can use a light-pen to draw on the display, move objects about, and point to the object that is to be affected by a command.

local area network (LAN)   A network interconnecting computers in a restricted locality, such as a single building.

machine language   The binary-coded instructions that can be understood and acted on by the central processing unit.

magnetic disk   See **disk.**

magnetic tape   Plastic tape coated with a magnetic material on which data can be recorded. Computer tape is similar to that used for audio and video recording.

main memory   High speed, random access memory used for temporary storage of programs and data. For long-term storage, programs and data must be transferred to auxiliary memory.

mainframe   A large-scale computer such as found in the computer rooms of such organizations as businesses, banks, universities, and government agencies.

megabyte (M or MB)   Approximately one million bytes; precisely 1,048,576 bytes.

memory   Electronic components for storing data. Some people and organizations prefer the term storage to memory.

memory location   A computer's main memory is made up of many individual memory locations, each of which holds a single data item and is designated by a unique address. If we picture main memory as a set of post office boxes, the individual boxes are the memory locations and the box numbers are the addresses.

memory-mapped display   A display that automatically shows the contents of a segment of main memory called display memory. Storing a new value in one of the memory locations of display memory instantly changes the corresponding part of the display. Highly interactive programs such as word processors and spreadsheet programs work best with a memory-mapped display.

microcomputer   A computer whose central processing unit is a microprocessor.

microprocessor   A central processing unit built on a single chip.

minicomputer   A computer intermediate between microcomputers and mainframes in cost and computing power. Also called a mid-range computer.

modem   A device that allows a computer to send and receive digital data over the existing analog telephone network. A modern "smart" or "intelligent" modem serves as a complete telephone set for a computer, dialing numbers at the computer's request and notifying the computer of incoming calls.

module   A part of a program that performs a well-defined function. Structured programming advocates building complex programs out of simple, easy-to-understand modules. Subroutines often serve as modules.

mouse   A pointing device consisting of a small box that rolls around on a desktop. Moving the mouse in a particular direction causes an arrow on the screen to move a corresponding distance in the same direction. The user presses or releases a button on the mouse to direct the computer's attention to the object at which the arrow is currently pointing.

multiprocessing   Using more than one processor to execute a number of programs concurrently. Contrast with multiprogramming, which achieves the same result (but less efficiently) using only a single processor.

multiprogramming   Using a single processor (the central processing unit) to execute a number of programs concurrently. The different programs take turns at being executed by the central processing unit; any program that is waiting on a peripheral device loses its turn until it is ready to continue execution. Also called multitasking.

near letter quality (NLQ)   The next-to-best print quality for dot-matrix printers. Characters are reasonably well formed and have a solid appearance, but they are not quite as sharp as in letter-quality printout. See **draft quality, letter quality.**

null modem   A cable used for connecting two computers via their RS-232 ports. The null modem crosses certain wires so that, for example, the wire on which one computer sends data is connected to the one on which the other computer receives data, and vice versa.

numeric keypad   A calculator-like arrangement of number keys designed to simplify entering numeric data into a computer. Computer keyboards often feature numeric keypads.

on-line Connected to or accessible through a computer system.

operating system The master control program responsible for the overall operation of the computer system. Both users and programs request services by means of commands to the operating system. Because one of its main tasks is managing the transfer of programs and data to and from disk, an operating system is often called a disk operating system (DOS).

operation code The part of a machine language instruction that specifies what operation the computer will carry out. The remainder of the instruction specifies such things as where the data to be manipulated will come from and where the result will be stored.

optical disc A disc on which information is stored and retrieved by means of a laser beam. The enormous storage capacity of these discs would allow them to store sounds and moving pictures in addition to programs and data. Currently the entertainment industry uses two forms of optical disc: video-discs for storing pictures and compact discs (CDs) for storing sounds. See **CD ROM.**

originate mode The mode in which a modem must be placed when making a call to another computer. Microcomputer modems are used far more frequently in the originate mode than in the answer mode used for receiving calls. See **answer mode.**

parallel port A port normally used for connecting a printer to the computer; the term *parallel* indicates that the eight bits making up each byte are transmitted simultaneously, in contrast to a serial port that transmits bits one at a time. See **serial port.**

peripheral An input, output, storage, or communications device such as a keyboard, printer, disk drive, or modem.

pixel One of the individual dots making up an image on a computer display. Also called a pel; both terms are abbreviations for picture element.

plotter A device for producing drawings under computer control. Usually used where the highest accuracy is required, as for maps, engineering drawings, and artwork for producing integrated circuits.

port A connector on the back of a computer through which data can be sent and received. The most commonly used ports are the parallel port used for connecting to a printer and the RS-232 or serial port used for connecting to a printer, modem, or another computer.

printer A device that enables a computer to print text and possibly also graphics. See **daisy-wheel printer, dot-matrix printer, laser printer.**

process A program in execution. A process consists of a program, the data it is manipulating, and a pointer to the next instruction to be executed. Program execution can be suspended and continued at a later time, as is often required when many processes share a single processor. A computer system can be viewed as a collection of concurrently executing processes that communicate with one another and with the user but otherwise lead independent existences.

processor A central processing unit. When several such are present in a computer system, the term *processor* is preferred, since no processor can be regarded as more central than the others. See **central processing unit.**

program A set of detailed, step-by-step instructions that govern the operation of a computer. See **algorithm.**

programming language A language for expressing programs in a form suitable for execution by a computer. Programs in machine language can be executed directly by the central processing unit. Programs in other languages can be executed only with the aid of a program called a language processor.

punch card A card in which data is stored as patterns of punched holes. Punch cards are now obsolete but played an important role in the history of computing.

RAM disk An area of main memory organized and used like a disk. Frequently used software is often stored on a RAM disk, allowing it to be loaded much faster than from a real disk.

random access Designates memory for which the time required to retrieve a particular data item is independent of the order in which the data items were stored and of the location of the retrieved item in memory. Main memory satisfies both of these requirements. Disk drives are usually considered random access devices even though the access time does depend somewhat on the location of the data.

random access memory (RAM) Main memory that allows data to be both retrieved (read) and stored (written). The name is poorly chosen, because the other kind of main memory, read-only memory, also has the property of random access. See **read-only memory.**

raster-scan display A video display in which an electron beam systematically scans the entire screen setting the color and brightness of each pixel it passes over. In the much-less-frequently used alternative, the vector display, the electron beam traces out the image to be displayed instead of methodically scanning the entire screen.

read-only memory (ROM) Main memory from which data can only be retrieved (read) during normal operation. The stored data is either permanent or can be changed only using special techniques. Frequently used software is often stored in read-only memory to save the user from having to load it from disk every time the computer is turned on.

read/write head The device that records (writes) data on a disk or plays back (reads) previously recorded data.

record A collection of related data items, often referring to a single individual (such as an employee) or object (such as an item of inventory). The positions occupied by the data items making up the record are called fields.

refresh The screen of a video display glows where it has been struck by an electron beam. Each glowing point begins to fade as soon as the electron beam moves on to other points. Therefore, the display must be repeatedly rescanned—refreshed—to prevent the image from fading.

relational database A database organized as a set of tables called relations. Some relations are stored in the database; others are created as needed using data extracted from one or more of the stored relations.

repetition The programming language control structure that causes some parts of a program to be executed more than once.

return key Another name for the enter key.

reverse video Displayed text in which the foreground and background colors are interchanged. For example, if a display normally shows white characters against a black background, reverse video would be black characters against a white background. Reverse video is often used for highlighting, for example, to designate a segment of text selected for manipulation by a word processor.

routine A general name for a program, or a part of a program, that does a specific job.

RS-232, RS-232C A standard for transmitting data serially—one bit at a time. An RS-232 port, also called a serial port, can be used to connect a computer to a printer, a modem, or another computer. Occasionally RS will be seen followed by another number, indicating the use of another standard for data transmission.

scroll Often a program has much more information to display than will fit on the display screen. Many programs treat the display as a window through which the user can see a small part of a large, imaginary document containing all the information to be displayed. Scrolling is the process of moving the display about on the large, imaginary document so as to view different parts of it.

sector A recording surface of a disk is divided into circular tracks, each of which is further divided into sectors (eight is a typical number of sectors per track). Data is usually transferred between main memory and disk one sector at a time.

selection The programming language control structure that allows the computer to select which instructions to execute based on the conditions that prevail when a program is executed. Selection gives computers their famed decision-making capability.

sequencing The programming language control structure that causes instructions to be carried out one after another in the order in which they appear in the program.

sequential access Designates memory from which data items can be retrieved only in the order in which they were stored. Magnetic tape is a sequential access medium, since for most purposes it is only practical to retrieve data items in the order in which they are recorded on the tape.

serial port A port through which data is transmitted one bit at a time. See **RS-232, parallel port.**

silicon The material from which computer chips are made. Pronounce it "silly cuhn" with the last syllable unaccented; not "silly CAHN" the way some TV reporters do. And don't confuse silicon with silicone (pronounced silly cone), a greaselike or rubberlike substance best known for its use in cosmetic surgery.

software The programs that control a computer.

special purpose computer A computer designed for a single application; computers embedded in other machines, such as household appliances and entertainment products, are always special purpose computers. The program for a special purpose computer is usually permanently installed in read-only memory and cannot be changed by the user. The user is allowed to supply only very limited programming, such as specifying when a microwave oven will turn on and how long it will run.

spreadsheet program A program that provides the user with an electronic version of an accountant's ledger sheet.

storage Another name for memory. People who dislike applying human-oriented terms to computers strongly prefer the term *storage* to *memory*. Storage is more common in the mainframe world than in the mini- and microcomputer worlds, and it is more common abroad than in the U.S.

structured programming An approach to programming that advocates (1) constructing large programs out of simpler modules and (2) using three simple control structures: sequencing, selection, and repetition.

Structured Query Language (SQL) A computer language for defining the structure of databases, inserting and deleting information in them, and retrieving information from them.

subroutine A part of a program that can be called from elsewhere in the program. When the subroutine completes its task, program execution continues from the point at which the subroutine called.

supercomputer A very fast, very expensive computer used for tasks that require massive amounts of numerical computation.

system unit The part of a computer that contains the central processing unit.

Some peripherals, such as keyboard, display, and disk drives, may also be installed in the system unit.

systems software   Programs designed to enhance the operation of the computer system rather than carry out specific applications for the user.

telecommunications   A general term for electronic communication; in a computer context it refers to electronic transmission of computer data. See **data communications.**

terminal   A combination of a keyboard and a display or printer used for communicating with a remote computer. Information typed on the keyboard is sent to the remote computer; information received from the remote computer is displayed or printed.

text editor   A program that allows the user to enter, modify, and print text. There are two types of text editors in common use: a program editor is designed for editing computer programs, and a word processor is designed for editing and formatting such conventional text as letters, reports, and manuscripts.

time sharing   A form of multiprogramming in which many users simultaneously interact with their programs via computer terminals. Time sharing differs from other forms of multiprogramming in that (1) a large number of programs may have to be executed concurrently and (2) each program's turn at the central processing unit must come up frequently enough so that the program can respond quickly to input from its user.

top-down design   An approach to program design in which we first block out the major operations a program is to perform, then decide what simpler operations are needed to carry out each of the major operations, then break each simpler operation down into still simpler ones, and so on until we reach operations simple enough for each to be expressed by a statement in a programming language.

track   On a disk, a circular path along which data is recorded.

trackball   A pointing device consisting of a ball that partly protrudes from a panel. Rotating the ball moves an arrow on the screen; the amount and direction of rotation determine the distance and in what direction the arrow moves. An advantage of a trackball over a mouse is that the trackball does not require desktop space to roll around on.

twisted pairs   Telephone wiring inside a building. Twisted pairs are sometimes used for local area networks, their major advantage being that they are probably already present in the building so that no new wiring need be installed for the local area network.

user-friendly   Designates a program or computer system that is easy for nonprogrammers to understand and use.

video display   A computer display that presents information on the cathode ray tube of a video monitor. The most common form of video display is a raster-scan display. See **cathode ray tube, raster-scan display.**

video display terminal (VDT)   A terminal for which information received from the remote computer is presented on a video display.

video monitor   A device similar to a television set that can display pictures, drawings, and text on the screen of a cathode ray tube. Like television sets, video monitors can be black and white or color, with color being the more expensive. For black and white video monitors designed for use with computers, "white" is often actually green or amber, which is considered more restful to the eyes than true white. See **video display.**

virtual memory   Main memory that is not actually present but is simulated by the operating system. To programmers and users the computer system seems to have a very large main memory. The actual main memory is much smaller, but the operating system swaps data between main memory and disk as needed, so that much of the data that appears always to be in main memory is actually stored on disk until its presence in main memory is required.

volatile   A property of main memory by which the data stored in it is lost when the power is turned off. One way to combat volatility is to use batteries to provide power to main memory even when the computer is not operating. Laptop computers use this principle to allow data to be retained even when the computer is turned off.

what you see is what you get (WYSIWYG)   A term referring to word processors that display text on the computer screen exactly as it will be printed on paper.

wide area network   A network interconnecting computers in widely separated locations, such as different cities, states, or countries. Because of the expense of constructing such a network, most organizations rely on the services of communications companies for wide-area communications. The telephone network is widely used for this purpose.

window   On a computer display, an area of the screen reserved for displaying information from a given source. For example, a word processor might display text from different documents in different windows. Or an operating system might allow several programs to execute simultaneously and present the output of each program in a different window.

word processor   A program that allows the user to enter text, edit it as needed, and print it in properly formatted pages with headers, footers, page numbers, and margins.

word wrap   The process by which a word processor automatically goes to a new line when the end of the current line is reached. A partially typed word is not broken: the part already typed is moved to the beginning of the new line.

WORM drive   An optical-disc drive that can both write to and read from the disc. Information, once written, cannot be erased, so the optical disc will eventually become full and have to be replaced.

Photo Credits

A SHITE TEACHER